PRAISE FOR *THE DICTATOR'S HANDBOOK*

"A lucidly written, shrewdly argued meditation on how democrats and dictators preserve political authority.... In a style reminiscent of *Freakonomics*, Messrs. Bueno de Mesquita and Smith present dozens of clever examples.... The most fascinating chapter in *The Dictator's Handbook* concerns the rewards that governments provide other governments. The authors make the obvious, but nevertheless controversial, argument that almost all aid money is dispersed not to alleviate poverty but to purchase loyalty and influence.... Bueno de Mesquita and Smith are polymathic, drawing on economics, history, and political science to make their points.... In other words, the reader will be hard-pressed to find a single government that doesn't largely operate according to Messrs. Bueno de Mesquita and Smith's model. So the next time a hand-wringing politician, Democrat or Republican, claims to be taking a position for the 'good of his country,' remember to replace the word 'country' with 'career.'"

—*Wall Street Journal*

"Machiavelli's *The Prince* has a new rival. It's *The Dictator's Handbook* by Bruce Bueno de Mesquita and Alastair Smith.... This is a fantastically thought-provoking read. I found myself not wanting to agree but actually, for the most part, being convinced that the cynical analysis is the true one."

—Diane Coyle, Enlightenment Economics

"In this fascinating book Bueno de Mesquita and Smith spin out their view of governance: that all successful leaders, dictators and democrats, can best be understood as almost entirely driven by their own political survival—a view they characterize as 'cynical, but we fear accurate.' Yet as we follow the authors through their brilliant historical assessments of leaders' choices—from Caesar to Tammany Hall and the Green Bay Packers—we gradually realize that their brand of cynicism yields extremely realistic guidance about spreading the rule of law, decent government, and democracy. James Madison would have loved this book."

—R. James Woolsey, Director of Central Intelligence, 1993–1995, and chairman, Foundation for Defense of Democracies

"In this book, Bruce Bueno de Mesquita and Alastair Smith teach us to see dictatorship as just another form of politics, and from this perspective they deepen our understanding of all political systems."

—Roger Myerson, Glen A. Lloyd Distinguished Service Professor of Economics at the University of Chicago

THE
DICTATOR'S
HANDBOOK

THE
DICTATOR'S
HANDBOOK

WHY BAD BEHAVIOR IS ALMOST ALWAYS GOOD POLITICS

BRUCE BUENO DE MESQUITA
AND ALASTAIR SMITH

PUBLICAFFAIRS
New York

PublicAffairs
Hachette Book Group
1290 Avenue of the Americas, New York, NY 10104
www.publicaffairsbooks.com
@Public_Affairs

Printed in the United States of America

Originally published in 2011 in the United States by PublicAffairs. Paperback first published in 2012 by PublicAffairs

Second Trade Paperback Edition: April 2022

Published by PublicAffairs, an imprint of Perseus Books, LLC, a subsidiary of Hachette Book Group, Inc. The PublicAffairs name and logo is a trademark of the Hachette Book Group.

The Hachette Speakers Bureau provides a wide range of authors for speaking events. To find out more, go to www.hachettespeakersbureau.com or call (866) 376-6591.

The publisher is not responsible for websites (or their content) that are not owned by the publisher.

The Library of Congress has cataloged the hardcover edition as follows:

Bueno de Mesquita, Bruce, 1946–
The dictator's handbook : why bad behavior is almost always good politics / Bruce Bueno de Mesquita and Alastair Smith.—1st ed.
p. cm.
Includes bibliographical references and index.
ISBN 978-1-61039-044-6 (hardcover : alk. paper)—
ISBN 978-1-61039-045-3 (e-book) 1. Political leadership—Philosophy.
2. Power (Social sciences) 3. Political corruption. I. Smith, Alastair, 1967–II. Title.
JC330.3.B84 2011
303.3'4—dc23
2011024164

ISBNs: 9781610390446 (hardcover), 9781610390453 (ebook), 9781610391849 (first trade paperback), 9781541701366 (trade paperback reissue)

LSC-C

Printing 1, 2022

To our dictators, who have treated us so well—
Arlene and Fiona and Susan

What is important here is cash. [A] leader needs money, gold, and diamonds to run his hundred castles, feed his thousand women, buy cars for the millions of boot-lickers under his heels, reinforce the loyal military forces, and still have enough change left to deposit into his numbered Swiss accounts.

—MOBUTU SESE SEKO OF ZAIRE,
probably apocryphal

Men at some time are masters of their fates. The fault, dear Brutus, is not in our stars, but in ourselves, that we are underlings.

—WILLIAM SHAKESPEARE,
Julius Caesar, act I, scene II,
lines 140–141

RULES TO RULE BY

What remarkable puzzles politics provides. Every day's headlines shock and surprise us. Daily we hear of frauds, chicanery, and double-dealing by corporate executives, new lies, thefts, cruelties, and even murders perpetrated by government leaders. We cannot help but wonder what flaws of culture, religion, upbringing, or historical circumstance explain the rise of these malevolent despots, greedy Wall Street bankers, and unctuous oil barons. Is it true, as Shakespeare's Cassius said, that the fault lies not in the stars but in ourselves? Or, more particularly, in those who lead us? Most of us are content to believe that. And yet the truth is far different.

Too often we accept the accounts of historians, journalists, pundits, and poets without probing beneath the surface to discover deeper truths that point neither to the stars nor to ourselves. The world of politics is dictated by rules. Short is the term of any ruler foolish enough to govern without submitting to these rules to rule by.

Journalists, authors, and academics have endeavored to explain politics through storytelling. They've explored why this or that leader seized power, or how the population of a far-flung country came to revolt against their government, or why a specific policy enacted last year has reversed the fortunes of millions of lives. And in the explanations of these cases, a journalist or historian can usually tell us what happened, and to whom, and maybe even why. But beneath the particulars of the many political stories and histories we read are a few questions that seem to emerge time after time, some profound, some seemingly minor, but all nagging and enduring in the back of our minds: How do tyrants hold on to power for so long? For that matter, why is the tenure of successful democratic leaders so brief? How can countries with such misguided and corrupt economic policies survive for so long? Why are countries that are prone to natural disasters so often unprepared when they happen? And why do lands rich with natural resources have populations stricken with poverty?

Equally, we may well wonder: Why are Wall Street executives so politically tone-deaf that they dole out billions in bonuses while plunging the global economy into recession? Why is the leadership of a corporation, on whose shoulders so much responsibility rests, decided by so few people? Why are failed CEOs retained and paid handsomely even as their company's shareholders lose their shirts?

In one form or another, these questions about political behavior pop up again and again. Each explanation, each story, treats the errant leader and his or her faulty decision-making as a one-off, one-of-a-kind situation. But there is nothing unique about political behavior.

These stories of the horrible things politicians or business executives do are appealing in their own perverse way because they free us to believe we would behave differently if given the opportunity. They liberate us to cast blame on the flawed person who somehow, inexplicably, had the authority to make monumental—and monumentally bad—decisions. We are confident that we would never act like Libya's Muammar al-Qaddafi, who bombed his own people to keep himself in power. We look at the huge losses suffered under Kenneth Lay's leadership by Enron's employees, retirees, and shareholders and think we aren't like Kenneth Lay. We look at each case and conclude they are different, uncharacteristic anomalies. Yet they are held together by the logic of politics, the rules ruling rulers.

The pundits of politics and the nabobs of news have left us ignorant of these rules. They are content to blame evildoers without inquiring why the worlds of politics and business seem to succor miscreants or turn good people into scoundrels. That's why we are still asking the same old questions. We're still surprised by the prevalence of drought-induced food shortages in Africa, 3,500 years after the pharaohs worked out how to store grain. We're still shocked by the devastation of earthquakes and tsunamis in places like Haiti, Iran, Myanmar, and Sri Lanka, and baffled that such natural disasters seem less intense in North America and Europe. We're still troubled by the friendly handshakes and winks exchanged between democratic leaders and the tyrants that they somehow justify empowering.

In this book, we're going to provide a way to make sense of the miserable behavior that characterizes many—maybe most—leaders, whether in government or business. Our aim is to explain both good and bad conduct without resorting to ad hominem claims. At its heart, this will entail untangling the reasoning and reasons behind how we are governed and how we organize.

The picture we paint will not be pretty. It will not strengthen hope for humankind's benevolence and altruism. But we believe it will be the truth, and it will point the way to a brighter future. After all, even if politics is nothing more than a game that leaders play, if only we learn the rules, it becomes a game we can win.

To improve the world, however, all of us must first suspend faith in conventional wisdom. Let logic and evidence be the guide and our eyes will be opened to the reasons why politics works the way it does. Knowing how and why things are as they are is the first, crucial step toward learning how to make them better.

BELL'S BOTTOMLESS BLUES

In politics, as in life, we all have desires and contend with obstacles that keep us from getting what we want. A government's rules and laws, for example, limit what we can do. Those in power differ from the rest of us: they can design rules to their advantage and make it easier for themselves to get what they want. Understanding what people want and how they get it can go a long way to clarifying why those in power often do bad things. In fact, bad behavior is more often than not good politics. This dictum holds up whether one governs a tiny town, a mom-and-pop business, a megacorporation, or a global empire.

Let's start with a tale of a small town's team of seemingly greedy, grasping, avaricious louts so that we can appreciate how the world looks from a leader's perspective. And yet it's vital that we remember that this is a story about politics, not personality. Whether or not we're discussing a cabal of corrupt reprobates, what really matters is that these are people who value power and recognize how to get it and keep it. Soon enough we will come to appreciate that this small tale of miserable conduct recurs at every level of politics and corporate governance, and that there is nothing out of the ordinary in the extraordinary story of Bell, California.

Robert Rizzo is a former city manager of the small town of Bell (population about thirty-six thousand). Bell, a suburb of Los Angeles, is a poor, mostly Hispanic and Latino town. Per capita income is about $36,000, way below both the California and national averages. More than 30 percent of the town's hardworking people live below the poverty line. Life is not easy in Bell.

Still, it is a community that takes pride in its accomplishments, its families, and its prospects. Despite its many challenges, Bell consistently outperforms other communities in California and the nation in keeping violent crime and property crime below average. A cursory glance at Bell's 2019 website suggests it's a thriving, happy community brimming with summer classes, library events, water play, and fun-filled family trips. And Bell seems to be a civic-minded community too. For instance, the town is a recipient of Housing and Urban Development (HUD) community grants, to the tune of nearly $800,000 in 2021–2022 aimed at improving housing.[1]

Back in 2010, Robert Rizzo had been Bell's city manager for seventeen years. That year, Bell's mayor, Oscar Hernandez (who was later convicted on corruption charges), said the town had been on the verge of bankruptcy in 1993 when Rizzo (also later convicted for corruption) was hired. For fifteen consecutive years of Rizzo's leadership, up until he stepped down in 2010, the city's budget had been balanced. Hernandez credited Rizzo with making the town solvent and helping to keep it that way. That, of course, was no mean feat. Surely Rizzo and the town leaders with whom he worked deserved praise and tangible rewards for their good service to the people of Bell.

Behind the idyllic facade, however, lies a story that embodies how politics really works. You see, Robert Rizzo, hired at $72,000 a year in 1993, at the end of his tenure seventeen years later was earning a staggering $787,000 per year.

Let's put that in perspective. If his salary had just kept up with inflation, he would have made $108,000 in 2010. He made seven times more! During long years of low inflation, his salary went up at an annual, compounded rate of more than 15 percent, almost exactly the return Bernie Madoff, the master Ponzi schemer, promised his hapless investors.

How does Rizzo's city manager's pay compare to other responsible government jobs? The president of the United States is paid $400,000.[2] The governor of California's salary is just over $200,000. The mayor of Los Angeles, just a hop, skip, and a jump from Bell, is paid only a bit over $200,000. To be sure, Robert Rizzo was not even close to the highest-paid public employee in California. That distinction, as in most states, went to the coach of a university football team: UC Berkeley's coach earned about $1,850,000 in 2010—but then he probably brought in a lot more revenue than Mr. Rizzo.[3] In 2020, being mindful of the pandemic, the coach generously took a pay cut, reducing his pay to a bit more than $3,725,000. Robert Rizzo, not close to the football coach's salary, was indeed credited with doing a good job for Bell, but was it really that good? It seems that he was the highest-paid city manager in the entire United States (at least until we discover another Bell).

The natural thought is that somehow Robert Rizzo must have been stealing money, dipping into the proverbial cookie jar, taking funds that were not rightfully and legally his, or at least doing something that was immoral and illegal. The California attorney general (and Democratic candidate for governor) at the time of the Bell scandal in the summer of 2010, Jerry Brown, promised an investigation to find out if any laws had been violated. The implicit message was clear: no one would voluntarily pay a small-town city manager nearly $800,000 a year. The truth, however, is quite a bit more complicated.

Let's be clear. Rizzo and all but one city council member were convicted of and served time for numerous criminal counts having to do with payments for committee memberships when the committees never met and for frauds they perpetrated. But none were convicted for receiving outrageously high salaries.

Being paid well is not a crime. Rizzo's actual story is one of clever (and reprehensible) political maneuvering implicitly sanctioned by Bell's voters and the city council members who represented them, supplemented only by a touch of larceny. Cities comparable to Bell pay their council members little or nothing. But four of Bell's five council members received close to $100,000 a year through the simple mechanism of being paid not only their (minimal) base council salaries but also nearly $8,000 per month to sit on bogus city committees. Only poor councilman Lorenzo Velez—not charged with any crimes—failed to reap such rewards. Velez apparently received only $8,076 a year as a council member, approximately equal to what his fellow council members were getting *each month*. How can we possibly explain these disparities, let alone the outrageous salaries and pensions provided not only to Mr. Rizzo but also to the assistant city manager and Bell's chief of police (all subsequently jailed on corruption charges)?

The answers lie in a clever manipulation of election timing. The city's leaders ensured that they depended on very few voters to hold on to power and to set their compensation. To see how a poor community could so handsomely reward its town leaders, we must start with the 2005 special election to convert Bell from a general city to a charter city. What, you may well ask between yawns, is the difference between a general city and a charter city? The answer is day and night: decisions are made in the open daylight in general cities and often in secret, behind closed doors, in charter cities. While a general city's governing system is dictated by state or federal law, a charter city's governance is defined by—well, as you would expect—its own charter.

The California legislature decided in 2005 to limit salaries for city council members in general cities. No sooner did the state legislature move to impose limits than creative politicians in Bell—some allege Robert Rizzo led the way—found a way to insulate themselves from the "whims" of those sent to California's state capital, Sacramento. A special election was called, supported by five council members, to turn Bell into a charter city. The selling point of the change to charter city was that it would give Bell greater autonomy and more freedom from decisions by distant state officials. Local authorities know best what is right for their community, better than distant politicians who are not in touch with local circumstances. Or so the leaders of Bell, California, argued.

Special elections on technical questions—to be a charter city or to remain a general city—are less than captivating to the general voter. Of course, if the vote had been held in the context of a major national or even statewide election, the proposition would likely have been scrutinized by many prospective voters, but as it happens—surely by political design—the special election, associated with no other ballot decisions, attracted fewer than 400 voters (336 in favor, 54 opposed) in a town of 36,000 people. And so the charter passed, placing within the control of a handful of people the right to allocate city revenues and form the city budget—and to do so behind closed doors. As best as we can tell, the charter changed nothing else of consequence concerning Bell's governance. It just provided a means to give vast discretion over taxing and spending decisions to a tiny group of people who were, as it happens, also making choices about their own compensation.

Lest one think the council members were stupid as well as venal, it is worth noting how clever they were in disguising what they had done. Should anyone have cared to ask about a city council member's part-time salary, the council member could say openly and honestly that they were paid just a few hundred dollars a month, a pittance, for their services. As we have already seen, the bulk of their pay—the part denied to Lorenzo Velez—was for participation on city committees. That, as it turns out, may ultimately have been their Achilles' heel.

All but Councilman Luis Artega (found not guilty) and Lorenzo Velez (not charged) among the principal players in Bell's scandal were charged and convicted on criminal counts that did not include their lavish salaries. As reprehensible as these may have been, it seems they were perfectly legal. No, they were jailed for receiving payments for meetings that never took place. It seems they collected a lot of money while overlooking their obligation to actually attend committee meetings. This is to say that the well-paid managers of Bell may have ended up falling victim to what one might describe as a legal technicality.

Outrageous salaries were okay, but getting paid for attending meetings while being absent from them was not. We cannot help but wonder how many government officials are held to that standard. How many senators and representatives, for instance, draw their full salaries while skipping meetings of the Senate or House so that they can raise campaign funds, give speeches, or participate in boondoggles?

You may well wonder how a little town like Bell could balance its budget—one of Mr. Rizzo's significant accomplishments—while paying such high salaries. (Indeed, now that Bell's governance is cleaned up, its spending involves paying off its indebtedness.) Remember, the town's leaders got to choose not only how to spend money but also how much tax to levy. And did they ever tax their constituents. Here's what the *Los Angeles Times* reported about property taxes in Bell:

> Bell's rate is 1.55%—nearly half again as much as those in such affluent enclaves as Beverly Hills and Palos Verdes Estates and Manhattan Beach, and significantly higher than just about everywhere else in Los Angeles County, according to records provided by the county Auditor-Controller's Office at the *Times* request. That means that the owner of a home in Bell with an assessed value of $400,000 would pay about $6,200 in annual property taxes. The owner of the same home in Malibu, whose rate is 1.10%, would pay just $4,400.[4]

In plain and simple terms, Bell's property tax was about 50 percent higher than those of nearby communities. With such high taxes, the city manager and council members certainly could balance the budget while enriching themselves and their key cronies.

Now that we have Bell's story, let's look at the subtext. In Bell, city council members are elected, although before 2007 their election was not contested for many years. That means that council members are beholden to the voters, or at least the voters whose support was needed to win office. Before 2007 that was hardly anyone because the elections were not contested. Since 2007, as it turns out, even with contested elections, it still takes very few votes to win a council seat. For instance, Bell had about 9,400 registered voters in 2009, of which only

2,285—that is, 24.3 percent—turned out to vote. Each voter could cast a ballot for two candidates for city council out of the six candidates seeking that office. The two winners, Luis Artiga and Teresa Jacobo, received 1,201 and 1,332 votes respectively, out of 2,285 votes that were cast, but they didn't need that many votes to win. Speaking generously, election was achieved with supportive votes from only about 13 percent of the registered electorate. We say "speaking generously" because to get elected to the city council in 2009 all that was necessary was to have one more vote than the *third*-largest vote-getter among the candidates. Remember, two were to be elected. The number three candidate had just 472 votes. So, 473 votes—about 5 percent of the registered voters, just over 1 percent of the city population, and only about one-fifth of those who actually turned out to vote—was all that was needed to win the election. Whatever the reason that the vote was divided among so many candidates, it is evident that election could have been achieved with support from only a tiny percentage of Bell's adult population. This goes a long way to explaining the city government's taxing and spending policies.

One thing we can be sure of: those on the city council could not have been eager for competing candidates (or even fellow council member Velez) to get wind of the truth about their compensation package. City manager Rizzo had to maintain the council's confidence to keep his job, and they needed his support to keep theirs. He could have exposed how deeply they were dipping into the public's hard-earned money, which would have sent them packing (as it eventually did). It is in this need for mutual loyalty that we see the seeds of Bell's practices and of politics in general. Rizzo served at the pleasure of the mayor and city council. They, in turn, served at the pleasure of a tiny group of Bell's citizens, the essential supporters among Bell's considerably larger prospective electorate. Without the council's support, Rizzo would have been out on his ear—albeit with a fabulous pension estimated at $650,000 to $880,000 per year. How best to keep their loyalty? That was easy: promote the means to transfer great private rewards in the form of lavish compensation packages to council members.[5]

Of course, if all were being done in the open, or if Bell had remained a general city subject to Sacramento's control over compensation,

Rizzo could not have provided the means to ensure that he would scratch the city council members' backs and they his. When a leader's hold on power—his or her political survival—depends on a small coalition of backers (remember the small percentage of voters needed to actually win a seat on the city council), then providing private rewards is the path to long tenure in office: Mr. Rizzo kept his job for seventeen years. Furthermore, when that small coalition is drawn from a relatively large pool—just five council members, elected under a city charter ratified by only 336 voters out of a registered voter population (in 2009) of 9,395—then not only is privately rewarding the small coalition an efficient way to govern, but so much budgetary and taxing discretion is created that the folks at the top have ample opportunity for handsome compensation, an opportunity that the city's top leadership did not fail to exploit.

Bell presents a number of lessons for us about the rules to rule by. First, politics is about getting and keeping political power. It is not about the general welfare of "we the people." Second, political survival is best assured by depending on few people to attain and retain office. That means dictators, dependent on a few cronies, are in a far better position to stay in office for decades, often dying in their sleep, than are democrats. Third, when the small group of cronies knows that there is a large pool of people waiting on the sidelines, hoping to replace them in the queue for gorging at the public trough, then the top leadership has great discretion over how revenue is spent and how much to tax. All that tax revenue and discretion opens the door to kleptocracy from many leaders, and public-spirited programs from a very few. And it means enhanced tenure in power. Fourth, dependence on a small coalition liberates leaders to tax at high rates, just as Bell's leaders did. Taxing at high rates has a propensity to foment the threat of popular uprisings. That risk was surely there once people found out what Bell's government was doing. There was no actual uprising, however, thanks to the media's exposés, which brought down Rizzo and Bell's other corrupt leaders. Of course, in Bell it was easy for the news media to end Rizzo's rule because it had essential freedoms: the rights to free speech and to a free press. We shall see that how the structure of government and the economy work explains variation in how many of these rights people have. This in turn accounts for whether the people take to the streets and whether they can succeed in orchestrating change, as we saw in some parts of the Middle East during the brief Arab Spring of 2011, or remain oppressed, as we saw in other parts during and shortly after the Arab Spring.

We will see that Bell's story offers a nearly perfect script for how to govern when the hold on office depends on very few people, especially when they are selected from among many. The politicians of Bell intuitively understood the rules of politics. Leaders who follow these rules faithfully truly can stay on top without ever having to do "the right thing" for their subjects. The people governing Bell clung to power for a very long time before probes from outside uncovered their means of holding on to office. As we will see, what works for those at the top usually works against those at the bottom; hence the public's shock and surprise at headlines about the misdeeds of so many in high positions. The way places like Bell are governed (which is the way most places and most businesses are governed) assure the Bell Bottom Blues.

One important lesson we will learn is that where politics are concerned, ideology, nationality, and culture don't matter all that much. The sooner we learn not to think or utter sentences such as "The United States should..." or "The American people want..." or "China's government ought to..." the better we will understand government, business, and all other forms of organization. When addressing politics, we must accustom ourselves to thinking and speaking about the actions and interests of specific, named leaders rather than thinking and speaking about fuzzy ideas like the national interest, the common good, and the general welfare. Once we think about what helps leaders come to and stay in power, we will also begin to see how to fix politics. Politics, like all of life, is about individuals, each motivated to do what is good for them, not what is good for others. And that surely is the story of Robert Rizzo of Bell, California.

GREAT THINKER CONFUSION

As Robert Rizzo's story highlights, politics is not terribly complicated. But by the same measure, history's most revered political philosophers haven't explained it very well. The fact is, people like Niccolò Machiavelli, Thomas Hobbes, James Madison, and Charles-Louis de Secondat (that is, Montesquieu), not to mention Plato and Aristotle, thought about government mostly in the narrow context of their times.

Hobbes sought the best form of government. He was blinded, however, by his experience of the English civil war, the rise of Cromwell, and his fear of rule by the masses. Hobbes saw monarchy as the natural path to order and good governance. Believing in the necessary benevolence of an absolute leader, the Leviathan, he also concluded that "no king can be rich, nor glorious, nor secure, whose subjects are either poor, or contemptible, or too weak through want, or dissension, to maintain a war against their enemies."[6] Taking a bit of liberty with Hobbes's more nuanced philosophy, we must wonder how Robert Rizzo, by Hobbesian lights, could grow so rich when his subjects, the citizens of Bell, were so demonstrably poor.

Machiavelli, an unemployed politician/civil servant who hoped to become a hired hand of the Medici family—that is, perhaps the Robert Rizzo of his day—wrote *The Prince* to demonstrate his value as an adviser. It seems the Medicis were not overly impressed—he didn't land the job. But he had, we believe, a better grasp than Hobbes on how politics can create self-aggrandizing practices such as those carried out in Bell half a millennium later. Writing in *The Discourses*, Machiavelli observed that anyone seeking to establish a government of liberty and equality will fail, "unless he withdraws from that general equality a number of the boldest and most ambitious spirits, and makes gentlemen of them, not merely in name but in fact, by giving them castles and possessions, as well as money and subjects; so that surrounded by these he may be able to maintain his power, and that by his support they may satisfy their ambition."[7]

Robert Rizzo might have done well to study Machiavelli as the best source of his defense against public opprobrium. He maintained his power for long years by satisfying the ambition for wealth and position of those loyal to him on Bell's city council, and they really were the only people whose support he had to have.

James Madison, a revolutionary trying to bring his brand of politics into power, was, like Hobbes, looking revolution in the face. Unlike Hobbes, however, Madison actually liked what he saw. In "Federalist 10," Madison contemplated the problem that was to bedevil the citizens of Bell a quarter of a millennium later: "whether small or extensive Republics are most favorable to the election of proper guardians of the public weal: and it is clearly decided in favor of the latter."[8] His conclusion—not easily reached, because he was fearful about tyranny of the majority—is close to what we argue is correct, although, as always, the devil is in the details and Madison, we believe, fell a bit short on the details of good governance. In describing a republic as large or small, he failed to distinguish between how many had a say in choosing leaders and how many were essential to keeping a leader in place. The two, as we will see, can be radically different.

Madison's view was at odds with that of Montesquieu, who maintained that "in a large republic the public good is sacrificed to a thousand views; it is subordinate to exceptions; and depends on accidents. In a small one, the interest of the public is easier perceived, better understood, and more within the reach of every citizen; abuses have a lesser extent, and of course are less protected."[9] Not so in Bell—and in Bell we trust.

For Montesquieu, the Enlightenment, the new Cartesian thinking, and the emerging constitutional monarchy of Britain all combined to stimulate his insightful ideas about political checks and balances. He hoped these checks and balances would prevent exactly the corruption of public welfare that the charter city election in Bell foisted on its citizens.

Of course, the option of forming a charter city was motivated, *in theory*, by a quest for checks on the authority of California's state legislature. But the electoral public in the charter city special election was a meager 390 souls, and even in Bell's contested elections before the scandal, fewer than a quarter of registered voters, themselves only a quarter of the city's population, bothered to vote. That's not enough to prevent the corruption Montesquieu hoped to avoid.

Now there is no doubt that Montesquieu, Madison, Hobbes, and Machiavelli were very clever and insightful thinkers (and surely brighter than us). However, they got an awful lot of politics wrong simply because they were coping with momentary circumstances. They were looking at but a small sample of data, the goings-on surrounding them, and bits and pieces of ancient history. They also lacked modern tools of analysis (which we, luckily, have at our disposal). Consequently, they leapt to partially right, but often deeply wrong, conclusions. In all fairness to these past luminaries, their shortcomings often have to do with the fact that, besides being bound by their then-present contexts, these thinkers were also caught up in "the big questions"—what the highest nature of man *ought* to be, or what the "right" state of government really is, or what "justice" truly means in political terms. This shortsightedness extends not only to history's legends in political thought but also to contemporary thinkers like Jürgen Habermas, Michel Foucault, and John Rawls—thinkers who someday may be viewed in the same light.

The big questions about how the world *ought* to be are indeed important. But they are not our focus. Questions about philosophical values and metaphorical abstractions—these simply don't apply to the view of politics that we'll present in the pages ahead. We do not start with a desire to say what we think ought to be. It is hard to imagine that anyone, including us, cares much about what we think ought to be. Neither do we exhort others to be better than they are. Not that we do not hope to find ways to improve the world according to our lights—but we believe that the world can only be improved if we first understand how it works and why. Working out what makes people do what they do in the realm of politics is fundamental to working out how to make it in *their* interest to do better things.

The modern vernacular of politics and international relations, from balances of power and hegemony to partisanship and national interest, is the stuff of high school civics and nightly news punditry. It has little to do with real politics. And so, you may be delighted—or disappointed—to hear, this particular book of politics is not concerned with any of this. Our account of politics is primarily about what *is*, and why what is, is. In this book, we hope to explain the most fundamental and puzzling questions about politics and, in the process, give all of us a better way to think about why the worlds of rulers and subjects, of authorities and rights, of war and peace, and, in no small way, of life and death all work in the ways that they do. And maybe, just maybe, from time to time we will see paths to betterment.

The origins of the ideas developed here came years ago during heated lunchtime discussions between one of the authors of this book—Bruce Bueno de Mesquita—and a coauthor of many earlier works, Randolph M. Siverson (now professor emeritus at the University of California, Davis). While munching on burritos, Randy Siverson and Bueno de Mesquita discussed a rather basic question: What are the consequences for leaders and their regimes when a war is lost?

Oddly, that question had not been much addressed in the copious research on international affairs, and yet surely any leader would want to know *before* getting involved in a risky business like war what was going to happen to him after it was over. This question hadn't been asked because the standard ideas about war and peace were rooted in notions about states, the international system, and balances of power and polarity, not in leader interests. From the conventional view of international relations, the question just didn't make sense. Even the term "inter*nationa*l relations" presumes that the subject is *nations* rather than what Joe Biden or Kim Jong-Un or any other leader wants. We so easily speak of the United States' grand strategy or China's human rights policy or Russia's ambitions to once more achieve great power status, and yet, from our point of view, such statements make little sense.

<u>States don't have interests. People do.</u> Amid all the debate about national interest, what did former president Barack Obama fret about when formulating his Afghan policy? If he did not announce a time-table for withdrawal from Afghanistan he would lose support from his Democratic—not his national, but his Democratic—electoral base. President Kennedy similarly fretted that if he took no action in what became the Cuban missile crisis, he would be impeached and the Democrats would pay a heavy price in the 1962 midterm

election.[10] National interest might have been on each of their minds, but their personal political welfare was front and center.

The prime mover of interests in any state (or corporation for that matter) is the person at the top—the leader. So we started from this single point: the self-interested calculations and actions of rulers are the driving force of all politics.

The calculations and actions that a leader makes and takes constitute how she governs. And what, for a leader, is the "best" way to govern? However is necessary first to come to power, then to stay in power, and to control as much national (or corporate) revenue as possible all along the way.

Why do leaders do what they do? To come to power, to stay in power and, to the extent that they can, to keep control over money.

Building on their lunchtime question about leaders and war, Siverson and Bueno de Mesquita wrote a couple of academic journal articles in which they looked at international relations as just ordinary politics in which leaders want, above all else, to survive in power. These articles caught on quickly. Researchers saw that this was a different way to think about politics, one tied to real people making real decisions—in their own interest—rather than metaphors like states, nations, and systems. (It seems obvious now, but among the dominant realist school of international relations this is still heresy.) But Siverson and Bueno de Mesquita also saw that the theory could be stretched across a bigger canvas. Every type of politics could be addressed from the point of view of leaders trying to survive.

The idea that the canvas was that big was scary. It meant trying to recast everything (or nearly everything) we knew or thought we knew about politics into a single theoretical whole. It was a humbling moment, and Bueno de Mesquita and Siverson felt in need of help. Enter James D. Morrow—now a professor at the University of Michigan but back then a senior research fellow at Stanford's Hoover Institution, where Bueno de Mesquita was also based—and Alastair Smith. And so a foursome was born (sometimes affectionately known as BdM^2S^2). Together we wrote a thick, dense, technical tome called *The Logic of Political Survival* as well as a long list of journal articles.[11] These are the foundation for this book, which presents our ideas in an account that we hope anyone can follow, argue with, and maybe even come to accept. Today the theory behind this body of research has inspired many spin-off studies by us and by other researchers, theoretical expansions and elaborations by us and by others, and some lively debate—and no shortage of controversy as well.

Using this foundation, we look at politics, the choices of public policies, and even decisions about war and peace as lying outside of conventional thinking about culture and history. We also put ideas of civic virtue and psychopathology aside as central to understanding what leaders do and why they do it. Instead, we look at politicians as self-interested louts, just the sort of people you wouldn't want to have over for dinner, but without whom you might not have dinner at all.

The structure of the book is simple. After the essentials of ruling are outlined in Chapter 1, each subsequent chapter will probe a specific feature of politics. We'll assess why taxes are higher in many poor countries than in rich countries and why leaders can spend a fortune on the military and yet have a weak and almost useless army when it comes to the national defense. We will see, encouragingly, that despite recent challenges, democratic governance—that is, dependence on a large coalition of essential backers—is robust and maybe even immune to successful revolution and coups d'état. Together, the chapters will detail how the logic of political survival—the rules to rule by—connects dots of political consequence across the widest canvas imaginable, deepening our understanding of the dynamics of all rulers and their populations. It is because of this capacity to connect the dots that many of our students have called our list of rules to rule by "The Theory of Everything." We are content to codify it simply as *The Dictator's Handbook*.

We fully admit that our view of politics requires us to step outside of well-entrenched habits of mind, out of conventional labels and vague generalities, and into a more precise world of self-interested thinking. We seek a simpler and, we hope, more compelling way to think about government. Our perspective, disheartening though it may often seem to some, offers a way to address other facets of life than just government. It easily describes businesses, charities, families, and just about any other organization. (We're sure many readers will be comforted to have confirmation that their companies really are run like tyrannical regimes.) All of this may be sacrilege to some, but we believe that, in the end, it's the best way to understand the political world—and the only way that we can begin to assess how to use the rules to rule by to rule for the better. If we are going to play the game of politics, and we all must from time to time, then we ought to learn how to win the game. We hope and believe that is just what we all can take away from this book: how to win the game of politics and perhaps even improve the world a bit as we do so.

CHAPTER ONE

THE RULES OF POLITICS

The logic of politics is not complex. In fact, it is surprisingly easy to grasp most of what goes on in the political world as long as we are ready to adjust our thinking ever so modestly. To understand politics properly, we must modify one assumption in particular: we must stop thinking that leaders can lead unilaterally.

No leader is monolithic. If we are to make any sense of how power works, we must stop thinking that North Korea's Kim Jong-Un can do whatever he wants. We must stop believing that Adolf Hitler or Joseph Stalin or Genghis Khan or anyone else is in sole control of their nation. We must give up the notion that Enron's Kenneth Lay or British Petroleum's Tony Hayward knew about everything that was going on in their companies or that they could have made all the big decisions. All of these notions are flat-out wrong because no emperor, no king, no sheikh, no tyrant, no chief executive officer, no family head, no leader whatsoever can govern alone.

Consider France's Louis XIV (1638–1715). Known as the Sun King, Louis reigned as monarch for over seventy years, presiding over the expansion of France and the creation of the modern political state. Under Louis, France became the dominant power in continental Europe and a major competitor in the colonization of the Americas. He and his inner circle invented a code of law that helped shape the Napoleonic code and that forms the basis of French law to this day. He modernized the military, forming a professional standing army that became a role model for the rest of Europe and, indeed, the world. He was certainly one of the preeminent rulers of his or any time. But he didn't do it alone.

The word *monarchy* may mean "rule by one," but such rule does not, has not, and cannot exist. Louis is famously (and probably falsely) thought to have proclaimed, "L'état, c'est moi" (The state, it is me). This declaration is often used to describe political life for supposedly absolute monarchs like Louis, likewise for tyrannical dictators. The declaration of absolutism, however, is never true. No leader, no matter how august or how revered, no matter how cruel or vindictive, ever stands alone. Indeed, Louis XIV, ostensibly an absolute monarch, is a wonderful example of just how false this idea of monolithic leadership is.

After the death of his father, Louis XIII (1601–1643), Louis rose to the throne when he was but four years old. During the early years actual power resided in the hands of a regent—his mother. Her inner circle helped themselves to France's wealth, stripping the cupboard bare. By the time Louis assumed actual control over the government in 1661, at the age of twenty-three, the state over which he reigned was nearly bankrupt.

While most of us think of a state's bankruptcy as a financial crisis, looking through the prism of political survival makes evident that it really amounts to a political crisis. When debt exceeds the ability to pay, the problem for a leader is not so much that good public works must be cut back but rather that the incumbent doesn't have the resources necessary to purchase political loyalty from key backers. Bad economic times in a democracy mean too little money to fund pork-barrel projects that buy political popularity. For kleptocrats they mean passing up vast sums of money and maybe even watching their secret bank accounts dwindle, along with the loyalty of their underpaid henchmen.

The prospect of bankruptcy put Louis's hold on power at risk because the old-guard aristocrats, including the generals and officers of the army, saw their sources of money and privilege drying up. Circumstances were ripe for these politically crucial but fickle friends to seek someone better able to ensure their wealth and prestige. Faced with such a danger, Louis needed to make changes or else risk losing his monarchy.

Louis's specific circumstances called for altering the group of people who had the possibility of becoming members of his inner circle—that is, the group whose support guaranteed his continued dignity as king. He moved quickly to expand the opportunities (and for a few, the actual power) of new aristocrats, called the *noblesse de robe*. Together with his chancellor, Michel Le Tellier, he acted to create a professional, relatively meretricious army. In a radical departure from the practice observed by just about all of his neighboring monarchs, Louis opened the doors to officer ranks—even at the highest levels—to make room for many more than the traditional old-guard military aristocrats, the *noblesse d'épée*. In so doing, Louis was converting his army into a more accessible, politically and militarily competitive organization.

Meanwhile, Louis had to do something about the old aristocracy. He was deeply aware of their earlier disloyalty as instigators and backers of the antimonarchy Fronde (a mix of revolution and civil war) at the time of his regency. To neutralize the old aristocracy's potential threat, he attached them to his court—literally, compelling them to be physically present in Versailles much of the time. This meant that their prospects of income from the crown depended on how well favored they were by the king. And that, of course, depended on how well they served him.

By elevating so many newcomers, Louis created a new class of people who were beholden to him. In the process, he centralized his own authority more fully and enhanced his ability to enforce his views at the cost of many of the court's old aristocrats. Thus he erected a system of "absolute" control whose success depended on the loyalty of the military and the new aristocrats, and on tying the hands of the old aristocrats so that his welfare translated directly into their welfare.

The French populace in general did not figure much into Louis's calculations of who needed to be paid off—they did not represent an imminent threat to him. Even so, it's clear that his absolutism was not absolute at all. He needed supporters, and he understood how to maintain their loyalty. They would be loyal to him only so long as being loyal was more profitable for them than supporting someone else.

Louis's strategy was to replace the "winning coalition" of essential supporters that he inherited with people he could more readily count on. In place of the old guard, he brought up and into the inner circle members of the *noblesse de robe* and even, in the bureaucracy and especially in the military, some commoners. By expanding the pool of people who could be in the inner circle, he made political survival for those already in that role more competitive. Those who were privileged to be in his winning coalition knew that with the enlarged pool of candidates for such positions, any one of them could easily be replaced if they did not prove sufficiently trustworthy and loyal to the king. That, in turn, meant they could lose their opportunity for wealth, power, and privilege. Few were foolish enough to take such a risk.

Like all leaders, Louis forged a symbiotic relationship with his inner circle. He could not hope to thrive in power without their help, and they could not hope to reap the benefits of their positions without remaining loyal to him. Loyal they were. Louis XIV survived in office for seventy-two years until he died quietly of old age in 1715.

Louis XIV's experience exemplifies the most fundamental fact of political life. No one rules alone; no one has absolute authority. All that varies is how many backs have to be scratched and how big the supply of backs available for scratching is.

THREE POLITICAL DIMENSIONS

For leaders, the political landscape can be broken down into three groups of people: the nominal selectorate, the real selectorate, and the winning coalition.

The nominal selectorate includes every person who has at least some legal say in choosing their leader. In the United States it is everyone eligible to vote, meaning all citizens aged eighteen and over. Of course, as every citizen of the United States must realize, the right to vote is important, but at the end of the day no individual voter has a lot of say over who leads the country. Members of the nominal selectorate in a universal-franchise democracy have a toe in the political door, but not much more. In that specific way, the nominal selectorate in the United States or Britain or France doesn't have much more power than its counterparts, the "voters," in the old Soviet Union. There, too, all adult citizens had the right to vote, although their choice was generally to say yes or no to the candidates chosen by the Communist Party rather than to pick among candidates. Still, every adult citizen of the Soviet Union, where voting was mandatory, was a member of the nominal selectorate.

The second stratum of politics consists of the real selectorate. This is the group that *actually* chooses the leader. In today's China (as in the old Soviet Union), it consists of all voting members of the Communist Party; in Saudi Arabia's monarchy it is the senior members of the royal family; in Great Britain, the voters backing members of Parliament from the majority party.

The most important of these groups is the third, the subset of the real selectorate that makes up the winning coalition. These are the people whose support is essential if a leader is to survive in office. In the USSR the winning coalition consisted of a small group of people inside the Communist Party who chose candidates and who controlled policy. Their support was essential to keep the commissars and general secretary in power. These were the folks with the power to overthrow their boss—and he knew it. In the United States, the winning coalition for the presidency is vastly larger than in the old Soviet system, but because of the peculiarities of the Electoral College, it is nowhere near a majority or even a plurality of voters. For Louis XIV, the winning coalition was a handful of members of the court, military officers, and senior civil servants without whom a rival could have replaced the king.

Fundamentally, the nominal selectorate is the pool of potential support for a leader; the real selectorate includes those whose support is truly influential; and the winning coalition extends only to those essential supporters without whom the leader would be finished. A simple way to think of these groups is as *interchangeables*, *influentials*, and *essentials*.

In the United States, the voters are the nominal selectorate— interchangeables. As for the real selectorate—influentials—the electors of the Electoral College *really* choose the president (just as the party faithful picked the general secretary back in the USSR), but the electors nowadays are normatively bound to vote the way their state's voters voted, so they don't really have much independent clout in practice. That is true, however, only if state legislatures do not change the rules for selection of their electors. If they do—in keeping with the US Constitution, by the way—then the winning coalition could be much, much smaller. We will come back to that possibility in Chapter 10 when we consider ways in which the rules for rulers might be used to distort or undo democracy. In the United States, the nominal selectorate and real selectorate so far have been pretty closely aligned. This is why, even though you're only one among many voters, interchangeable with others, you still feel like your vote is influential—that it counts and is counted. The winning coalition—essentials—in the United States is the smallest bunch of voters, properly distributed among the states, whose support for a candidate translates into a presidential win in the Electoral College. The winning candidate may, of course, garner many more votes than the essential minimum they need to win the presidency. Those extra voters plus the essentials make up the support coalition. The support coalition must not be confused with the winning coalition. As we will see, essentials get goodies that the excess supporters may not receive. It is easy to confuse the support coalition and the essential, winning coalition in a democracy. Their differences are much more obvious when the essential group is very small.

With the distinction between essentials and the support coalition firmly in mind, we can see that while the winning coalition (essentials) is a pretty big fraction of the nominal selectorate (interchangeables) in the United States, it doesn't have to be even close to a majority of the US population. In fact, given the federal structure of American elections, it's possible to control the executive and legislative branches of government with as little as about one-fifth of the vote, if the votes are really efficiently placed. (Abraham Lincoln—and Donald Trump— were masters at just such voter efficiency.) Indeed, the absolute popular vote margin tells us almost nothing in a great many places, including, distressingly, the United States. Still, it is worth observing that the United States has one of the world's biggest winning coalitions both in absolute numbers and, most importantly, as a proportion of the electorate. But it is not the biggest. Britain's parliamentary structure requires the prime minister to have the support of a little over 25 percent of the electorate in two-party elections to Parliament. That is, the prime minister generally needs at least half the members of Parliament to be from her party and for each of them to win half the vote (plus one) in each two-party parliamentary race: half of half of the voters, or one-quarter. France's runoff system can be even more demanding. Election requires that a candidate win a majority in the final, two-candidate runoff, but, of course, to make the runoff it is only necessary to have one more vote than the third-place finisher. If, say, ten candidates ran, then getting into the runoff might require few votes indeed!

Looking elsewhere we see that there can be a vast range in the size of the nominal selectorate, the real selectorate, and the winning coalition. Some places, like North Korea, have a mass nominal selectorate in which everyone gets to vote—it's a joke, of course—a tiny real selectorate that actually picks the leader, and a winning coalition that surely is no more than maybe a couple of hundred people (if that) and without whom even North Korea's first leader, Kim Il-Sung, could have been reduced to ashes. Other nations, like Saudi Arabia, have tiny nominal and real selectorates, made up of the royal family and a few crucial merchants and religious leaders. The Saudi winning coalition is perhaps even smaller than North Korea's.

How does Bell, California, measure up? We saw that in 2009, the interchangeables in Bell consisted of 9,395 registered voters; the influentials, the 2,235 who actually voted; and the essentials, not more than the 473 voters whose support was *essential* to win a seat on the city council. Bell definitely looks better than North Korea or Saudi Arabia—we'd hope so. It looks alarmingly close, however, to the setup of a regime with mostly phony elections, such as today's Egypt, Venezuela, Cambodia, and Russia. Most publicly traded corporations have this structure as well. They have millions of shareholders who are the interchangeables. They have big institutional shareholders and some others who are the influentials. And the essentials are pretty much those who get to pick actual board members and senior management. Bell doesn't look much like Madison's or Montesquieu's idealization of democracy, and neither do corporations, regardless of how many shareholders cast proxy ballots.

Think about the company you work for. Who is your leader? Who are the essentials whose support he or she *must* have? What individuals, though not essential to your CEO's power, are nonetheless influential in the governance of the company? And then, of course, who is there every day at the office—working hard (or not), just hoping for the breakthrough or the break that will catapult them into a bigger role?

These three groups provide the foundation for all that's to come in the rest of this book and, more importantly, the foundation for the working of politics in all organizations, big and small. Variations in the sizes of these three groups give politics a three-dimensional structure that clarifies the complexity of political life. By working out how these dimensions intersect—that is, each organization's mix in the size of its interchangeable, influential, and essential groups—we can come to grips with the puzzles of politics. Differences in the size of these groups across states, businesses, and any other organization, as you will see, decide almost *everything* that happens in politics—what leaders can do, what they can and can't get away with, to whom they answer, and the relative qualities of life that everyone under them enjoys (or, too often, doesn't enjoy).

VIRTUES OF 3-D POLITICS

You may find it hard to believe that just these three dimensions govern all of the varied systems of leadership in the world. After all, our experience tends to confirm that on one end of the political spectrum we have autocrats and tyrants—horrible, selfish thugs who occasionally stray into psychopathology. On the other end, we have democrats—elected representatives, presidents, and prime ministers who we like to think are the benevolent guardians of freedom. Leaders from these two worlds, we assure ourselves, must be worlds apart!

It's a convenient fiction but a fiction nonetheless. Governments do not differ in kind. They differ along the dimensions of their selectorates and winning coalitions. These dimensions limit or liberate what leaders can and should do to keep their jobs. How limited or liberated a leader is depends on how selectorates and winning coalitions interact.

No question, it is tough to break the habit of talking about democracies and dictatorships as if either of these terms is sufficient to convey the differences across regimes, even though no two "democracies" are alike and neither are any two "dictatorships." In fact, it is so hard to break that habit that we will continue to use these terms much of the time throughout this book—but it is important to emphasize that the term *dictatorship* really means a government based on a particularly small number of essentials drawn from a very large group of interchangeables and, usually, a relatively small batch of influentials. On the other hand, if we talk about democracy, we really mean a government founded on a very large number of essentials and a very large number of interchangeables, with the influential group being almost as big as the interchangeable group. When we mention monarchy or military junta, we have in mind that the number of interchangeables, influentials, and essentials is small.

The beauty of talking about organizations in terms of essentials, influentials, and interchangeables is that these categories permit us to refrain from arbitrarily drawing a line between forms of governance, pronouncing one "democratic" and another "autocratic," or one a large republic and another small, or any of the other mostly one-dimensional views of politics expressed by some of history's leading political philosophers.

The truth is, no two governments or organizations are exactly alike. No two democracies are alike. Indeed, they can be radically different one from the other and still qualify perfectly well as democracies. The more significant and observable differences in the behavior of governments and organizations depend on the absolute and relative size of the interchangeable, influential, and essential groups. The seemingly subtle differences between, say, France's government and Britain's, or Canada's and the United States', are not inconsequential. However, the variations in their policies are the product of the incentives leaders face as they contend with their particular mix of interchangeable, influential, and essential groups.

There is incredible variety among political systems, mainly because people are amazingly inventive in manipulating politics to work to their advantage. Leaders make rules to give all citizens the vote—creating lots of new interchangeables—but then impose electoral boundaries, stacking the deck of essential voters to ensure that their preferred candidates win. Democratic elites may decide to require a plurality to win a particular race, giving themselves a way to impose what a majority may otherwise reject. Or they might favor having runoff elections to create a majority, even though it may end up being a majority of the interchangables' second-place choices. Alternatively, democratic leaders might represent political views in proportion to how many votes each view got, forging governments out of coalitions of minorities. Each of these and countless other rules easily can fall within our definition of democracy, yet each can—and does—produce radically different results.

Figure 1.1 makes clear, using a "normalized" measure of coalition size that varies between 0—the smallest coalition, proportionally speaking—and 1—the largest proportional coalition—that there is a great deal of variation in the size of coalitions across places we think of as democracies and also within each of those countries over time. As the figure shows us, Costa Rica—surprised?—topped the list for most of the half-century that is graphed. The United States did excellently most of the time after about 1976, but it was in decline for several years near the end of the graph, turning back up around 2020. India plummeted in the late 1970s when Indira Gandhi worked to amend the constitution to give herself and her party an electoral advantage. In response, the voters tossed her out and the coalition expanded back to a solid level. However, it has begun another retreat as Prime Minister Narendra Modi works to amend the constitution to tilt representation more in favor of his supporters. Will India continue to shrink its coalition, or will it stay in the "democratic" fold? We will have more to say on that later. The most disturbing element of the graph is that all of the countries that are plotted saw their coalition size decrease after 2010. So it is not just that the world has been on a bit of a populist binge; democracy has been in retreat even in supposedly well-established democratic societies. Will they self-correct? We think so!

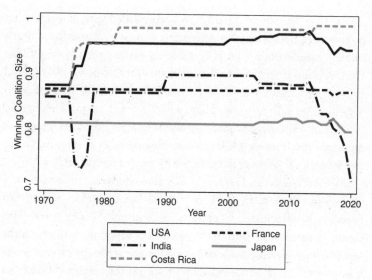

Figure 1.1: No Two Democracies Are Alike

Figure 1.1 urges us to remember that labels like *democracy* or *dictatorship* are a convenience—but only a convenience.

CHANGE THE SIZE OF DIMENSIONS AND CHANGE THE WORLD

Changing the relative size of interchangeables, influentials, and essentials can make a real difference in basic political outcomes.[1] As an example, we can look to the past, seemingly prosaic election of members of San Francisco's board of supervisors.

San Francisco used to elect its board of supervisors in citywide elections. That meant that the selectorate consisted of the city's voters, and the essentials were the minimum number needed to elect a member to the board. In 1977 the method changed, and at-large, citywide elections were replaced by district voting. Under the old rules, members of the board of supervisors were elected by and represented the whole city as if it were one large constituency. Under the new rules, they were elected by and represented their district—that is, their neighborhood—so each supervisor was chosen by a much smaller constituency. The policy and candidate preferences of San Francisco residents as a whole were little different between 1975 and 1977; nevertheless, a candidate named Harvey Milk who failed in his bid to be elected to the board in 1975 went on to be elected in 1977 (and tragically assassinated not long after). As *Time* magazine reported later, Harvey Milk was "the first openly gay man elected to any substantial political office in the history of the planet."[2]

What changed in Harvey Milk's favor between 1975 and 1977 was simple enough. In 1975, he needed broad support among San Francisco's influentials to get elected. He got 52,996 votes. This meant he finished seventh in the election of supervisors, in which the top five were elected. Milk did not have enough support, and so he lost. In 1977 he only needed support within the neighborhood from which he ran, the Castro, a dominantly gay area. He was, as he well knew, popular within his district. He received 5,925 votes, giving him a plurality of support with 29.42 percent of the vote in district 5, which placed him first in the 5th Supervisory District contest, and so he was elected. So in 1977, with a little more than 10 percent of the votes that he'd garnered in his losing 1975 campaign, Milk won, thanks to the change in how election outcomes were determined.

Strange as it may seem, the same ideas and subtle differences that held true in San Francisco can be applied to illiberal governments like Zimbabwe, China, and Cuba, and even to the somewhat more ambiguous sorts of governments like Russia or Venezuela or Singapore. Each is easily and uniquely placed on the three organizational dimensions: interchangeables, influentials, and essentials.

Once we learn to think along these three dimensions, we can begin to unravel some of politics' most enduring puzzles. Our starting point is the realization that any leader worth her salt wants as much power as she can get, and she wants to keep it for as long as possible. Managing the interchangeables, influentials, and essentials to that end *is* the act, art, and science of governing.

RULES RULING RULERS

Money, it is said, is the root of all evil. That can be true, but in some cases, money can serve as the root of all that is good about governance. It depends on what leaders do with the money they generate. They may use it to benefit everyone, as is largely true for expenditures directed toward protecting the personal well-being of all citizens and their property. Much public policy can be thought of as an effort to invest in the welfare of the people. But government revenue can also be spent on buying the loyalty of a few key cronies at the expense of general welfare. It can also be used to promote corruption, black marketeering, and a host of even less pleasant policies.

The first step in understanding how politics really works is to ask what kinds of policies leaders spend money on. Do they spend it on *public goods* that benefit everyone? Or do they spend mostly on *private goods* that benefit only a few? The answer, for any savvy politician, depends on how many people the leader needs to keep loyal—that is, the number of essentials in the coalition.

In a democracy, or any other system where a leader's critical coalition is really large, it becomes too costly to buy loyalty exclusively through private rewards. The money has to be spread too thinly. So more democratic types of governments, dependent as they are on large coalitions, tend to emphasize spending to create effective public policies that improve general welfare pretty much as suggested by James Madison. In such a government there is little difference between the benefits enjoyed by the winning coalition, the larger support coalition, and the people in general.

By contrast, dictators, monarchs, military junta leaders, and most CEOs all rely on a smaller set of essentials. As intimated by Machiavelli, it is more efficient for them to govern by spending a chunk of revenue to buy the loyalty of their coalition through private benefits, even though these benefits come at the expense of the larger taxpaying public or millions of small shareholders. Thus small coalitions encourage stable, corrupt, private goods–oriented regimes in which the essentials do great while even the broader support coalition does pretty poorly. The choice between enhancing social welfare and enriching a privileged few is not a question of how benevolent a leader is. Honorable motives might seem important, but they are overwhelmed by the need to keep essential supporters happy, and the means of keeping them happy depends on how many need rewarding.

TAXING

To keep backers happy a leader needs money. Anyone aspiring to rule must first ask how much he can extract from his constituents—whether they are citizens of a nation or shareholders in a corporation. This extraction can take many forms—personal income taxes, property taxes, duties on imports, licenses, and government fees—but we will refer to it generically as taxation to keep the discussion from wandering too far afield. As we've already seen, those who rule based on a large coalition cannot efficiently sustain themselves in power by focusing on private benefits. Their bloc of essential supporters is too large for that. Since they must sustain themselves by emphasizing public goods more than private rewards, they must also keep tax rates low, relatively speaking. People prefer to keep their money for themselves, except when that money can be pooled to provide something they value that they cannot afford to buy on their own.

For example, we all want to be sure that a reliable fire department will put out a fire that threatens our home. We could conceivably hire a personal firefighter to protect our house alone. However, not only is that expensive, but we would also have to worry about whether our neighbor's house is well enough protected that it won't catch fire and threaten our home. Furthermore, our neighbor, realizing that we won't want his house to burn if in doing so it threatens ours, may attempt to hitch a free ride on the fact that we hired a personal firefighter who will have to step in to protect the neighbor's house as well. In no time we are in the position of paying for neighborhood-wide fire protection single-handedly, a very costly proposition. The easiest way to get neighbors to share the burden of fire protection is to let government leaders take the responsibility for fire protection. To provide such protection we happily pay taxes.

Though we may willingly pay taxes for programs that provide tangible benefits to us, such as protection from fire, felons, and foreign foes, we would not be so willing to see our tax money used to pay a tremendous salary to our president or prime minister—or, in the case of Bell, California, to our local government officials. As a result, heads of governments reliant on a large coalition tend not to be among the world's best-paid executives.

Because the acceptable uses of taxation in a regime that depends on a large coalition are few—just those expenditures thought to buy more welfare than people can buy on their own—taxes tend to be low when coalitions are large. But when the coalition of essential backers is small and private goods are an efficient way to stay in power, then the well-being of the broader population falls by the wayside, contrary to the view expressed by Hobbes. In this setting leaders want to tax heavily, redistributing wealth by taking as much as they can from the poor interchangeables and the disenfranchised and giving that wealth to the members of the winning coalition, making them fat, rich, and loyal. Chapter 4 will show us that taxes really are higher in autocracies than in democracies once we compare apples to apples. That will help explain why per capita incomes are typically much higher in societies with lots of essentials than in those with few.

Obviously, self-interest plays a large role in taxation and spending equations. We must wonder, therefore, why incumbents don't take all the revenue they've raised and sock it away in their personal bank accounts. This question is especially pertinent for corporate executives. Once investors have entrusted money in the hands of a CEO or chairman of the board, what can the investors do to assure themselves that the money will be invested wisely to produce benefits for them? Investors want increased value. They want share prices to rise, their portion of ownership to go up, and dividend payments to be large and predictably regular. To be sure, focusing on self-interest tells us that rulers and business leaders, and in fact all of us, would love to take other people's money and keep it for ourselves, much as Robert

Rizzo and his cronies did. This means that the next step in explaining the calculus of politics is to figure out how much a leader can keep and how much *must* be spent on the coalition and on the public if the incumbent is to stay in power.

SHUFFLING THE ESSENTIAL DECK

Staying in power, as we now know, requires the support of others. This support is only forthcoming if a leader provides his essentials with more benefits than they might expect to receive under alternative leadership or government. When essential followers expect to be better off under the wing of some political challenger, they desert.

Incumbents have a tough job. They need to offer their supporters more than any rival can. While this can be difficult, the logic of politics tells us that incumbents have a huge advantage over rivals, especially when officeholders rely on relatively few people and when the pool of replacements for coalition members is large. Lenin designed precisely such a political system in Russia after the revolution. This explains why, from the October 1917 revolution through to Gorbachev's reforms in the late 1980s, only one Soviet leader, Nikita Khrushchev, was successfully deposed in a coup. All the other Soviet leaders died of old age or infirmity, but Khrushchev failed to deliver what he'd promised to his cronies. It is the successful, reliable implementation of political promises to those who count that provides the basis for any incumbent's advantage.

The story of survival is not much different, although the particulars are very different, in political settings that rely on many essential backers. As even a casual observer of election campaigns knows, there is a big discrepancy between what politicians promise when making a bid for power and what they actually deliver. Once in power, a new leader might well discard those who helped her get to the top and replace them with others whom she deems more loyal.

Not only that, but essential supporters can't just compare what the challenger and incumbent each offer today. The incumbent might pay less now, for instance, but the pay is expected to continue for those kept on or brought into the new incumbent's inner circle. True, the challenger may offer more today, but his promises of future rewards may be nothing more than political promises without any real substance behind them. Essentials must compare the benefits expected to come their way in the future because that future flow adds up in time to bigger rewards. Placing a supporter in his coalition after a leader is ensconced as the new incumbent is a good indicator that he will continue to rely on and reward that supporter, exactly because the new incumbent has made a concerted effort to sort out those most likely to remain loyal from opportunists who might bring him down in the future. The challenger might promise to keep backers on if she reaches the heights of power, but it is a political promise that might very well not be honored in the long run.

Lest there be doubt that those who share the risks of coming to power are often thrown aside—or worse—let us reflect on the all-too-typical case of the backers of Fidel Castro's revolution in Cuba. Of the twenty-one ministers appointed by Castro in January 1959, immediately after the success of his revolution, twelve had resigned or been ousted by the end of the year. Four more were removed in 1960 as Castro further consolidated his hold on power. These people, once among Fidel's closest, most intimate backers, ultimately faced the two big "exes" of politics. For the luckier among them, divorce from Castro came in the form of exile. For others, it meant execution. This included even Castro's most famous fellow revolutionary, Che Guevara.

Che may have been second in power only to Fidel himself. Indeed, that was likely his greatest fault. Castro forced Che out of Cuba in 1965 partly because of Che's popularity, which made him a potential rival for authority. Castro sent Che on a mission to Bolivia, but toward the end of March 1967 Castro simply cut off Guevara's support, leaving him stranded. Captain Gary Prado Salmon, the Bolivian officer who captured Che, confirmed that Guevara told him that the decision to come to Bolivia was not his own; it was Castro's. One of Fidel's biographers remarked,

> In a very real sense Che followed in the shadows of Frank Pais, Camilo Cienfuegos, Huber Matos, and Humberto Sori Marin

[all close backers of Castro during the revolution]. Like them, he was viewed by Castro as a "competitor" for power and like them, he had to be moved aside "in one manner or another." Che Guevara was killed in Bolivia but at least he escaped the ignominy of execution by his revolutionary ally, Fidel Castro. Humberto Sori Marin was not so "fortunate." Marin, the commander of Castro's rebel army, was accused of conspiring against the revolution. In April 1961, like so many other erstwhile backers of Fidel Castro, he too was executed.[3]

Political transitions are filled with examples of supporters who help a leader to power only to be replaced. This is true whether we look at national or local governments, corporations, organized crime families, or, for that matter, any other organization. Each member of a winning coalition, knowing that many are standing on the sidelines to replace them, will be careful not to give the incumbent reasons to look for replacements.

This was the relationship Louis XIV managed so well. If a small bloc of backers is needed and can be drawn from a large pool of potential supporters (as with the small coalition needed in places like Zimbabwe, North Korea, or Afghanistan), then the incumbent doesn't need to spend a huge proportion of the regime's revenue to buy the coalition's loyalty. On the other hand, more must be spent to keep the coalition loyal if there are relatively few people who could replace its members. That is true in two circumstances: when the coalition and real selectorate are both small (as in a monarchy or military junta), or the coalition and selectorate (whether real or nominal) are both large (as in a democracy). In these circumstances, the incumbent's ability to replace coalition members is pretty constrained. Essentials can therefore drive up the price for staying loyal. The upshot is that there is less revenue available to be spent at the incumbent's discretion because more has to be spent to keep the coalition loyal, fending off credible counteroffers by political foes.

When the ratio of essentials to interchangeables is small (as in rigged-election autocracies and most publicly traded corporations), coalition loyalty is purchased cheaply and incumbents have massive discretion. They can choose to spend the money they control on themselves or on pet public projects. Kleptocrats, of course, sock the money away in secret bank accounts or in offshore investments to serve as a rainy-day fund in the event that they are overthrown. A few civic-minded autocrats slip a little into secret accounts, preferring to fend off the threat of revolt by using their discretionary funds (the leftover tax revenue not spent on coalition loyalty) to invest in public works. Those public works may prove successful, as was true for Lee Kuan Yew's efforts in Singapore and Deng Xiaoping's in China. They may also prove to be dismal failures, as was true for Kwame Nkrumah's civic-minded industrial program in Ghana and Mao Zedong's Great Leap Forward, which turned out to be a great leap backward for China.

We have seen how the desire to survive in office shapes some key revenue-generation decisions, key allocation decisions, and the pot of money at the incumbent's discretion. Whether the tax rate is high or low, whether money is spent more on public or private rewards, and how much is spent in whatever way the incumbent wants all dictate political success within the confines of the governance structure the leader inherits or creates. And our notion of governing for political survival tells us that there are five basic rules leaders can use to succeed in any system:

RULE 1: *Keep your winning coalition as small as possible.* A small coalition allows a leader to rely on very few people to stay in power. Fewer essentials equals more control and contributes to more discretion over expenditures.

Bravo for Kim Jong-Un of North Korea. He is a contemporary master at ensuring dependence on a small coalition. Bravo to Donald Trump. He tried to shrink the coalition by manipulating vote counting in the world's oldest democracy. That's not an easy thing to do.

RULE 2: *Keep your nominal selectorate as large as possible.* Maintain a large selectorate of interchangeables and you can easily replace any troublemakers in your coalition, influentials and essentials alike. After all, a large nominal selectorate provides a big supply of substitute supporters to put the essentials on notice that they should be loyal and well behaved or else face being replaced.

Bravo to Vladimir Ilyich Lenin for introducing universal adult suffrage in Russia's old rigged election system. Lenin mastered the art of creating a vast supply of interchangeables. Boo to Donald Trump. He foolishly tried to suppress turnout by America's interchangeables, inducing more people to turn out to vote in 2020 and swelling the size of the selectorate, which resulted in his unintentionally swelling the size of the essential coalition needed for victory in 2020, making it bigger than had been true in 2016. Big error!

RULE 3: *Control the flow of revenue.* It's always better for a ruler to determine who eats than it is to have a larger pie from which the people can feed themselves. The most effective cash flow for leaders is one that makes lots of people poor and redistributes money to keep select people—their supporters—wealthy.

Bravo to Pakistan's former president, Asif Ali Zardari, estimated to be worth up to $4 billion even as he governed a country near the world's bottom in per capita income. Bravo to Donald Trump. He found a way to tax his foes (Democrats) heavily while lightening the tax burden on his supporters (especially wealthy Republicans).

RULE 4: *Pay your key supporters just enough to keep them loyal.* Remember, your backers would rather *be* you than be dependent on you. Your big advantage over them is that you know where the money is and they don't. Give your coalition just enough that they don't shop around for someone to replace you and not a penny more.

Bravo to Zimbabwe's Robert Mugabe, who, whenever facing a threat of a military coup, managed to pay his army, keeping their loyalty against all odds well into his nineties.

RULE 5: *Don't take money out of your supporters' pockets to make the people's lives better.* The flip side of rule 4 is not to be too cheap toward your coalition of essential supporters. If you're good to the people at the expense of your coalition, it won't be long until your "friends" will be gunning for you. Effective policy for the masses doesn't necessarily produce loyalty among essentials, and it's darn expensive to boot. Hungry people are not likely to have the energy to overthrow you, so don't worry about them. Disappointed coalition members, in contrast, can defect, leaving you in deep trouble.

Bravo to Senior General Than Shwe of Myanmar, who made sure following Cyclone Nargis in 2008 that food relief was controlled and sold on the black market by his military supporters rather than letting aid go to the people—at least 138,000 and maybe as many as 500,000 of whom died in the disaster.[4]

DO THE RULES WORK IN DEMOCRACIES?

At this point, you may be saying, *Hold on! If an elected leader followed these rules she'd be out of the job in no time flat.* That's almost right, but not quite. Donald Trump followed all but one of these rules about as closely as any freely elected leader in modern history, and he was voted out after one term. Breaking even one rule is dangerous for anyone, including democratically elected leaders.

As we'll see throughout the chapters to follow, a democratic leader does indeed have a really tough time maintaining her position while looting her country and siphoning off funds. She's constrained by the laws of the land, which also determine—through election procedures—the size of the coalition that she needs in order to come to power. The coalition has to be relatively large and she has to be responsive to it, so she does have a problem with rule 1. But that doesn't mean she doesn't try to follow rule 1 as closely as she can (and all of the other rules too).

Why, for example, do state legislatures gerrymander districts? Precisely because of rule 1: Keep the coalition as small as possible.

Why do some political parties favor immigration? Rule 2: Expand the number of interchangeables, a rule Donald Trump did not adequately understand and manipulate.

Why are there so many battles over the tax code? Rule 3: Take control of the sources of revenue.

Why do Democrats spend so much tax money on welfare and social programs? Or why on earth do we have earmarks? Rule 4: Reward your essentials at all costs.

Why do Republicans wish the top tax rate were lower and have so many problems with the idea of national health care? Rule 5: Don't rob your supporters to give to your opposition.

Just like autocrats and tyrants, leaders of democratic nations try to follow these rules because they, like every other leader, want to get power and keep it. Even democrats almost never step down unless they're forced to.[5] The problem for democrats is that they face different constraints and have to be a little more creative than their autocratic counterparts. And they succeed less often. Even though they generally provide a much higher standard of living for their citizens than do tyrants, democrats generally have shorter terms in office.

Political distinctions are truly continuous across the intersection of the three dimensions that govern how organizations work. Some "kings" in history have actually been elected. Some "democrats" rule their nations with the authority of a despot. In other words, the distinction between autocrats and democrats isn't cut-and-dried.

Having laid the foundation for our new theory of politics and having revealed the five rules of leadership, we'll turn to the big questions at the heart of the book, often using the terms *autocrats* and *democrats* throughout, to show how the games of leadership change as you slide from one extreme to the other on the spectrum of small and large coalitions. But just remember, there's always a little mix of both words regardless of the country or organization in question. The lessons from both extremes apply whether you're talking about Saddam Hussein or George Washington. After all, the old saw still holds true—politicians are all the same.

CHAPTER TWO

COMING TO POWER

For centuries, "John Doe" has served as the placeholder name assigned to unidentified nobodies. And while his first name may have been Samuel, not John, in every other respect Liberia's Sergeant Doe was just such a nobody until April 12, 1980. Born in a remote part of Liberia's interior and virtually illiterate, he, like hundreds of thousands of others in his predicament, moved out of the West African jungle in search of work. He headed to the capital city, Monrovia, where he found that the army held great opportunities even for men like him who had no skills. One of these opportunities presented itself when Doe found himself in President William Tolbert's bedroom on April 12. As the president slept, he seized the day, bayoneted the president, threw his entrails to the dogs, and declared himself Liberia's new president.[1] Thus did he rise from obscurity to claim the highest office in his land.

Together with sixteen other noncommissioned officers, Doe had scaled the fence at the Executive Mansion, hoping to confront the president and find out why they had not been paid. Seeing the opportunity before him, he ended the dominance of Tolbert's True Whig Party, a political regime created by slaves repatriated from America in 1847. He immediately rounded up thirteen cabinet ministers, who were then publicly executed on the beach in front of cheering crowds. Many more deaths would follow. Doe then headed the People's Redemption Council, which suspended the constitution and banned all political activity.

Doe had no idea what a president was supposed to do and even less idea how to govern a country. What he *did* know was how to seize power and keep it: remove the previous ruler, find the money, form a small coalition, and pay the coalition just enough to keep them loyal. In short order, he proceeded to replace virtually everyone who had been in the government or the army with members of his own small Krahn tribe, which made up only about 4 percent of the population. He increased the pay of army privates from $85 to $250 per month. He purged everyone he did not trust. Following secret trials, he had no fewer than fifty of his original collaborators executed.

Doe funded his government, as his predecessors had, with revenues from Firestone, which leased large tracts of land for rubber; from the Liberian Iron Mining Company, which exported iron ore; and by registering more than 2,500 ocean-going ships without requiring safety inspections. Further, he received direct financial backing from the United States government. The United States gave Doe's government $500 million over ten years. In exchange the United States received basing rights and made Liberia a center for US intelligence and propaganda. It is believed that Doe and his cronies personally amassed $300 million.

As for Doe's policies, they couldn't be called successful. Indeed, he produced virtually no policies at all. He was lazy and spent his days hanging out with the wives of his presidential guards. The economy collapsed, foreign debt soared, and criminal enterprises became virtually the only successful businesses in Liberia. Monrovian banks became money-laundering operations. Little wonder that the people of Liberia ended up hating Doe. And yet, because he knew where the money was and who needed paying off, he managed to survive in power.

Damn the idea of good governance and don't elevate the concerns of the people over your own and those of your supporters: that's a good mantra for would-be dictators. In such a way any John Doe—even a Samuel Doe—can seize power, and even keep it.

PATHS TO POWER WITH FEW ESSENTIALS

To come to power a challenger need only do three things. First, he must remove the incumbent. Second, he needs to seize the apparatus of government. Third, he needs to form a coalition of supporters sufficient to sustain him as the new incumbent. Each of these actions has its own unique challenges. The relative ease with which they all can be accomplished differs between democracies and autocracies.

There are three ways for an incumbent leader to leave office, making room for a new leader. The first, and easiest, is for the leader to die. If that convenience does not offer itself, a challenger can make an offer to the essential members of the incumbent's coalition that is sufficiently attractive that they defect to the challenger's cause. Third, the current political system can be overwhelmed from the outside, whether through military defeat by a foreign power or through revolution and rebellion, in which the masses rise up, depose the current leader, and destroy existing institutions.

While rebellion requires skill and coordination, its success ultimately depends heavily upon coalition loyalty, or, more precisely, the absence of loyalty to the old regime. Hosni Mubarak's defeat by a mass uprising in Egypt is a case in point. The most critical factor behind Mubarak's defeat in February 2011 was the decision by Egypt's top generals to allow demonstrators to take to the streets without fear of military suppression. And why was that the case? As explained in a talk given on May 5, 2010, based on the logic set out here, cuts in US foreign aid to Egypt, combined with serious economic constraints that produced high unemployment, meant that Mubarak's coalition was likely underpaid and the people were likely to believe the risks and costs of rebellion were smaller than normal.[2] That is, the general rule of thumb for rebellion is that revolutions occur when those who preserve the current system are sufficiently dissatisfied with their rewards that they are willing to look for someone new to take care of them. On the other hand, revolts are defeated through suppression of the people—always an unpleasant task—so coalition members need to receive enough benefits from their leader that they are willing to do horribly distasteful things to ensure that the existing system is maintained. If they do not get enough goodies under the current system, then they will not stop the people from rising up against the regime.

SPEED IS ESSENTIAL

Once the old leader is gone, it is essential for a new leader to seize the instruments of power, such as the treasury, as quickly as possible. This is particularly important in small-coalition systems. Anyone who waits will be a loser in the competition for power.

Speed is of the essence. In most political systems the coalition is much smaller than a majority of the nominal selectorate. Furthermore, even though we tend to think that if one leader has enough votes or supporters, then the other potential candidates must be short, this is wrong. There can be many different groups simultaneously trying to organize to overthrow a regime, and each might have sufficient numbers of lukewarm or double-dealing coalition members who could aid them in securing power—or just as easily aid someone else, if the price is right. This is why it is absolutely essential to seize the reins of power quickly: so you can make sure that your group gets to control the instruments of the state, and not someone else's.

Samuel Doe ruled because his group had the guns. He did not need half the nation to support him. He needed just enough confederates so that he could control the army and suppress the rest of the population. There were many other coalitions that could have formed, but Doe grabbed hold of power first and suppressed the rest. This is the essence of coming to power.

Consider a room filled with one hundred people. Anyone could take complete control if she had five supporters with automatic weapons pointed at the rest. She would remain in power so long as the five gunmen continue to back her. But there need be nothing special about her or about the gunmen beyond the fact that they grabbed the guns first. Had someone else secured the guns and given them to five supporters of their own, then it would have been someone else telling everyone what to do.

Waiting is risky business. There is no prize for coming in second.

PAY TO PLAY

Paying supporters, not good governance or representing the general will, is the essence of ruling. Buying loyalty is particularly difficult when a leader first comes to power. When deciding whether to support a new leader, prudent backers must think not only about how much their leader gives them today but also what they can expect to receive in the future.

The supporting cast in any upstart's transitional coalition must recognize that they might not be kept on for long. After Doe took over the Liberian government, he greatly increased army salaries. This made it immediately attractive for his fellow army buddies to back him. But they were mindful that they might not be rewarded forever. Don't forget that fifty of his initial backers were eventually executed.

Allaying supporters' fears of being abandoned is a key element of coming to power. Of course, supporters are not so naive that they will be convinced by political promises that their position in the coalition is secure. But such political promises are much better than tipping your hand and revealing your true plans. Once word gets out that supporters are going to be replaced, they will turn on their patron. For instance, Ronald Reagan won the pro-choice vote in the 1980 US presidential election over the pro-life incumbent, Jimmy Carter. When Reagan's true abortion stance became apparent, the pro-choice voters abandoned him in droves. Walter Mondale won the pro-choice vote in the 1984 presidential election, although Reagan was reelected in a landslide.

Leaders understand the conditions that can cost them their heads. That is why they do their level best to pay essential cronies enough that these partners really want to stay loyal. This makes it tough for someone new to come to power. But sometimes circumstances conspire to open the door to a new ruler.

MORTALITY: THE BEST OPPORTUNITY FOR POWER

Most unavoidably, and therefore first, on the list of risks of being deposed is the simple, inescapable fact of mortality. Dead leaders cannot deliver rewards to their coalition. Dying leaders face almost as grave a problem. If essential backers know their leader is dying, then they also know that they need someone new to assure the flow of revenue into their pockets. That's a good reason to keep terminal illnesses secret: a terminal ailment is likely to provoke an uprising, either within the ranks of the essential coalition or among outsiders who see an opportunity to step in and take control of the palace.

Ayatollah Ruhollah Khomeini in Iran and Corazon Aquino in the Philippines both chose the right time to seize power. Take the case of Ayatollah Khomeini. He was one of the most senior Shia clerics in Iran and a vehement opponent of Mohammad Reza Shah Pahlavi's secular regime. During the early 1960s he spoke out against the regime and organized protests. His activities resulted in his being repeatedly arrested. In 1964 he went into exile, first to Turkey, then to Iraq, and eventually to France, continuing to preach his opposition to the shah wherever he was. Tapes of his speeches were popular throughout Iran.

In 1977, with the death of the shah's rival, Ali Shariati, Khomeini became the most influential opposition leader. Although he urged others to oppose the shah, he refused to return to Iran until the shah was gone. Except for a privileged few, almost everyone in Iran hungered for change. The shah's regime and those associated with it were widely disliked. Seeing that there was a chance for real change, people threw their support behind the one clearly viable alternative: Khomeini. After the shah fled the country, an estimated six million people turned out to cheer Khomeini's return. Judging from what he did next, they may have cheered too soon.

Immediately after his return, Khomeini challenged the interim government, which was headed by the shah's former prime minister. Much of the army defected and joined Khomeini, and when he ordered a jihad against soldiers remaining loyal to the old regime, resistance collapsed. Then he ordered a referendum in which the people would choose between the old monarchy of the shah or an Islamic republic. With 98 percent of people endorsing the latter, he rewrote the constitution and based it on rule by clerics. After some dubious electoral practices this constitution was approved, and he became the Supreme Leader with a Council of Guardians to veto non-Islamic laws and candidates. The many secular and moderate religious groups who had taken to the streets on his behalf, providing the critical support needed for his rise to power, found they were left out, excluded from running the new regime. The group of essentials dropped precipitously once Khomeini's regime was locked into power, shrinking on our 0-to-1 scale for coalition size from 0.47 to 0.26 between 1979 and 1983.

Khomeini became leader because he provided a focal point for opposition to the shah's regime and because the army did not stop the people from rising up against the monarchy. Once the shah was gone, Khomeini quickly asserted that it was he, not an interim government or a council representing all interests, who was in charge. Although the masses brought down the old regime in hopes of obtaining a more democratic government, Khomeini ensured that real power was retained by a small group of clerics, closely following rule 1. The parliament, while popularly elected, could only contain politicians who supported and were supported by the Council of Guardians.

There was nothing special or unique about Khomeini's success. That millions wanted the shah's regime overturned is unsurprising. The shah ran a brutal, oppressive government under which thousands disappeared. Imprisonment, torture, and death were commonplace. But that had been equally true fourteen years earlier when Khomeini went into exile and the shah's government seemed invulnerable. The key to Khomeini's success at the end of the 1970s was that the army refused to stop the unhappy millions from taking to the streets. They had not allowed such protests before. What had changed? The army was no longer willing to fight to preserve the regime because they knew that the shah was dying. The *New York Times Magazine* published an account of the farce of a sick leader desperate to hide the progression of his cancer.[3] A dead shah couldn't guarantee rewards. Neither could his successor. The incumbency advantage unraveled. Faced with the unpleasant task of suppressing the people with only a modest prospect of continuing to enjoy the lavish rewards of coalition membership, the army sat on its hands, smoothing the way for revolution.

The story of the rise of democracy in the Philippines is not much different. Benigno Aquino Jr. was an outstanding man. At the age of eighteen he was awarded the Philippine Legion of Honor for his journalism during the Korean War. He then negotiated the surrender of a rebel group. He was mayor of Concepcion by age twenty-two, governor of Tarlac Province at twenty-nine, and a senator by thirty-four. In a dangerous move, he became an outspoken critic of President Ferdinand Marcos. His outspokenness resulted in his imprisonment. In 1980, while in prison, he suffered two heart attacks. Doctors had political (not medical) concerns about performing bypass surgery, and he feared that they might be in cahoots with Marcos. He asked for and was granted the opportunity to exile himself to the United States in exchange for the promise that he would not speak out against Marcos, a promise he broke after a successful surgery in Dallas. In 1983, Benigno returned from exile in the United States. On the flight back to Manila he warned journalists that it might all be over in minutes. And it was. He was immediately taken from the plane and assassinated on the tarmac. He should have followed Khomeini's example and bided his time.

His wife, Corazon, did not have his political skills or experience, but she had one critical advantage: she was alive! In late 1985 Ferdinand Marcos announced snap elections a year earlier than scheduled. Corazon Aquino stepped in as her late husband's surrogate and ran as the main opposition candidate. There was widespread fraud at the elections on February 7, 1986, so it was of little surprise when, just over a week later, the electoral commission declared Marcos the winner. But Marcos's supporters swiftly deserted him. President Ronald Reagan expressed concern about the electoral result. Jaime Cardinal Sin, influential leader of the Catholic Church in the Philippines, spoke out. At Corazon Aquino's urging, the people protested. Key members of the army and other leading political figures resigned from the government and joined the demonstrations. Without the army to stop them, hundreds of thousands of people joined the protest, resulting in the defection of still more military leaders.

In an attempt to avoid bloodshed, Marcos and his family sought sanctuary in the United States. They left the Philippines and settled in Hawaii, but, as insiders and many others knew, Marcos would not live long. That, in fact, had been his problem all along. He was dying of lupus, and all his key backers knew it. He could not deliver goodies from beyond the grave, so his supporters sought to ingratiate themselves with someone who might benefit them. Corazon Aquino had no experience in government. Yet she succeeded where her more accomplished husband had failed. She challenged Marcos at a time when his supporters knew his life was coming to an end. They were looking for a new partner to defend in exchange for rewards. Corazon Aquino was inaugurated as president and was *Time* magazine's Woman of the Year for 1986.

These are not isolated examples. Laurent Kabila, once maligned by Che Guevara as lacking "revolutionary seriousness" and being "too addicted to alcohol and women," took on the mighty Mobutu Sese Seko of Zaire and won.[4] Kabila lacked talent, but his timing was excellent. Mobutu was dying of prostate cancer, and everybody knew it. His military simply refused to fight back as Kabila's insurgents captured more and more territory. Mobutu's erstwhile backers knew that their own future would be brighter if they abandoned their dying patron, a sentiment captured in the announcement, "The king is dead; long live the king!"

Legitimate health concerns for North Korea's Kim Jong Il and Cuba's Fidel Castro engendered similarly intense political speculation. Both attempted to stave off defection by their essential coalition members by nominating heirs. Kim Jong Il promoted his youngest son, Kim Jong-Un, to a variety of posts, including the rank of four-star general, even though his son had no military experience. Fidel Castro likewise promoted his brother, Raúl, to president when Fidel's survival was in doubt following major surgery. Raúl, in turn, stepped down in April 2021, just two months ahead of his ninetieth birthday. Of course, like Kim Jong Il and Fidel, Raúl named his own successor, Miguel Díaz-Canel. By designating heirs who might keep the existing winning coalition largely intact, these leaders sought to prevent the incumbency advantage from disappearing as their ability to deliver on political promises was brought into jeopardy. Fidel and Kim died peacefully and their designated heirs took over. It will be interesting to watch what happens in Cuba now that Raúl has also stepped down. Resignation, as in the case of Fidel, often leads to a successful, controlled power transition—but, most assuredly, not always. After all, once the king is dead, he is, well, dead, and unable to control the unfolding events. It would be wise for these modern dynastic dictators to recall that half of Europe's dynastic monarchs in the past were not succeeded by the chosen heir.

Impending death often induces political death. For this reason a leader's health is the most important state secret. However, once a leader is dead the need for secrecy vanishes, so to gauge the importance of health we were able to collect data on the date and cause of death of political leaders from sources such as obituaries. On average, the risk of being deposed in any particular year is about 19 percent. However, for leaders like Marcos and the shah who have a serious chronic health condition that will lead to death within three years, this deposition risk nearly doubles. Health concerns particularly exacerbate the risk of removal by revolution and coup.[5] The epitaph "died in office" is generally reserved for leaders who hide their illness.

The sad truth is that if you want to come to power in an autocracy, you are better off stealing medical records than you are devising fixes for your nation's ills. Power mostly belongs to the healthy—that is, to people whose promise to deliver future goodies to loyal backers can be believed.

INHERITANCE AND THE PROBLEM OF RELATIVES

We don't mean to say that healthy leaders don't face hazards of their own. If an incumbent runs out of money, he cannot continue to pay his supporters. Why might he run out of money? Because he has taxed so heavily and stolen so much that the masses choose siestas over labor, stymieing the future flow of revenue into the government's treasury. Worse, the masses could choose revolution over siestas, emboldened by the realization that things will only get worse if they do not act now to overthrow their masters. Mismanagement of coalition dynamics and the incentives of revolutionary entrepreneurs can create changes in institutions that topple the incumbent regime and bring new leaders to power.

Normally one of the most difficult tasks a challenger faces is removing the incumbent. But this is instantly achieved when a leader dies or, as in the case of William Tolbert, is murdered. Once an incumbent is dead, there is still the issue of fending off competitors for the dead leader's job. Ambitious challengers still need to grab control of the state apparatus, reward supporters, and eliminate rivals. To resolve this issue, the Ottomans, who ruled what is today's Turkey from 1299 until 1923, eventually instituted the law of fratricide.[6]

When the sultan died, the succession depended upon who could capture control of the state and reward his coalition. In practice this meant grabbing the treasury and paying off the army. Succession became a battle of survival of the fittest to see which son would become the next sultan. Each of the sultan's sons governed a province of his own. When the sultan died, the sons raced back to the capital, Constantinople, in an attempt to seize the treasury and pay the army for its loyalty. The result could often be civil war, as each brother used his provincial force to try to achieve sole, total control of the state. The sultan could have already shown favor to one son over others simply by giving him a province to govern that was closer to the capital, thereby favoring that son even from the grave.

Ottoman succession was most unpleasant and bloody. Unsuccessful brothers were typically killed. Mehmed II (1432–1481) institutionalized this practice with the fratricide law, under which all unsuccessful male heirs were strangled with a silk cord. A century later, Mehmed III (1566–1603) allegedly killed nineteen brothers, two sons, and fifteen slaves who were pregnant by his own father, thereby eliminating all present and future potential rivals. By the middle of the seventeenth century this practice was replaced by the kinder, gentler practice of locking all male relatives in the Fourth Court of the Topkapi Palace—quite literally the original Golden

Cage. With relatives like this, it is perhaps no wonder that Shakespeare's Hamlet or Robert Graves's Claudius chose to feign madness.

The general dilemma of succession is hardly unique to the Ottomans. England's King Richard the Lionheart died in 1199. Since Richard had no direct heirs, at least three people had a strong claim to the English throne following his death. Richard's father was the previous king, Henry II, meaning that succession could be claimed by Henry II's wife, Eleanor of Aquitaine, then nearing eighty years old; by Henry's eldest surviving son, John; or by Henry's older—but deceased—son Geoffrey's eldest surviving male child (himself but eleven years old), Arthur.

Eleanor was too pragmatic to put herself at risk for the crown, especially given her advanced years. She understood the likely consequences for her if she pushed her claim. Being the loving mother and grandmother that she surely must have been, she stepped aside, leaving John and Arthur to fight it out. Or, more precisely, she looked at who was likely to win and threw her support in that direction, allowing herself to change directions as the winds of fortune switched from time to time.

Would-be autocrats must be prepared to kill all comers—even immediate family members. The Ottomans formalized this practice while the English merely relied on the tradition of doing in their rivals. Murder seems to be a favored solution under the extreme conditions of fear and insecurity that accompany monarchic and autocratic successions. What did John do? Even after assuming the crown he continued to fear Arthur's quest for power, a quest that grew more intense as the boy aged into his teenage years. Finally, in 1203, John had Arthur taken prisoner and murdered. Some rumors suggested that he killed his nephew personally. With Arthur out of the way, no one stood as a further threat to John's crown—not until the nobles rose up against him and forced him to sign the Magna Carta, twelve years later.

Inheritance holds a number of advantages for leaders and their supporters alike. Paying off the right people is the essence of good government—and princes are well equipped to continue to reward supporters. They know where the money is and who to pay off. Even so, why should the court be so keen to go along with inheritance? After all, if the prince takes the top job, then the other courtiers cannot be king (or dictator or president) in his place. Supporting inheritance inevitably means giving up the chance to become king yourself. Yet that is just one side of the calculation. With so many people who would like to be king, the chance of landing the top job is tiny. In reality, supporters of the late king are often best off elevating his son and hoping that he then dances with the one who brought him to the ball.

You may be thinking that murdering family is out of fashion in this allegedly more civilized time. Sad to say, living family members are no less of a threat today in some regimes than was true in the time of King John. Stalin had loads of relatives executed. Several of Saddam Hussein's cousins and in-laws were executed or met their death indirectly at the hands of other family members. And how about North Korea's Kim Jong-Un? He ordered the execution of his beloved uncle Jang Song-Thaek in 2013 and seems to have had his brother, Kim Jong-Nam, murdered in 2017. It can be exceedingly dangerous to be related to a ruler even today, but then it can also be exceedingly profitable.

New leaders need supporters to stay in power, and with inheritance those supporters are all already in place. The prince knows who they are and how to pay them. Of course, as we saw with France's Louis XIV, the prince might radically alter the coalition. But supporters of the old king correctly believe in the old adage, "Like father, like son." It's not a bad gamble for them. Essential supporters have a much greater chance of retaining their privileged position when power passes within a family, from father to son, from king to prince, than when power passes to an outsider. If you are a prince and you want to be king, then you should do nothing to dissuade your father's supporters from believing they will be important to you too. They will curry favor with you. You should let them. You will need them to secure a smooth transition. If you want them gone (and you may not), then banish them from court later. But the first time they need to know your true feelings for them is when you banish them from court, well after your investiture.

Naturally, if you're a young prince who hopes to be king, you'll have to make sure to outlive your "supporters." History has shown that regents are notoriously bad caregivers. Provided a regent is prepared to kill his charge, being entrusted with the care of the would-be future king is a great way to become king. England's King Richard III provides an example. When Edward IV died in 1483, the crown fell to his twelve-year-old son, Edward V. Richard III, King Edward IV's brother, was appointed Lord Protector of the Commonwealth and charged with looking after the prince's interests. He was supposed to manage the crown for a few years and then hand it over. Like many leaders, however, Richard didn't relish the idea of giving up power.

As the trusted executor of King Edward IV's wishes, Richard was able to manipulate events to his own benefit. First he had twelve-year-old Edward and his younger brother taken to the Tower of London. Richard then had Parliament declare both princes illegitimate by questioning the legitimacy of their parents' marriage. The princes were never seen again. Richard may not have been much of an executor, but he seems to have had no trouble with execution. (It is believed that two skeletons found under a staircase in 1674 belonged to the two young boys.)

Even in systems that rely on inheritance, a door can nevertheless be opened for a designated successor who is not a blood relative. Leaders often nominate their successor and sometimes choose someone outside of their immediate relations, perhaps because they understand the dire risks to family if they turn to one member and not another. For instance, the first Roman emperor, Augustus, formally adopted his successor, Tiberius. Mob bosses often do the same. Carlo Gambino nominated "Big Paulie" Castellano to succeed him as head of his New York mafia family. In each case, the designated successor was seen as someone likely to continue the programs and projects of the prior leader. Therefore, there wasn't much rush to replace the old leader. The designated successors might even enhance the old boss's reputation.

For sick and decrepit leaders, nominating an heir can help them live out the rest of their life in power. Provided the essentials in the coalition believe the heir will retain sufficient continuity in the coalition's makeup, inheritance or nominated succession can make it very difficult for outsiders to offer essential coalition members more than they expect from the father-son succession.

Of course, for such dynastic succession to work, a leader must ⎤
nominate the *right* successor—the one that the coalition believes will ⎥
act in their interest. It was in this criterion that Robert Mugabe, a ⎦
master of maintaining coalition loyalty, finally slipped up. At the age
of ninety-four and in declining health, Mugabe was deposed by a
coup in 2017, having ruled Zimbabwe since 1980. His wife, Grace,
had publicly urged him to appoint her as his successor.[7] Unfortunately
for the old guard of Mugabe's ZANU-PF party, Grace was associated
with a younger faction of the party.[8] Her ascension would almost certainly have curtailed their access to wealth and privilege, and so they
deposed him. Better for them to take the gamble that their choice of
successor would keep them on than stay loyal knowing they would
be replaced once Mugabe eventually passed away. He died in 2019.

PAPAL BULL(YING) FOR POWER

Some of the greatest stories and movies of all time portray how the
fate of whole nations, peoples, and faiths comes down to the actions
of a single individual. Whether it is Luke Skywalker wrestling with
father issues or Frodo disposing of a ring, massed battles have only
secondary importance compared to an individual's triumph. It makes
for great fiction, certainly, but such events happen in fact too.

For Christianity's first several hundred years, the Bishop of Rome—
the pope—was not the leading figure even within the Christian community. Bishops were the arbiters of Christian practice and belief, but
not until Damasus I, pope from 366 to 384, was the Bishop of Rome
truly elevated above other Roman Catholic bishops, becoming the
head of the western Roman Catholic Church.[9] Eventually sainted for
his extraordinary accomplishments, Damasus is a case study in the
manipulation of essentials, influentials, and interchangeables.

By the late 300s, the East had a seemingly insurmountable advantage in the long struggle between the eastern and western branches
of Christianity. The apostles and, of course, Jesus himself all came
from the East. The holy places were in Jerusalem and Galilee and
nearby cities in today's Israel, Palestine, Jordan, and Syria. With such

incontestable credentials, how could Christianity be seen first and foremost as anything other than an eastern religion? Damasus had the insight to find an answer. True, the apostles came from the East, but Peter and Paul were martyred in Rome, and it was in Rome that they were buried. Thus he could argue that Rome was privileged by being the scene of apostolic missions intended to spread the word and by the profound example of martyrdom carried out of the East and to Rome.

Damasus made the compelling case that only the See of Peter in Rome could be the heart of Christianity because, as Jesus reportedly said (Matthew 16:17–20), "I tell you that you are Peter, and on this rock I will build my church, and the gates of Hell will not overcome it. I will give you the keys of the kingdom of heaven; whatever you bind on earth will be bound in heaven, and whatever you loose on earth will be loosed in heaven." Rome, then, must have a superior claim compared to the eastern Sees. On the surface, this may seem to be an explicitly religious argument—but powerful though it is, it obscures the coalition-building strategies that actually made Damasus pope and made the Roman Church the new locus of power.

Nowadays a new pope is elected by the College of Cardinals upon the death of the pope. In Damasus's day, the method was different. The interchangeables—the nominal selectorate—consisted of all of the Christians in the Roman diocese. The influentials included at least the local clergy and other bishops from the province. Defining the winning coalition—the essentials—is where the tale of Damasus's success must begin.

Damasus had a rival for election as pope, Ursinus. Ursinus was popular with the lay Christians and with much of the clergy. Damasus, in contrast, enjoyed the support of the aristocracy. Both men had worked closely with the previous pope, Liberius. When Liberius was exiled to Berea by Emperor Constantius II in 354, Damasus, like Ursinus, followed him into exile. Unlike Ursinus, however, Damasus wasted no time returning to Rome, abandoning Liberius and throwing his support behind the antipope Felix II, who was favored by the emperor. This most assuredly helped cement Damasus's popularity with the controlling classes while alienating the lay Christian community and clergy.

When Liberius died in 366, parallel papal elections were held, resulting in both Damasus and Ursinus claiming election. Ursinus was chosen by the faithful plebian worshippers and Damasus by the powerful. Riots ensued, leading to a bloody massacre in which 137 people were slaughtered in the Basilica of Sicininus, a popular Roman church. The city's prefects—the secular leaders of Rome—stepped in and restored order by establishing Damasus as the one and only pope. They dealt with the threat Ursinus represented by exiling him to Gaul. So it was that Ursinus's larger coalition of lay worshippers was defeated by the smaller but much more powerful coalition behind Damasus. As we shall see when we discuss nation building in chapter 7, undermining democratic institutions is a tried and trusted means of maintaining influence. Although Christianity became Rome's official religion in 380, it wasn't until after the collapse of Rome in 476 that the papacy gained its independence from Rome.

Damasus did not come by his upper-crust backing by accident. We have already seen that he supported Felix II over Liberius. He assiduously pursued support from the upper classes of Romans, many of them pagans, before (and during) his papacy, thereby ensuring their loyalty to him in return for his loyal pursuit of policies that benefited them. For instance, he made a habit of cultivating the upper-class women of Rome. His detractors, noting his close associations with Rome's leading ladies, accused him of adultery (and murder). He was exonerated thanks to direct intervention by the emperor himself. His promoters, in contrast, noted that he had converted many aristocratic pagan women to Christianity and they, in turn, had brought their husbands into the fold, thereby expanding the selectorate and perhaps the influentials in Rome's Christian community. That, of course, was good for the growth of the Church, but it also was good for Damasus's ability to secure and hold power. He relied on a small coalition—unlike Ursinus—and he worked on drawing that coalition from an enlarged set of influentials and interchangeables.

Being a sophisticated strategist, he also worked to further expand the set of interchangeables by reaching out to the Christian masses of Rome. This could only help him shore up his political power and his discretionary authority over Church funds, discretionary authority he later used to build important public works and to employ (Saint) Jerome to write the Vulgate, the first accessible Latin translation of the Bible, which further solidified the Roman pope's ability to dictate the meaning of the gospels.

How did Damasus expand his appeal to the masses—the interchangeables—many of whom had opposed his papacy? It seems that many of the recently converted laypeople of the declining Roman Empire missed their many pagan Roman gods. Damasus recognized that these same people seemed happy to substitute the many Christian martyrs for those gods. Damasus focused his energy on discovering the burial places of martyrs and erecting great marble monuments. Some of his monuments and inscriptions to martyrs can still be seen in Rome to this day.

Damasus's efforts bore fruit. He won over and expanded the Christian laity, gained support among the upper classes, and even captured the support of the emperor himself, who endorsed Damasus's view of the preeminence of the See of Rome. On February 28, 380, Emperor Theodosius declared that everyone must abide by the Christian principles as declared by "the Apostle Peter to the Romans, and now followed by Bishop Damasus and Peter of Alexandria."[10]

Damasus understood what to do to come to power and how to retain it. Indeed, after his ignominious road to election as pope, he did good works from the perspective of the Roman Catholic Church and achieved sainthood for himself. The door to his coming to power was opened by the errors of Liberius, his predecessor, who alienated the emperor instead of cultivating him as an ally. Damasus did not make that error. He built a small winning coalition drawn from an expanded set of influentials and interchangeables, thereby ensuring loyal, long-lasting support for himself and his papacy. And, in the process, his battle for power shifted Christianity away from its Eastern origins and set it on the path to becoming a Western faith.

Leaders who fail to do the right thing, like Liberius, provide opportunities for someone new to come to power. But remember, what constitutes doing the right thing must be understood from the perspective of a potential supporter; it may have nothing to do with what is best for a community or nation. Anyone who thinks leaders *do what they ought to do*—that is, what is best for their nation of subjects—ought to become an academic rather than enter political life. In politics, coming to power is never about doing the right thing. It is always about doing what is expedient.

SEIZING POWER FROM THE BANKRUPT

As it turns out, one thing that is always expedient is remaining solvent. If a ruler runs out of money with which to pay his supporters, it becomes far easier for someone else to make coalition members an attractive offer. Financial crises are an opportune time to strike.

The Russian Revolution is often portrayed through the prism of Marxist ideology and class warfare. The reality might be much simpler. Kerensky's revolutionaries were able to storm the Winter Palace in February 1917 because the army did not stop them. And the army did not bother to stop them because the czar did not pay them enough. The czar could not pay them enough because he had foolishly lost one of his major sources of revenue, the vodka tax, at the same time that he was fighting World War I.

Czar Nicholas confused what might seem like good public policy with bad political decision-making. He had the silly idea that a sober army would prove more effective than an army that was falling-over drunk. Nicholas, it seems, thought that a ban on vodka would improve the performance of Russia's troops in World War I. He missed the obvious downsides, however. Vodka was vastly popular with the general populace and, most assuredly, with the troops. So popular and widely consumed was vodka that its sale provided about a third of the government's revenue. With vodka banned, his revenue diminished sharply. His expenses, in contrast, kept on rising because of the costs of the war.

Soon Nicholas was no longer able to buy loyalty. As a result, his army refused to stop strikers and protesters. Alexander Kerensky formed Russia's short-lived democratic government after toppling the czar's regime. But he couldn't hang on to power for long. His mistake was operating a democratic government, which necessitated a large coalition, while implementing an unpopular policy—continuing the czar's war—thereby alienating his coalition right from the start. Lenin and the Bolsheviks made no such mistakes.

The czar fell once there was no one to stop the revolution. Louis XVI suffered much the same fate in the French Revolution. Successful leaders must learn the lesson of these examples and put raising revenue and paying supporters above all else. Consider Robert Mugabe's success in staying on as Zimbabwe's president until he was in his mid-nineties. The economy collapsed in Zimbabwe thanks to Mugabe's terrible policies. Starvation was common, and epidemics of cholera regularly swept the country. Mugabe "succeeded" because he understood that it did not matter what happened to the people provided that he made sure to pay the army. He reduced a once-thriving agricultural exporting nation into one that became dependent on foreign aid. Mugabe was certainly horrible for what he did to the people he ruled, but he was a master of the rules to rule by. Where policy matters most, paying off cronies, he delivered. That is why he survived in power for decades, until he was just too old to be counted on to provide future bounty for his essential supporters.

Myanmar's generals seem to have taken a ream of pages from Mugabe's playbook. They govern a country that routinely swings into economic misery and mass starvation, but they make sure to pay the loyal military well, murder anyone they suspect of disloyalty, and soak in economic support from the United States, China, and others, playing each against the others when they can. They bemoan the people's misery, blame it on others, and promise better times but only deliver those better times to the few whose support they need. Like Mugabe and so many other "successful" leaders before him, Myanmar's leaders have mastered the rules to rule by.

SILENCE IS GOLDEN

We all grew up hearing the lesson that silence is golden. As it turns out, violating that basic principle is yet another path by which incumbents can succumb to their political rivals.

The incumbent's advantage in offering rewards disappears as soon as coalition members come to suspect their access to personal benefits will end. An incumbent's failure to reassure his coalition that he will continue to take care of them provides competitors with a golden opportunity to seize power. Houari Boumedienne was able to seize the Algerian presidency from Ahmed Ben Bella in 1965 after Ben Bella foolishly opened his mouth. Silence would have served him better.

Ben Bella achieved fame both on the soccer pitch and as a war hero. He joined the French army in 1936 and, while posted to Marseille, played for its professional soccer team. He was awarded the Croix de Guerre and the Médaille militaire for his gallantry during World War II. After the war he joined the struggle to liberate Algeria from France. He became a popular figure in the independence movement and was elected president of Algeria in 1963. But despite his many talents, he made a serious mistake. On June 12, 1966, he announced that there would be a Politburo meeting a week later and that the purpose of the meeting was to discuss three major issues: (1) changes in the cabinet; (2) changes in the army command; and (3) the liquidation of the military opposition. He then left Algiers for Oran.

This announcement was tantamount to telling his essential supporters that he was getting rid of some of them. Since he did not say who was to go, he created a common interest among the whole group in getting rid of him.

Ben Bella's foolish announcement was just the opening that Houari Boumedienne needed. No one was certain who would be replaced, but given Ben Bella's sweeping statement, clearly many would be. In this unforced error, Ben Bella threw away his incumbency advantage and left Boumedienne a week to organize a plot of his own. Ben Bella returned to Algiers the day before the scheduled meeting and was awakened at gunpoint by his friend Colonel Tahar Zbiri. Boumedienne grasped his opportunity, and Ben Bella's essential supporters defected.[11] Silence, as Ben Bella learned far too late, truly is golden. There is never any point in showing your hand before you have to; that is just a way to give the game away.

INSTITUTIONAL CHANGE

There is a common adage that politicians don't change the rules that brought them to power. This is false. They are ever ready and eager to reduce coalition size. What politicians seek to avoid are any institutional changes that increase the number of people to whom they are beholden. Yet as much as they try to avoid these changes, circumstances do arise when institutions must become more inclusive. This can make autocrats vulnerable because the coalition they have established and the rewards they provide are then no longer sufficient to maintain power.

Under the old Soviet system, Boris Yeltsin had no chance of rising to power.[12] His first effort at becoming a major player relied on a proposal every bit as foolish as Czar Nicholas's decision to ban vodka sales. He sought to end Communist Party members' access to special stores, privileged access to the best universities, and other benefits not shared by the working people of the Soviet Union. Sure, that was popular with the masses, but the masses didn't have much say in choosing who ran the Soviet Union—party members did. Mikhail Gorbachev, seeing that Yeltsin was a loose cannon, sent him packing. After this setback, Yeltsin only survived by being resilient and inventive in the face of a changed environment.

By the late 1980s the Soviet economy had stagnated. This left the recently promoted Soviet leader, Gorbachev, with a serious dilemma. Unless he could somehow resuscitate the economy, he was liable to run out of money. As we have seen, this situation can get leaders into serious trouble. In order to get the economy moving so that there would continue to be enough money, Gorbachev needed to loosen control over the people, freeing their suppressed entrepreneurial potential.

Economic liberalization wasn't a simple matter for the Soviets. It entailed giving Soviet citizens many more personal and political freedoms. On the upside, this allowed the people to communicate, coordinate, and interact, which can be good for economic growth. On the downside, allowing people to communicate, coordinate, and interact facilitates mass political protest. Gorbachev was no fool and presumably knew liberalization could get him in trouble. Unfortunately for him, he was between a rock and a hard place. Without a stronger economy his Soviet Union could not hope to compete with the United States and maintain its superpower status. And, more importantly, he could not pay party members the rewards they were used to. To get a stronger economy he had to put his political control at risk, both from the masses, who wanted a speedier path to prosperity, and from his coalition, who feared losing their privileges. Gorbachev rolled the dice and ultimately lost.

First Gorbachev faced a coup from within his own coalition. In 1991, harder-line antireform party members, fearful of losing their special privileges (a loss openly advocated by Boris Yeltsin), deposed Gorbachev and took control of the government. But then Boris Yeltsin, standing atop a tank in Red Square, ensured that the Soviet military would not fire on protesters who wanted reform. The mass movement, with Boris Yeltsin at its head, overthrew the coup that wanted to return to the Soviet Union's more repressive policies of the past. The mass movement returned Gorbachev ever so briefly to power, leaving him with a much-diminished rump Soviet Union and paving the way for the dissolution of the Soviet empire just a few months later.

Yeltsin, having gotten over his privileges fiasco, understood that he could not forge a winning coalition out of the inner circles of the Communist Party, but he could win over the apparatchiks by promoting greater budgetary autonomy for the Russian republic within the Soviet structure. They could become richer and more powerful in Russia than they had been in the Soviet Union. In this way, Yeltsin picked off essential members of Gorbachev's coalition and made himself a winner. Yeltsin was, as it turned out, much better at working out how to come to power than he was at governing well, but that is a tale for another time.

COMING TO POWER IN A DEMOCRACY

Most of the examples we have discussed so far have involved autocracies. Although generally much less violent, leader transitions in democracies operate via the same mechanisms. Just as in an autocracy, a challenger in a democracy needs to ensure the deposition of the incumbent, seize command of the instruments of state, and sufficiently reward a coalition of supporters so that they back her as the new incumbent. Yet the way these goals are achieved is quite different in democracies.

In some respects, it is easier. In a democracy it is less difficult, for instance, to detach supporters from the dominant coalition, because democrats need such a large number of supporters. Leaders rely heavily on public goods to reward their backers, but precisely because so many of the rewards are public goods that benefit everyone, those *in* the coalition are not much better off than those *outside* the coalition. Furthermore, since personal rewards are relatively modest once the essential bloc is so large, loyalty is further diluted. The risk of exclusion from the next leader's coalition remains relatively small—after all, the next leader will need a lot of backers too—further weakening the incumbency advantage.

Challengers succeed when they offer better rewards than the existing government. Given that there are so many who need rewarding, this means coming up with better, or at least more popular, public policies. Unfortunately, because it is easy to erode the support of the incumbent's coalition, it remains difficult for the challenger to pay off her own supporters.

When democratic leaders come to power they need to seize control of the government, but there is not the frenzied rush that we observe in autocracies. In the United States, for instance, leaders elected in November are not sworn in until the following January. This lag gives incoming presidents time to prepare, nominating their cabinet and appointing people to positions that need to be filled. Originally the delay (which once lasted until March) was required because leaders needed months to travel to the capital from the state where they lived. Contenders to become a new dictator or monarch never extend the courtesy of waiting for their more distant kin to travel great distances to compete with them. Democrats lack urgency when assuming power because the democratic rules that determine that the

incumbent has been defeated simultaneously create a coalition of supporters for the new leader.

DEMOCRATIC INHERITANCE

Democrats, because they rely on a large coalition, cannot lavish
great wealth on their supporters personally. They simply do not have
enough money to go around. Instead democrats need to find effective
public policies that their supporters like and reward their loyalty that
way. But this is not to say there are no private goods in democratic
politics. There are. And this explains why dynastic rule is common
even in democracies. It may be surprising to learn, for instance, that
a careful study finds that 31.2 percent of American female legislators
(and 8.4 percent of men) had a close relative precede them in their
political role.[13] Nearly 20 percent of American presidents have been
close relatives of each other. That's a lot more than chance and fair
competition suggest.

Dynastic rule is commonplace in democracies for exactly the
same reasons that it is popular among autocrats and monarchs. Who
better to protect the wealth and prestige of the family than family
members? Elected officials get to dole out money and enjoy power and
money in return. They are as eager to see their progeny enjoy the same
benefits—and protect their own legacy—as Emperor Augustus or
Carlo Gambino. And so it is that the Tafts of Ohio have held high office generation after generation. Ohio's governor from 1999 to 2007,
Bob Taft, for instance, enjoyed an illustrious pedigree. His father
and his grandfather were both US senators, his great-grandfather was
president of the United States, and his great-great-grandfather was attorney general and secretary of war. The Kennedys, the Rockefellers,
the Roosevelts, the Bushes, and many other American families also
have long and distinguished political histories. And this is not only an
American phenomenon. Kenya's 2017 election was a contest between
two candidates: Uhuru Kenyatta, the son of Kenya's first president,
and Raila Odinga, the son of Kenya's first vice president. Despite a

population of fifty-two million, the leading candidates were drawn from a few leading families.

Of course, dynastic rule is more common outside of democracies. Even if you don't have the good fortune to be born into a political dynasty, you can come to power in a democracy if you have good, or at least popular, ideas. Good ideas that help the people are rarely the path to power in a dictatorship.

DEMOCRACY IS AN ARMS RACE FOR GOOD IDEAS

Competition in democracies is cerebral, not physical. Killing foes works for dictators, but it is a pretty surefire path to political oblivion in a democracy. That's a good thing from a moral standpoint, of course. But from a democrat's point of view, the corollary is that even good public policy does not buy much loyalty.

Everyone in a democracy receives policy benefits, whether they support the incumbent or not. If a leader cleans up the environment or solves climate change, then everyone is a winner, although of course the extent to which individuals value these things will vary. But past deeds don't buy loyalty. When a rival proposes a cheaper way to fix the environment or finds policy fixes for other problems that people care about more, then the rival can seize power through the ballot box. Autocratic politics is a battle for private rewards, for a bigger slice of a relatively small pie. Democratic politics is a battle for good policy ideas. If you reward your cronies lavishly and at the expense of the broader public, as you would in a dictatorship, then you will be out on your ear so long as you rely on a massive coalition of essential backers. It's fine to give backers a big hunk of pie, but that hunk had better be a small portion of the whole pie if a democrat wants to have a chance to survive in power.

Winston Churchill is certainly a candidate for Britain's greatest statesman. He is deservedly famous for his wonderful oratory. Yet patriotic rhetoric alone was not enough to defeat Hitler's Nazi Germany in World War II. Churchill did not just deliver rhetoric; he delivered policy results too. He convinced President Franklin D. Roosevelt to implement the lend-lease program that enabled a virtually bankrupt Britain to keep fighting. He converted the British economy to an efficient wartime footing and found ways to pressure the Axis powers on multiple fronts. He was fondly admired and praised by the vast majority of Britons at the end of the war. Yet Clement Attlee's Labour Party decisively defeated Churchill's Conservative Party in elections held in July 1945. Technically speaking, World War II—a war that Winston Churchill, as much as any single individual, might be credited with having won—wasn't even over yet. And already the people of Britain were ready to toss Winston out.

Churchill famously stated in November 1942, following Britain's victory at El Alamein, "I have not become the King's First Minister in order to preside over the liquidation of the British Empire." British voters ensured he did not have to. Churchill offered the policies of continued austerity to make Britain great again. After six hard years of war, rationing, and sacrifice, these policies had little appeal. Attlee chose to promote the National Health Service and the creation of a welfare state over the reestablishment of international dominance. He won the battle for good ideas. Few would deny Churchill did a magnificent job as prime minister, and he was much loved. But it was Attlee who won.

COALITION DYNAMICS

That democrats need so many supporters makes them vulnerable. If you can find an issue over which the incumbent's supporters disagree, then it will soon be your turn to lead. Divide and conquer is a terrific principle for coming to power in a democracy—and one of the greatest practitioners of this strategy was Abraham Lincoln, who propelled himself to the US presidency by splitting the support for the Democratic Party in 1860.

During the 1858 US Senate race in Illinois, Republican Abraham Lincoln forced Democrat Stephen Douglas to declare his position on slavery just one year after the Supreme Court's *Dred Scott* decision made clear that Congress did not have the right to ban slavery in federal territories. Douglas was cornered. If he said that slavery could be banned, he would win the election in Illinois but he would shake the foundations of his party; if he said that it couldn't, he would lose the election and thereby diminish his chances of being the Democrats' presidential nominee in 1860. Douglas declared that the people could exclude slavery and won the race, of course, but his response on slavery came at the expense of dividing the Democratic Party two years later in the 1860 presidential election, clearing the way for Lincoln's coalition to elect him president despite a very poor showing in popular votes.

Lincoln, more than any other winner of the presidency, foresaw that he would not be popular among a vast segment of voters in the presidential election. He understood that his best chance, maybe even his only chance, for election in 1860 lay in dividing and conquering. Had Douglas answered Lincoln's question with a pro-slavery response (that is, in support of the *Dred Scott* decision as the law of the land), he almost certainly would have lost the Senate race to Lincoln. That might have kept the Democrats united in 1860, but it would have boosted Lincoln's prospects for the presidency as the Senate incumbent with a popular following. By answering as he did, Douglas guaranteed that his own party would divide over his presidential bid. With southerners John C. Breckinridge and John Bell also contesting the presidency, Douglas lost his opportunity to win the southern vote, dooming him—and his Democratic rivals—to defeat, even though Lincoln's vote total was slim. Lincoln beat the divided Democrats with less than 40 percent of the popular vote and almost no votes in the South. Similarly, in 1992 Bill Clinton beat the incumbent president George H. W. Bush with 43 percent of the popular vote compared to Bush's 38 percent, thanks in no small measure to the run by H. Ross Perot (who got 19 percent of the vote).[14] Lincoln understood that he needed to keep the coalition as small as possible—even in a system with an inherently large coalition.

Lincoln did not lose sight of this important principle as he sought reelection in 1864. Seeing that his prospects were not great, he maneuvered to expand the set of interchangeables and influentials so that he could forge a winning coalition out of those who had previously had no say at all. How did he do this? He introduced absentee ballots so that soldiers could vote, which had an especially important impact in New York. It is widely believed that the votes of soldiers carried the state for Lincoln in his 1864 race against General George B. McClellan. Lincoln was a master at using the rules of politics to his advantage, winning while being unpopular with a large swath of the American people.

In democracies, politics is an arms race of ideas. Just as the democrat has to be responsive to the people when governing, when seeking office it helps to propose policies that the voters like, and it pays to want to do more (as opposed to less)—even if the economic consequences are damaging down the road (when you're no longer in office). Satisfy the coalition in the short run. When democratic politicians lament "mortgaging our children's future," they're really regretting that it was not they who came up with the popular policy that voters actually want. Sure, voters might feel guilty about the latest $1 trillion program, but see if they actually vote to reject it. With parents like that, what children need enemies?

A LAST WORD ON COMING TO POWER: THE ULTIMATE FATE OF SERGEANT DOE

Our account of coming to power began with the story of Liberia's Sergeant Doe. His end provides a useful cautionary tale for those seeking power. Coming to power and staying in power, as the rest of this book makes clear, are very different things.

Sergeant Doe knew where Liberia's money was. And so long as he knew where it was and used it to keep the army faithful, he was able to survive numerous attempts to overthrow him. The trouble is that you only have to lose once, and the question *Where's the money?* ended up being the last thing that Sergeant Doe ever heard.

With the end of the Cold War, the United States no longer needed Doe's assistance, and in 1989 the US government cut off his aid. Rivals Charles Taylor and Prince Johnson, backed by the governments of Burkina Faso and Côte d'Ivoire, saw their opportunity and launched an insurgency. Doe sent soldiers to counter them, but rather than act as a professional army ought to, his soldiers proceeded to rape, pillage, and murder, not exactly endearing themselves to the very people whose support might have saved Doe.

Civilians flocked to join the revolt. Showing his characteristic lack of statesmanship or judgment, Doe decided to take a car and personally go off in search of recently arrived Nigerian peacekeepers. Following a gun battle that killed all of Doe's entourage, Prince Johnson captured the president and videotaped his subsequent interrogation. The interrogators repeated the same questions over and over again before Johnson turned to cutting off Doe's ear and eating it: "Where is the money? What is the bank account number?" Doe didn't answer. Maybe, knowing he was going to die regardless, he figured that if he kept silent at least his family could enjoy the fruits of his labor and live out their lives in a comfortable exile.

Doe was incompetent at running a country. He drove an already-poor nation into even deeper poverty and civil war. But he knew the essence of coming to power. Although dressed up in many forms, basic principles are followed by all successful challengers. They offer greater rewards to the essential supporters of the current leader than those essentials currently receive. Unfortunately for the challenger, the incumbent has a significant advantage because the members of the established winning coalition can be confident that their leader will keep on lining their pockets or providing the public policies they want. But if the incumbent is believed to be dying, takes too much for himself, chooses the wrong policies, or is seen to have only weak loyalty from his critical backers, then the door swings wide open for a challenger to step in and depose the incumbent.

To achieve power means recognizing the moment of opportunity and moving fast and decisively to seize the day. And, for good measure, coming to power also means seizing any opponents, figuratively in democracies and physically in dictatorships. Coming to power is not for the faint of heart.

Politics, however, does not end with becoming a leader. Even as you take up the reins of power and enjoy its rewards, others are gunning for you. They want the same job that you so desperately sought! Politics is a risky business. As we will see, successful leaders manage these risks by locking in a loyal coalition. Those who fail at this first task open the door for someone else to overthrow them.

CHAPTER THREE

STAYING IN POWER

At long last, the aspirant to high office has triumphed. Whether through inheritance, coup, election, revolt, murder, or mayhem, he has seized power. Now he faces a new challenge: hanging on to it.

As Sergeant Doe's brutal career has taught us, rising to a high position often requires skills altogether different from those needed to maintain control. And even the rules for surviving in power do not always resemble the skills necessary for ruling *well*. The novelist Italo Calvino has clearly and succinctly described the tribulations of those who have risen to power: "The throne, once you have been crowned, is where you had best remain seated, without moving, day and night. All your previous life has been only a waiting to become king; now you are king; you have only to reign. And what is reigning if not this long wait? Waiting for the moment when you will be deposed, when you will have to take leave of the throne, the scepter, the crown, and your head."[1]

What, then, must a newly minted leader do to keep his (or her) head? A good starting place is shoring up the coalition of supporters. This may seem like a simple enough task. After all, as we've seen, the heights of power are unattainable without the backing of a coalition strong enough to beat back rivals. However, a wise leader does not count too much on those who helped her gain power. Remember the fate of many of Fidel Castro's closest allies. After toppling the previous leader, it's only a matter of time until they realize that they can do the same again.

A prudent new incumbent will act swiftly to get some of them out of the way and bring in others whose interests more strongly assure their future loyalty. Only after sacking, shuffling, and shrinking their particular set of essentials can leaders assure their future tenure.

Nor is this only true of dictators. To see this urge to build a modified coalition at work in the seemingly less ferocious world of business, let's take a look at Carly Fiorina's rise and fall as CEO at Hewlett-Packard.

GOVERNANCE IN PURSUIT OF HEADS

CEOs, just like national leaders, are susceptible to removal. Being vulnerable to a coup, they need to modify the corporate coalition (usually the board of directors and senior management) by bringing in loyalists and getting rid of potential troublemakers. Usually they have a large potential pool of people to draw from and prior experience to help guide their choices. But, also like national leaders, they face resistance from some members of their inherited coalition, and that may be hard to overcome.

Most publicly traded corporations have millions of interchangeables (their shareholders), a considerably smaller set of influentials (big individual shareholders and institutional shareholders), and a small group of essentials, often not more than ten to fifteen people. In a group of this size, even seemingly minor variations in the number of coalition members can have profound consequences for how a company is run. As we will see, this was particularly true for Hewlett-Packard (HP), because, as in all companies, small shifts in coalition numbers can lead to large percentage changes in the expected mix of corporate rewards.

In the case of HP, the CEO's winning coalition made up a relatively large fraction of the real selectorate because ownership is heavily concentrated in a few hands. That is, we might count corporate coalition size in terms of the number of its members or in terms of the number of shares they own. In HP's case, the essential bloc and the influential bloc have very few members compared to the total selectorate because the families of the company's founders, William Hewlett and David Packard, retain significant ownership, just as was true of Ford Motor Company, Hallmark Cards, and quite a few other businesses for many years.

Involvement in a corporation can yield benefits, just like involvement in any form of government. These benefits can take the form of rewards given to everyone or private payments directed just to the essentials. In a corporate setting, private benefits typically come as personal compensation in the form of salary, perks, and stock options. Rewards to everyone—what economists call "public goods"—take the shape of dividends (an equal amount per share) and increased stock value. When the winning coalition is sufficiently large that private rewards are an inefficient mechanism for the CEO to buy the loyalty of essentials, public goods tend to be the benefit of choice. Usually, coalition members are eager to receive private benefits. However, dividends and growth in share value are preferred over private rewards by very large shareholders who also happen to be in the winning coalition—this makes them the biggest recipients of the rewards that go to all shareholders. That was precisely the situation in HP, where the Hewlett and Packard families owned a substantial percentage of the company.

Who makes up the essentials in a corporation? The coalition typically includes no more than a few people in senior management and the members of the board of directors. The board usually includes a mix of senior managers in the company, representatives from large institutional shareholders, handpicked friends and relatives of the CEO (generally described as "civic leaders," no doubt), and the CEO herself. In the parlance of economists who study corporations, the makeup of these boards boils down to insiders (employees), gray members (friends, relatives), and outsiders. One part of any corporate board's duties is to appoint, retain, or remove CEOs. Generally CEOs keep their job for a long time, and that certainly was true of HP's first CEO, founder David Packard. He was replaced in 1992 by an insider, Lewis Platt, who had worked for the firm since the 1960s. Platt retired in 1999 and was replaced by outsider Carly Fiorina. The HP board has repeatedly deposed CEOs since then.

It should be obvious that any board members involved in deposing the former CEO have the potential to be a problem for a new CEO. Since they have already been coup makers, there is little reason to doubt that they stand ready to start trouble once again if they think the circumstances warrant it. And what could those circumstances be but application of one or more of the rules of governance we set out earlier, especially if that application harms their interests?

Research into CEO longevity teaches us, not surprisingly, that time in office lengthens as one maintains close personal ties to members of the board. Just as sons and daughters may make attractive inheritors of the mantle of power in a dictatorship, friends, relatives, and fellow employees can generate the expectation of more loyal supporters after power is achieved. This logic probably contributed to Lewis Platt's elevation to CEO of HP. Putting more outsiders on a board translates on average into better returns for shareholders, a benefit to everyone. At the same time, it also translates into greater risk for the CEO.[2] Since the CEO's interest is rarely the same as the shareholders' interest, CEOs prefer to avoid outsider board members if they can.

Corporate problems, especially those serious enough to result in the ousting of a sitting CEO, can serve to galvanize attention and enhance oversight by the board, making existing coalitions less reliable. Furthermore, it is likely that the new CEO will face real impediments to his efforts to create and shape a board of directors in the wake of an older CEO's deposition. After all, the old board members did not get rid of the prior incumbent with the idea that they would also make it easy for the successor CEO to get rid of them. Nevertheless, any new CEO worth her salt will try to do just that. The long-lasting CEOs are the ones who succeed.

Carly Fiorina became Hewlett-Packard's CEO in 1999. After six turbulent years she was deposed from that position and as chairwoman of the board. Prior to being removed she was the target of an unsuccessful proxy fight mounted by Walter Hewlett and David Woodley Packard, sons of HP's founders. The board, in keeping with the power of inherited insider influence, also included Susan Orr, founder David Packard's daughter. All were individuals with big financial stakes in HP. Furthermore, as big shareholders Hewlett, Packard, and Orr were more concerned about HP's overall performance than about any private benefits they got from being on the board. Good news for shareholders—potentially bad news for Fiorina.

The board that selected Fiorina as CEO consisted of fourteen members. As we've seen, three were relatives of HP's founders; three more were current or retired HP employees.[3] Fiorina's initial board, in other words, had a substantial group of insiders and gray members who were not of her choosing and who had big stakes in the corporation's stock value. It is not hard to see that Carly Fiorina needed to make changes to build a leaner board with stronger attachments to her. It would not be easy—while the board had selected her to be CEO, they were not *her* handpicked loyalists.

She achieved results nonetheless. A year after Fiorina's ascension, in 2000, HP's proxy statement to its shareholders listed only eleven board members, 20 percent fewer than the group that selected her. Three, including David Woodley Packard, were gone. As Fiorina became more entrenched in her position, the board continued to shrink—the 2001 statement listed only ten board members, a reduction of nearly 30 percent from the board she'd originally inherited. Seemingly growing more secure in her control, Fiorina launched an effort to merge HP with Compaq, an effort with both beneficial prospects and serious risks for her continued rule.

Naturally, Fiorina presented the merger as a boon for HP and its shareholders. As Fiorina explained in a speech at a conference on February 4, 2002, "It is a rare opportunity when a technology company can advance its market position substantially and reduce its cost structure substantially at the same time. And this is possible because Compaq and HP are in the same businesses, pursuing the same strategies, in the same markets, with complementary capabilities. So, yes, we thought about a go-slow approach. But, we concluded, after two-and-a-half years of careful deliberation and preparation, that standing still had enormous risks. . . . Standing still means choosing the path of retreat, not leadership."[4]

There is no reason to doubt the sincerity of Fiorina's expectations for the Compaq merger. But it is instructive to examine a major indicator of how Fiorina's appointment and her views meshed with broader market sentiments. The day before the announcement of Carly Fiorina's appointment as HP's new CEO, HP's shares traded at $53.43. The market's reaction to her appointment can reasonably be described as uncertain. The price of HP shares was flat immediately following the announcement and then began to decline, falling to under $39 by mid-October 1999, about three months later. Of course, markets are forward looking, and so investors were watching and learning, modifying their expectations as Fiorina took charge. The news and modified expectations must have been good for a while because by early April 2000, HP's shares had risen markedly, to about $78. But good feelings and good circumstances were not to prevail for long. After April 7, 2000, the share price went into a tailspin, bottoming out in September 2002 at around $12 a share and significantly underperforming the major stock market indexes. By the time Fiorina resigned in February 2005, HP's share price had only rebounded to about $20.

With respect to the Compaq merger, the market was similarly pessimistic. The plan to merge with Compaq was announced on September 3, 2001. Share prices rose on the news, with a peak in December of that year of about $23, though that was still well below the value the day before Carly Fiorina became CEO. Over the period from July 1999 (the announcement of Fiorina's appointment) to the end of December 2001, the adjusted Dow Jones index fell 9.4 percent while HP's adjusted share price fell 47 percent.

From the perspective of any big investor in HP, including the Hewlett and Packard families, Fiorina must have looked like a disaster. Their company was doing worse than the general stock market; their fortunes were being hammered. She was a CEO in trouble. Nevertheless, the upward tick in the share value indicated a renewed, if temporary, boost of optimism at the announced intention to merge with Compaq. But markets don't like infighting, and when Walter Hewlett and David Woodley Packard declared their opposition to the merger, the gains were reversed. Soon the price collapsed even further, halving as it became apparent that there was to be a proxy fight in which Hewlett and Packard sought to muster support from enough shareholders to defeat the board's proposed slate at the corporation's annual meeting. No doubt Fiorina realized that she was going to be in for a tough time, perhaps even before her public announcement of the intended and eventually successfully completed merger. It also seems likely that she would already have known Hewlett's and Packard's views. We can only conclude that this was an intentional gamble on a major policy shift, one that could—and did—adversely affect the wealth of HP's large shareholders (such as now-former board members Hewlett and Packard).

Looking at the Compaq-HP merger politically, we can see several critical themes emerging. Fiorina was already in some trouble because of declining share value. She had successfully diminished the board's size and shuffled its membership, both wise choices for a CEO seeking longevity in office. Yet despite these actions, she still faced significant opposition from the inner circle of essentials and influentials. She had not yet secured the board's loyalty. The Compaq merger might have made good business sense and could therefore have been good for the stock price, thus softening internal opposition to her. Or else, seeing the merger as a fait accompli, her opponents might have given up their fight. That didn't happen. And the disgruntled board members, heavily invested as they were in HP's stock value, could not be mollified with private rewards.

However, what in retrospect may seem like a political nonstarter held at the time great *political* advantages. For instance, what had to be an implication of Fiorina's multibillion-dollar merger with Compaq for the board composition? Once the deal was sealed, Fiorina would have to bring some Compaq leaders onto the postmerger HP board. This could be done either by expanding the existing board to accommodate Compaq influentials or by pruning the existing board to make room for the new Compaq representatives drawn from Compaq's selectorate. Fiorina apparently saw that the merger would provide an opportunity to reconstitute the board and potentially weaken the board faction that opposed her. That seems to be exactly what she tried to do.

Of course, her rivals would not sit idly by and be purged. Unless such a purge can be accomplished in the dark, presented as a fait accompli to the old group of influentials, the risk of failure is real. As it happens, Securities and Exchange Commission regulations require disclosures, which makes turning a board purge into a fait accompli extremely difficult when the opportunity to purge the board depends on a prospective merger.

There are two potential responses to a rebellion such as the one Fiorina faced over HP's weak share price and the Compaq merger. CEOs can either purge some essentials and boost the private benefits to remaining coalition members, or they can expand the coalition and increase rewards to the general selectorate of interchangeables (that is, shareholders). Having survived the proxy fight in 2002, Fiorina faced an eleven-member board that included five new members carried over from Compaq as part of the merger. HP's board had shifted materially, with only six previous HP board members on it. Since Fiorina had been the mover and shaker behind the Compaq deal, it is reasonable to believe that she assumed the new members would be likely to work with her as opposed to lining up with board members who had supported Walter Hewlett's fight against the merger. Walter Hewlett and Robert P. Wayman, meanwhile, had left the board. By this time, in 2002, Fiorina had expanded the total board size by only one, from ten to eleven, while overseeing the departure of several old board members at the same time to make room for five Compaq representatives. Surely she had reason to believe she now enjoyed the support of a majority of the new board.

Perhaps in an effort to shore up the support of remaining old hands on the board, or perhaps coincidentally, there also was a notable shift in board compensation. Just before Fiorina became HP's head, board members earned compensation (that is, private benefits) that ranged from $105,700 to $110,700. With Fiorina in office and the board diminished in size, this amount dropped slightly to $100,000–$105,000 and remained there in the years 2000–2003. But in 2004, according to HP's 2005 proxy statement, board members received between $200,000 and $220,000. During the same period, dividends remained steady at thirty-two cents a share annually and HP's shares significantly underperformed the main stock market indexes. Clearly something was up: HP's stock price performance was poor; dividends were steady; and directors' pay had doubled.

Fiorina's board shuffling and their improved compensation seem aimed at getting the right loyalists in place to help her survive. Although the Compaq merger resulted in the board's growing from ten to eleven, what is most noteworthy is that this net growth of one member was achieved while adding five new members (one of whom stepped down at the end of the year). So the old members constituted only about half the board, shifting the potential balance of power toward Fiorina. Presumably that is just what she hoped, although it is not how things turned out.

Expanding the board was not, and generally is not, the optimal response to a threat from within. To her credit, in terms of political logic, she significantly expanded the size of the interchangeables by adding Compaq's shareholders to HP's shareholders. This normally helps to induce strengthened loyalty, but declining share value could not have been good for new HP board members who had been heavily invested in Compaq, since their economic well-being was now tied to HP's share performance. Nor could Fiorina mollify HP's large shareholders on the board with better board compensation, since their welfare depended on producing the public good of greater returns to shareholders. Those gray board members who owned lots of shares made the seemingly small board of eleven actually pretty large in terms of shares they could vote.

Under enormous pressure, Carly Fiorina stepped down. She was replaced by Patricia Dunn as chairwoman, with HP's chief financial officer, Robert Wayman, emerging again as a significant HP player. He was made interim CEO. Wayman, unable or uninterested in translating his interim position into a full-time job, stepped down a month later while continuing in his role as a member of the board and an HP employee. Mark Hurd replaced him as CEO.

In the immediate aftermath of Fiorina's ouster, the board separated two key positions, CEO and chairperson, presumably in a good Montesquieu-like effort to promote the separation of powers and protect themselves against future adverse choices by the CEO. If that was their intention, they certainly failed. Following Hurd's ascent to the position of CEO, he successfully brought the two posts back under one person's control: his own.

Within a year of Fiorina's ouster, all the leading coup makers who acted against her were gone. Mark Hurd had risen to the top, and, as suggested by the quote from Italo Calvino, he had to watch day and night to keep his head. Four years later, despite stellar HP performance, Hurd was forced out amid a personal scandal. This is the essential lesson of politics: in the end, ruling is the objective, not ruling well.

THE PERILS OF MERITOCRACY

One lesson to be learned from Mark Hurd's ultimate removal at HP is that doing a good job is not enough to ensure political survival. That is true whether one is running a business, a charity, or a national government. How much a leader's performance influences the length of his tenure in office is a highly subjective matter. It might seem obvious that it is important to have people in the coalition of key backers who are competent at implementing the leader's policies. But autocracy isn't about good governance. It's about what's good for the leader, not what's good for the people. In fact, having competent ministers or competent corporate board members can be a dangerous mistake. Competent people, after all, are potential (and potentially competent) rivals.

The three most important characteristics of a coalition are (1) loyalty, (2) loyalty, and (3) loyalty. Successful leaders surround themselves with trusted friends and family, and rid themselves of any ambitious supporters. Carly Fiorina had a hard time achieving that objective, and as a result she failed to last long. Fidel Castro, by contrast, was a master (of course, he had fewer impediments to overcome in what he could do than did Fiorina), and he lasted in power for nearly half a century.

The implications of this aspect of political logic are profound, particularly in small-coalition governments. Saddam Hussein in Iraq, like Idi Amin in Uganda and so many other national leaders, started as a street thug. Autocrats don't need West Point graduates to protect them. Once in power, people like Amin and Hussein wisely surround themselves with trusted members of their own tribe or clan, install-ing them in the most important positions—those involving force and money—and killing anyone who may turn out to be a rival.

Saddam Hussein came to power after compelling his predecessor (and cousin), Ahmed Hassan al-Bakr, to resign in 1979. Before that, however, he had carefully laid the groundwork for his control over Iraq. In 1972, for instance, he had spearheaded the nationalization of international oil interests in Iraq. Oil, of course, was and is where the money is in Iraq, so he had fulfilled the essential ingredient of coming to power: he knew where the money was. Once in power, he ruthlessly pruned his support base.

Just six days after President al-Bakr "resigned," Saddam Hussein convened a national assembly of the ruling Ba'ath Party's leaders, the Revolutionary Command Council. The assembly was videotaped at Saddam Hussein's insistence. During the session, Muhyi Abdel-Hussein, secretary of the Revolutionary Command Council, read out a confession that he had plotted against Saddam Hussein, and then sixty-eight more "enemies of the state" were named as coconspirators. Each, one at a time, was removed from the assembly. Twenty-two were sentenced to death by firing squad and summarily executed by members of the Ba'ath Party, each branch of which was required to send a delegate with a rifle to participate in the executions. Hundreds more were executed within the next few days. Saddam Hussein's bi-ographer later asked Saddam about the decision to eliminate these people, most of whom had risen in the ranks of the Ba'ath Party with Saddam's support. He reported, "The answer was that as long as there is a revolution, there will be a counter-revolution."[5] As we said before, those who can bring a leader to power can also bring the leader down. It is best to shrink the ranks of those who represent a threat and keep those who are most trusted to be loyal.

How competent were the approximately 450 Ba'ath leaders who were executed as part of Saddam's consolidation of power? It is diffi-cult to say from this remove, but we do know that among their ranks were professors, military officers, lawyers, judges, business leaders, journalists, religious leaders, and many other well-educated and ac-complished men. For good measure, Hussein also threw in leaders of competing political parties, who, after all, might have conspired to replace him.

Survivors included people like Saddam's cousin "Chemical Ali," Ali Hassan al-Majid. Chemical Ali most notably demonstrated his loyalty in 1988 when, under orders from Saddam, he launched a successful campaign to commit genocide against Iraq's restive Kurds. But long before that al-Majid had established his commitment to Saddam Hussein. In the infamous videotape mentioned earlier, al-Majid is seen speaking to Saddam, saying, "What you have done in the past was good. What you will do in the future is good. But there's one small point. You have been too gentle, too merciful."[6] Unlike many who were executed following the July 22, 1979, party assembly, al-Majid, previously a motorcycle courier/delivery boy, had little formal education. Although he held the posts of defense minister, interior minister, and head of Iraq's intelligence service, it seems his main area of competence was murder.

Saddam Hussein's pattern of appointments is quite typical. His successor, Prime Minister Nouri al-Maliki, purged the security services of all Sunnis and replaced them with Shia supporters, albeit with a gentler hand than his predecessor.[7] These replacements did not have the experience and training of the existing security personnel. Both leaders knew that it is better to have loyal incompetents than competent rivals.

Post-Saddam Iraq, for all its many troubles, not only looks very different; it looks much better. Cabinet ministers are more likely to be college educated, many have postgraduate degrees, and a great many have actual expertise in the subject matter of their ministry. Of course, those are some of the benefits that follow from having shifted the size of the essential group from 0.27 on our 0-to-1 scale during Saddam's time in power to 0.71 after he was overthrown. Not surprisingly, that improvement in government has been a disaster for national leaders. Saddam survived in office for twenty-four years, whereas since 2003 Iraq has had at least six different governments and counting. The new, more democratic leaders get tossed out pretty regularly. There is always a trade-off between better government and longer-lasting leaders.

Sometimes, of course, having competent advisers is unavoidable even for truly undemocratic rulers. Byzantine, Mughal, Chinese, Caliphate, and other emperors devised a creative solution that guaranteed that these advisers didn't become rivals: they all relied on eunuchs at various times. In the Byzantine Empire in the ninth and tenth centuries, the three most senior posts below emperor were held almost exclusively by eunuchs. The most senior position of grand administrator had evolved from the position of prefect of the sacred bedchamber and included the duties of posting eunuch guards and watching over the sleeping emperor. Michael III made an exception and gave his position to his favorite, Basil, rather than a eunuch. This decision cost him his life. When Basil perceived that Michael was starting to favor another courtier, he murdered the emperor and seized the throne.[8]

Even in modern times the principle of choosing close advisers who cannot rise to the top spot remains good advice. It is surely no coincidence that Saddam Hussein as president of Islamic Iraq had a Christian, Tariq Aziz, as his number two.

KEEP ESSENTIALS OFF-BALANCE

What we can begin to appreciate is that no matter how well a tyrant builds his coalition, it is important to keep the coalition itself off-balance. Familiarity breeds contempt. As noted, the best way to stay in power is to keep the coalition small and, crucially, to make sure that everyone in it knows that there are plenty of replacements for them. This is why you will often read about regular elections in tyrannical states. Everyone knows that these elections don't count, and yet people go along with them. Rigged elections are not about picking leaders. They are not about gaining legitimacy. How can an election be legitimate when its outcome is known before the vote even occurs? Rigged elections are a warning to powerful politicians that they are expendable if they deviate from the leader's desired path.

Vladimir Ilyich Lenin was the first to really exploit the idea of substitute coalition members. In a one-party state, he nonetheless perfected a system of rigged elections and universal adult suffrage. Any action he took—say, sending so-and-so to Siberia—was the will of the people, and any of the people in the replacement pool had a chance, albeit a slight one, of being called up to serve as an influential or maybe even an essential somewhere down the line. Everybody in the Soviet selectorate could, with a very small probability, grow up to be general secretary of the Communist Party, just like the petty criminal Joseph Stalin and the uneducated Nikita Khrushchev. Those already in the inner circle knew they had to stay in line to keep their day jobs. Bravo, Lenin.

Although Lenin perfected the system and probably came up with it on his own, the always-fascinating country of Liberia had experimented earlier with the same phenomenon. Prior to Samuel Doe's takeover, Liberia had been ruled by the True Whig Party. The country originated when a number of liberal American organizations, appalled by the evils of slavery, paid to repatriate former slaves to West Africa. Despite the nation's philanthropic origins, the most important lesson the former slaves took from their experiences appears to be that slavery and forced labor worked much better for the masters than the slaves. These former slaves instituted universal adult suffrage in 1904, but with a property qualification that effectively excluded Indigenous Africans from becoming insiders, making the selectorate large but the influential group relatively small. Thus, they established a system run for a small group of insiders despite the appearance of a universal franchise. This structure provided for strong loyalty to the incumbent and ensured the incumbent had the opportunity to suppress any opposition that might arise to their forced labor policies—a system whose policies differed from Soviet ones but whose promise of security in office was the same.[9]

Virtually every publicly traded company in the world has adopted the Leninist rigged-election system, and for much the same reasons. Along with a packed board, it is one of the major factors ensuring that poorly performing CEOs hardly ever get fired. Carly Fiorina had the misfortune of heading a company that might have *looked* like a rigged-election autocracy but up close and personal remained more akin to a monarchy. Although there were millions of shareholders who in theory could shape HP policy, so many shares were concentrated in a few hands that HP had more of the characteristics of a small coalition drawn from a small group of influentials within a mostly small, concentrated group of interchangeables—that is, members of the Hewlett and Packard families.

The essence of keeping coalition members off-balance is making sure that their loyalty is paid for and that they know they will be ousted if their reliability is in doubt. The USSR's Mikhail Gorbachev, thought to be a good guy in Western political circles, certainly understood the necessity of rewarding loyalty and shucking off all those whose faithfulness was questionable. He replaced much of the Politburo within his first two years in office, picking and choosing from the Communist Party (the real selectorate) those most loyal to him. It turns out, though, that Gorbachev was much less ruthless than contemporaries of the autocratic class. To be sure, he forced adversaries, like Boris Yeltsin, out of the Politburo. But, as Yeltsin surely realized, he would have been killed under Stalin. Equally, he and many others must have known that it was much better to cross swords with Gorbachev, an intellectual reformer, than with such contemporaries as Mobutu Sese Seko of Zaire or even Deng Xiaoping of China. Deng, after all, used ruthless force to end the prodemocracy uprising at Tiananmen Square in 1989. Gorbachev, as we will see, did not hesitate to use force outside of Russia, but he also did not go around killing his political rivals. His reward was a short time in power, first because he left himself vulnerable to a coup by hard-line Communists and then because he allowed Yeltsin to resurrect himself politically, defeat the coup, and make himself into Gorbachev's replacement. Yeltsin's own successor, Vladimir Putin, learned the errors of Gorbachev's approach. Putin allegedly has had around a dozen of his more influential opponents assassinated or, in a few cases, unsuccessfully targeted for death.

The execution of opponents is a long-standing practice among most autocrats. We should not fail to appreciate the moral significance of Gorbachev's restraint. Adolf Hitler, Mao Zedong, Fidel Castro, Samuel Doe, and so many others showed no such restraint. They had their erstwhile backers murdered once they worked out who was most likely to be loyal and who was not. We see a nicer version of such behavior as a routine part of corporate changes when there's a new

CEO. Although the CEO is supposed to answer to the board, it is commonplace for boards to be reconstituted after a new CEO comes to power; the tail apparently wags the dog.

Being purged from the initial coalition is often fatal. Hitler became chancellor of Germany on January 30, 1933. During his rise to power he had relied heavily on the Sturmabteilung, a paramilitary force also known by the abbreviation SA or by a description of their uniforms, the Brownshirts. Hitler perceived the SA's leader, Ernst Röhm, as a threat. He built up an alternative paramilitary, the Schutzstaffel, or SS, and then, on what became known as the Night of the Long Knives, he ordered the assassination of at least eighty-five and possibly many hundreds of people between June 30 and July 2, 1934. Thousands more were imprisoned. Despite Röhm's long-term and essential backing of Hitler (Röhm had been with him during his failed 1923 Beer Hall Putsch), Hitler showed no sentimentality. He replaced him with men like SS leader Heinrich Himmler, whom he deemed more loyal.

Robert Mugabe was likewise a master at keeping his coalition off-balance. He was elected president of Zimbabwe in 1980 following a negotiated settlement to a long civil war. The struggle against the white-only rule of the previous Rhodesian regime was led by two factions that crystallized into political parties behind their respective leaders: Robert Mugabe's ZANU (Zimbabwe African National Union) and Joshua Nkomo's ZAPU (Zimbabwe African People's Union). Initially, Mugabe preached reconciliation:

> If yesterday I fought you as an enemy, today you have become a friend and ally with the same national interest, loyalty, rights and duties as myself. If yesterday you hated me, you cannot avoid the love that binds you to me and me to you.... Draw a line under the past.... The wrongs of the past must now stand forgiven and forgotten. If ever we look to the past, let us do so for the lesson the past has taught us, namely that oppression and racism are inequalities that must never find scope in our political and social system. It could never be a correct justification that because the whites oppressed us yesterday when they had power, the blacks

must oppress them today because they have power. An evil remains an evil whether practiced by white against black or black against white.[10]

A naive observer might have thought that Mugabe planned to bring ZAPU elites into his winning coalition. That might have made sense at the outset, but once ZANU's power was consolidated there would be no reason to keep ZAPU loyalists around. And once Mugabe's power was consolidated, he'd have no need to keep some of his old friends from ZANU around either.

Mugabe also reached out to many in the white community, particularly former leaders and administrators, to help him run the country. Many whites who had feared the transition began to refer to him as "good old Bob." Mugabe needed their support. He could not run the country without them, and he needed to know where the money was. In this he was greatly assisted by the international community. They pledged $900 million in aid during his first year. However, once he was ensconced in power, Mugabe's attitude changed.

In 1981 he called for a one-party state and began arresting whites, saying, "We will kill those snakes among us, we will smash them completely." Mugabe was even harsher toward his former comrades in arms. He forced Nkomo out of the cabinet and sent a North Korean–trained paramilitary group, the Fifth Brigade, to terrorize Matabeleland, Nkomo's regional stronghold. As one ZANU minister put it, "Nkomo and his guerillas are germs in the country's wounds and they will have to be cleaned up with iodine. The patient will scream a bit."[11] The operation was called Gukurahundi—a Shona word that means "wind that blows away the chaff before the spring rains." Many veterans from the fight against white rule resisted. In retaliation Matabeleland was effectively sealed off and four hundred thousand people faced starvation. As one of Mugabe's henchmen, a brigade officer, stated, "First you will eat your chickens, then your goats, then your cattle, then your donkeys. Then you will eat your children and finally you will eat the dissidents."[12]

Mugabe needed the assistance of ZAPU fighters to defeat white-only rule. He needed the assistance of white farmers and administrators and the international community to find the money to solidify his control over the state. Only when he was entrenched in power did "good old Bob" show his true colors.

DEMOCRATS AREN'T ANGELS

As we all know, history is written by the victors. Leaders should therefore never refrain from cheating if they can get away with it. Politicians in democracies may have to put up with real and meaningful elections in order to stay in power, but it shouldn't be shocking to see that whenever they can, they'll happily take a page out of Lenin's book. There's no election better than a rigged one, so long as you're the one rigging it.

Indeed, Donald Trump's refrain in 2020, from the moment the polls turned against him, was that the Democrats somehow were going to rig the election against him, even though they were not in power in key swing states. And when he lost what even his own attorney general declared was an honest election, he continued to claim it was rigged against him and tried to stop Congress from making his loss official. Honest elections are good, but winning, by whatever means, is better.

The list of tried-and-true means of cheating is long. Just as quickly as electoral rules are created to outlaw corrupt practices, politicians find other means. For instance, leaders can restrict who is eligible and registered to vote. In Malaysia, under a system known as Operation IC, immigration is controlled so as to create demographics favorable to the incumbent party. Tammany Hall, New York City's infamous Democratic Party machine, acquired its Irish flavor by meeting and recruiting immigrants as they left the boat, promising citizenship and jobs in exchange for their vote. The British were really good at rigging elections. In the rotten boroughs of England's eighteenth and nineteenth centuries, there were places where a handful of voters—maybe just one family—could elect a member of Parliament. Malaysians, Brits, Republicans, Democrats: everyone looks for ways to shrink how much support they need to win while maximizing how much support their foes require.

When leaders can't restrict who is eligible to vote or are unable to buy enough votes, they can use intimidation and violence to restrict access to polling places. North Indian states, such as Bihar and Uttar Pradesh, experience "booth capture," where party supporters capture the polling place and cast every eligible voter's vote for their party. The US state of Georgia won't allow anyone to hand out water bottles to people who might spend hours waiting in line to vote. After all, that bottle of water just might change someone's vote.

Cheating does not stop once ballots are cast, of course. Leaders never hesitate to miscount or destroy ballots. Coming to power and staying in power are the most important things in politics. And candidates who aren't willing to cheat are typically beaten by those who are. Since democracies typically work out myriad ways to make cheating difficult, politicians in power in democracies have innovated any number of perfectly legal means to ensure their electoral victories and continued rule.

One counterintuitive strategy is for leaders to encourage additional competitors. This is why some states have so many political parties, even though only one really wins. The conventional wisdom about America's two-party system tells us that fringe parties allow for a more vibrant and responsive government. But even in multiparty states, there are always leading parties—you have to ask yourself whether the leading parties would allow the fringe parties to exist if they weren't somehow serving their interests.

Tanzania's parliament and presidency are perennially controlled by the Chama Cha Mapinduzi party (CCM), even though as many as fifteen parties competed for the presidency in 2020. This is especially surprising because Tanzania follows electoral rules very similar to the Westminster system in which a plurality wins. Such systems are expected to have only two major parties. In fact, this is such a well-established regularity that it is known as Duverger's law.[13]

Why so many parties in Tanzania, apparently in defiance of Duverger's law? Well, the CCM government actually provided campaign financing, as we would expect, in an opaque way, to small parties until quite recently, thereby encouraging them to compete and divide the opposition vote. This makes it easier for the relatively centrist

CCM to win. Although the CCM wins a large percentage of the vote, all it *needs* to win is one more vote than the second-largest party in half the parliamentary constituencies. That turns out to mean the CCM needs much less than 10 percent in most districts. The number of supporters a party needs affects the kinds of policies it pursues. In those constituencies in Tanzania where an opposition party generates lots of votes, the CCM needs to appeal to many voters and therefore generally provides better health care, education, and services. In constituencies where the CCM needs fewer votes, cash transfers, such as vouchers for subsidized fertilizer, are more common.[14]

Multiparty democracy provides a similar means for one or two parties to dominate governments in democracies from Botswana to Japan and Israel. There is more to representing the people than just allowing them to vote, even when the vote is done honestly.

Designated seats for underrepresented minorities is another means by which leaders reduce the number of people upon whom they are dependent. Such policies are advertised as empowering minorities or underrepresented groups, whether women or members of a particular caste or religion. In reality they empower leaders. That a candidate is elected by a small subset of the population reduces the number of essentials required to retain power. At a very basic level, electoral victory in a two-party parliamentary system requires the support of half the people in half the districts—that is, in principle, 25 percent of the voters. Suppose 10 percent of the seats were reserved for election by one specific group that happens to be geographically concentrated (such as gay voters in the Castro in our earlier account of Harvey Milk's election in San Francisco). To retain half the seats in parliament, the incumbent party need only retain 40 percent of the regular single-member district seats, which is readily done with just over 22 percent of the vote. So by focusing on districts in which the privileged minority is prevalent, a party can reduce the number of votes it requires by 12 percent.

Delegated positions also make it easier to form a small coalition. Consider Tanzania's parliament, the Bunge. There are 264 directly elected seats, 113 additional seats reserved for women who are nominated by the parties in relation to the number of seats they capture in the election, and 5 seats nominated by the Zanzibar Assembly. (Zanzibar is a beautiful island off the mainland that united with mainland Tanganyika in 1964 to form Tanzania.) In addition, the president gets to nominate ten cabinet appointees and an attorney general to serve in the parliament. This gives a total of 393 seats, of which the president needs 197 to control the Bunge. Given that he appoints eleven and that the CCM is regionally based in Zanzibar, he already controls sixteen seats. If the CCM wins 141 elected seats, then he controls parliament—that is, 141 directly elected seats (equal to 35.8 percent of parliament), 16 appointed seats, and .358 × 113 of the appointed women's seats (that is, 41 such seats), together total 198, rounding having forced an extra seat to be held. The CCM not only needs only 35.8 percent of the directly elected seats; by funding many opposition parties the CCM can win many seats with less than a 10 percent vote share. In practice the president actually controls nearly all the women's appointments, and he tends to appoint women who lack an independent base of support. Indeed, few women win direct election to Tanzania's parliament.

While Tanzania may have free and fair elections (though this was strongly questioned in 2020 when there were widespread allegations that leading opposition candidates were restricted in their ability to campaign), the reality is that the incumbent CCM party can sustain itself in office with a very small percentage of the vote. Of course, in most districts they get much more support than they need because politicians find inventive ways to incentivize voters. One of these ways is the creation of voting blocs.[15]

BLOC VOTING

Bloc voting is a feature common in many fledgling democracies. It was also the norm under party machines in large US cities. For instance, under the influence of Tammany Hall, whole neighborhoods in New York City would turn up to vote Democratic. Many of India's electoral districts have followed a pattern similar to the old Tammany Hall: a small group of local notables or village patrons can deliver their community's vote and extract great rewards for themselves in return.

During Bueno de Mesquita's time doing fieldwork in India in 1969–1970, he observed firsthand how the quest for power coupled with the influence of power blocs undermined any notion of the pursuit of political principles other than the principles of winning and getting paid off.

Senior people in villages and towns—and indeed, up and down the levels of governance in India's states—would pledge to a particular party the support of those they led. In return, they would receive benefits and privileges. By and large, all the "clients" of these "patrons" followed their patron's lead and voted for the designated party. What is most fascinating is that the affiliations between voters and parties didn't need to have any ideological rhyme or reason. In Uttar Pradesh, India's most populous state, for instance, the free-market, anticommunist Swatantra Party, the socially conservative and anticommunist Jana Sangh party (a Hindu-nationalist party that was a precursor to today's BJP), and the Communist Party of India formed a coalition government with each other following India's 1967 election. This was true despite the Swatantra Party leadership's description of the Communist Party of India as "public enemy number 1." What did these parties have in common? Only their desire to band together and beat the Congress Party so as to enjoy the benefits of power. This sort of odd-bedfellows, coalition-building strategy was long rampant throughout India.[16]

Perhaps the most egregious case of bald opportunism occurred in the state of Bihar. There, ideologically disparate parties formed a government by relying heavily on currying favor with the Raja of Ramgarh. The raja, owner of many of the mining interests in Bihar, switched parties every few months, bringing coalition governments down—and up—with him. Each time he switched, he garnered greater private goods for himself and his backers, including the dismissal of criminal charges against him. As noted in an analysis of one of the raja's frequent defections to an alternative coalition, which led to the formation of a new government, "The Raja who had been able to get his terms from Mr. Mahamaya Prasad [the former head of the Bihar government] assumed that he could demand from Mr. Paswan [the new head of the Bihar government] a higher price. This amounted to Deputy Chief Ministership and the Mines portfolio for himself and withdrawal of the innumerable cases filed against him and members of his family by the Bihar government."[17] The raja understood that he could manipulate his bloc of backers to make or break governments and that, in doing so, he could enrich himself a lot and help his followers a little bit. That, indeed, is the lesson of bloc voting whether based on personal ties in Bihar, trade union membership among American teachers, corporate membership in a lobbying group like the American Petroleum Institute, tribal clans in Iraq, linguistic divisions in Belgium, or religion in Northern Ireland. Bloc leaders gain a lot, their members gain less, and the rest of society pays the price.

Bloc voting takes seemingly democratic institutions and makes them appear like publicly traded companies. Every voter or share has a nominal right to vote, but effectively all the power lies with a few key actors who can control the votes of large numbers of shares or deliver many votes from their village. Bloc voting makes nominally democratic systems with large coalitions function as if they are autocratic by making the number of influentials—that is, the people whose choices actually matter—much smaller than the nominal selectorate of the rest of the voters. Since this is such an important aspect of winning elections, we are obliged to explore how politicians do it.

The traditional approach has been to treat emerging democracies as patronage systems in which politicians deliver small bribes to individual voters. For instance, the *New York Times* reported on September 17, 2010, in an article with the headline "Afghan Votes Come Cheap, and Often in Bulk," that the typical price paid for an Afghan voter's support was about five or six dollars. But the article also noted that widespread vote fraud probably made vote buying unnecessary in any event.

The explanation for fraudulent electoral outcomes based on vote buying in exchange for patronage is simple, but it is also incomplete. First, parties don't bribe enough people, and second, once in the voting booth, voters can renege. Historically parties used to issue their own ballots. For instance, your party might print a ballot on pink paper, so party representatives could check that those who took bribes voted with pink ballots. Although we could fill a whole book with the tricks parties use to monitor vote choices, the reality is that today votes are likely to be anonymous, at least in real democracies.

Bribing voters works far better at the bloc level. Suppose there are just three villages, and suppose a party, call it party A, negotiates with senior community figures in the villages and makes the following offer: if party A wins, it will build a new hospital (or pick up the trash, send police patrols, plow the snow, and so on) in the most supportive of the three villages. Once a village elder declares for party A, voters in that village can do little better than support party A, even if they don't like it. The reality is that there are so many voters that the chance that any individual's vote matters is inconsequential. Yet voters have much more influence on where the hospital gets built or whose streets get swept than they have on who wins the election. To see why, consider the case where two or three of the village elders declare in favor of party A and most voters in these villages go along with them.

Consider the incentives of an individual voter. Since at least two of three villages have declared for party A, an alternative party is unlikely to win, so an individual's vote has little influence on the electoral outcome. Voting for party B is a waste of time. Yet the voter could influence where the hospital is built by turning out to vote for A. If everyone else supports A but she does not, then her village gives one less vote for A than another village and so loses out on the hospital. If she votes for A, then her village has a shot at getting the hospital. In the extreme case, where absolutely everyone votes for party A, our voter would give up a one-third chance of getting the hospital in her village if she did not vote for party A. Voters have little incentive to do anything but go along with their village elders.

By rewarding supportive groups over others, individual voters are motivated to follow the choice of their group leader, be that a village elder, a ward organizer, a church leader, or a union boss. The real decisions are made by the group leaders who deliver blocs of votes. They are the true influentials. It is therefore unsurprising that it is common for the rewards to flow through them, so that they can take their cut, rather than go directly to the people. Political scientist Milton Rakove describes the process of handing out rewards to different ethnic groups under Mayor Richard Daley's party machine in Chicago in the early 1970s: "The machine co-opts those emerging leaders in the black and Spanish-speaking communities who are willing to cooperate; reallocates perquisites and prerogatives to the blacks and the Spanish speaking, taking them from ethnic groups such as the Jews and Germans, who do not support the machine as loyally as their fathers did."[18]

Of course, leaders can use sticks as well as carrots. Lee Kuan Yew ruled Singapore from 1959 until 1990, making him, we believe, the longest-serving prime minister anywhere. His party, the People's Action Party (PAP), dominated elections, and that dominance was reinforced by the allocation of public housing, upon which most people in Singapore rely. Neighborhoods that fail to deliver PAP votes come election time found the provision and maintenance of housing cut off.[19] In Zimbabwe, Robert Mugabe went one step further. In an operation called Murambatsvina (Operation Drive Out the Rubbish), he used bulldozers to demolish the houses and markets in neighborhoods that failed to support him in the 2005 election.

Of course, there are nicer ways to reward bloc voting than rushing out to bulldoze the homes of opponents. These nicer ways nevertheless are tremendously effective in dampening opposition. Consider that even in a seemingly staid, rule-oriented democracy like Japan, bloc voting is commonplace and successfully delivers the goods. A study of more than 3,300 Japanese municipalities revealed that municipalities that gave more support to Japan's Liberal Democratic Party winners got disproportionately more government support within the district than they seemed to be entitled to. That seems surprising because the support they got was supposed to be allocated according to a formula intended to even out the quality of services despite inequalities in wealth.[20]

Ownership of a public company works in the same way as bloc voting. We could hold our shares in our own names and vote at stockholder meetings. However, except for a very wealthy few of us, our votes are inconsequential, and turning up at meetings is burdensome. Thus we hold stock via mutual funds and pensions (there are tax and management reasons to do so, too, but then think about who has the incentive to lobby for these regulations). These institutional investors, like village elders, are influential enough that CEOs court their support. But it is much cheaper to buy the loyalty of the institutional investor with private goods, such as fees for board membership, than it is to reward all the little investors he represents with great stock performance.

So what can a politician do when elections are fair and the risk of electoral defeat is rising? When an incumbent is at risk of electoral defeat, he can always mitigate that risk by redrawing the boundaries of the constituency to exclude opposition voters—that is to say, the district can be gerrymandered, although the opportunity to redraw district boundaries only comes once in a while, so it may come too late to save an unpopular incumbent. The practice of gerrymandering has made the odds of an incumbent being voted out of a US congressional seat not that different from the odds of defeat faced by members of the Supreme Soviet under the Soviet Union's one-party Communist regime. And while gerrymandering virtually ensures reelection, it also makes the voters in a congressional district happy. After all, the gerrymander means that they get the candidate favored by a majority in the district. If gerrymandering isn't an option, then other rule

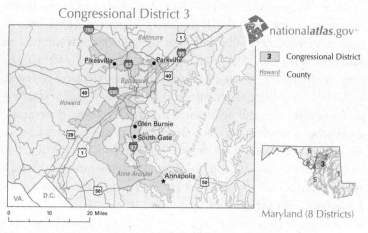

Figure 3.1: Maryland's 3rd Congressional District

changes can be instituted, such as the prohibition of rallies—in the name of public safety, of course.

Have a look at the map of Maryland's 3rd Congressional District in Figure 3.1. Need any more be said about why, in many districts, one party always wins?

LEADER SURVIVAL

Building a small coalition is key to survival. The smaller the number of people to whom a leader is beholden, the easier it is for her to persist in office. Autocrats and democrats alike try to cull supporters. Let's arrange political systems into broad groups of autocrats and democrats to make it easy to see big differences in coalition size. Doing so, we can compare the survival of different political leaders.

Figure 3.2 looks at democrats' and autocrats' risk of being replaced based on how long they have been in office. On average, democrats who make it through the first six months in office have about a 38 percent chance of being out by the end of their first year; autocrats have about a 28 percent chance of being ousted in the same amount of time.[21] The figure demonstrates that the farther out leaders go in time, the more likely it is that they are ousted if they are democrats. Autocrats are removed at a much lower rate. The effect of this higher rate of democratic deposition is that about 12 percent of autocrats survive ten years in office while only 5 percent of democrats survive that long. The figure ends after just ten years because there are virtually no democrats with longer tenures. However, if the chart were extended, we would see that of the autocrats that make it to ten years, two-thirds of them will still be in office after twenty years. These simple comparisons, however, miss an interesting and important detail. Although autocrats survive longer, they find surviving the initial period in office particularly difficult. During their first six months they are nearly twice as likely to be deposed as their democratic counterparts. However, if they survive those first turbulent months, then they have a much better chance of staying in power than democrats. Those early months are difficult because they have not yet worked out where the

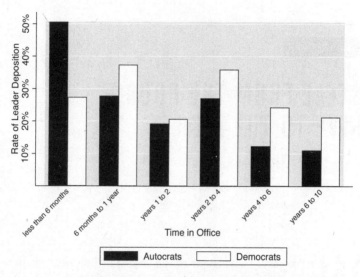

Figure 3.2: The Risk of Ouster by Type of Government

money is, making them unreliable sources of wealth for their coalition, and they have yet to work out whose support they really need and whom they can dump from their transitional coalition. But once autocrats have reshaped their group of supporters through a purge, survival becomes easier. Democrats, in contrast, are constantly engaged in a battle for the best policy ideas to keep their large constituencies happy. As a result, although democrats survive the early months in office more easily (they get a honeymoon), the perpetual quest for good policy takes a toll.

Staying in power right after coming to power is tough, but a successful leader will seize power and then reshuffle the coalition that brought him there to redouble his strength. A smart leader sacks some early backers and replaces them with more reliable and cheaper supporters. But no matter how much he packs the coalition with his friends and supporters, they will not remain loyal unless he rewards them. And as we will see in the next chapter, rewards don't come cheaply.

CHAPTER FOUR

STEAL FROM THE POOR, GIVE TO THE RICH

Whether you're taking charge of the Ottoman Empire, a corporation, or Liberia, controlling the flow of funds is essential to buying support. However, once you've emptied the state's or corporation's coffers in order to buy off both your essential supporters and their replacements, if necessary, you must reckon with the entirely new challenge of *refilling* the treasury. If a leader cannot find a reliable source of income, then it is only a matter of time until someone else will offer his supporters greater rewards than he can.

Money is essential for anyone who wants to run any organization. Without their share of the state's rewards, hardly anyone will stick with an incumbent for long. Liberia's Prince Johnson knew this when he tortured Samuel Doe and demanded the numbers of the bank accounts where the state's treasure had been hidden. Without getting his question answered, Johnson would not be able to secure power for himself. In fact, neither he nor rival insurgent Charles Taylor could secure enough state revenue to buy control of Liberia's government immediately after Doe was overthrown. The upshot: Samuel Doe died under Prince Johnson's torture without answering the question "Where's the money?" and Liberia degenerated into civil war. Each faction was able to extract enough resources to buy support in a small region, but no one could control the state as a whole.

The succession process in the Ottoman Empire is another illustration of the same point. Upon the death of their father, the Ottoman princes rushed from their provinces to secure the treasury, buy the loyalty of the army, and have all their potential rivals (also known as their brothers) strangled. Whoever secured control over the money first was likely to win. If no one son triumphed, cleanly wresting the treasury out of his siblings' control, then no one could summon the necessary revenues to pay his backers. The common result was, as in Liberia, civil war.

Knowing where the money is, is particularly important in autocracies—and particularly difficult. Such regimes are shrouded in secrecy. Supporters must be paid, but there are no accurate accounts detailing stocks and flows of wealth. Of course, this lack of transparency is by design.[1] Thus does chaotic bookkeeping become a kind of insurance policy: it becomes vastly more difficult for a rival to promise to pay supporters if he cannot match existing bribes or, for that matter, put his hands on the money. Indeed, secrecy not only provides insurance against rivals, but it also keeps supporters in the dark about what other supporters are getting. Anyone who has tried to read the annual reports of publicly traded firms will quickly realize that this is a practice induced by dependence on a small winning coalition. In the corporate setting there is opacity even though the company has to satisfy strict regulations and accounting standards. Secrecy ensures that everyone gets the deal they can negotiate, not knowing how much it might cost to replace them. Thus every supporter's price is kept as low as possible, and woe to any supporter who is discovered trying to coordinate with his fellow coalition members to raise their price.

As we saw at the end of the last chapter, it is very difficult for autocrats to survive their early months in office. Good governance is a luxury they cannot afford at a time when they must scramble to find revenues. Little surprise, then, that we so often see looting, confiscations, extraction, and fire sales during political transitions—or conversely, and perhaps ironically, temporary liberal reforms by would-be dictators who are mindful that it is easier for a public goods–producing democrat than an autocrat to survive the first months in office. Thus it is that in the immediate aftermath of a leadership transition we see a few new leaders acting as if they care about the people and many new leaders seizing the people's wealth and property. Such confiscations of property might well damage revenue in the long run, but if a leader does not find money in the short term, then the long run is someone else's problem.

Democrats are generally fortunate enough to know where most of the money is. When Boris Johnson became prime minister of Britain or Joe Biden became president of the United States, neither needed to torture their predecessor to find the money. Sure, the Trump administration delayed providing transition assistance to the incoming Biden administration until the very end. Still, despite every effort to hamper the transition, the simple fact was that the accounts were public enough that the Biden team could sort out where most of the money was and hit the ground running. Because democracies have well-organized and relatively transparent treasuries, their flow of funds is undisturbed by leader turnover. There are two reasons for this transparency. First, as we are about to explore, democratic leaders best promote their survival through policies of open government. Second, a larger proportion of revenue in democracies than in autocracies tends to be from the taxation of people at work. Such taxes need to be levied in a clear and transparent way, because just as surely as leaders need money, their constituents want to avoid taxes.

TAXATION

We all hate taxes and are impressively inventive in looking for ways to avoid them. Leaders, however, are rather fond of taxes—as long as they don't have to pay them. Being a dictator can be a terrific job, but it also can be terribly stressful, especially if money is in short supply. Taxes are one of the great antidotes to stress for heads of governments. Taxes, after all, generate much-needed revenue, which can then be used to reward supporters. As a general principle, leaders always want to increase taxes. That gives them more resources with which to reward their backers—and, not to be forgotten, themselves. Nevertheless, they find it difficult to raise taxes with impunity.

Leaders face three constraints on how much money they can skim from their subjects. First, taxes diminish how hard people work. Second, some of the tax burden inevitably will fall on the essential backers of the leader. (In general, the first constraint limits taxes in autocracies and the second constraint sets the boundary on taxes in democracies.) The third consideration is that tax collection requires both expertise and resources. The costs associated with collecting taxes limit what leaders can extract and shape the choice of taxation methods.

The first and most common complaint about taxes is that they discourage hard work, enterprise, and investment. This is true. People are unlikely to work as hard to put money in government coffers as they do to put money in their own pocket. Economists often like to express taxation and economic activity in terms of pies: when taxes are low, they say, the people work hard to enlarge the pie, but the government only gets a thin slice of the pie. As the government increases taxes, its share of the pie increases but people begin to do less work, so the overall size of the pie shrinks. If the government sets tax rates extremely low or extremely high, its take will approach zero. In the first case it gets very little of a large pie; in the latter case there is hardly any pie because hardly anyone works. Somewhere between these extremes there is an ideal tax rate that produces the most revenue the state can get from taxation. What that ideal rate is depends on the precise size of the winning coalition. That, in fact, is one of many reasons that it is more helpful to talk about organizations in terms of how many essentials they depend on than in terms of imprecise notions such as autocracy or democracy. The general rule is that the larger the group of essentials, the lower the tax rate. Having said that, we return to the less precise vocabulary of autocracy and democracy, always mindful that we really mean smaller or bigger coalitions.

Autocrats aim for the rate that maximizes revenue. They want as much money as possible for themselves and their cronies. In contrast, good governance dictates that taxes should only be taken to pay for things that the market is poor at providing, such as national defense, a social safety net, and large infrastructure projects. Taking relatively little in taxes therefore encourages people to lead more productive lives, creating a bigger pie. Democrats are closer to this good governance ideal than autocrats, but they too overtax. The centerpiece of Reaganomics, the economic plan of US president Ronald Reagan (1981–1989), was that US taxes were mistakenly set higher than this revenue-maximizing level. If taxes were reduced, he argued, people would do so much extra work that government revenue would actually go up; that is, a smaller share of a bigger pie would be larger than the bigger share of a smaller pie. Such a win-win policy proved popular. Of course, it did not quite work out that way.

To a certain extent, Reagan was right: lower taxes encouraged people to work and so the pie grew, and it did so again during Donald Trump's term following his big tax cut for top earners (before the COVID-19 pandemic). However, crucially, in democracies it is the coalition's willingness to bear taxes that is the true constraint on the tax level. Since taxes had not been so high as to squash entrepreneurial zeal in the first place, there wasn't much appreciable change as a result of Reagan's or Trump's tax cuts. The pie grew, but not by so much that revenues could keep up with increased spending. The net effect of the tax cuts was, therefore, higher debt rather than a pie growing fast enough to outpace government spending.

Politicians who raise or even maintain current taxes are politically vulnerable, but then so too are politicians who fail to deliver the policies their coalition wants. Herein lies the rub. It may well be that cutting taxes, while increasing the size of the economic pie, fails to make the pie big enough to generate both more wealth and more effective government policies. The question is and always must be the degree to which the private sector's efficient but unequal distribution of wealth trumps government's more equitable, less efficient, but popular economic programs.

Ruling is about staying in power, not good governance. To this end, leaders buy support by rewarding their essential backers relative to others. Taxation plays a dual role in generating this kind of loyalty. First, it provides leaders with the resources to enrich their most essential supporters. Second, it reduces the welfare of those outside of the coalition. Taxation, especially in small-coalition settings, re-distributes from those outside the coalition (the poor) to those inside the coalition (the rich). Small-coalition systems amply demonstrate this principle, for these are places where rich people are rich precisely because they are in the winning coalition and others are poor because they are not. Phillip Chiyangwa, a protégé of the late Robert Mugabe in Zimbabwe (possibly even his nephew), stated it bluntly: "I am rich because I belong to Zanu-PF [Mugabe's ruling party]."[2] When the coalition changes, so does who is rich and who is poor. Today, poor Mr. Chiyangwa has been ousted from numerous lucrative positions, including being banned for life from ZIFA, Zimbabwe's football (soccer) association, which he formerly headed and from which he allegedly embezzled $2 million.[3]

Nor is Zimbabwe an isolated case. Robert Bates, a professor of government at Harvard University, described the link between wealth and political backing in Kenya:

> I recall working in western Kenya shortly after Daniel Arap Moi succeeded Jomo Kenyatta as president of Kenya. With the shift in power, the political fortunes of elite politicians had changed. As I drove through the highlands, I encountered boldly lettered signs posted on the gateways of farms announcing the auction of cattle, farm machinery, and buildings and lands. Once they were no longer in favor, politicians found their loans cancelled or called in, their subsidies withdrawn, or their lines of business, which had once been sheltered by the state, exposed to competition. Some whom I had once seen in the hotels of Nairobi, looking sleek and satisfied, I now encountered in rural bars, looking lean and apprehensive, as they contemplated the magnitude of their reversal.[4]

Needless to say, people want to be sleek and satisfied and not lean and apprehensive. That is why they remain loyal. A heavy tax burden emphasizes the difference between being rich and being poor—in or out of the coalition. At the same time, the resulting revenues fund spoils for the lucky few, leaving little for everyone else. Further, the misery such heavy taxes inflict on the general population makes participation in the coalition even more valuable. Fearing exclusion and poverty under an alternative leadership, supporters are all the more fiercely loyal. They will do anything to keep what they have and keep on collecting goodies. Gerard Padró i Miquel of Yale University has shown that the leaders of numerous African nations tax too highly (that is, beyond the maximum revenue point) and then turn around and provide subsidies to chosen groups. This may be economic madness, but it is also political genius.[5]

Democratic governments may tax heavily, too, and for the same reason as autocrats: they provide subsidies to groups that favor them at the polls at the expense of those who oppose them. We will see, for instance, that Democrats and Republicans in the United States each use taxation when they can to redistribute wealth from their opponents to their supporters. So democratic governments also have an appetite for taxation, but they cannot indulge that appetite to the extent autocrats can. Since his essential backers are few, an autocrat can easily compensate them for the tax burden that falls on them. This option is not available to a democrat because his number of supporters is so large. Tax rates are therefore limited by the need to make coalition members better off than they can expect to be under alternative leadership. Donald Trump's tax legislation, for instance, greatly reduced the deductibility of state and local government taxes. Since states controlled by Democrats generally have higher state and local taxes than Republican states, Trump reduced Republican taxes disproportionately at the expense of his Democratic opponents. No wonder so many Republicans loved him and so many Democrats reviled him, but then they weren't going to vote for Trump anyway. He had no need to make those who vote for the Democrats happy. Of course, all leaders want to generate revenue with which to reward supporters, but democratic incumbents are constrained to keep taxes relatively low. A democrat may tax above the good governance minimum, but he does not raise taxes to the autocrat's revenue maximization point.

The relationship between regime type and taxation can be seen in the recent history of Mexico. Mexico began a transition toward democracy following a massive earthquake in 1985 (as discussed in chapter 8). Its first free election came in 1994, and the incumbent party, the Partido Revolucionario Institucional (PRI), lost nationally for the first time in 2000. As can be seen in Figure 4.1, the onset of democratization marks the start of the decline in government revenue as a percentage of gross domestic product (GDP). As the size of the winning coalition enlarged, Mexico's tax rates followed suit by declining, just as they should when politicians need to curry favor with many instead of a few. For instance, the highest marginal tax rate in Mexico in 1979, with the PRI firmly in control, was 55 percent. As the PRI's one-party rule declined, so did tax rates. By 2000, marking the first truly free, competitive presidential election, Mexico's highest tax rate was 40 percent.[6] Today it is only 35 percent.

Members of any autocrat's small coalition also dislike paying taxes, but they readily endorse high taxes when those taxes are used to funnel great wealth back to them. This was just the case in Bell, California. City manager Robert Rizzo raised property taxes. The city council could have stopped such increases, but had they done so, the city could not have afforded their bloated consultancy fees. Suppose for simplicity that Rizzo's coalition was composed of 1 percent of Bell's thirty-six thousand residents. For every dollar increase in tax

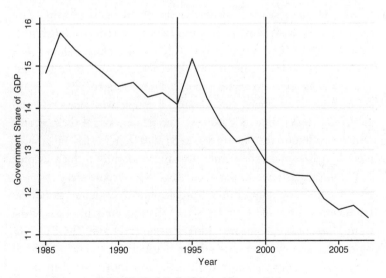

Figure 4.1: Mexico's Tax Take and Democratization

per person, Rizzo would have been able to transfer up to $100 of services and payments to each coalition member. Had his coalition been composed of half of Bell's residents, each dollar increase in tax per person would provide only $2 to transfer to each coalition member. It is easy to see why the coalition would sooner endorse higher taxes in the former setup than in the latter.

Nevertheless, to most of us who live in democracies, the idea that our taxes are lower than in other systems might sound frankly absurd. If you live in New York City, as we do, you pay federal, state, and local taxes (as well as Social Security, Medicare, and sales tax). If you earn a reasonably good income, then income taxes suck up about 40 percent of your earnings. By the time you factor in sales, property, and other taxes, a reasonably wealthy New Yorker will have paid more than half her marginal income in tax—hardly a low figure. European democracies, with their extensive social safety nets and universal health care, can tax at even higher rates. In contrast, some autocracies don't even have income taxes. But the comparison of average tax rates is misleading.

At the income levels taxed in much of the world's poor autocracies, the tax rate in Europe and the United States is zero. We have to compare taxes at given income levels, not across the board, since most income tax systems are designed to be progressive, taxing higher incomes at higher rates than lower incomes. By looking at how much tax has to be paid at a given income level across countries we get close to comparing apples to apples and oranges to oranges.

In the United States, for example, a couple with one child and an income under about $32,400 pays no income tax. If their income were, say, $20,000 they would *receive* $1,000 from the federal government to help support their child. In China, a family with an income of $32,400 is expected to pay about $6,725 in income tax.[7]

Of course you might think it problematic to compare tax rates at US incomes, since these are far higher than incomes in much of the world. Instead, let's compare China, Russia, and India. These nations differ substantially in terms of governance institutions and wealth, although all are poor compared to the US. India is the most democratic of these nations, but it is also the poorest. China has the smallest

winning coalition and ranks in the middle in terms of average income, about $8,000. Russia is the wealthiest of these nations and
has an intermediate coalition size. Each nation's taxation structure
differs. Russia has a flat 13 percent tax rate; all income is taxed at the
same rate: bad for the poor, but probably great news for Putin's rich
oligarch backers. India and China both have progressive tax schemes;
tax rates rise with incomes. However, there are important differences.
China has a higher maximum tax rate than India (45 percent vs 30
percent) and higher tax thresholds kick in at lower income levels compared to India. What are the net results for people in each nation?

On an average Indian income, a family would pay no income tax
in India, an average tax of about 13 percent in China, and an average
tax of exactly 13 percent in Russia. As incomes increase, the average
tax rate increases in both India and China, but much more slowly in
India. At the income level of an average Russian family (the wealthiest of the three nations), the tax rate would still be 13 percent in
Russia. In China, the system with the smallest coalition, the tax rate
would average about 25 percent, while in India the average tax would
equate to about 9 percent. The pattern is clear. If you don't like paying
taxes—and who does—then you want to live in a democratic nation.
The sticker price of living in New York seems huge, but it would become astronomical if the government were not reliant on the support
of so many people.

Many small-coalition systems appear to have low nominal rates of
taxation. But those looking to keep the rewards of their labor should
beware. Autocracies have high implicit taxes—if you have something
valuable then it simply gets taken.[8] North Korea has no formal income tax system. Yet when Kim Jong-Un sends many thousands of
North Koreans to work overseas, often in Russia or China, he taxes
their earnings at 67 percent.[9] It's worth remembering that when the
wealthiest man in China, Jack Ma (founder of Alibaba), spoke out in
the fall of 2020 against the government's efforts to stifle innovation,
"the government suspended the debut of the Ant Group, a spinoff of
Alibaba…a move that cost the company $37 billion."[10]

The former richest man in Russia (disregarding allegations about
Putin's wealth), Mikhail Khodorkovsky, spent years in prison. Back in

2004, Khodorkovsky, then the sixteenth-wealthiest man in the world, had made his money building up Yukos, an oil company founded during the privatization wave in Russia in 1993. Yukos was the largest nonstate oil company in the world and accounted for about 20 percent of Russian oil production. Khodorkovsky, who had initially been close to the government, spoke out against Putin's autocratic rule of Russia and funded several opposition political parties. In 2003, he was arrested on fraud charges, and he was subsequently convicted. The Russian government also accused Yukos of tax evasion. According to a Yukos spokesperson, the tax take claimed by Russia from Yukos was substantially higher than that levied on other oil companies and, in some years, exceeded gross revenue. These enormous tax burdens forced Yukos into bankruptcy. At the end of his first eight-year sentence, Khodorkovsky, apparently still seen as a liability by the Russian government, was given a second sentence for embezzlement and money laundering. Wisely, he left Russia in 2015 and now lives in exile in London. One can only wonder whether Jack Ma, his Chinese counterpart, is looking at a similar future or whether he has been taught by his government that it is prudent to keep his mouth shut.

In autocracies, it is unwise to be rich unless it is the government that made you rich. And if this is the case, it is important to be loyal above all else. Of course, it is possible that Khodorkovsky and the many Chinese entrepreneurs and former leaders who have been convicted of corruption were, in fact, guilty. That is the nature of business in their countries. Even so, many others were surely guilty of the same crimes and yet walk free today. What singled out Khodorkovsky and others was that they did not support the government and they had enormous wealth. White farmers in Zimbabwe suffered a similar fate. Robert Mugabe's government seized their land. The cover for these seizures was land redistribution to poor Blacks who were dispossessed under colonial and white minority rule. The reality was much different. The redistributed land invariably ended up in the hands of government cronies, none of whom were farmers. When the new owners invariably allowed the land to fall into disuse, the farmers lost their investments, farmworkers were evicted from their houses, and

Zimbabwe, once a huge agricultural exporter, became hungrier. But on the other side of the ledger, Robert Mugabe survived in power into his nineties.

Democrats are less inclined to rewrite the rules and seize wealth. Tempting though extra revenue is, it comes at the cost of lost productivity to the masses. In Shakespeare's *The Merchant of Venice*, the heroine, Portia, disguises herself as a judge and adjudicates the case between Antonio, who pledged his person as security on a loan, and Shylock, who demands his pound of Antonio's flesh when Antonio does not pay on time.[11] Bassanio, Antonio's friend (and Portia's husband), offers to pay many times the debt due, and when Shylock refuses, he appeals to the mercy of the court:

> *And I beseech you,*
> *Wrest once the law to your authority:*
> *To do a great right, do a little wrong.*

But Portia recognizes the sanctity of the law:

> *It must not be: there is no power in Venice*
> *Can alter a decree established:*
> *'Twill be recorded for a precedent;*
> *And many an error, by the same example,*
> *Will rush into the state: it cannot be.*

The many messages of *The Merchant of Venice* are complicated and controversial, but one message, epitomized by the passage just quoted (but not the reversal in the enforcement of contracts just a bit later in the play), reminds us that rule of law is essential to successful commerce. As one examination of the demands of commerce in *The Merchant of Venice* makes clear, both for Venice and in general, "Contract does not require friendship, but it does require a degree of trust that the market is well-regulated or that the institutions of contract enforcement are appropriately strong."[12]

TAX COLLECTORS

Democrats need resources so they can reward their coalition, but they can't take too much or they risk alienating those very same supporters. Similar concerns shape how taxes are collected. Leaders want to collect taxes in a fair or at least transparent way. Few US citizens would regard the Internal Revenue Service (IRS) as a transparent tax authority, but it is at least governed by rules (albeit an awful lot of them) that are overseen by an independent judiciary. As for all the rules and exceptions that make the US tax code so complicated, these inevitably result from politicians doing what politicians inevitably do: reward their supporters at the expense of everybody else. This is why sheaves of pages in the tax code are dedicated to farmers—a crucial coalition for some politicians and a group that needs to receive their rewards if their senators and representatives are to remain in power.

As poor Mikhail Khodorkovsky learned, when the opportunity arises autocrats will grab whatever they can. Yet even as they work without being bound by people's feelings, autocrats face real issues in the realm of collecting taxes. High taxes will inevitably drive people to hide their work and profits. This makes monitoring their income difficult. Furthermore, the large bureaucracy required to run a comprehensive tax system, such as the one in the United States, can be prohibitively expensive. To put this in context, the IRS spends about $38 per person, or about 0.5 percent of the IRS take, to collect an average of $7,614 in tax per person.[13] This is fine in a nation with a per capita GDP of $64,000, but in nations where the average income is only $1,000 per year, such a cost of collecting taxes would be about 23 percent of the revenue. Further, setting up a large bureaucracy makes an autocrat beholden to those who run it. The first rule of officeholding is to minimize the number of people whose support you need. To avoid becoming a slave of their own tax collectors, autocrats often use indirect taxation instead. With indirect taxes, the cost of the tax is passed on to someone other than the person actually paying it. For instance, sellers pay sales tax to municipal governments but pass the cost on to buyers, making sales taxes indirect.

Agricultural marketing boards are a common indirect means of taxing poor farmers in autocracies. In principle such organizations are designed to fulfill a similar function as the European Union's Common Agricultural Policy (CAP). The CAP guarantees farmers minimum prices for their goods—thus it provides a benefit to the farmers. In many democracies, including the United States, rural areas are overrepresented electorally. Given the desire to rule with as few supporters as possible, it should be of little surprise that democrats often include farm groups in their coalition and reward them accordingly.[14]

In contrast, farmers are rarely key supporters in autocracies. Farm marketing boards are set up to exploit rather than help them. Consider Ghana's Cocoa Marketing Board (CMB), reconstituted as CocoBod in 1979. Cocoa is Ghana's major agricultural export. The CMB/CocoBod fixes a price for cocoa—an implicit tax—and insists that farmers sell all their cocoa to the board at that price, an indirect tax. The board then historically resold the cocoa on world markets at a *higher* price and pocketed the difference: "The first rung in the long ladder of leeches that feed on the sweat of the cocoa farmers was the Cocoa Marketing Board."[15] These excessive profits were a major source of government revenue in Ghana. But after Ghana became a democracy in the early 1990s, following the collapse of its economy, CocoBod turned itself around. Today, "farmers receive a relatively large share of export earnings. Product quality is world renowned, and it regularly exceeds the most stringent international standards. Exports are handled professionally and efficiently. International loans are repaid reliably. Internal marketing is relatively uncorrupt and effective."[16] The change in Ghana's governmental exploitation of cocoa farmers illustrates both the pitfalls of small coalitions and the enormous benefits—for the people if not the politicians—of political reform.

Taxing the poor to pay the rich has plenty of bad economic consequences, but these tend to be "in the long run"—that is, on another leader's watch. For instance, when Ghana heavily taxed its farmers, the longer-term consequence was reduced production. Ghanaian farmers simply stopped planting and caring for cocoa trees. By the 1980s cocoa production had collapsed, and farmers tried to smuggle what little they did grow to neighboring Côte d'Ivoire. Case after case proves the point: when taxes are too high, people either stop working or find ways to avoid the formal economy. And when governments become more accountable, as Ghana did, taxes drop and farmers are incentivized again to grow crops.

PRIVATIZED TAX COLLECTION

When even indirect taxation proves to be too much trouble, autocrats sometimes turn to outsiders for help extracting funds from their people. For autocrats and for their tax collectors this has a virtue and a liability. People hired to extract money for the government, keeping a portion of what they collect for themselves, have a strong incentive to take in lots of tax revenue. That's good for them and good for the leader who receives the substantial remainder not kept by prudent tax collectors. But people hired to extract money can also use the power of that money to become a threat to a leader, and that, of course, is dangerous for them and for the incumbent.

The Caliphate was the Muslim empire created by military conquest following the death of the Prophet Muhammad in 632. It ruled much of the Middle East, North Africa, and parts of Europe until 1258. In the tradition of the Romans before them, the caliphs avoided the technical difficulties of tax collection by outsourcing the task altogether. A tax farmer would pay the treasury for the right to collect taxes from a particular territory. Obviously, once they had paid for the privilege, tax farmers extracted everything they could. They were notoriously brutal and always looking for ingenious ways to take more. For instance, they would demand payment in silver coins rather than crops and then collude with merchants to fix prices. Those who could not pay were punished or even killed.

Naturally, the people resisted. Tax farmers contended with a persistent problem of people fleeing the land rather than paying their property taxes. To prevent this, tax farmers set up patrols to check identities. Non-Muslims were often tattooed or forced to wear "dog tags" with their name and address to prevent them from fleeing.[17] Initially some of the taxes collected by the tax farmers were only applicable to non-Muslims. This proved to be a very successful, if not wholly intended, means of encouraging religious conversion. It seems that many non-Muslims, realizing that they could reduce the tax collectors' reach by becoming Muslim, put their religious beliefs aside and converted. As long as these conversions did not assume massive proportions, the tax farmers made themselves incredibly rich at the expense of the average citizen. When conversion became commonplace, tax farmers adjusted, no longer excluding Muslims from some of the taxes they levied. And from the perspective of the caliph, they ensured reliable revenue. That they terrorized the people was of no political importance: impoverished and persecuted farmers were not part of the winning coalition.

Autocrats can avoid the technical difficulties of gathering and redistributing wealth by authorizing their supporters to reward themselves directly. For many leaders, corruption is not something bad that needs to be eliminated. Rather, it is an essential political tool. Leaders implicitly or sometimes even explicitly condone corruption. Effectively they license the right to extract bribes from the citizens. This avoids the administrative headache of organizing taxation and transferring the funds to supporters. Saddam Hussein's sons were notorious for smuggling during the 1990s when Iraq was subject to sanctions. They made a fortune from the sanctions that were supposed to harm the regime.

EXTRACTION

"Oil is the Devil's excrement," at least according to Juan Pablo Pérez Alfonzo, a Venezuelan who founded the Organization of Petroleum Exporting Countries (OPEC), the cartel of oil-producing nations. "Ten years from now, twenty years from now, you will see: oil will bring us ruin."[18] And he was right.

As many leaders have learned, the problem with raising revenue through taxation is that it requires people to work. Tax too aggressively or fail to provide an environment conducive to economic activity, and people simply don't produce. Actually extracting revenue from the land itself provides a convenient alternative, cutting the people out of the equation altogether.

Take oil, for example. It flows out of the ground whether it is taxed at 0 percent or 100 percent. Labor represents but a small part of the value of oil extraction. This makes it a leader's dream and a people's nightmare. In a phenomenon often called the resource curse, nations with readily extractable natural resources systematically underperform nations without such resources.[19] Resource-rich nations have worse economic growth, are more prone to civil wars, and become more autocratic than their resource-poor counterparts.

Nigeria, the most populous nation in Africa, achieved independence from Britain in 1960. At the time of independence it was a poor nation, but expectations were high. These expectations grew with the discovery of oil. Nigeria is believed to have the world's tenth-largest reserves. With the rise in oil prices during the oil crises in the early and late 1970s, Nigeria found itself awash with funds. And yet by the early 1980s the country was swamped by debt and poverty. From 1970 to 2019, Nigeria accumulated hundreds of billions of dollars in oil revenue.[20] That money has not helped the Nigerian people much. Over the same years, average annual income per capita went from $1,691 in 1970 (in constant US 2010 dollars) to US$1,376 in 2000 and up to US$2,374 in 2019, making Nigeria still one of the poorest nations in the world, in spite of its vast oil wealth. Poverty has risen too. Earning less than one dollar per day is a common standard used for assessing poverty. In 1970, 36 percent of Nigerians lived on less; by 2000 this figure had jumped to nearly 70 percent. In 2020, with the dollar's value inflated, things were still worse than in 1970, with 40 percent of Nigerians living on less than one dollar per day.

Nigeria is not exceptional, as Figure 4.2 shows. The horizontal axis shows natural resource exports as a percentage of GDP in 1970. The vertical axis shows the average level of economic growth between 1970 and 1990. The trend is clear. Nations flush with oil, copper, gold, diamond, or other minerals grow more slowly.

Nevertheless, natural resources are wonderful for leaders. Natural resources don't require freedoms to be productive, and so they allow a leader to pay her coalition without the risk of empowering the people.

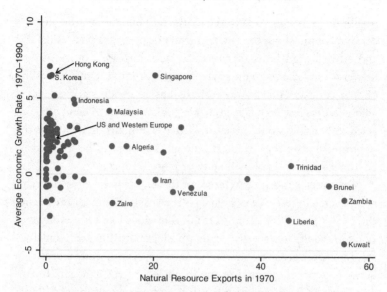

Figure 4.2: Growth and Natural Resource Abundance, 1970–1990

A leader who can afford to keep the people isolated, uneducated, and ignorant and chooses not to do so is a fool. Just such foolishness led to Muammar al-Qaddafi's demise. Given the derision he is usually subject to, it will probably surprise most people that his undoing was that he was too enlightened rather than too despotic. While we would never claim that the Libyan press was free, it had more freedom to publish what it wanted than Libya's neighbors, which were not so blessed with oil. Qaddafi also allowed Libyans to gain more education than he needed to. And the reward for his unnecessary benevolence was that the people rose up against him. When NATO intervened to prevent him from using heavy weapons to suppress the rebels, he lost power. A clear case of "no good deed goes unpunished."

Leaders in Qaddafi's position don't need their subjects to work. Admittedly the minerals need to be extracted, but by and large autocrats can achieve this without the participation of the local population. In Nigeria, for instance, the oil is concentrated in the Niger Delta region. Foreign firms with foreign workers do most of the extraction. Few Nigerians participate. The oil companies run security firms, effectively small private armies, to keep the locals from obstructing the business or complaining about the environmental degradation that results. BP and other foreign firms are free to act with impunity, provided they deliver royalty checks to the government. This is not so much a failing of these companies as the way business must be conducted in countries whose leaders rely on a few cronies to back them up. A company that acted responsibly would necessarily have less money to deliver to the government, and that would be enough for them to be replaced by another company that is willing to be more "cooperative."

One interesting manifestation of the differences between wealth and poverty in resource-rich lands is the cost of living for expatriates there. While it is tempting to think that cities like Oslo, Tokyo, or London would top the list of the most expensive places, and they are, indeed, expensive cities, for many years—until quite recently, in fact—Luanda, the capital of the southwestern African state of Angola, was the most expensive city. It used to cost upwards of $10,000 per month for housing in a reasonable neighborhood, and even then, water and electricity were intermittent. What made this so shocking was the surrounding poverty. According to the United Nations Development Program, back in 2000, 68 percent of Angola's population lived below the poverty line, more than a quarter of Angolan children died before their fifth birthday, and male life expectancy in Angola was below forty-five years. Angola ranked 143 out of 182 nations in terms of overall human development. Prices in Angola, as in many other West African states, were fueled by oil and by corruption.

Today, in 2021, with oil prices deflated by the global pandemic, Luanda ranks as only the 123rd most expensive city for foreign workers to live in. But it held the top spot as recently as 2017, and as much as it has remained expensive for foreigners, it has remained miserable for its citizens. While Angola's Human Development Index has risen slightly since 2000, as of 2020 it still ranked only 148th out of 189 nations.[21] Unfortunately, little is likely to change. The size of Angola's winning coalition has improved little over the last three decades, although it did expand substantially in 1992. Although Angola elected a new president, João Lourenço, in 2017, he was the handpicked successor of José Eduardo dos Santos. Dos Santos had ruled since 1979,

amassed a huge personal fortune, and appears to have stepped down
only due to ill health. *resource curse*

The story of Angola reminds us that the resource curse enables
autocrats to massively reward their supporters and accumulate enormous wealth. This drives prices to the stratospheric heights as seen
in Luanda, where wealthy expatriates and lucky coalition members
could have foie gras flown in from France every day. Yet to make sure
the people cannot coordinate, rebel, and take control of the state,
leaders endeavor to keep those outside the coalition poor, ignorant,
and unorganized. It is ironic that while oil revenues provide the resources to fix societal problems, they create political incentives to
make them far worse.

The effect of natural resource wealth is much less pernicious in
democracies. Angola, still far from being a smoothly functioning democracy, nevertheless shows us how expanding the winning coalition
can change things for the better. But Angola's transformation is unusual. The trouble is that once a state profits from mineral wealth, it
is unlikely to democratize. The easiest way to incentivize the leader
to liberalize policy is to force him to rely on tax revenue to generate
funds. Once this happens, the incumbent can no longer suppress the
population because the people won't work if he does.

The upshot is that the resource curse can be lifted. If aid organizations want to help the peoples of oil-rich nations, then the logic of
our survival-based argument suggests they would achieve more by
lobbying governments in the developed world to increase the tax on
petroleum than by providing assistance overseas. By raising the price
of oil and gas, such taxes would reduce worldwide demand for oil.
This in turn would reduce oil revenues and make leaders of oil-rich
countries more reliant on taxation.

Effective taxation requires that the people are motivated to work,
but people cannot produce as effectively if they are forbidden such
freedoms as freedom to assemble with their fellow workers and freedom of speech. These freedoms facilitate formal and informal discussions and debates over how to make the workplace perform more
effectively and how to make government regulations less of a burden
on the workers.

BORROWING

Borrowing is a wonderful thing for leaders. They get to spend the money to make their supporters happy today and, if they are sensible, set some aside for themselves. Unless they are fortunate enough to survive in office for a really long time, repaying today's loan will be another leader's problem. Autocratic leaders borrow as much as they can, and democratic leaders are enthusiastic borrowers as well.

We are all at least a little bit impatient. It's in our nature to buy things today when better financial acumen might suggest saving our money. Politics makes financial decision-making even more suspect. To understand the logic and see why politicians are profligate borrowers, suppose everyone in a country earns $100 per year and is expected to do so in the future too. The more we spend today, the more we must pay in interest and debt repayment tomorrow. Suppose, for instance, that to spend an extra $100 today we have to give up $10 per year as interest payments in the future. It is reasonable to see that people could differ on whether this is a good idea or not, but politics certainly makes it more attractive. To simplify the issue vastly, suppose leaders simply divide the money they borrow among the members of their coalition. This encourages leaders to borrow more. If a leader has a coalition of half the people and he borrows an amount equivalent to $100 per person, then everyone has to give up $10 in each future year (as taxes to pay the interest). However, since the coalition is only half the population, each coalition member's immediate benefit from the borrowing is $200. While to some this might still not seem like an attractive deal, it is certainly better than incurring the same debt obligation for $100. Governments of all flavors are more profligate spenders and borrowers than the citizens they rule. And that profligacy is greatly multiplied when we look at small-coalition regimes.

As the size of the coalition shrinks, the benefits that the coalition gains from indebtedness go up. If, for instance, the coalition includes one person per hundred, then, in exchange for the debt obligation, each coalition member receives $10,000 today instead of the mere $200 in the 50 percent coalition example. This is surely a deal that most of us would jump at. As the coalition size becomes smaller, the incentive to borrow increases.

Of course, borrowing more today means more indebtedness and reduced ability to borrow tomorrow. But such arguments are rarely persuasive to a leader. If he takes a financially reasonable position by refusing to incur debt, then he has less to spend on rewards. No such problem will arise for a challenger who offers to take on such debt in exchange for support from members of the current incumbent's coalition. This makes the current leader vulnerable. Incurring debt today is attractive because, after all, the debt will be inherited by the next administration. That way, it also ties the hands of any future challenger.

A leader should borrow as much as the coalition will endorse and markets will provide. There is surely a challenger out there who will borrow this much and, in doing so, use the money to grab power away from the incumbent. So not borrowing jeopardizes a leader's hold on power. Heavy borrowing is a feature of small-coalition settings. It is not the result, as some economists argue, of ignorance of basic economics by third-world leaders.

In an autocracy, the small size of the coalition means that leaders are virtually always willing to take on more debt. The only effective limit on how much autocrats borrow is how much people are willing to lend them. Earlier we saw the paradoxical result that as Nigeria's oil revenues grew so did its debt. It wasn't that the oil itself encouraged borrowing—autocrats *always* want to borrow more. Rather, revenues from oil meant that Nigeria could service a larger debt and so people were more willing to lend.

Although the large coalition size in a democracy places some restrictions on the level of borrowing, democratic leaders are still inclined to be financially irresponsible. Remember, while the debt is paid by all, the benefits disproportionately flow to coalition members. Over the last ten years the economies of many Western nations boomed. This would have been a perfect time to reduce debt. Yet in many cases this did not happen. In 1990, US debt was $2.41 trillion, which was equivalent to 42 percent of GDP. By 2000 this debt had grown in nominal terms to $3.41 trillion, although in relative terms this was a decline to 35.1 percent of GDP. However, as the economy prospered during the

2000s (other than during the several years of global recession), debt continued to slowly accumulate instead of shrink. By the end of 2020, US debt stood at $27 trillion, 82 percent of the pandemic-affected GDP. To compare apples to apples, the 2019—pre-pandemic—debt, during a time of economic expansion, was a whopping $16.8 trillion, equal to 79 percent of GDP. A bigger economy means a greater ability to service debt and a capacity to borrow more.

We may be inclined to explain the expansion of the debt by citing the party politics of the leader in charge. However, ideology offers a poor account of these trends. The major accumulations of US debt in the postwar period began under Republican administrations: Ronald Reagan (1981–1989), George W. Bush (2001–2009), and Donald Trump (2017–2021). This debt grew at a staggering pace during the 2007–2009 recession as the United States underwrote troubled banks and embarked on Keynesian policies of fiscal stimulus. It grew at an even more staggering pace during the Trump years, including the pre-pandemic period. British debt follows a similar pattern. In 2002 debt stood at 34 percent of GDP, by 2007 it was 41.5 percent, and it exploded in the wake of the 2008 financial crisis and continued to grow through good economic times, reaching 85.4 percent of GDP by the end of 2019.

From a Keynesian perspective, many governments were taking the perverse steps of trying to cut spending during the Great Recession of 2007–2009 instead of stimulating demand. This did not reflect a desire by politicians to borrow less. Rather, debt crises in Iceland, Greece, and Ireland led many investors to doubt the ability of nations to repay their loans. This pushed up the cost of borrowing and made it much harder to secure new loans. It was supply, not demand, that had shrunk.

Markets limit how much a nation can borrow. If individuals borrow too much and either cannot or will not repay it, then banks and other creditors can seize assets to recover the debt. With sovereign lending to countries, however, creditors cannot repossess property. On a few occasions creditors have tried. For instance, France invaded Mexico in 1862 in an attempt to get Mexico to repay loans. France also invaded the Ruhr, an industrial area of Germany, in 1923 to collect reparation payments from World War I that Germany had not paid. Both attempts failed. In practice, the only leverage lenders have over nations is to cut them off from future credit. Nevertheless, this has a profound effect, as the ability to engage in borrowing in financial markets is valuable. For this reason nations generally pay their debts.

However, once the value of access to credit is worth less than the cost of servicing the debt, then leaders should default. If they don't, surely a challenger will come along who will offer to do so. This was one of the appeals of Adolf Hitler to the German people in the 1930s. Germany faced a huge debt, in part to pay reparations from World War I. Hitler defaulted on this debt. It was a popular policy with the German people because the cost of servicing the debt was so high.

As debt approaches the balance point where the value of access to credit equals the cost of debt service, lenders refuse to increase the overall size of debt. At this point, if leaders want to borrow more, then they need to increase revenues such that they could service this additional debt. As in the Nigerian case, the discovery of exploitable natural resources provides one means to increase debt service and hence borrowing. However, without such discoveries, the only way to increase borrowing is to increase tax revenue. For autocratic leaders this means liberalizing their policies to encourage people to work harder, because they already tax at a high (implicit) rate. Only when facing financial problems are leaders willing to even consider undertaking such politically risky liberalization. They don't do it frequently or happily. They liberalize, opening the door to a more democratic, representative, and accountable government only when they have no other path to save themselves from being deposed today.

DEBT FORGIVENESS

Debt forgiveness is a popular policy but one that is generally misguided. Those in favor of forgiving the debt of highly indebted poor countries argue that the debt burden falls on the poor people of the nation who did not benefit in a consequential way from the borrowed funds. This is certainly true. As we have explained, the benefits go to the leader and the coalition while the debt obligation falls on everyone. But people who argue for debt forgiveness construct their arguments in terms of how they think the world *should* operate rather than how it actually works.

In the late 1980s, as many poor nations struggled to repay debts, creditors coordinated to reschedule and forgive debt. The French Ministry of the Economy, Finance, and Industry became an important center for negotiations, helping ensure that creditors shared similar losses. The group of creditors that met to help poor debtor countries became known as the Paris Club. In 1996 the International Monetary Fund (IMF) and World Bank launched the Heavily Indebted Poor Countries (HIPC) Initiative. Instead of the previous case-by-case approach, this program provided systematic help to poor nations with writing down their debts. However, nations could only receive debt relief when they met or made substantial progress toward meeting explicit criteria concerned with poverty alleviation and budget reform. The program received a huge boost under the UN's Millennium Development Goals program. From 2006 onward many HIPCs saw very large reductions in their debt. How well did these countries do after receiving the benefits of massive debt relief?

The HIPC Initiative was the policy consequence of important research into what is known as debt overhang, a term introduced by Paul Krugman in 1988 and built on by Jeffrey Sachs in 1989.[22] The core idea was, to be a little technical and jargony, that a country's total factor productivity—basically how well its resources, like labor and capital, are converted into output—is held down by too much debt. In actuality, the HIPC program failed to produce the expected benefits. In a comparison of poor countries that participated in the program and poor countries that did not, the evidence shows that "the debt overhang hypothesis would appear to be erroneous."[23] Bad governance rather than misguided economic policy were and are almost certainly the source of national impoverishment, indebtedness, and failure to grow. This is true for those who were part of the HIPC experiment and those who were not.

The record of debt forgiveness just is not a happy one. Consider that as a percentage of debt, the largest debt reliefs prior to 2000 were given to Ethiopia in 1999 (42 percent of debt), Yemen in 1997 (34 percent), Belarus in 1996 (33 percent), Angola in 1996 (33 percent), Nicaragua in 1996 (30 percent), and Mozambique in 1990 (27 percent).[24] With the exceptions of Angola and Nicaragua, each of these nations promptly started reaccumulating debt. For instance, after a series of small debt reductions, in 1999, with the forgiveness of $4.4 billion, Ethiopia had its debt reduced to $5.7 billion. But by 2003 this debt had risen to $6.9 billion. Despite the forgiveness of $589 million of debt in 1996, Belarus's debt has steadily risen from $1.8 billion in 1995 to over $4.1 billion in 2005 to a staggering $21.4 billion in 2019. Even though debt-reduction programs vet candidates, these examples suggest that in many cases forgiveness without institutional reform simply allows leaders to start borrowing again.

Democrats also like to borrow, but they are not as profligate as autocrats; they prefer lower levels of indebtedness. Democratization promotes successful debt reduction, as the history of Mozambique illustrates. In 1990, 27 percent of Mozambique's debt was forgiven. The result was the further accumulation of debt. By the time Mozambique democratized in 1994, its debt was over $8 billion. However,

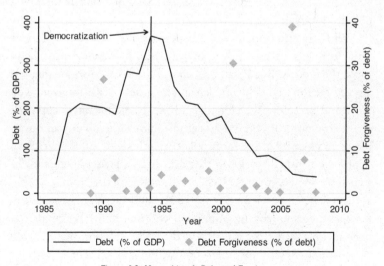

Figure 4.3: Mozambique's Debt and Forgiveness

this debt has gradually been reduced, as seen in Figure 4.3, aided in part by further forgiveness.

The HIPC program received much misguided criticism for its slow pace in reducing the debt of poor nations. Our criticism of the HIPC Initiative is the opposite: it's actually too eager to forgive debt. Debt forgiveness simply allows autocratic leaders to start borrowing more money. As we'll see a little later, financial crises are one of the important reasons that leaders are compelled to democratize. Debt reduction, however, relieves financial pressure and enables autocrats to stay in office without reform, continuing to make the lives of their subjects miserable.

It is no wonder that autocrats love debt relief. But how does debt relief look to those who would like to improve governance and who want to start, as we do, from understanding how leaders behave rather than engaging in wishful thinking? We depart for the moment from looking at governance through a leader's eyes and instead turn our attention to how to change an autocrat's vision. That is, we turn for the moment to thinking about how we can use the logic of dictatorial rule to give autocrats the right incentives to change their government for the better. We wonder, Can we create a desire in at least some autocrats to govern for the people as the best way to ensure their own political survival?

Debt reduction might work in democracies. Since such nations want to reduce excessive debt anyway, debt reduction clearly helps speed the process. But as can be seen in Figure 4.3, Mozambique was already tackling its debt problem prior to large-scale forgiveness in 2001 and in 2006. Therefore, we advocate a conservative approach of little or no debt relief as a way to improve the quality of governance and quality of life for people currently living under wretched, oppressive regimes. We know that debt relief allows autocrats to entrench themselves in office. Debt forgiveness with the promise of subsequent democratization never works. An autocrat might be sincere in his willingness to have meaningful elections in return for funds. Yet once the financial crisis is over and the leader can borrow to pay off the coalition, any promised election will be a sham. For democrats, debt relief, while helpful, is unnecessary. By eliminating debt relief for autocrats we can help precipitate the sorts of rebellions seen in the Middle East in 2011, rebellions that, if properly motivated and timed, as discussed later, may very well open the door to better governments in the future.

Taxation, resource extraction, and borrowing are the foremost ways of acquiring funds for enriching a coalition. Discussions that portray taxation differently are either window dressing to make the process seem more palatable or are making arguments based on how people would like the world to work. Leaders tax because they need to spend on their coalition. Successful leaders raise as much revenue as they can. The limits of taxation are (1) the willingness of people to work as they are taxed; (2) what tax burden the coalition is willing to bear; and (3) the cost of collecting taxes.

Having filled government coffers, leaders spend resources in three ways. First, they provide public goods—that is, policies that benefit all. Second, they deliver private rewards to their coalition members. This mix of private and public benefits differs across political systems, and it's worth noting that any resources left over after paying off the coalition are discretionary. Leaders therefore have a third choice to make about spending money. They can spend discretionary money promoting their pet projects. Alternatively, and all too commonly, as we shall see, they can hide it in a rainy-day fund.

financial crisis →
forced to
democratize

CHAPTER FIVE

GETTING AND SPENDING

A**t last, a new ruler** has shaken up the coalition that first brought him to power and has the right supporters in place. Money is coming in thanks to the taxes being levied. Now comes the real task of governing: allocating money to keep the coalition happy—but not too happy—and providing just enough to keep the interchangeables from rising up in revolt. As we saw in North Africa and the Middle East in the 2010s, and in Eastern Europe in the 1980s and 1990s, this can be an awkward tightrope for any leader to traverse. The last few decades encourage us by showing that in time many autocrats fall off that tightrope, but they also discourage us by showing that sometimes they manage to climb right back on. It is really hard to strike just the right balance between benefits for leaders, for their coalition, and for the mass of interchangeables.

Any new incumbent who wants to be around for a long time needs to fine-tune the art of spending money. Of course, he can err on the side of generosity to the coalition or to the people—but only with any money that is left for his own discretionary use after taking care of the coalition's needs. He had better not err on the side of shortchanging anyone who could mount a coup or a revolution. If he shortchanges the wrong people, any leader's fate will confirm our abuse of William Wordsworth's famous line "Getting and spending, we lay waste our powers."

Thus we turn to the essential question of all democracies: how to allocate resources aimed at providing policies of benefit to everyone in a society. These public goods come in a variety of different forms depending on the tastes of those in a position to demand such policies. Those in such a position, of course, are the incumbent's essential backers. Different groups of essentials will have different baskets of public goods–oriented policies in mind. Some will want to spend more on a social safety net; others on education; still others on benefits for the elderly or for the young, benefits to the arts, and so forth. Although all of these are of interest and will be touched upon, however briefly, we are especially interested in core public benefits like education, health care, and such freedoms as a free press, free speech, and freedom of assembly.

Although security against foreign invasion certainly is a central public good, we leave consideration of foreign threats to a later chapter and focus here on domestic policy choices. For now, let's have a look at how public goods can help society as a whole and how they help entrenched leaders.

EFFECTIVE POLICY NEED NOT BE CIVIC MINDED

To balance between spending policies that benefit the masses and those that favor the essentials, leaders would do well to reflect on those parts of Thomas Hobbes's philosophy of government that we touched on briefly in the introduction. He had a lot right, but Hobbes's ideas about government weren't infallible. While he realized that anyone who enriched society would avoid a revolution such as the one he lived through in England, he failed to distinguish between what it takes to keep the people at bay and what it takes to keep essential backers from betraying their leader—whether that leader is Hobbes's Leviathan, Plato's philosopher king, Rousseau's general will, or Madison's faction-ridden representatives of the people. Hobbes was sure his Leviathan had to be a benign ruler. That, Hobbes seems to have thought, was the way to prevent a revolution such as he had experienced. Without a ruler who enriched his people, Hobbes feared, for many, life would be, in his well-coined phrase, "solitary, poor, nasty, brutish, and short."

Hobbes was only half-right. It is true, as Hobbes believed, that happy, well-cared-for people are unlikely to revolt. China's prolonged economic growth seems to have verified that belief (at least for now). Keep them fat and happy, and the masses are unlikely to rise up against you. It seems equally true, however, that sick, starving, ignorant people are also unlikely to revolt. All seems quiet among North Korea's masses, who deify their Great Successor and Supreme Leader as the sole source of whatever meager, life-sustaining resources they have. Who makes revolution? It is the great in-between: those who are neither immiserated nor coddled. The former are too weak and cowed to revolt. The latter are content and have no reason to revolt. Truly, it is the great in-between who are a threat to the stability of a regime and its leaders. Therefore, a prudent leader balances resources between keeping the coalition content and the people just fit enough to produce the wealth needed to enrich the essentials and the incumbent. We should not be surprised that those countries whose governments rely on the fewest essential backers—that is, those that are least democratic—are the very places where Hobbes's state of nature is most likely to be an apt description of life for the masses. They are also, as we saw earlier, the places where leaders have the best prospect of staying in control for years and years.

Leaders who depend on a large coalition have to work hard to make sure that their citizens' lives are not solitary, poor, nasty, brutish, and short. That doesn't mean democratic rulers have to be civic minded, or that they need to harbor warm and cuddly feelings for their citizens. All they need is to ensure that there are ample public benefits to provide a high quality of life. They just need to follow the rules by which successful leaders rule, adapting them to the difficult circumstances that any democrat faces: stuck depending on an unruly crowd of essentials to stay in power.

Just as democrats have no need to be civic visionaries, dictators likewise aren't bound to make life miserable. It just happens, more often than not, to work out better for them to do so. There are exceptions, but those exceptions tend simply to reaffirm the importance of obeying the rules of politics. As we have noted, it is okay for a leader to spend her pot of discretionary money on trying to bring the good life to her citizenry. By definition, discretionary money is money that is not required to keep the coalition loyal; the coalition has already been paid off before any resources become discretionary. Singapore, for example, has managed through benevolent dictatorship to produce a high quality of material life for its citizens, albeit without many of the freedoms that others hold dear. Maybe Lee Kuan Yew, Singapore's longtime benefactor, was the embodiment of Hobbes's Leviathan. But benevolent dictators like Singapore's late LKY are hard to find.

The most reliable means to a good life for ordinary people remains the presence of institutional incentives in the form of dependence on a big coalition, which compels power-seeking politicians to govern for the people. Democracy, especially with little or no organized bloc voting (one of India's great political constraints), aligns incentives such that politicians can best serve their own self-interest, especially their interest in staying in office, by promoting the welfare of a large proportion of the people. That, we believe, is why most democracies are prosperous, stable, and secure places to live.

Perhaps you doubt that the path to a good life is ensured by the presence of a big coalition. You wouldn't be alone. Many distinguished economists, even quite a few with a Nobel Prize under their belt, are convinced that the best way to promote democracy is by promoting prosperity. That is why whenever they see an economic crisis looming on the horizon, such as a government so indebted that it is on the verge of default and bankruptcy, they call for debt forgiveness, new loans, lots of foreign aid, and other economic fixes. They resist the cry of people like us who demand improved governance before any bailout money is offered up to rescue a troubled autocratic economy. They are convinced that wealth—not politics—is the best route to escape Hobbes's state of nature. Simply reviewing the history of economic bailouts, as we outlined in the previous chapter, makes clear that the very forgiveness without political change so eagerly embraced for third-world financial crises is rarely sought when the crisis arises in a society that relies on a large coalition.

money is carrot

BAILOUTS AND COALITION SIZE

The politics of economic bailouts can be quite different in small- and large-coalition regimes. Bailouts come in many forms: shifts in domestic taxing and spending; loans, whether from banks at home or abroad; debt forgiveness; or foreign aid. Any bailout is accompanied by demands for economic reform, whether the money comes from the IMF, the Deutsche Bundesbank, or the taxpayers. A big difference between large- and small-coalition bailout recipients is that the former almost always institute reforms and the latter only infrequently do.

Just like debt forgiveness, a bailout in the face of economic stress for autocrats is a way to solve an impending political crisis. When their economy becomes too feeble to provide sufficient money to buy political loyalty, autocrats face being overthrown by either a rival or a revolution. This, in a nutshell, is the story of the politico-economic crises in small-coalition, autocratic places like Tunisia and Egypt in 2011. A bailout, whether generated from within or through outside loans or aid, can buy off opposition and thwart the threat to the leader's hold on power. Therefore, during an economic crisis autocrats shop around for bailout money from others to save themselves in the name of relieving their country's financial woes.

For large-coalition leaders bailouts are a curse, or at least a necessary evil. Voters are likely to see a poorly performing economy as the consequence of a policy failure, resulting in the leadership's being thrown out by the voters at the first opportunity. That was very much a part of the story of the defeat of the Republican Party in 2008 and, when the economy did not turn around fast enough to satisfy voters, the defeat of the Democrats in the House of Representatives in 2010. Similarly, Trump's mishandling of the COVID-19 pandemic and the economic crisis it induced contributed to his electoral defeat in 2020. He and his party were reluctant to provide a large bailout during the presidential campaign, and voilà, out he went. So the need for an economic bailout strongly signals voters to find new leaders with new policy ideas. Foreign aid rarely comes to the rescue of democrats, for reasons we will explain later. Therefore, financial crises and the need for a bailout are just about always bad news for democratic leaders in power.

The rich countries of the world faced a severe economic crisis in 2008 and 2009. Both the Bush and Obama administrations sought to stem the worst of the crisis by providing massive financial bailouts to save the banking industry and other large businesses, restore liquidity in the market, and bring the US economy back onto a path toward sustained growth. Much the same was done in Europe. These bailouts were accompanied by regulatory change. The Dodd-Frank Wall Street Reform and Consumer Protection Act, signed by President Obama in 2010, is a case in point. Faced with a severe recession, Congress passed the largest regulatory reform since the presidency of Franklin Roosevelt.

In contrast, in small-coalition regimes, bailouts all too often are the means to preserve business as usual. Economic bailouts in autocracies rarely precipitate a serious review of economic or business policies. They are almost never accompanied by regulatory reform. Consequently, economic crises happen more often than in democracies and, so long as rich nations feel an urge to provide loans, debt forgiveness, or aid, rarely result in betterment for the society—although they do result in security for lousy leaders.

IS DEMOCRACY A LUXURY?

Are dictators and economists right that economic solvency needs to come ahead of political change? Is becoming materially rich the precursor for the luxury of democracy? We think not. There are plenty of well-to-do places that nevertheless suffer under oppressive governments that keep ordinary people's lives as solitary, poor, nasty, brutish, and short as their neighbors' in poorer nations. Take a look at just about any nondemocratic oil-rich or diamond-studded regime.

Yes, the world has produced wise, well-intentioned leaders even among those who depend on few essentials, but it neither produces a lot of them nor ensures that they have good ideas about how to make life better for others. Indeed, a common refrain among small-coalition rulers is that the very freedoms that promote welfare-improving government policies, like free speech, free press, and especially freedom of assembly, are luxuries to be doled out only after prosperity is achieved and not before. This seems to be the self-serving claim of leaders who keep their people poor and oppressed. The People's Republic of China is the poster boy for this view.

When Deng Xiaoping introduced economic liberalization to China in the 1980s, experts in wealthy Western countries contended that China's economy would grow and the growth would lead to rapid democratization. Today, after more than forty years of sustained rapid growth in China, we still await these anticipated political reforms. Instead, we see the opposite in China's policy toward Hong Kong. Despite China's commitment to economic growth, it is prepared to crush democracy in Hong Kong even if doing so puts Hong Kong's successful economy, created during a century of British rule, at risk. Apparently, China's fear that Hong Kong's freedoms might stimulate revolution on the mainland is stronger than its urge to achieve prosperity. Indeed, governance in China demonstrates how wrong Western experts were about the ties between prosperity and democratization. As China's per capita income improved over the past four decades, the size of its winning coalition held pretty steady for a while and then went into a prolonged period of shrinkage between 2000 and the present. Growth does not guarantee political improvement, but neither does it preclude it. The Republic of China (a.k.a. Taiwan) and the Republic of Korea (a.k.a. South Korea) are models of building prosperity ahead of democracy. Needless to say, the People's Republic of China certainly is not fond of promoting either of those countries' experiences.

Many economists arrive at the same inference as dictators, though from an entirely different perspective. For many economists, the contention that nations must work on becoming rich before becoming free follows from how they think about politics. They treat politics as just so much friction, to be written off instead of dealt with. But reality is very different. True, some countries that become rich then become democratic, but many nondemocratic regimes, like China, become even less democratic as they become richer. In contrast, poor autocratic regimes that become more democratic are highly likely to subsequently become rich, or at least richer. Political improvement is more successful at encouraging economic growth than economic improvement is at producing political reform.

No doubt it is good to be rich, and many of the world's rich countries are democratic. But dependence on a large coalition of essentials is a powerful explanation for quality of life even when wealth is absent, just as it seems to be a harbinger of future wealth. Economic growth and success, in contrast, does not seem to be an assurance of improved governance and, indeed, may hinder it.[1] This is a question worth exploring in greater depth, though for now our subject is how variations in the size of the group of essentials and interchangeables determines how resources are allocated between public and private rewards so as to pay just the right amount to one's coalition while also paying just enough to keep the citizenry from making trouble.

PUBLIC GOODS NOT FOR THE PUBLIC'S GOOD

From a leader's point of view, the most important function of the people is to pay taxes. All regimes need money. As a result, certain basic public goods must be made available even by the meanest autocrat, unless he has access to significant revenue from sources that are not based on taxing workers, like oil or foreign aid. Public benefits like essential infrastructure, education, and health care need to be readily available to ensure that labor is productive enough to pay taxes to line the pockets of rulers and their essential supporters. These policies are not instituted for the betterment of the masses, even though, of course, some members of the masses, especially workers, benefit from them.

Education, as a means for getting ahead in life, is a big deal for any country's citizenry. Indeed, a popular refrain among many liberal-minded thinkers is to extol the quality of education in otherwise oppressive states like Cuba or even North Korea. And they have a good point. Both Cuba and North Korea have impressive primary education. For instance, a 2014 USAID study found that Cuban third and fourth graders far outperform their counterparts in other Latin American countries. As for North Korea, like Cuba, it has a 100 percent literacy rate. In contrast, only 74 percent of democratic India's people can read.[2] But these facts can be misleading or even downright wrong. That basic education is mandatory and extensive in autocratic nations often is used to argue that autocracy isn't so bad.

Rarely do any of us stop to probe beneath these observations to find out why dictators pay to have well-educated third graders—but do not carry that quality of education forward to higher learning. The logic behind political survival teaches us to be suspicious. We cannot help but believe that these public goods are not intended to uplift and assist the people unfortunate enough to live in such places. The rules of politics, as we know, instruct leaders to do no more for the people than is absolutely essential to prevent rebellion. Leaders who spend on public welfare *at the expense of their essentials* are courting disaster.

Leaders, whether dictators or democrats, are all grappling with the same question: How much education is the right amount? For those who rely on few essential backers, the answer is straightforward: educational opportunity should not be so extensive as to equip ordinary folks, the interchangeables, to question government authority. A naive person might look at any number of awful regimes and yet come to the conclusion that, because they provide such public benefits as nationalized health care or sound primary education, they're actually better to their people than many democratic states are to theirs. This is nonsense, of course—in the vast majority of cases autocrats are simply keeping the peasants healthy enough to work and educated enough to do their jobs. Either way, literate or not, they're still peasants and they're going to stay that way.

A far better measure of leaders' interest in education is the distribution of top universities. With the exceptions of China, Russia, and Singapore, no nondemocratic country has even one university rated among the world's top two hundred. Despite China's size, the best-ranked Chinese university—not counting universities in Hong Kong, where academic freedom was once protected by the agreement that transferred Hong Kong from Britain to China in July 1997—is only in twentieth place despite China's opportunity to draw top minds from its vast population. The highest-ranking Russian university, with Russia's long history of dictatorship, is 174th. By contrast, countries with relatively few people but with dependence on many essential backers, like Israel, Finland, Norway, the Netherlands, Belgium, and Canada, have several universities ranked among the top two hundred.[3] Switzerland, with one-third the population of the city of Shanghai, has a university that is ranked fourteenth in the world. That this uneven distribution of top-notch universities favors large-coalition locales is no accident.

Highly educated people are a potential threat to autocrats, and so autocrats make sure to limit educational opportunity. Autocrats want workers to have basic labor skills, like literacy, but they want their *own* children—their most likely successors—to be truly well educated, and so they send them off to schools in places like Switzerland, where Kim Jong-Un, Kim Jong Il's youngest son, was educated. Dictators also like to have their children educated at leading universities in the United States and, especially, at Oxford University in the United Kingdom. In fact, one might almost conclude that Oxford is a breeding ground for authoritarians. It certainly is the alma mater of many, including Zimbabwe's late Robert Mugabe; the Bhutto family of Pakistan; and the kings of Jordan, Bhutan, Malaysia, and even little Tonga. England's big-coalition system opens the door pretty broadly to give access to higher education.

When the leadership relies on few essentials, higher education is for the children of the powerful; when the bloc of essentials is big, it is for the betterment of everyone. One of the features of the old Soviet regime that Boris Yeltsin balked at, for instance, was exactly the privileged access that children of Communist Party leaders had to the best universities regardless of their ability. Kids of loyal families were helped to get ahead. The capable children of potentially dissident families were kept down by being excluded from the best schools.[4]

One thing that dictatorships and democracies have in common is the special advantage insiders seem to have when it comes to the top universities. Even places with lots of essentials seem to work that way, although the privileged access is voluntarily granted by the universities and not imposed on them by the government. The president of the

United States doesn't get to tell Harvard who to admit. A closer look at the system demonstrates the reasoning: Harvard and many other prestigious universities favor "legacies"—that is, the children of alumni—because admitting such students is likely to bring the university more donations from its wealthy graduates. What may seem like a case of privileged access in an otherwise open, large-coalition system actually reflects the internal dynamics of universities themselves.

We shouldn't fail to notice that universities in their own right constitute small-coalition political systems with a pretty big batch of interchangeables. No surprise, then, that they behave like autocracies, favoring the rich and connected at the expense of those who lack political clout. If you doubt it, have a look one day at how many administrators university presidents like to hire compared to faculty. It seems you can never have too many supporting-cast administrators whose jobs depend on keeping the person at the top happy. Faculty, on the other hand, don't have to keep their "bosses" happy; they have to keep their colleagues happy long enough to get tenure and then they are pretty free to do whatever they want—why do you think we can write this passage! There is a delicate balance to be struck, to be sure, and so successful university leaders are especially skilled at doling out private rewards to anyone who could be a threat. People who raise money for the university frequently get a percentage of what they bring in to incentivize them. Faculty who are cooperative are likely to more readily be granted sabbaticals, get research funds, pick the classes (usually small) that they teach, and so forth. So we shouldn't be surprised by distortions in merit in universities; they really are small-coalition regimes.

We might hope for a rosier picture when it comes to secondary education in places that need few essentials. Why wouldn't all political leaders favor open access to secondary school, where students learn higher levels of math, science, language, literature, history, and social thought? That's easy to answer. These are dangerous public goods that should be doled out carefully. It just isn't necessary to have lots of people around with skills that are not absolutely required to produce revenue for the autocrat's regime. Why, for instance, would any autocrat eager to stay in power want to open the secondary schools to people who are not likely to contribute to the coalition's wealth and security? Math and science are great subjects for study in China; sociology and political science are subjects for study in democracies.

WHO DOESN'T LOVE A CUTE BABY?

The incentives to provide good health care are not so different from the incentives to provide basic education. Keeping the labor force humming is the primary concern for leaders of small-coalition countries—everything, and everyone, else is inessential. There is no point in spending lots of money on the health of people who are not in the labor force and who won't be in the labor force for a long time. One of the more depressing ways in which this can be seen is in the relation between the performance of health-care systems for infants and the size of a government's winning coalition.

It seems that a lot of dictators and their essential backers don't love babies. This is true whether we think of seeming monsters like Saddam Hussein or leaders like Fidel Castro, who was often praised for his efforts to foster high-quality health care in Cuba.

Saddam Hussein built lavish palaces while his people suffered under the impact of economic sanctions. The UN provided baby formula with the intention of offsetting the impact of this hardship on little children—however, Hussein allowed his cronies to steal it. The formula found its way to markets throughout the Middle East, yielding profits for Hussein even as shortages in Iraq resulted in a doubling of the infant mortality rate. There is no doubt that Hussein was a miserable human being—it may be that his record is no better or worse than any other heartless brute. Alternatively, it could be that dependence on a small group of cronies made him act as if he were a brute. Perhaps in a different place and circumstance he might have gone around kissing babies to garner political support. Perhaps Chemical Ali was right that Saddam was too merciful.[5] Indeed, it so happens that even in many autocracies with reportedly good health-care systems, infant mortality is high. This may be because helping little children does not particularly help leaders survive in power. It's not that they don't like a cute baby as much as the next guy; they simply recognize that helping babies doesn't help them.

Cuba has the lowest infant mortality rate in Latin America. It's a commendable accomplishment at one-twelfth the rate of Haiti, which has the highest. However, the real question is whether we should attribute this to Fidel Castro's beneficence in building a quality health-care system over the nearly half century he was in power or whether he just inherited a good health-care system from his predecessor, Fulgencio Batista, a petty dictator who first rose to power—as did a good health system—in a democratic Cuba in the 1940s.

Batista originally rose in prominence as a participant in Cuba's 1933 coup. Although a succession of other figures became president of Cuba, Batista, as army chief of staff, remained a key figure behind the throne throughout this transitional period. He defeated former president (under the coup regime) Ramón Grau San Martín in the free, democratic election of 1940. Batista then served as Cuba's democratically elected president from 1940 until his term ended in 1944. It is noteworthy that during this period Batista enjoyed the support of Cuba's Communist Party because of his strongly pro-labor and pro–labor union policies. Indeed, during his period as a democratic leader under the rules of Cuba's 1940 constitution, Batista proved to be an effective social reformer who also helped promote successful economic policies.[6] In short, he governed just the way we would expect a large-coalition leader to govern.

After his term expired, Batista moved to the United States. His preferred successor for the presidency lost to Grau in the 1944 Cuban presidential election. Although still in the United States in 1948, Batista was elected to the Cuban senate. He returned home to serve and then ran again for the presidency in 1952, but he was a distant third in the polls to Robert Agramonte, the front-runner, and Carlos Hevia. Seeing that he had no chance to be elected and possessing the backing of the United States government, pro-American Batista launched a coup before the election took place. Backed by the army, Batista now assumed the presidency as a small-coalition dictator, gradually shrinking the coalition from 0.66 at its democratic peak to an autocratic low of 0.39, then bringing it back to 0.52 before he fell to Castro's revolution. From the time Fidel Castro came to power to the present, Cuba's winning-coalition score has oscillated between 0.16 and 0.12, leading us to suspect that Cuba's infant mortality success has more to do with the relatively more democratic period than with the revolution. Let's see what the record reveals.

The Cuban economy depended largely on agriculture, especially growing sugarcane, a highly labor-intensive activity. As a result, both Batista's and Castro's regimes, bereft of natural-resource wealth, had to rely on workers to generate revenue. Each did have the benefit of supplementing that revenue with a significant amount of foreign aid, from the United States in Batista's case and from the Soviet Union in Castro's. Nevertheless, to stay afloat, both needed to maintain a healthy and reasonably educated workforce. Therefore, both Batista's Cuba and Castro's Cuba needed good health care as well as good basic education.

We should not expect vast differences between the public goods provided by Batista after he became a dictator and those provided by Castro, but we should expect some, favoring Batista, since his coalition was larger. To be sure, their ideological songs were radically different, but they both depended on a small clique to keep them in power. In both cases, the military was essential and so were loyal bureaucrats. So, putting aside the window dressing each used to justify their rule and stripping out the ideology, they were running similar regimes. The main difference in our terms was that Batista had a (larger) small coalition and a small selectorate once he overthrew the constitution. Castro ran a rigged-election regime, so he, like Batista, had a small coalition, but unlike Batista his nominal selectorate was pretty big. Of course, the real Cuban selectorate under Castro, the influentials, was probably no bigger than Batista's real selectorate. So we should anticipate that both of them were good at producing good health care and good primary education. And the facts bear out these expectations.

Although a headline fact is that Cuba has Latin America's best infant mortality rate, the details reveal that the relative quality of infant care has declined. Cuba had Latin America's best infant mortality rate under Batista as well as under the Castros. In general, small-coalition regimes gradually run their economy into the ground through inefficiencies designed to benefit the leader and essentials in the short run, at the expense of longer-term productivity. How quickly welfare erodes depends in part on what foreign aid comes in to off-set the economic woes brought on by small-coalition governance. We should see trends indicating declining quality of health care in Cuba under Castro compared to Batista, not necessarily because one was more civic minded than the other but because time inexorably dimin-ishes the quality of life for ordinary people in most petty dictatorships.

Cuba's absolute infant mortality rate has improved markedly since Batista's overthrow, but Cuba's relative quality of infant care has not kept pace with the rest of the world's. Medical technology has improved health care substantially since the end of World War II, and especially since Castro's revolution succeeded in 1959. Cuba's improvements in infant mortality, though substantial, have lagged behind improvements in infant mortality in many other countries. In 1957, not long before Batista was overthrown by Castro's revolu-tion, Cuba's infant mortality rate was thirty-two per one thousand live births. This was the thirteenth best in the world at the time. To put this impressive record in perspective, Cuba was outperforming Austria, Belgium, France, Israel, Japan, Spain, Portugal, and West Germany. Today, all of these countries outrank Cuba in infant mor-tality rates except for France—the two are tied according to the World Bank. Yet, until the demise of the Soviet Union, Cuba's economic growth rate was one of the highest in Latin America, and its abortion rate (25; that is, twenty-five abortions per one thousand women of childbearing age) is among the highest in the world. By compari-son, among countries that allow abortion—the relevant comparison group—the average abortion rate is 15.7, well below Cuba's.[7]

Cuba's infant mortality story is one of the better ones among coun-tries with long histories of petty dictatorship. Indeed, even wealth proves a poor way to inoculate little children from untimely deaths. But having a big coalition is the best vaccine. Like all medicine, it is not perfect, but it makes a huge difference.

The world's thirty governments that depend on the largest groups of essentials have twenty fewer infant deaths per one thousand births than the thirty governments that depend on the smallest groups of essentials. Having a high per capita income reduces the infant mortality rate even more, but then almost every rich country is a democracy, dependent on a large coalition, and almost every poor country relies on a small coalition. Being rich and being democratic facilitates saving babies' lives!

CLEAN DRINKING WATER

For autocrats, money spent on people who are years away from contributing to the economy—like infants and little children—is money wasted. Resources should instead be focused on those who help the ruler stay in power *now*, not those who might be valuable in the distant future. When you see images flowing out of populations in crisis, it's apparent that suffering at the extremes of the life span is hardly uncommon in autocracies. It's not that these terrible conditions can't be reversed; it's that the autocrat chooses not to reverse them as a simple matter of cost. Funds diverted in such a fashion would be taken right out of her own pocket and the pockets of the coalition.

Consider the availability of as basic and essential a public good as clean drinking water. In a world in which easily prevented waterborne diseases like cholera, dysentery, and diarrhea kill millions of the young and old—that is, nonworkers—clean water would be a tremendous lifesaver. The problem is that these are lives that autocrats seem not to value. Sure enough, drinking water is cleaner and more widely available in democratic countries than in small-coalition regimes, independent of the separate and significant impact of per capita income. Honduras, for instance, is a pretty poor country. Its per capita income is only about $5,728 (in current US dollars) according to the latest World Bank estimates. Yet 95 percent of the people in Honduras have access to clean drinking water. Per capita income in Equatorial Guinea is $18,558, more than three times higher than in Honduras.[8] And yet only about 68 percent of its people enjoy clean potable water. This is true even though both places have the same burden of a tropical climate; both were Spanish colonies; and both are predominantly Christian societies. The big difference: Honduras is considerably more democratic, with a larger group of essentials, than Equatorial Guinea.

Is this comparison out of the ordinary? Not at all! Kuwait, awash in oil wealth but cursed with a small-coalition regime, has much worse access to clean drinking water than its not-oil-rich neighbor Israel. Israel enjoys one of the world's highest scores on water quality. To be sure, higher-income countries on average do enjoy higher-quality drinking water than poorer countries. Looking within approximately equal per-capita-income slices of the world, however, those regimes that depend on a big coalition on average make quality drinking water readily accessible to almost their entire population, and those that depend on a smaller coalition lag behind by 20 percent or more. The availability and technology of clean water doesn't favor democratic societies; democratic regimes favor ensuring that drinking water is clean.

BUILDING INFRASTRUCTURE

As we've demonstrated, even a nasty dictator provides the people with basic education and essential health care so that they can work at making the autocrat rich. There is one more public goods program that is necessary to translate labor into his or her wealth. Everything the workers make has to get out to the market so that the leader can sell the product of the workers' labor for money. That means there is a need for roads to transport what's been made to markets where people have money.

Nevertheless, there is still a balance when it comes to infrastructure. Since roads run in two directions, one must be careful not to build too many roads or, especially, roads to the wrong places. Roads are very costly to build, and it is easy to hide their true costs. This makes them a good source of graft, which in turn makes constructing them attractive. But having a country *too well connected* can lead to new regional power centers—political, economic, or otherwise—that undermine the autocrat. And if things ever heat up sufficiently to encourage rebellion, the roads that autocrats build can come back to haunt them. Shoddy infrastructure is often an intentionally designed feature of many countries, not a misfortune suffered unwillingly.

Mobutu Sese Seko of Zaire (today's Democratic Republic of the Congo) once told Rwanda's president, Juvénal Habyarimana, "I've been in power in Zaire for thirty years, and I never built one road." Why? As he explained to Habyarimana, "Now they are driving down your roads to get you."[9] Indeed, when Mobutu came to power in 1965, Zaire had about ninety thousand miles of roads. Thirty-two years later, when he was finally deposed, only about six thousand miles remained, just enough to sell goods and not enough to make it easy to get to Mobutu. So, roads to market: yes. Roads to get you out of the country: yes. Other roads: no.

Consider how straight or curvy the roads are from the center of capital cities to the city's largest airport. Of course, just how straight a road is depends on a number of factors. There's topography, how sprawling the capital city is, the technology when the road was built, and how wealthy the society is. And then there is the size of the winning coalition.

Wealth is not randomly distributed. Places that depend on broad-based support to keep the government in power tend to be wealthy too. That might lead us to think that airport highways are especially straight in wealthy—read: large-coalition—societies, since rich governments can most easily compensate people for tearing down their houses to make efficient roads from the city to the airport. And yet that isn't the case.

Topography, unlike wealth, isn't dictated by politics. A landscape spattered with wide waterways and high mountains is likely to make the road from the capital city to its airport pretty curvy regardless of the type of government that runs the society. To just plow straight ahead in such circumstances means building tunnels and long bridges. Those are expensive. Tearing through villages is expensive, too, if the townspeople need to be properly compensated when the government invokes its right of eminent domain to knock down houses. And the people who need to be compensated in such circumstances may well happen to be both influential and essential. If the townsfolk whose houses are in the way of an airport road are not influential or essential, then it is cheaper to go straight ahead than to skirt village after village.

If the choice of route were just about economics, one might think that straight roads from city to airport would be especially prevalent in rich countries. But if politics trumps economics, then straight roads would more often be the province of petty dictatorships rather than of representative—and rich—democracies. That the difference between driving distance and the distance as the crow flies is related to politics, and especially to how many essentials a leader needs, is rather interesting and perhaps surprising, but related they are.

We calculated the ratio of driving distance to the distance as the crow flies from the major airport serving each national capital for 158 countries.[10] A low ratio means a fairly straight road; higher ratios mean more curves. Only two of the thirty lowest ratios—places where the driving distance is almost equal to the distance as the crow flies—fall in democracies, taking the average coalition requirements for governance into account over the thirty years from 1981 to 2010. Portugal and Canada have the straightest roads to their respective capital-city airports among societies whose leaders rely on lots of essentials to hold power. Portugal has the world's thirteenth-lowest ratio and Canada is twenty-eighth. Which countries have the ten lowest ratios? Guinea, Cuba, Dominica, Colombia, Afghanistan, Pakistan, Yemen, Ecuador, Ethiopia, and Equatorial Guinea. This certainly is not a who's who of democracy. Only Ecuador's and Colombia's governments, among this motley crew, are making real progress toward dependence on a large coalition. The average coalition size for these ten by our estimation method is 0.54 out of a possible score of 1.00.[11] The world's average in 2020 was 0.68—that is, substantially higher than this set of countries, with the caveat that Colombia scores 0.78 and Ecuador 0.67![12]

The lesson is that when an autocrat needs a road to the airport (a good route of escape), he can just confiscate people's property to make the road as straight and as quickly traveled as possible. As President Obama observed in his State of the Union address on January 25, 2011, when discussing the similar issue of building railroads, "If the central government wants a railroad, they get a railroad—no matter how many homes are bulldozed." He was contrasting what autocrats can do with what he, as a democratic leader, cannot.

Democrats find using eminent domain politically costly and so are more likely to go around a village or house than to knock it down. In the event that a democrat ignores property rights, it's likely that all the freedoms she must provide will culminate in people taking to the courts and the streets to redress any perceived wrong. A smart democrat, of course, tries to avoid such troubles, using eminent domain only when it benefits many people, especially members of the democrat's constituency (the influentials). It is incredible to see how easily leaders can take people's property in the *People's* Republic of China and how hard it has been to do the same in Hong Kong. When essentials are few, pretty much anything goes. Sadly, that probably means it will be getting easier to bulldoze property for government purposes in Hong Kong as China extends its control.

Roads are not the only infrastructure whose construction seems to emphasize private benefits in autocracies and public benefits in democracies. Autocrats and democrats need electric grids. For instance, an excellent study showed that when governments expand reliance on a large coalition, they shift electricity pricing and availability away from policies that favor industry and toward policies that help consumers— that is, the masses instead of the wealthiest in society.[13] And then there are the Mobutu Sese Sekos of the world, who have worked out how to use electric power to advance their political survival.

Mobutu famously replaced local electricity-generating capacity near Zaire's copper mines with a hydroelectric station that was more than a thousand miles away. This empowered him to cut off electricity at the touch of a button, guaranteeing that he, and not some local entrepreneur, controlled the flow of copper wealth. It's worth noting that the power lines bypassed all the people along the way. That's the right sort of infrastructure project for someone who wants to use public policy to secure his hold on power.

Massive construction projects, like the Aswan Dam in Egypt and China's Three Gorges Dam, are very much like Mobutu's power grid. These sorts of projects are great for autocrats. Although they dislocate

vast numbers of people, they also generate vast corruption opportunities, making them gems of private rewards as well as providers of basic
public infrastructure. It is noteworthy that they also cost far more to
build than comparable dams in the United States or other democratic
countries, where such projects serve primarily to advance public—not
private—welfare.

All leaders need to provide some public goods so that the people
can work to pay taxes. This is just as true in other organizational
settings. Corporate bosses cannot expect their employees to produce
in isolation. Communications, training, and team-building skills
promote productivity, although they also facilitate the coordination
of protest against the boss. For this reason, not all corporate phones
connect to everywhere.

Even the heads of crime families provide public goods (or, technically, "club goods"—benefits to the members of the crime family)
that help mobsters earn, of which perhaps the most important is reputation. Mobsters would find it much harder to demand protection
money if people did not believe they were backed by muscle. Mafias
also provide muscle and deterrence to protect their members. Killing
a mafioso is not to be undertaken lightly. Mobs also provide lawyers.
Each of these services is a valuable reward. But more importantly,
they keep the mafia earning. Like autocrats, mob bosses provide those
public goods (or, more accurately, club goods enjoyed within a mafia
family) that help mobsters produce the wealth that their bosses need
to stay on top.

PUBLIC GOODS FOR THE PUBLIC GOOD

In small-coalition polities, public goods often serve the narrow interests of the leadership and only indirectly the interests of citizens.
The situation is almost entirely different for those who rely on a big
coalition. For such leaders, the desire to stay in office dictates that
they must satisfy the large coalition's desire for access to good education at all levels; to quality health care at all levels; and, most
importantly, to the means to make the wishes of the coalition easily

known by the government at all levels. It is surely no coincidence that, excluding Kuwait and Bahrain—petrostates—all but one (Singapore) of the twenty-five countries in the contemporary world with the highest per capita incomes are liberal democracies—that is, societies that enjoy rule of law, with transparent and accountable government, a free press, and freedom of assembly. These are places that foster rather than suppress or obstruct political competition. They foster such competition not out of civic-mindedness but rather out of the necessity of assembling a large coalition of supporters.

Some of the richest people in the world live in tiny countries with tiny populations, like Iceland, Malta, and Luxembourg. Others live in countries with vast populations—such as the United States or Japan—while still others live in expansive territories with relatively modest populations, like Canada or Australia. Some of the wealthiest people live in religiously homogeneous societies like Denmark or Italy, but others reside in religiously heterogeneous nations such as the United Kingdom or the United States. Many of the richest countries are in Europe, but others are in Asia, North America, or Oceania. Some were imperial powers, like Britain and France; others were themselves colonies, like Canada and New Zealand.

What, then, do these countries have in common? It is not their geographic locale, their culture, religion, history, or size. What they all have in common is that they are democracies and therefore depend on a large coalition, albeit of different shapes and sizes. And being dependent on many essentials, all of these regimes share in common the provision of the cheap and yet hugely valuable public good called *freedom*.

Although such crucial freedoms as free speech, free assembly, and a free press are cheap to provide, autocrats avoid them like the plague. Democratic leaders no doubt wish they could avoid these freedoms, since it is these public goods that make it easy for opponents to organize to overthrow them. But those who depend on a large coalition can't escape them because they cannot amass a winning coalition without guaranteeing large numbers of people the right to say, read, and write what they want, and to come together to discuss and debate at will. And then democrats must listen and deliver what their constituents want or else someone else will come to power and do so.

But when incumbents rely on a small coalition of cronies, then coalition members are readily satisfied by being made rich through corruption and cronyism. They do not risk these riches by demanding that incumbents siphon money away from them and into effective public policies. Under these conditions, leaders can readily limit the provision of public goods in general and freedom in particular if they so choose. Hence, democracies escape Hobbes's state of nature and autocracies generally don't. Indeed, we can see just how dramatic the difference is in escaping the state of nature by looking at what happens when nature exercises its freedom to wreak havoc. We have in mind the consequences of natural disasters like earthquakes, cyclones, tsunamis, and droughts. These certainly are not political events, but their consequences are the product of how rulers allocate revenue and how people's freedom to organize shapes allocation decisions.

EARTHQUAKES AND GOVERNANCE

An earthquake of magnitude 7 on the Richter scale is ten times larger than one of magnitude 6, just as an 8 is ten times larger than a 7 and a hundred times bigger than a 6. The city of Bam in Iran suffered a terrible earthquake on December 26, 2003. Its magnitude was between 6.5 and 6.6. Of the city's approximately 97,000 residents, 26,271 were killed. Chile, with a similar per capita income to Iran, experienced a magnitude 7.9 earthquake on June 14, 2005. That is twenty-five times bigger than the Bam earthquake, and it struck in a more populous area. The Chilean quake hit the city of Iquique, which had a population of about 238,000. Remarkably, it killed only eleven people. Was this good luck or good policy at work?

Chile and Iran both regularly experience substantial seismic activity. Therefore, we should expect that their governments are attentive to the risks of earthquakes and the devastation that can befall their people. But everything we have argued urges us to be cautious about such an optimistic view of governance.

Just looking at the past sixty years of history, Iran has consistently been a small-coalition regime. The shah's government may well have depended on a somewhat smaller group of essentials than Iran's current theocracy, but the two regimes are in practice not so different. To our way of thinking, therefore, Iran is not a place we would expect to foster the kinds of political freedoms that make it easy for people to express what they want and for the government to make a serious effort to fulfill those wants.

Chile's last half century was a bit more complex. The country was a fairly democratic polity from 1960 until 1973, when it was plunged into a small-coalition regime that lasted until the end of the 1980s. By 1989 it was well on its way back to dependence on a relatively large coalition to sustain the government. This means that we should expect a substantially more public goods–oriented approach to seismic activity in Chile than in Iran at least during the 1960s and since 1990.

Chile experienced an extraordinary 9.5 earthquake in 1960. It killed 1,655 Chileans (as well as 61 in faraway Hawaii following the tsunami that resulted) and left about 2 million people homeless. Chile's fairly democratic government (at the time) immediately set about developing a new, rigorous seismic code for all new construction to protect its citizens from such destruction in the future. Left largely unaltered during the long years of military dictatorship, the code was revisited in 1993 when the once-again democratic Chile made upgrades to reflect improvements in technology. A recent study comparing Chile's seismic code to conditions in the United States reported that "overall, seismic design requirements in Chile and the United States are similar. Standards in Chile are comparable to U.S. codes and standards in regions of high seismicity during the mid-1990s."[14] It seems that Chile's seismic code was not only rigorous but also well enforced, resulting in greatly enhanced public safety in the face of the ominous threat of earthquakes.

Unlike Chile, Iran enjoyed no such period of democratic rule during the last half century. As a result, there was no impetus for the government to strengthen its policies for protecting the public from disaster. As reported by the Iranian studies group at the Massachusetts Institute of Technology following the Bam earthquake, "Considering the high seismicity of Iran, a comprehensive hazard reduction program was launched in 1991, *but the effectiveness of the measures have [sic] been limited by lack of adequate funding and in-stitutional coordination.... The principal causes of vulnerability in the region include... inefficient public policies, and lagging and misguided investments in infrastructure"* (emphasis added).[15] Translation: the small-coalition Iranian regimes of the shah and the ayatollahs have siphoned off funds for their private benefit instead of directing them toward improved public security against the predictable threat of seis-mic disasters. They provide no means for the people to make clear their desires, and they take few actions to secure their citizens against the predictable danger of death and destruction from seismic shocks.

The comparison of Iran and Chile is far from unusual. China, like Chile, has suffered a 7.9 earthquake of its own. It struck in May 2008, bringing down many shoddily constructed schools and apart-ment buildings and killing nearly seventy thousand people. Even accounting for variations between Chile's and China's populations and incomes, it is impossible to reconcile the difference between Chi-na's death toll and Chile's, except by reflecting on the incentives to enforce proper building standards in democratic Chile—incentives missing in autocratic China and Iran. And lest it is thought these are special cases, it is worth noting that democratic Honduras had a 7.1 earthquake in May 2009 with 6 deaths and Italy a 6.3 in April 2009 with 207 deaths. Even Japan's horrendous death toll following its massive 8.9 magnitude earthquake and tsunami in March 2011 was surely lower than a comparable event's death toll would have been in a small-coalition regime. Japan spent a fortune on quality construction to withstand earthquakes, but almost no one can afford to protect against a seismic event and tsunami of the magnitude Japan expe-rienced. Big coalitions save lives because big-coalition leaders know that if they don't protect their ordinary citizens, they'll be turned out of office in favor of someone who will.

Earthquakes and tsunamis are hard to foresee. But their after-math is not. When there are lots of essential supporters, rescue is swift and repair is quick and effective. If it isn't as swift and effective as people expect—and in large-coalition systems they expect it to be remarkably swift and effective—then political heads roll. This is what happened, as we will see later, following Hurricane Katrina in the

United States. We will also see that when there are few essentials, poor relief does not lead to heads rolling. Rather, autocrats actually prefer to exaggerate damage to attract more relief funds. Once aid is secured, it is redirected into the private accounts of political elites rather than steered toward rebuilding. Consider the relief effort in Sri Lanka following the tsunami of 2004.

Such differences can be observed within nations too. Edward Luce toured refugee camps in Tamil Nadu on the east coast of southern India in the wake of the 2004 tsunami.[16] Although fifteen thousand to twenty thousand people were killed and there was widespread devastation, within a year virtually everyone had been resettled and the government had provided compensation for the losses of life and property. The people, although relatively poor, were kept well informed about the process. The reason: elections in Tamil Nadu are highly competitive, as the patronage style of bloc voting that is still prevalent in northern India has broken down. When Luce toured the more northerly state of Orissa in 2006, he found people still housed in tent villages. But these were not victims of the 2004 tsunami: they were still coping with the aftermath of a cyclone that had happened in 1999.

Each of these examples of natural disasters tells a variation upon the same story. When governments depend on many essentials, they need to allocate the government's resources and provide valuable public goods like reliable building codes, relief efforts to rescue the victims of disaster, and, when possible, protective barriers like levees and dikes to forestall disaster. To know what the people need, governments need to make it easy for the public to make clear what basket of public goodies they desire. That is best done by allowing the least costly and most precious public good of all: freedom.

Public goods can be for the public's good. Yet they can also be a means of exploiting the public. In large-coalition environments, public goods overwhelmingly enhance public well-being. In small-coalition settings this is not true.

Democracies are not lucky. They do not attract civic-minded leaders by chance. Rather, they attract survival-oriented leaders who understand that, given their dependence on many essentials, they can only come to and stay in power if they figure out the right basket of public goods to provide. Small-coalition leaders figure out their solution to the exact same survival problem. It is just that when the coalition on which they rely is small, then the mix of public goods is slimmer and trimmer. It is designed for survival purposes in both cases.

We don't need to appeal to civic spirit to explain why people have so much better a life in a democracy than in an autocracy. Higher levels of education are accessible to everyone when the coalition is large; education is basic when the coalition is small. Health care is for those who are productive when the coalition is small; babies and the elderly are not excluded from health care when the coalition is large. Good water is for everyone when the coalition is large; otherwise, it is only for the privileged. And most importantly, freedom to say what you want and to dissent when you don't get it is abundant when the coalition is large and scarce in the extreme when the coalition is small. Sure, freedom means that different people can express different points of view, that they are polarized politically. Better to debate the issues that create polarization than to suppress dissenting opinions, pretending that everyone agrees with whatever the government leaders do for their own good. Large-coalition governments are about easily throwing the rascals out; they are not about consensus. Dictatorships, as the word indicates, *dictate* consensus and punish those who openly disagree.

After this exploration of the benefits of living in a large-coalition system, in the next chapter we will see the dark side of democracy—for large-coalition regimes are not immune from providing private benefits to a select set of their citizenry. We will also see that corruption is a boon to small-coalition leaders and that, in fact, corruption, bribery, and other private benefits to their cronies help small-coalition leaders stay in power. These same benefits could cost large-coalition leaders their jobs. That is why the world's most corrupt regimes are always small coalition.

CHAPTER SIX

IF CORRUPTION EMPOWERS, THEN ABSOLUTE CORRUPTION EMPOWERS ABSOLUTELY

We have seen how leaders come to power, find money, and provide public goods, sometimes even for the benefit of society. Yet precious few successful leaders are motivated primarily by the desire to do good works on behalf of their subjects. Everyone likes to be liked, and there's no reason to think that the powerful have anything against being beloved and honored by their people. Indeed, it could well be the case that there are many candidates for high office who pursue power with the intention of being benevolent leaders. The problem is that doing what is best for the people can be awfully bad for staying in power.

The logic of political survival teaches us that leaders, whether they rule countries, companies, or committees, first and foremost want to get and keep power. Second, they want to exercise as much control over the expenditure of revenue as they possibly can. While they can indulge their desires to do good deeds with any money at their discretion, to come to power and survive in office, leaders must rivet their attention on building and maintaining a coalition loyal enough that the ruler can beat back any and all rivals. To do that, leaders must reward their coalition of essential backers before they reward the people in general and even before they reward themselves.

We have seen how the coalition's rewards can come in the form of public goods, especially when the group of essentials is large. However, as the essential coalition gets smaller, the efficient thing for any ruler to do is to emphasize more and more the allocation of resources in the form of private benefits to her cronies. Why? Private goods to a few cost less in total than public goods for the many, even when the few get really lavish rewards. This is all the more true when the coalition not only is small but also is drawn from a very large pool of interchangeable selectorate members, each clamoring to become a member of the winning coalition with its access to myriad private gains.

Successful leaders must place the urge to do good deeds a distant third behind their own political survival and their degree of discretionary control. Private goods are the benefits that most help rulers keep coalition loyalty. It is only the private gains that separate the essentials from the masses.

For this reason, it's crucial that we next explore the use of private rewards as the means to survive in power. It remains to be seen what rulers do with money they do not have to spend on buying their coalition's loyalty—that is, any money whose use is at the incumbent's discretion. As we investigate these uses of revenue, we will see that Lord Acton's adage, "Power tends to corrupt, absolute power corrupts absolutely," holds generally true—however, it doesn't quite capture the causality. The causal ties run both ways: power leads to corruption and corruption leads to power. As the title of this chapter instructs us, corruption empowers leaders and absolute corruption empowers them absolutely—or almost so. Remember, as we saw with Louis XIV, no leader ever has absolute power. That's why leaders need coalition members who support them, and why coalition members need opportunities for enrichment if they are to remain loyal to their leader, empowering her to stay on in office and get and spend money—on them.

POWER AND CORRUPTION

Corrupt politicians are attractive to would-be supporters, and politicians eager for power find it easiest to attract corrupt people to their cause. Leaders want to stay in power and must take whatever actions are needed to do so. Successful leaders are not above repression, suppression, oppression, or even killing their rivals, real and imagined. Anyone unwilling to undertake the dirty work that so many leaders are called on to do should not pursue becoming a leader. Certainly anyone reluctant to be a brute will not last long if everyone knows he is unprepared to engage in the vicious behavior that may be essential to political survival. If an aspiring leader won't do terrible things, they can be sure that there are plenty of others who will. And if they don't pay their backers to do terrible things, they can be pretty confident that those cronies will be bought off, exchanging terrible deeds for riches and power.

Genghis Khan (1162–1227) understood this principle. If he came across a town that did not immediately surrender to him, he killed everyone who lived there and then made sure the next town knew he had done so. That way, in aggregate, he didn't actually have to slaughter that many townspeople. They worked out that things would be better for them if they gave up, turned their wealth over to him, and accepted that the Mongols would then pass through, leaving the survivors to fend for themselves. Genghis went on to rule much of the known world and to die in his sleep of old age at sixty-five. True, he doesn't have the greatest reputation in the West (although he is revered in his homeland of Mongolia), but he most assuredly was a successful leader.

It is fair to say that England's Henry V (1387–1422) has a better reputation than Genghis Khan.[1] His St. Crispin's Day speech in Shakespeare's play *Henry V* is received even by the modern reader with admiration. We sometimes forget that Henry was capable of brutality. Much as the English revere him, it may be that he is less warmly received in France, where, at the siege of Harfleur, Shakespeare had him announce, in a properly brutal leader's terms, what he would do if the town's governor did not surrender:

> If I begin the battery once again,
> I will not leave the half-achieved Harfleur
> Till in her ashes she lie buried.

The gates of mercy shall be all shut up,
And the flesh'd soldier, rough and hard of heart,
In liberty of bloody hand shall range
With conscience wide as hell, mowing like grass
Your fresh-fair virgins and your flowering infants....
What say you? Will you yield, and this avoid,
Or, guilty in defence, be thus destroy'd?[2]

Fortunately for Harfleur, on hearing Henry's words, the governor surrendered.

The most powerful leaders in history, people like Genghis Khan, Henry V, or Russia's Catherine the Great, tend to be autocrats beholden to only a small coalition. Those who are most successful, especially in the modern world, also enjoy a secure means of extracting vast revenues, such as mineral wealth. Provided they remain healthy, such leaders are practically unassailable. That is to say, they are as close to being absolute leaders as one can get.

What, then, is an autocrat to do once in power? They should tax excessively—Genghis Khan is said to have levied a tax of 100 percent following a conquest. Being a nomad, he didn't need those he defeated to produce for the next year, since by then he and his horde would be elsewhere. They should enthusiastically suppress the people—Joseph Stalin worked out that killing many to catch but a few "enemies of the people" was worth the expense and loss of innocent lives. He therefore made clear to his commissars that an exorbitant error rate in executing potential enemies of the people was perfectly acceptable. They should hand out lavish rewards to essential supporters—Catherine the Great made sure that even her ex-lovers remained loyal by giving them control over vast tracts of land, thousands of serfs, and the income that came with them. And finally, they should sock money away for their personal use, giving themselves a rainy-day fund to bail themselves out of trouble or assure a soft landing when their luck runs out and they are overthrown—Haiti's Jean-Claude "Baby Doc" Duvalier did just that, living lavishly in exile in France until he lost most of his fortune to his ex-wife in a nasty divorce.[3]

How should nearly absolute leaders behave? In short: *be corrupt.*

Leaders, essentials, and influentials of autocratic states can flaunt a dauntingly extravagant degree of wealth, especially when you consider that their general populations are destitute, starving, and often dying. Nevertheless, their monopoly on power and force keeps the people down, and the money keeps the select few happy to enforce the regime's will and protect the leader's power.

Lest anyone jump to the conclusion that this is an apt description only of dictators, private goods in the democrat's domain are indeed worthy of examination. Needing the help of so many, they don't pay as much as autocrats, but still, even backers of democrats must have their rewards.

HOW PRIVATE GOODS WORK

Our version of political logic tells us that private rewards capture a larger percentage of government spending when there are fewer essentials. That is surely one reason why we are so much more conscious of gross corruption in dictatorships than in democracies, and rightfully so. Transparency International, which rates government corruption every year, shows that our expectation about dictatorships and autocracies is generally right. Of the twenty-five most corrupt regimes, according to Transparency International's 2020 corruption index, not even one is a mature democracy.[4] Only a very few—Madagascar, for instance—might be described by some as quasi-democratic, at least in the sense that it appears to have multiparty elections. We say "appears" because the opposition parties are severely restricted in their access to the media and in their ability even to hold public rallies; and the size of the country's winning coalition is below the global average. So, to be sure, the highest levels of corruption do belong to illiberal, small-coalition regimes. But that does not mean that dependence on a big coalition exempts a government from corruption. It doesn't even mean that large-coalition regimes spend absolutely less on corruption than their more autocratic counterparts.

Because democratic settings foster lower taxes and more spending on productivity-enhancing public goods than small-coalition regimes, dependence on lots of essentials tends to correlate with a successful economy. Consequently, it is likely to promote a bigger revenue pie than small-coalition settings, as we discussed earlier. Less of the total income pie is taken by big-coalition governments, but they are taking a smaller share of a bigger pie, so they could have more revenue at their disposal. Even though the private-public goods mix favors more private benefits in small-coalition regimes, the total amount of private rewards can be greater in a large-coalition environment. After all, if you divide an eighteen-inch pizza into twelve slices and a twelve-inch pizza into only eight slices, one slice of the bigger pie gives you 50 percent more pizza than a slice of the smaller pie! We can see just how this works by comparing two countries that are similar in many respects but different when it comes to coalition size.

Nicaragua and the Dominican Republic have much in common. Both, for instance, are Spanish-speaking nations, are former colonies, and have Caribbean coastlines. But they differ noticeably in how democratic they are and in how wealthy they are.

Back in 1975, the two countries had almost identical per capita income (around $2,300). At the time, Nicaragua's coalition size was 0.44 and the Dominican Republic's coalition size was 0.53, just 0.09 larger. Today, the Dominican Republic's per capita income is about $8,000 while Nicaragua's has declined to just under $2,000. The Nicaraguan coalition size today is 0.55 while the Dominican Republic's coalition size is 0.76, 0.21 larger, a meaningful difference. As the number of essentials in the countries pulled apart, so too did income.

With these numbers in mind, we are going to do a back-of-the-envelope calculation to illustrate two important characteristics of corruption in democracies and autocracies: first, autocracies spend a large portion of their revenue on private rewards, and second, they may spend absolutely less on corruption than a more democratic polity does.

Nicaragua's average tax take is 16 percent of the economy. As expected, the Dominican Republic's tax take is lower, 13 percent. That means that Nicaragua's president, Daniel Ortega, has about $320 per person available for public and private goods. Let's suppose he spends half of that on public goods ($160) and half on private goods ($160), with no discretionary money left over for himself (hmm). The president of the Dominican Republic, Luis Abinader, with 13 percent of a larger economy, has $1,040 per person to spend on public and private goods. Because he relies on a larger coalition, we assume he spends 75 percent ($780) on public goods and 25 percent ($260) on private goods, again with no leftover discretionary funds. In that case, on a per capita basis, President Abinader spends $100 more on private goods than does President Ortega. However, Abinader's slice of the revenue pie going to private goods is, as we have assumed for illustrative purposes, much smaller than Ortega's—25 percent of the total pie compared to 50 percent. That is why the Dominican Republic's corruption score on a 0 to 1 scale, with lower numbers being better, is 0.68, consequentially better than Nicaragua's score of 0.81.

Before we discard our envelope, it is useful to do one final calculation to show why private goods are so much more politically important in Nicaragua than in the Dominican Republic. Daniel Ortega's ability to restrict media and opposition activities and "influence" the counting of votes means that he is beholden to a smaller number of supporters than Luis Abinader is. In particular, under the election rules in the Dominican Republic and in Nicaragua (even if conducted honestly), Abinader needs 2.5 times more electoral support to be president than Ortega needs. Although the Dominican Republic is richer and, in absolute terms, might distribute more private goods, it is the essentials in Nicaragua who receive the most private goods. Indeed, they get 50 percent more than the essential supporters in the Dominican Republic receive. Obviously, essentials in Nicaragua are likely to be more loyal and beholden to their leader than are their counterparts in the Dominican Republic!

What, then, are the private rewards that are provided to essentials in democracies? How might public policy be distorted to create benefits for some and costs for others?

In more democratic systems, private rewards are likely to come in the form of distorted public policy rather than more overt forms such as outright bribery, black marketeering, or extreme favoritism. Tax structures that favor coalition members, for instance, are a common way of rewarding the loyal while punishing the opposition.

Government subsidies for the arts—say, the opera—favor a different constituency than subsidies for preschool, each saving a favored constituency money and using money from the opposed constituency, at least in part, to pay for the subsidies.

It is fashionable to talk about politics in terms of concepts like ideology or left-right continuums. The standard mantras from either side of the left-right continuum go something like this: Liberals care about the poor and are dedicated to alleviating their misery. They are often stymied by the rich and powerful. The very rich and powerful tend to be conservative. Conservatives care about the rich and are dedicated to protecting them from the tax-and-spend inclinations of liberals, whose supporters, not surprisingly, tend to be relatively poor compared to conservative backers. As a simplification of politics, that works fine. We do not challenge this view so much as offer a completely different way to think about politics.

The rules governing how people rule inevitably divorce the policies politicians really desire from what they say and do. Not that we doubt that politicians hold sincere views about good and bad public policy—rather, those views are not terribly important, and besides, there are few ways to tell the difference between declarations based on opportunistic political expediency and true beliefs.

From the perspective of this book, so-called liberals and so-called conservatives appear simply to have carved out separate electoral niches that give them a good chance of winning office. Members of the Democratic Party in the United States like to raise taxes on the rich, improve welfare for the poor, and seek heavy doses of benefits for the middle-class swing voters. Republicans in the United States like to reduce taxes on the rich, decrease welfare for the poor and emphasize back-to-work programs instead, and, like Democrats, look for a heavy dose of benefits for the middle-class swing voters. Many of the tax-and-spend policies, pork-barrel programs, and the like are simply private goods distributed to the relevant party's coalition of essentials. Both parties pay special attention to the middle class because there are an awful lot of middle-class voters and they can be tipped either way. They like to define the rich—those who might be asked to pay higher taxes—as anyone whose income is higher than their own. They like to think of welfare systems as rife with fraud and cheating that need to be ferreted out. And they are very happy to have government programs that disproportionately benefit them—no surprise there—such as tax deductions on mortgage interest, expanded Medicare benefits, subsidies for university tuition for their children or student loan forgiveness, and increases in social security payments even in the absence of inflation.

The very poor are not likely to vote, but the working poor are, and, of course, they are likely to vote for people who adopt policies that benefit them. The less well-off love progressive taxes and hate sales taxes. Those who hope for expanded and more effective programs for jobs training, Medicaid, long-term unemployment insurance, and low or no taxes at their income level tend to turn to candidates most likely to fulfill their wishes. These wishes are public policies, to be sure, but they are public policies that benefit primarily the select group whose voting bloc is essential to the winning candidate. Working-class voters used to vote Democratic because that was the party that advocated on their behalf. Donald Trump, building on an insight articulated by Ronald Reagan in 1977—that blue-collar workers are socially conservative—saw a way to capture that voting group with promises about job creation and social policies they like, such as stricter limits on immigration, a ban on abortion, and protection of gun ownership rights. Because of Trump's insight, the less well-off are up for grabs today. The politician who is likely to succeed in grabbing their votes is the one who adopts the policies that provide the greatest perceived benefits for their political support. And, of course, no politician worth his or her salt will pay any more or any less than necessary to get that support. Adopting the policies that selectively benefit this or that voter bloc is just another way of paying out a private reward.

Winning over the relatively low-turnout poorer voters is great, but by themselves they are probably not enough to form a winning coalition. And besides, the rich like subsidies too, just like the poor and the middle class. Republican candidates trying to build a coalition around the support of the relatively well-to-do are the candidates most likely to provide these subsidies. The well-off, typically Republican candidates by and large favor, for instance, government support for medical research on cancer, Alzheimer's disease, and other ailments of the elderly, who happen to be the wealthiest age cohort in the United States. What is more, the well-to-do are more likely to live long enough to suffer from these diseases. They like lower capital gains taxes because they have enough money that they can invest in the pursuit of equity gains, and they don't like inheritance taxes because they can save enough to leave a tidy sum to their heirs. The poor rarely consume any of these benefits, but if they pay taxes, they pay for these benefits to help the rich. But with Democrats controlling numerous legislatures at the state level, as well as (at the time of this writing) Congress, it is worth noting that more than 40 percent of Americans—mostly at the lower income levels—pay no income taxes at all.[5] That, after all, is one of the private rewards they covet, just as in smaller-coalition regimes the rich pay few taxes and covet their private gains.

Private benefits, whether in large- or small-coalition environments, distort economies in exactly the self-serving ways we should expect. And even in the most democratic of polities, these private benefits are perfectly explainable without appeal to highfalutin principles of equity, efficiency, or ideology. People support leaders who deliver policies— whether monetary, cultural, or social—that specifically benefit them. That's why earmarks—*pork*, in colloquial terms—are reviled in general and beloved by each constituency when the money goes to them.

This is true outside of the United States as well. As governments shift toward or away from democracy, or as leaders experience different degrees of dependence on large or small coalitions in different parts of their domain, they adjust their private goods–giving accordingly. We can see this by comparing two countries that inspired hopes for democratization in the first few years after the Arab Spring: Tunisia and Turkey.

Tunisia, though bound to hit lots of bumps in the road, seems on a mostly positive path. To be sure, its economy could be doing better, and we must never forget that leaders always prefer to shrink their coalition rather than expand it. Still, Tunisia has definitely moved toward more accountable governance in the last ten years. Between 2010 and 2020, Tunisia increased the size of its winning coalition by 0.43 points, reaching a score of 0.86 in 2020 (down a bit from its peak of 0.90 in 2013–2014).

Turkey, in contrast, has retreated from the brink of solidly ensconced democracy. While it was on the cusp of entry into the European Union as a democratic Muslim country in 1999, its bid for EU membership was put on hold in 2016. Why? Because its government was transitioning in the wrong direction. Turkey had made a pretty robust move toward democracy by the onset of the Arab Spring, seemingly insulating it from the rebellions to its south. Its coalition score was a solid 0.77 in 2011, up from 0.70 in 2000, but then, following a series of questionable elections and oppressive policies, Turkey's democracy began a slow retreat, and the size of its essential group fell to 0.66 by 2020.

The changes in the essential group in Tunisia and in Turkey should be harbingers of very different choices over quashing or promoting corruption. Hence, we are compelled to ask, have these changes really mattered? Did they matter in the way the logic of the selectorate perspective tells us they should have mattered? The answer is a resounding yes to both.

Figure 6.1 shows us levels of corruption and coalition size in Tunisia and Turkey between the years 2000 and 2020. The graphs couldn't tell a clearer story. Expanded coalitions translate into reduced corruption and contracted coalitions stimulate corruption. Just as our cynical theory led us to expect, corruption varied almost perfectly with shifts in the size of Turkey's and Tunisia's respective winning coalitions.

Between 2000 and 2010, the sizes of the coalitions in Tunisia and Turkey were stable, and they both had stable scores on corruption (higher scores mean worse behavior). Turkey, dependent on a larger coalition, had appreciably less corruption than Tunisia. But then Tunisia's government hugely increased its winning coalition following the Arab Spring in 2011, and corruption there plummeted. In contrast—and also starting, perhaps coincidentally, right around the time of the Arab

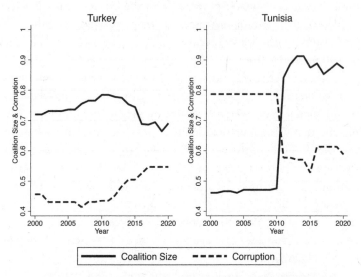

Figure 6.1: Coalition Size and Corruption: The Tales of Turkey and Tunisia

Spring—Turkey's coalition size slowly but steadily declined. Corruption rose apace. Then, following an attempted coup in 2015, the decline in the coalition size began to level off, and so too did the rise in corruption.

Many explanations for the changes in Turkey and Tunisia have been offered. Some look at Turkish president Recep Tayyip Erdoğan's tilt toward stronger Islamic identification as the cause of the coup attempt and other problems Turkey faced. Certainly Islam is compatible with smaller-coalition regimes. Yet Islam is strongly opposed to corruption, making it a poor explanation for the rise in Turkey's private-goods orientation. If Islamic leanings were the right explanation, we should have seen corruption fall as Islamic influence rose, but instead we saw the opposite.

Tunisia's transformation is sometimes traced to the self-immolation of Mohamed Bouazizi, a poor street vendor. Indeed, he is often credited as the inspiration for the Arab Spring. Maybe his death was the immediate cause, but much else was going on that seems to us essential. As we have noted, autocrats get toppled when they are thought to be near death and therefore unable to keep on delivering ample rewards to their cronies. Tunisian president Ben Ali, nearly seventy-five years old when Mr. Bouazizi killed himself, was widely rumored to be deathly ill. Indeed, *Le Monde* reported on February 17, 2011, just a few weeks after the start of demonstrations that brought down his government, that Ben Ali had had a stroke and was in a coma. Of course, the claims that he was gravely ill within days of his ouster may have been a convenient fiction. Whether true or not, according to selectorate logic, the *belief* that he was gravely ill and coming to the end of his life (he actually lived until 2019) would have been sufficient to jeopardize his hold on power in 2011. That same logic tells us that under those circumstances, ruling coalitions are more likely to expand than to contract, and as it happens, that is just what happened in Tunisia. Ben Ali fled into exile, and Tunisia set off on a path of democratization followed by diminished corruption.

Without a doubt, corruption is endemic to small-coalition regimes. Governments that transition from autocracy to democracy diminish corruption in the process. That is what we saw in Tunisia. We saw the opposite in Turkey as it began a transition from democracy toward autocracy. It just doesn't seem that the pursuit or demise of corruption is all that hard to fathom. It doesn't seem to depend so much on culture, religion, altruism, personality, or history as it does on the size of the essential coalition of key supporters.

Corruption is ubiquitous and an essential part of political survival in smaller-coalition regimes. Let's take a look at the record in Russia, one of the world's most corrupt states—as such, the political logic of private goods can be seen vividly at work at the street level.

Low salaries for police forces are a common feature of small-coalition regimes, and Russia is no exception. At first blush this might seem surprising. The police are crucial to a regime's survival. Police officers are charged with maintaining civil order—which often boils down to crushing antigovernment protests and bashing in the heads of antigovernment activists. Surely such behavior must be induced by either great commitment to the regime or good compensation. But as elsewhere, the logic of corruption takes a more complex turn.

Though private rewards can be provided directly out of the government's treasury, the easiest way to compensate the police for their loyalty—including their willingness to oppress their fellow citizens—is to give them free rein to be corrupt. Pay them so little that they can't help but realize that it is not only acceptable but necessary for them to be corrupt. Then they will be doubly beholden to the regime: first, they will be grateful for the wealth the regime lets them accumulate; second, they will understand that if they waver in loyalty, they will be at risk of losing their privileges and being prosecuted. Remember Mikhail Khodorkovsky? He used to be the richest man in Russia. We do not know whether he was corrupt or not, but we do know that he was not loyal to the Putin government and duly found himself prosecuted for corruption. Police face the same threat.

Consider former police major and whistleblower Alexei Dymovsky.[6] Mr. Dymovsky, by his own admission, was a corrupt policeman in Novorossiysk, a city of 225,000 people. He noted that on a new recruit's salary of $413 (12,000 rubles) a month, he could not make ends meet and so had to turn to corruption. Dymovsky claimed he personally only took very small amounts of money. Whether that is true or not, we cannot know. What we do know is what happened next.

In a video he made and sent to Vladimir Putin before it became famous on YouTube, "Mr. Dymovsky also described a practice that is considered common in Russia: When officers end their shifts, they have to turn over a portion of their bribes to the so-called cashier, a senior member of the department. Typically, $25 to $100 a day. If officers do not pay up, they are disciplined." According to his own account, Mr. Dymovsky eventually grew tired of being corrupt and feeling compelled to be corrupt. As the *New York Times* reported, he inquired of Vladimir Putin, "How can a police officer accept bribes? . . . Do you understand where our society is heading?" He continued, "You talk about reducing corruption. You say that it should not be just a crime, that it should be immoral. But it is not like that. I told my boss that the police are corrupt. And he told me that it cannot be done away with."

Dymovsky became something of a folk hero in Russia. It seems his whistleblowing was much appreciated by many ordinary Russians. The official governmental response, however, was quite different. He was shunned, fired, persecuted, prosecuted, and imprisoned. The public uproar that followed led eventually to his release. No longer a police officer, he established a business guiding tours of the luxurious homes of some of his police colleagues. Most notable among these was the home of police chief Vladimir Chernositov. The chief's salary was about $25,000 a year—yet he owned a beachfront home on land estimated to be worth $800,000. The chief offered no account of how he could afford his home, and, it should be noted, he remained in his position as chief. He certainly did not face imprisonment for his apparent corruption, but then, unlike Mikhail Khodorkovsky or Alexei Dymovsky, Novorossiysk's police chief remained loyal to the governing regime. As for Dymovsky's whistleblowing, it did prompt a response from the Kremlin. Russia's central government passed a law imposing tough penalties on police officers who criticize their superiors. As the *Times* noted, the law came to be known as the "Dymovsky law." And then in 2019, Mr. Dymovsky was arrested, while in a taxicab, for possession of the explosive TNT. How did the police know he had TNT with him? Well, he had posted a video pointing to the TNT as real evidence in a crime that the police had chosen to throw away. That's his version of the story, anyway.

Corruption is a private good of choice for exactly the reasons captured by the Dymovsky affair. It ensures loyalty to a regime without the cost of good salaries, and it guarantees the prosecutorial means to ferret out any beneficiaries who fail to remain loyal. From a leader's perspective, what could be better?

PRIVATE GOODS IN SMALL-COALITION SETTINGS

Liberia's Sergeant Doe, our by now all-too-familiar example of a "right-thinking" small-coalition ruler, understood the importance of private rewards for his cronies. As a US government report observed of his use of US aid funds, "The President's primary concern is for political and physical survival. His priorities are very different from and inconsistent with economic recovery.... President Doe has great allegiance to his tribespeople and inner circle. His support of local groups on ill designed projects undercut larger social objectives."[7] That, in a nutshell, is what private rewards are all about—physical and political survival, not larger social objectives. What is most significant about Sergeant Doe's "misuse" of government money is that it kept him in power for a decade.

Doe's story is not unique to him, nor is it unique to Africa; it is not even unique to governments. It applies to all organizations, especially when they rely on a small group of essentials. Before reporting on the world's many dictators, let's look at how private rewards work in a small-coalition regime that most of us think of as benign and even praiseworthy. We have in mind two sports organizations, the International Olympic Committee (IOC) and Fédération Internationale de Football Association (FIFA), the international governing body of football—or, to people in the United States, soccer. What, after all, could be more important to the IOC than advancing the quality (and maybe the quantity) of international sports competition, free from political and personal distortions? The answer: lavish entertainment and money.

The 2002 Salt Lake City Olympic Winter Games are perhaps remembered almost as much for scandal and bribery as they are for athletic excellence. The Salt Lake Organizing Committee (SLOC) spent millions of dollars on entertainment and bribes, which included cash, lavish entertainment and travel, scholarships and jobs for relatives of IOC members, real estate deals, and even plastic surgery. All of this was done in the hope that Salt Lake City would be chosen to host the 2002 games. In the fallout, ten IOC members were removed or resigned, ten others were reprimanded, and Tom Welch and Dave Johnson, who headed the SLOC, were prosecuted for fraud and bribery.

Yet this was not an isolated incident. Indeed, the Salt Lake bid committee felt they had been unfairly overlooked as a potential host for the 1998 Winter Games. The Japanese city of Nagano, which won the opportunity to host those games, spent over $4.4 million on entertainment for IOC officials. Improprieties of this sort abound behind virtually all hosting bids. During its bid to host the 1996 games, Melbourne, Australia, arranged a special concert of the Melbourne Symphony Orchestra to showcase the piano playing of the daughter of a South Korean IOC official. Clearly, any city that wants a serious chance at hosting the games needs to lay on lavish travel and entertainment.

Corruption and private dealing are not limited to big bribes; money to be converted into private gains for backers is sought at every level. Indeed, the 1996 Summer Games, held in Atlanta, demonstrate that no threat to the IOC's ability to shift money to its cronies and essential backers is too small to capture their attention. As the British newspaper *The Independent* reported in its business section on March 26, 1995:

> Even small entrepreneurs, from T-shirt vendors to Greek restaurants, need to beware. Under a 1978 US law—the Amateur Sports Act—the United States Olympic Committee (USOC) has a "super trademark" over any Olympic symbols or words....
>
> The promise of strict action has been critical to attempts by the Atlanta Committee for the Olympic Games (ACOG) to attract official sponsors, some of which must pay up to $40 million for the privilege. Those already signed up include Coca-Cola, which is based in Atlanta, IBM, Kodak, Xerox and the car makers General Motors and BMW....
>
> Eyebrows have been raised, however, at steps taken to protect the Olympic trademark. An Atlanta artist wanted the trademark "USAtlanta" to market her works. ACOG objected, saying that it evoked the 1996 games.
>
> "I think that's stepping over the line a little bit. I find it hard to believe that anyone is going to misconstrue her logo as being designed to profit from the games," said John Bevilaqua, a sports sponsorship consultant in Atlanta, who nonetheless sympathizes with the organizers.
>
> Perhaps the oddest case is that of Theodorus Vatzakas, who opened a Greek restaurant in Atlanta in 1983—long before the city won the right to stage the 1996 games—and called it the "Olympic." In 1991, he was advised by ACOG that he was infringing the 1978 Act and would have to change the name. Eventually he did, at a cost to himself of $1,000, calling it "Olympia Restaurant and Pizza."

"I am very upset about this," he complained, "but I changed the name because I don't have any money to fight these kind of people. Really, I think it's crazy."[8]

Even one of the authors of this book—Bueno de Mesquita— experienced firsthand how eager Olympic committees are to control the flow of money and the opportunities for private gains. His wife, Arlene, together with two friends, founded a company called Cartwheels (which they eventually sold) to make fun products, like T-shirts, jewelry, stationery, and music CDs, all on a gymnastics theme, for competitive gymnasts. As Arlene recalled about Cartwheels' experience with regulations from the IOC and the USOC leading up to the 1996 Atlanta Olympics,

> Our company designed t-shirts and other products for gymnasts. Prior to the Atlanta Olympics we tried to design some with rings, a torch, or any other "Olympic" related logo, but were told that no one would print them and we would wind up with big legal problems. It didn't matter if we used completely different styles or colors from the official designs. We could not use any form of the word "Olympic," nor any allusion to rings or a torch. We even had to stay away from the official colors. In order to fulfill our clients' demands for Olympic goods, we had to buy only official USOC products at greatly inflated prices. Some of the quality was awful, making us wonder about how some of these companies got their sponsorship.

The answer, according to our way of thinking, is straightforward. Cartwheels, like many others, was compelled to pay high prices and buy from vendors chosen by the IOC or ACOG to fund the pot of money that the IOC and ACOG used to enrich themselves and pay for the lavish private rewards they doled out to others. And just as we should expect, quality was as low as prices were high.

The scandalous corruption that seemed to accompany almost all business aspects of the Olympics appeared finally to come to a head with Salt Lake City. The negative publicity surrounding the corruption scandal did inspire the IOC to promise reforms and to place restrictions on gifts, luxury travel, and perks in bidding cities. But as the dictates of political survival lead us to expect, this was unlikely to last because the Olympic organizations are all small-coalition operations. In fact, an undercover investigation by the BBC's news program *Panorama* suggested bribery was still active after the Salt Lake City incident. In the run-up to the announcement of the location of the 2012 games, secretly taped meetings suggested a price on the order of around \$100,000–\$200,000 per IOC vote.[9] Distressing to sports lovers, to be sure, but no surprise to anyone who thinks about political survival.

That the IOC is plagued by bribery and corruption allegations is exactly what we should expect based on its institutional structure. The IOC, created in 1894, runs all aspects of the modern Olympics. The IOC is composed of no more than 115 members: up to fifteen current athletes, up to fifteen members of international sporting federations (IFs), up to fifteen senior members of National Olympic Committees (NOCs), and up to seventy unaffiliated members. IOC members are nominated and voted in by existing IOC members. The IOC is responsible for selecting the senior Olympic executives and executive committees, regulating IFs and NOCs, and selecting the sites of future games.

Only fifty-eight votes are needed to elect someone IOC president or select a city to host the games. Not surprisingly, IOC presidents keep their jobs for a long time and maintain lavish expense accounts. Since 1896, the date of the first modern Olympic games, there have been only nine IOC presidents, and five of them served for at least seventeen years. In practice, often even fewer than fifty-eight votes are required because not all 115 positions on the IOC are filled (in 2021 there were 103 members) and representatives are ineligible to vote on motions involving their home nation.

The design of the IOC lies at the heart of the scandals it faces. When fifty-eight votes guarantee victory and the IOC president can handpick IOC members, politics and control will always revolve around corruption and bribery. As long as the IOC's institutions remain as they are, vote buying and graft will persist because it is the "right" strategy for any IOC president who wants to survive. Regulating gifts and travel cannot change the underlying incentives for cities to compete on the basis of private rewards rather than better management and facilities for the games.

When billions of dollars are at stake and winning requires the support of a mere fifty-eight people, any nation that relies solely on the quality of its sporting bid will be a loser. Salt Lake City learned this lesson bidding for the 1998 Winter Games. It was an error they did not repeat for the 2002 games, although they got caught in the process. Many in Salt Lake might have feigned outrage at the corruption, but many might also have been glad. After all, in spite of the allegations, the games were not moved to another city.

The IOC is not alone in engendering corruption. FIFA, soccer's international governing body, is even worse. On December 1, 2010, FIFA announced that it had chosen Russia and Qatar as the sites for the 2018 and 2022 World Cup Finals. Russia beat out bids from European rivals including England, Belgium and the Netherlands (which put forth a joint bid), and the Iberian Peninsula (in another joint bid). While there were many attractive features of Russia's bid, it is difficult to understand why Qatar was chosen over Australia, Japan, South Korea, and the United States.

Qatar, a tiny state in the Persian Gulf, had the world's third-largest gas reserves and possibly the highest per capita income in the world. However, as a site for a soccer tournament, it was problematic. Sharia formed the basis of its legal code. Alcohol consumption was harshly punished and homosexuality was banned, and Sepp Blatter, FIFA president, was condemned for making insensitive remarks on this topic. Beyond these concerns, the weather remained the most serious impediment to Qatar's sponsorship. It is so hot and humid in Qatar that many of its residents leave for the summer months. To make it possible for the players to compete, Qatar's bid entailed constructing new, fully air-conditioned stadiums. FIFA ultimately agreed to move the tournament to November and December, when the temperature is much cooler. However, this shift will severely disrupt domestic competition in the European football leagues, where many of the world's top players ply their trade.

The locations of the 2018 and 2022 tournaments were determined by the twenty-four members of FIFA's executive committee, meaning that the location of the finals required the support of only thirteen members—if that. In the December 2010 vote, only twelve votes were required after two members were suspended for allegedly trying to sell their votes. One of these members, Amos Adamu, was caught asking for an $800,000 bribe in a sting operation by the *Sunday Times* newspaper. While the money was nominally for building artificial pitches, the deal required that the $800,000 be paid directly to him. Three days prior to the location vote the BBC's *Panorama* once again exercised its penchant for unearthing corruption in sports by airing a documentary entitled *FIFA's Dirty Secret*, which detailed bribery and corruption among a number of senior FIFA officials. It is thought that this severely harmed England's bid to host the 2018 finals, since three of the officials accused were among the twenty-two executive committee voters. Perhaps the fact that the backers of England's bids, including then British prime minister David Cameron, immediately expressed full confidence in the fidelity of the accused FIFA officials was a telling sign that bribery was the modus operandi at FIFA. Why call for an investigation, after all, when it could only imperil England's future prospects?

In 2015 the US Department of Justice indicted nine FIFA executives on charges including racketeering, wire fraud, and money laundering. Swiss police raided a hotel and arrested seven high-ranking executives on charges related to bribes worth an alleged $100 million. How did FIFA respond? Naively, one might have expected them to clean house, but an Associated Press news report suggested a response more akin to the "Dymovsky law."[10] Revisions to FIFA rules included the removal of references to corruption, the addition of a ten-year statute of limitations for fraud and bribery, and the insertion of a defamation clause: "Persons bound by this code are forbidden from making any public statements of a defamatory nature towards FIFA and/or towards any other person bound by this code in the context of FIFA events."[11] It would appear that FIFA took the *revelation* of corruption and bribery much more seriously than the *occurrence* of such crimes.

FIFA is a truly small-coalition organization with access to enormous wealth. In 2018, the year the World Cup Finals were in Russia, it had revenue of \$4.6 billion. To put that figure in perspective, it had a larger revenue than 38 of the 127 nations for whom the World Bank reported data in 2018 (and the World Bank revenue figures are disproportionately missing for small, poor nations). As of 2021, the executive committee has grown in size to thirty-seven members: a substantial increase, but major decisions still only require the support of nineteen people. Admittedly, FIFA has seen a considerable turnover in its senior leadership in the last decade; Sepp Blatter was replaced by Giovanni Vincenzo. But this had much more to do with the actions of Swiss law enforcement than a lack of coalition loyalty.

The experiences of FIFA and the IOC remind us of how much reform is needed to limit corruption. Fortunately, devising reforms that would promote sport and competition over bribery and corruption is straightforward, and a comparison of bribery at the two institutions shows why. To buy the Olympics took approximately four times as many votes as to buy the World Cup, fifty-eight versus thirteen for the games we discussed. And, if the details of alleged corruption are to be believed, the size of bribes was substantially smaller, \$100,000–\$200,000 per vote versus \$800,000. This is a direct illustration of the role of institutions in action, and it makes the solution clear.

As the number of supporters needed increases, private goods become less important. Bribery could easily be made a thing of the past by simply expanding the IOC. For instance, all Olympians might be made eligible to vote for the executive officers and the sites of future games. There were over eleven thousand athletes at the 2016 Summer Games in Rio de Janeiro and nearly three thousand at the 2018 Winter Games in Pyeongchang. Alternatively, medalists—or, to prevent overrepresentation of team sports, one representative per team medal—could become IOC members. Given that there were 306 sets of medals at the Rio games, if gold, silver, and bronze medalists become voters, then the Summer Games alone would add nearly one thousand voters every four years. Within a few years the body of the IOC would swell, and officials and bidding cities would have to compete on the quality of leadership, games, and facilities rather than on lavish travel trips. (Fixing the English football team, alas, poses a far greater challenge.)

WALL STREET: SMALL COALITIONS AT WORK

From any boss's perspective, the best way to organize a business is exactly the same as the best way to organize a government: rely on a small group of essentials, drawn from a small group of influential selectors, who are drawn from millions of interchangeable selectors. That, of course, is a perfect description of most modern, publicly traded corporations. It also happens to be a pretty good description of organized crime families. A coincidence? Probably not—and not for the reasons you may be thinking.

Big corporations do not coerce people to consume their services. In fact, they provide valuable services that lead people voluntarily to spend money on them and to make themselves generally better off for having done so. But, like the mafia and petty dictatorships, publicly traded corporations are made up of a small coalition, a small group of influentials, and masses of interchangeables. That means that for their leaders—the CEOs, CFOs, and other senior management—to survive in office, they must provide lots of private goods to their coalition of essential supporters.

The media (itself made up of just such corporations) like to portray Wall Street businesses as tone-deaf and greedy. We take a broader view: pretty much all of us are greedy, some for money, some for adulation, some for power, but all are greedy nevertheless. A few among us have the opportunity to act on our greed, while most of us are confined to pursuing our greed in minor ways. Wall Street bankers have the opportunity to satisfy their desire for money and power in a big way, and we should not be surprised that they do so.

As we all know, the world economy went through a massive tumble between 2007 and 2009. The recovery was slow. Even years after the near-depression's onset, unemployment remained high and economic growth meager. And yet—and here is the basis for the media's accusation of tone-deafness—Wall Street bonuses remained huge even as the banks lost their proverbial shirts. Wall Street financial houses distributed $18.4 billion in bonuses in 2008, even though many of the largest Wall Street firms begged for and got billions in bailout money from the federal government. Of course, these bonuses, distributed among the leaders, their coalition, and their influential backers, were the very private goods that helped keep the existing managers in their jobs. It is equally worth noting that these bonuses were more than 40 percent lower than in 2007, the year before the economic collapse. Private goods are doled out from revenue. If revenue is down, private goods are likely to go down too, because, after all, leaders want to keep as much for their discretionary purposes as possible, and when there isn't much money around it is not as if those getting private goods can easily find a better deal by defecting to some alternative leadership. And when revenues swell, so too do private goods. Despite the COVID-19 pandemic ravaging many sectors of the economy in 2020, finance did well and Wall Street paid out over $31 billion in bonuses.

DEALING WITH GOOD-DEED DOERS

We commented earlier that "successful leaders are not above repression, suppression, oppression, or even killing their rivals, real and imagined." The truth of this statement is demonstrated routinely in the world's smallest-coalition environments. Alexei Dymovsky's unhappy experience in Russia is nothing compared to what happens when anticorruption campaigns are mounted in really small coalition settings.

Africa provides many of the worst cases. Daniel Kaufmann, a senior fellow at the Brookings Institution, estimates that more than a trillion dollars is spent annually on bribes worldwide, presumably with most of it going to government officials. With so much money on the line, it is no wonder that he also reports, "We are witnessing an era of major backtracking on the anticorruption drive. And one of the most poignant illustrations is the fate of the few anticorruption commissions that have had courageous leadership. They're either embattled or dead."[12] Two examples among many are the deaths of Ernest Manirumva of Burundi and Bruno Jacquet Ossebi in the Congo. Mr. Manirumva was investigating corruption at high levels in Burundi when he was stabbed to death. Although he apparently was not robbed of his personal possessions, the president of the nonprofit organization he was working with reported, according to the *New York Times*, that "a bloodstained folder lay empty on his bed. Documents and a computer flash drive were missing."[13] Coincidence, no doubt!

Mr. Ossebi's error was to cooperate with Transparency International in its lawsuit to recover wealth allegedly stolen by Congo's president. Mr. Ossebi died as the result of a suspicious fire in his home. Alexei Dymovsky, if he knows these facts, must count his good fortune in living in a country that is transitioning away from democracy rather than in one that never got close to such a status in his lifetime.

CAUTIONARY TALES: NEVER TAKE THE COALITION FOR GRANTED

Whistleblowing is not the only way to get in trouble. Leaders can put themselves at dire risk if they take their coalition's loyalty for granted. The rules governing rulers teach us that leaders should never underpay their coalition, whether they do so to reward themselves or to reward the common people. Those who want to enrich themselves must do so out of discretionary funds, not coalition money. Those who want to make the people's lives better likewise should do so only with money from their own pockets and not at the expense of the coalition. Leaders sometimes miscalculate what is needed to keep the coalition happy. When they make this mistake it costs them their leadership role and, very often, their life. The stories of crime boss "Big Paulie" Castellano and Roman emperor Julius Caesar are cautionary tales for any who would make the mistake of not giving the coalition its due.

"Big Paulie" Castellano, who inherited control of the Gambino crime family in 1976, made just such a mistake. He shifted the focus of the family business to racketeering and shaking down the construction industry. Indeed, it was said that no concrete could be poured on projects worth over $2 million in New York City without the mafia's permission. That would have been fine for his crime family if the wealth from these new activities flowed to its members, or if he continued to pay sufficient attention to their traditional revenue sources.

Instead, he neglected the traditional businesses, such as extortion, loan sharking, and prostitution, that were the source of income for his coalition of mafiosi. When a moment of opportunity presented itself, triggered by the death of a key supporter, Aniello "Neil" Dellacroce, and the pressures from the ongoing Mafia Commission Trial prosecuted by Rudy Giuliani, Castellano's erstwhile backers turned on him. John "the Dapper Don" Gotti, Frank DeCicco, Sammy "the Bull" Gravano, and other captains worked together to gun down Castellano outside of Sparks Steak House on Forty-Sixth Street in New York.[14]

Castellano rewarded himself at the expense of his supporters, and it cost him his life. A couple of thousand years earlier, Julius Caesar's mistake was to help the people at the expense of his backers, and this cost him his life, too. Julius Caesar's death at the hands of some of his closest supporters is often portrayed as the slaying of a despot. But the facts don't support this interpretation.

Julius Caesar was a reformer. He undertook important public works, from redoing the calendar to relieving traffic congestion to stabilizing food availability. He also took steps specifically designed to help the poor. For instance, he provided land grants to former soldiers and got rid of the system of tax farming, replacing it with a more orderly and predictable tax system. Not only that, he relieved the people's debt burden by about 25 percent.

Not surprisingly, though these policies were popular with the people, many came at the expense of Rome's prominent citizens. Tax farming was, of course, lucrative for those lucky few who got to extract money from the people. High indebtedness was also lucrative for those who were owed money. These groups found Caesar's reforms hitting them straight in their anachronistic pocketbooks and therefore not at all to their liking. Popular though many of his reforms might have been with the woman or man on the street, they harmed the welfare of the powerful influentials and essentials, and it was of course these people who cut him down.[15]

Caesar made the mistake of trying to help the people by using a portion of the coalition's share of rewards. It is fine for leaders to enrich the people's lives, but it has to come out of the leader's pocket, not the coalition's. The stories of Caesar and Castellano remind us that too many good deeds and too much greed are equally punished if the coalition loses out as a result.

As we have seen, there is a fine balance between giving enough private goods to keep the coalition loyal and giving too much or too little. When money is spent elsewhere that "rightfully" belongs to the coalition, there is a serious risk of a coup d'état. When more money is spent on the coalition than is their due, then the incumbent wastes funds that would otherwise have been his.

DISCRETIONARY MONEY

What is a leader to do with any money that need not go to the coalition to buy loyalty? There are two answers to this question: sock it away in a secret account or lavish it on the people. Those who are most successful at stealing for their own benefit open the door to joining our "Haul" of Fame. Those who are more civic-minded spend discretionary money to help the people, but only some of them are good at it. The successful join our Hall of Fame and the unsuccessful, those with bad ideas about civic improvement, become members of our Hall of Shame.

According to Hank Gonzalez, a politician in Mexico before democratization, "A politician who stays poor is poor at politics."[16] On this basis, Zaire's Mobutu Sese Seko was a political genius. He allegedly stole billions. His biographer, Michela Wrong, observed that "no other African autocrat had proved such a wily survivor. No other president had been presented with a country of such potential, yet achieved so little. No other leader had plundered his economy so effectively or lived the high life to such excess."[17] Indeed, the word *kleptocrat*, meaning "rule by theft," was coined to describe Mobutu's style of governance. But though Mobutu made kleptocracy famous, he didn't invent it.

King Solomon is reported to have had seven hundred wives. One can only wonder for how many of them the choice was theirs or his alone. And then who can forget the economic looting of the Caliphate. A serious estimate of the Caliphate's income for the years 918–919 is 15.5 million dinars, 10.5 million of which—that is, two-thirds of the economy—was spent on the caliph's household.[18] To put that in perspective, if President Joseph Biden had that proportion of the US economy available for his household's discretionary use, he and Jill would personally control a cool $14 trillion, give or take a few hundred billion. There, indeed, is the reason people took such great risks to become the caliph.

Small-coalition leaders have tons of money to use as they see fit. Even though they compensate their coalition of essential backers well, with so few who need to be bribed, plenty is left over. Some incumbents may choose to use their discretionary pile of money for civic-minded purposes—we'll talk about them when we discuss Hall of Shame and Hall of Fame leaders—but an awful lot just want to sock the money away for a rainy day. It is to accommodate just such leaders that secret bank accounts exist.

The prevalence of master thieves among world leaders is striking. Some succeed on a relatively small scale, such as Alberto Fujimori, Peru's president from 1990 to 2000 (including a so-called self-coup in 1992, in which he suspended his own congress and constitution). He probably didn't take more than a few hundred million. And with Peru's return to democracy, Fujimori, who went into self-imposed exile, found himself extradited, returned to Peru, put on trial, and convicted of murder, human rights violations, bribery, and a host of other crimes, for which he was imprisoned. He just did what any small-coalition leader does, but he had the misfortune of being removed following popular discontent with his corruption and being replaced by a large-coalition regime.

Others do considerably better considering the meager means of their society. Serbia's Slobodan Milošević, for instance, is believed to have accumulated $1 billion in a country where per capita income fell by 50 percent during his rule. He followed key political principles: his coalition was small; he taxed heavily, allowing him to make a fortune on the backs of the poor Serbs; and he made sure to keep the people downtrodden. Reliable reports indicate that he precipitated food shortages and massive unemployment for Serbs who opposed him, leaving millions in desperate circumstances while enriching ten thousand influential supporters.

Moving up the ladder of success when it comes to treating the national treasury as one's personal account, we come to Iraq's Saddam Hussein. He built billion-dollar palaces for himself while his country's infants died of easily treated diseases. Other notable national thieves distinguished by their relative take given the impoverishment of their societies are such figures as Uganda's Idi Amin, Haiti's Papa Doc Duvalier, and then his son, Baby Doc Duvalier, and the list goes on. They all typify the rule of successful autocrats—they know how to build, manage, and finance tight coalitions while enriching themselves. But they are all—except for Mobutu—Little Leaguers when compared to the champion Haul of Famers.

When it comes to the crème de la crème of kleptocrats, some of the greats include Indonesia's Suharto (president from 1967 to 1997), Zaire's Mobutu (president from 1965 to 1997), the Philippines' Ferdinand Marcos (ruled from 1965 to 1986), and perhaps the former president of Sudan, Omar al-Bashir. He came to power in 1993 and was in office until he was deposed by a coup in 2019. Estimates of his net worth vary from $1 billion to $9 billion, probably enough to get by for the rest of his life. Mr. Suharto, whom *The Economist* referred to as the king of kleptocrats, is alleged by Transparency International to have stolen up to $35 billion from his country.[19] His late wife, Madame Tien, was often known as "Madame Tien percent." Of course we cannot know what the true amount captured by his family was, but we do know that he depended on a small coalition, he had lots of discretionary power, he survived in office for more than thirty years, and he lived out his life as a free man in Indonesia (he died in 2008). Apparently he was considered too ill to prosecute.

Like Suharto, Zaire's Mobutu lasted in power for more than thirty years, ousted only once he was known to be suffering from terminal cancer. Mobutu stole billions and lived the high life, whereas Suharto lived more modestly considering his alleged means. Mobutu owned villas in the Swiss Alps, Portugal, the French Riviera, and numerous residences in Brussels. In addition he had a presidential palace in just about every major town in Zaire, including his hometown of Gbadolite. With a population of about 114,000, one would not have thought the town needed an airport that could handle the supersonic Concorde, but then one of the 114,000 sometime-residents was Mobutu. He apparently rented the Concorde from Air France for his personal use, and, needing a proper airfield for it to land and take off, he built one for himself.

Ferdinand Marcos, like Suharto, seemingly ran a successful economy. The growth rate during many of Marcos's years was quite good, but then the Philippine population was growing faster than the economy. Whereas Suharto had been successful at controlling population growth, Marcos did not do so well. But he certainly did well in enriching his coalition and himself through his so-called crony-capitalism system. Transparency International estimated that Marcos looted billions from his country. His wife, Imelda, notorious for her enormous shoe collection, was brought up on charges related to the family's theft of Philippine wealth, and the government succeeded in recovering $684 million, a relatively small portion of the total allegedly taken by Marcos and his family. Despite their alleged thievery, the Marcos family, remarkably, has made a political comeback in the Philippines. It seems money really makes the world—of politics—go round!

Returning to Omar al-Bashir, he was accused of having taken up to $9 billion from his country. This was one of the revelations that came to light when Wikileaks released US diplomatic cables in late 2010. The claim, made by Luis Moreno Ocampo, chief prosecutor for the International Criminal Court, included the allegation that Bashir's money was held by Lloyd's of London. They denied it, and, of course, so did Bashir. Indeed, the *Guardian* reported that Khalid al-Mubarak, government spokesperson at the Sudanese embassy in London while Bashir was still in power, said, "To claim that the president can control the treasury and take money to put into his own accounts is ludicrous—it is a laughable claim by the ICC prosecutor."[20] When he was deposed in 2019 there was allegedly $130 million in cash in his house. He was convicted and sentenced to two years in jail for money laundering.

Discretion means leaders have choices. So far we have looked at leaders who use their discretion to enrich themselves, but we do not mean to suggest that people in power *must* be greedy louts like Marcos, Mobutu, Suharto, and Bashir. It is entirely possible for autocrats to be civic-minded, well-intentioned people, eager to do what's best for the people they govern. The trouble with relying on such well-intentioned people is that they are unconstrained by the accountability of a large coalition. It is hard for a leader to know what the people really want unless they have been chosen through the ballot box and they allow a free media and freely assembled groups to articulate their wishes. Without the accountability of free and fair elections, a free press, free speech, and freedom of assembly, even well-intentioned small-coalition rulers can only do whatever they and their coalition advisers think is best.

We close by reflecting on exemplars among well-intentioned leaders of what we call the Hall of Shame and the Hall of Fame—that is, those who wanted to do well and didn't, and those who wanted to do well and did. The Soviet Union's Nikita Khrushchev well illustrates a member of the Hall of Shame.

Khrushchev visited the United States in 1959 and announced a new agricultural policy. He asserted that the USSR would overtake the United States in the production of meat, milk, and butter. He neither knew much about agriculture nor was directly accountable to the people who did and who would be burdened with trying to achieve his goals. There is no reason to believe that Khrushchev hoped to gain personally from his ill-conceived agricultural policies. Indeed, there is no evidence that he socked away public money for his personal use. Rather, he seems genuinely to have wanted to improve the lot of the Soviet people.

Good intentions notwithstanding, his agricultural program and its implementation were a disaster. Local officials, wishing to please Khrushchev and sensitive to the potential political consequences of failing to meet his expectations, committed to fulfilling his demand for increased production. But his goals could not be met with the primitive farming technology available in the Soviet Union. The upshot of Khrushchev's civic-minded ideas was that farmers had to slaughter even their breeding cattle to meet the meat quotas to which they were committed. They even went as far as to buy meat from state stores and later pretend that they had produced it when they sold it back to the government. This created both a false sense of improved production and subsequent increases in prices as the slaughter of the breeding cattle reduced the size of future herds.

A few short years into his program, food prices skyrocketed, leading to mass movements against the government. Official Soviet reports indicate that 22 people were killed, 87 were wounded, 116 demonstrators were imprisoned, and 7 were executed in response to the people's taking to the streets.[21] Two years later, with the Soviet economy in shambles, the nation rife with food shortages, and the leadership humiliated in the Cuban missile crisis, Khrushchev was overthrown in a peaceful coup. A bit more than twenty years later, Mikhail Gorbachev followed in Khrushchev's footsteps by introducing economic reforms to mobilize the economy. His programs also failed to have the effect he desired, but in his case they led not only to his ouster but also to the end of the Soviet Union.

Mao Zedong and Deng Xiaoping in China mirrored Khrushchev and Gorbachev, but with an important difference. All of these leaders seem to have been initially motivated by the sincere desire to improve the economy. All seemed to have recognized that failing to get the economy moving could pose a threat to their hold on power. But unlike Mao, Mikhail, and Nikita, Deng belongs squarely in the Hall of Fame. Like them, he was not accountable to the people, and like them, he did not hesitate to put down mass movements against his rule. The horrors of Tiananmen Square should not be forgotten. But *unlike* his fellow dictators, he actually had good ideas about how to improve economic performance.

Deng and Singapore's Lee Kuan Yew are surely among the contemporary world's greatest icons of the authoritarians' Hall of Fame. They did not sock fortunes away in secret bank accounts (to the best of our knowledge). They did not live the lavish lifestyles of Mobutu Sese Seko or Saddam Hussein. They used their discretionary power over revenue to institute successful, market-oriented economic reforms that, respectively, made Singaporeans among the world's wealthiest people and lifted millions of Chinese out of abject poverty. Nothing about their actions contradicts the rules of successful, long-lasting governance. They were brutal when that served their interest in staying in power, Deng with murderous violence and Lee Kuan Yew through the power of the courts to drive his opponents into bankruptcy. Lee's approach was vastly more civilized than Deng's, but nevertheless it was the arbitrary and tough use of power dictated by the logic of political survival. And that, in the end, is what politics is all about.

Most people think that reducing corruption is a desirable goal. One common approach is to pass additional legislation and increase sentences for corruption. Unfortunately, such approaches are counterproductive. When a system is structured around corruption, everyone who matters, leaders and backers alike, is tarred by that corruption. They would not be where they are if they had not had their hand in the till at some point. Increasing sentences simply provides leaders with an additional tool with which to enforce discipline. It is all too common for reformers and whistleblowers to be prosecuted for one reason or another. It is rumored that Yasser Arafat kept a record of all the corrupt activities of the cabinet members in his government in the Palestinian Authority. Increasing the punishment for corruption only increases the leverage people like Arafat have over their cronies. Arafat effectively induced loyalty to him by both allowing and monitoring crony corruption within his inner circle. And, while claiming that the Palestinian Authority was bankrupt, he allegedly personally socked away a vast fortune, between $4.2 billion and $6.5 billion according to ArabNews.[22]

Legal approaches to eliminating corruption won't ever work and can often make the situation worse. The best way to deal with corruption is to change the underlying incentives. As coalition size increases, corruption becomes a thing of the past. As we proposed for the IOC and FIFA, increasing the number of members responsible for choosing the sites of the games could end graft. The same logic prevails in all organizations. If politicians want to end massive bonuses for bankers, then they need to pass legislation that fosters the restructuring of corporate government so that chief executive officers and board chairs really depend on the will of their millions of shareholders (and not on a handful of government regulators). As long as corporate bosses are beholden to relatively few people, they will provide those few key supporters with fat bonuses. Big bonuses might not be popular with the public or even with their many shareholders, but the public and unorganized shareholders can't simply depose corporate executives. Insiders at the bank can. Legislating limits on compensation will simply force CEOs to resort to convoluted and quasi-legal means. Such measures cannot improve corporate transparency or make balance sheets easier to understand.

Those seeking to regulate corporate compensation and put businesses on the straight and narrow path to enhancing shareholder welfare would do well to examine closely the rules by which corporations are ruled. First-blush fixes, such as are often proposed by government officials, play well with their political constituencies but also violate the fundamental logic of governance and so are likely to undermine good corporate governance. Consider the problem of corporate fraud. We have amassed considerable evidence that securities fraud is more likely to be committed by firms with financial problems *and* a large coalition than by firms with comparable financial problems and a small coalition. After all, executives who depend on a relatively large coalition are particularly vulnerable to being replaced when corporate performance is poor. Being at greater risk of deposition, larger-coalition executives try to hide poor corporate performance through fraudulent reporting.[23] What is more, one of the best early indicators of corporate fraud is that senior management is paid less—not more—than one would expect given the firm's reported performance!

The same issues hold when examining governments. Politicians can introduce all sorts of legislation and structure administrations to seek out and prosecute corruption. This looks good to the voters. But such measures either are a facade behind which it is business as usual or are designed as a weapon to be used against political opponents. Neither a smokescreen nor a witch hunt will root out sleaze. But make political leaders accountable to more people and politics becomes a competition for good ideas, not bribes and corruption.

Of course, leaders don't want to be more accountable. It reduces their tenure in office and gives them less discretion. That's why we must next turn to the difficult problem of how to get leaders to agree to changes that benefit the people.

CHAPTER SEVEN

FOREIGN AID

A **democrat's lot is** not a happy one. She must continually try to find better policy solutions to reward her large number of supporters. And yet her hands are tied. She has little discretion in her policy choices. Her pet projects must be subjugated to the wishes of her large body of supporters, and she can steal virtually nothing for herself. She is like a selfless angel, appearing to place the concerns of her people over her own interests—that is, until she turns her attention overseas.

When it comes to foreign policy, a democrat is prone to behave more like a devil than an angel. In fact, in targeting her policies at foreign governments she is likely to be little better than the tyrannical leaders who rule those foreign regimes.

In this chapter we explore five questions about foreign aid: Who gives aid to whom? How much do they give? Why do they give it? What are the political and economic consequences of aid? And what do the answers to these questions teach us about nation building?

For any who were starting to think of democrats as the good guys, this will serve as a wake-up call. Most of us would like to believe that foreign aid is about helping impoverished people. The United States Agency for International Development (USAID), the primary organization for allocating US aid, advertises itself as "extending a helping hand to those people overseas struggling to make a better life, recover from a disaster or striving to live in a free and democratic country. It is this caring that stands as a hallmark of the United States around the world."[1] Making the world a better place is a laudable goal for donors. Yet the people in recipient nations often develop a hatred for the donor. And recipient governments (and donors too) often have different views about what the money should be for. As we will see, democrats are constrained by their big coalition to do the right thing at home. However, these very domestic constraints can lead them to exploit the peoples of other nations almost without mercy.

THE POLITICAL LOGIC OF AID

Heart-wrenching images of starving children are a surefire way to stimulate aid donations. Since the technology to store grain has been known since the time of the pharaohs, we cannot help but wonder why the children of North Africa remain vulnerable to famine. A possible explanation lies in the observations of Polish writer Ryszard Kapuscinski. Writing about the court of the Ethiopian emperor Haile Selassie, Kapuscinski described its response to efforts by aid agencies to assist millions of Ethiopians affected by drought and famine in 1972 by seeking bribes for the regime's insiders:

> Suddenly reports came in that those overseas benefactors who had taken upon themselves the trouble of feeding our ever-insatiable people had rebelled and were suspending shipments because our Finance Minister, Mr. Yelma Deresa, wanting to enrich the Imperial treasury, had ordered the benefactors to pay high customs fees on the aid. "You want to help?" the minister asked. "Please do, but you must pay." And they said, "What do you mean, pay? We give help! And we're supposed to pay?" "Yes," says the minister, "those are the regulations. Do you want to help in such a way that our Empire gains nothing by it?"[2]

The antics of the Ethiopian government should perhaps come as little surprise. Autocrats need money to pay their coalition. Haile Selassie, although temporarily displaced by Italy's invasion in the 1930s, held the throne from 1930 until he was overcome by decrepitude in

1974. As a long-term, successful autocrat, Selassie knew not to put the needs of the people above the wants of his essential supporters. To continue with Kapuscinski's description:

> First of all, death from hunger had existed in our Empire for hundreds of years, an everyday, natural thing, and it never occurred to anyone to make any noise about it. Drought would come and the earth would dry up, the cattle would drop dead, the peasants would starve. Ordinary, in accordance with the laws of nature and the eternal order of things. Since this was eternal and normal, none of the dignitaries would dare to bother His Most Exalted Highness with the news that in such and such a province a given person had died of hunger.... So how were we to know that there was unusual hunger up north?[3]

Selassie fed his supporters first and himself second; the starving masses had to wait their turn, which might never come. His callous disregard for the suffering of the people is chilling, at least until you compare it to his successor. Mengistu Haile Mariam led the Derg military regime that followed Selassie's reign. He carried out policies that exacerbated drought in the northern provinces of Tigray and Wollo in the mid-1980s.[4] With civil war raging in these provinces and a two-year drought, he engaged in forced collectivization. Millions were forced into collective farms and hundreds of thousands were forced out of the province entirely. Mass starvation resulted. Estimates of the death toll are between three hundred thousand and one million people. From the Derg's perspective the famine seriously weakened the rebels, a good thing as Mengistu saw it. Some may still remember Live Aid, a series of records and concerts organized by Bob Geldof to raise disaster relief money for Ethiopia in 1985. Unfortunately, as well intentioned as these efforts were, much of the aid fell under the influence of the Ethiopian government.[5] For instance, trucks meant for delivering aid were requisitioned to forcibly move people into collective farms all around the country. Perhaps a hundred thousand people died in these relocations.

There is no shortage of similar instances, where aid is misappropriated and misdirected by the recipient governments. To take just one prominent example, the United States gave Pakistan $6.6 billion in military aid to combat the Taliban between 2001 and 2008. Only $500 million is estimated to have ever reached the army.[6] Nevertheless, aid continued to flow into Pakistani coffers. Given the stated goals of aid agencies, one would expect that once it becomes clear money is being stolen, they would stop giving. Alas, they do not.

Indeed, to dispel any pretense that donors are having the wool pulled over their eyes, it is worthwhile to consider the Kenyan case. In her book *It's Our Turn to Eat*, Michela Wrong described the exploits of an idealistic bureaucrat, John Githongo. He was appointed anticorruption czar by the Kenyan president Mwai Kibaki.[7] Given the notorious corruption of his predecessor, Daniel arap Moi, Kibaki ran on an anticorruption ticket. International aid agencies began once again to lend to Kenya at attractive rates. When the IMF gave Kenya a $252.8 million loan, the *Economist* reported that the finance minister was overheard whistling "Pennies from Heaven."[8]

Githongo quickly discovered that the government thought his agency's function was more to cover up corruption than to root it out. When he realized the corruption went all the way to the president, he made secret recordings and then fled to Britain and provided international organizations and banks with documentary evidence of the corruption. He was not alone in his claims. The British ambassador to Kenya, Edward Clay, in beautifully florid language, described the corruption as ministers eating "like gluttons" and "vomiting on the shoes" of donors.[9]

Although some years later the IMF and World Bank eventually stopped lending to Kenya, this was not the immediate reaction to proof of the corruption. Indeed, the international financial community shunned Githongo rather than the wrongdoers. His information was ignored, and he became a pariah at development meetings. Banks and bureaucrats acted like people so desperate to eat at a restaurant that they ignored the health department's warning that the kitchen was overrun by rats. Githongo is now a prominent activist promoter of good government and recipient of numerous prestigious awards for his courage and his actions. But in the immediate aftermath of his revelations it was all he could do to make a meager living as a lecturer and consultant. Edward Clay became persona non grata in Kenya and was discreetly retired by the British government. Both Githongo and Clay effectively ended their careers in Kenya's government by "doing the right thing."

It is hard to believe that aid agencies remain so naive as to not understand how misused their funds are. Perhaps the truth lies in another aim of the USAID—"furthering America's foreign policy interests."[10] Perhaps the United States is more interested in having a reliable ally in its fight against global terrorism and in whatever is the political struggle of the day; remember that governments once perceived a strong need for assistance in combating Somali pirates in the Indian Ocean.

Against this harsh view, that aid is about recipients selling favors overseas, is the rhetoric of Kenya's first president, Jomo Kenyatta, who at his Independence Day speech in 1963 said:

> We shall never agree to friendship through any form of bribery. And I want all those nations who are present today—whether from West or from East—to understand our aim. We want to befriend all, and we want aid from everyone. But we do not want assistance from any person or country who will say: Kenyatta, if you want aid, you must agree to this or that. I believe, my brothers, and I tell you now, that it is better to be poor and remain free, than be technically free but still kept on a string. A horse cannot choose: reins can be put on him so he can be led around as his owner desires. We will not be prepared to accept any aid that will tie us like a horse by its reins.[11]

As upright as this speech may initially sound, Kenyatta was in fact being disingenuous. Are aid agencies willingly throwing away money? Or are they getting something in return? We suspect that the key statement in Kenyatta's speech was "whether from West or from East." In spite of his idealistic words, he was covertly telegraphing that his government remained open to bids from both sides.

Political logic suggests that democratic donors are ready to turn a blind eye to theft and corruption when they need a favor. If you remember, Sergeant Doe of Liberia received over $500 million from the United States during his decade in power. And the United States got a lot in return: As claimed by a senior American foreign-policy maker, "We [the United States] were getting fabulous support from him on international issues. He never wavered [in] his support for us against Libya and Iran. He was somebody we had to live with. We didn't feel that he was such a monster that we couldn't deal with him. All our interests were impeccably protected by Doe."[12]

With the end of the Cold War, the United States had much less need for Doe's support. Only then did it find its moral scruples. In 1989 it published a report, which we quoted earlier but is nonetheless worth repeating:

> [Liberia] was managed with far greater priority given to short-term political survival and deal-making than to any long-term recovery or nation-building efforts.... The President's primary concern is for political and physical survival. His priorities are very different from and inconsistent with economic recovery.... President Doe has great allegiance to his tribes people and inner circle. His support of local groups on ill designed projects undercut larger social objectives.[13]

The truth is, foreign-aid deals have a logic of their own. Aid is decidedly *not* given primarily to alleviate poverty or misery; it is given to make the constituents in donor states better off. Aid's failure to eliminate poverty has not been a result of donors giving too little money to help the world's poor. Rather, the right amount of aid is given to achieve its purpose: improving the welfare of the donor's constituents so that they want to reelect their incumbent leadership. Likewise, aid is not given to the wrong people—that is, to governments that steal it rather than to local entrepreneurs or charities that will use it wisely. Yes, it is true that a lot of aid is given to corrupt governments, but that is by design, not by accident or out of ignorance. Rather, aid is given to thieving governments exactly because they will sell out their people for their own political security. Donors give them that security in exchange for policies that make donors more secure, too, by improving the welfare of their own constituents.

The fact is, aid does a little bit of good in the world and vastly more harm. Unless and until it is restructured, aid will continue to be a force for evil with negative consequences. Moreover, it will continue to be promoted by well-meaning citizens who, while making themselves feel good, are oblivious of the harm they are inflicting on many poor people who deserve a better lot in life.

Let's be clear, democrats act as if they care about the welfare of *their* people because they need their support. They are not helping out of the goodness of their hearts, and their concern extends only as far as *their own* people—the ones from whom they need a lot of supporters. Democrats cannot greatly enrich their essential backers by handing out cash. There are simply too many people who need rewarding. Democrats need to deliver the public policies their coalition wants.

Autocrats, on the other hand, can richly reward their limited number of essential backers by disbursing cash. Money, which good governance suggests should be spent on public goods for the masses, can instead more usefully (from the autocrat's perspective) be handed out as rewards to supporters. And since private goods generate such concentrated benefits to the people who matter (and a good leader never forgets that *who matters* is all that matters), autocrats forsake the public policy goals of the people. It is not that they necessarily care less about the people's welfare than do democrats; it is just that promoting the people's interest jeopardizes their hold on power. Remember the story of Julius Caesar!

Herein lies the basis for making foreign-aid deals. Each side has something to give that the other side holds dear. A democrat wants policies his people like, and the autocrat wants cash to pay off his coalition.

Suppose there are two nations, A and B, each with a population of one hundred people. The leader in each nation has $100 with which to buy political support. Suppose nation A is a democracy and its leader needs to keep fifty people happy in order to stay in power. In contrast, nation B is an autocracy and its leader needs to keep five people happy.

Suppose the people of both nations care about some policy initiative taken up by nation B—for instance, to take a common Cold War situation, the policy might be nation B's stance towards the Soviet Union. The citizens in nation A prefer that nation B adopt an anti-Soviet stance. Suppose the value of such a stance to each of the people in nation A is equivalent to $1. The citizens of nation B don't want socialism outlawed, and they don't want their government to take an anti-Soviet stance. Indeed, since it is their country's policy at stake, let's assume that the people of nation B care about their government's policy much more than the people in nation A do. To keep our example simple, suppose that if B takes the anti-Soviet policy, then this is equivalent to a $2 loss in welfare for each of the hundred people in B.

In nation A, the leader has $100 to make fifty people happy. If he hands out the money to his supporters, then each gets $2. The leader in nation B has fewer people to satisfy. If he hands out all his money, then each of his five supporters gets $20. Now, suppose the leader in B agrees to change to the anti-Soviet policy in exchange for cash. The essential questions are, How much does B need, and how much is A willing to pay to make this deal work?

The leader of B would only agree to trade policy for aid if it made his coalition better off. The switch in policy is equivalent to a $2 loss for each of his supporters (and each of the inconsequential remaining ninety-five people in B who are not influential), because they don't like the policy. So the leader of B would never agree to the anti-Soviet stance unless the "aid" money he gets for doing so is larger than this loss. Since he has five supporters to keep happy and each supporter suffers a $2 loss, he needs at least $10 in aid to offset the political cost of turning anti-Soviet. That is, an extra $2 for each of his five essential backers is the minimum required to change B's policy to anti-Soviet.

The leader in nation A only "buys" the anti-Soviet policy if its value to his supporters is greater than the amount given up by each. Since the fifty coalition members in A value the anti-Soviet policy at $1 each, the money they give up so that their government can buy an anti-Soviet stance from country B must be less than $1 each. Otherwise, they prefer the cash to the policy concession. Since the policy shift is worth $1 to each supporter in nation A and there are fifty members of the coalition, this means the leader in A would pay up to $50 in "aid" to B's government to get B to become anti-Soviet.

Provided the aid transfer is between $10 and $50, the essential backers in both nations are made better off by trading policy for aid. This enhances the survival of both leaders. However, it makes each of the remaining ninety-five people in nation B—those not in the winning coalition—the equivalent of $2 worse off. They are not compensated for the anti-Soviet policy that they don't like.

This example, while extremely simple, captures the logic of Cold War aid flows. The United States provided Liberia's Sergeant Doe with an average of $50 million per year in exchange for his anti-Soviet stance. This aid did not provide for the welfare of his people and is coincidentally close to the amount of money Doe and his cronies are alleged to have stolen during his decade in power. From the perspective of survival-oriented leaders, the rationale for aid becomes clear. When the Cold War ended, the United States no longer valued anti-Soviet policies and was no longer willing to pay for them. Doe's government didn't have much else to offer the United States that American voters valued, so he was cut off. Without aid revenue, Doe could no longer pay his supporters enough for them to suppress insurgencies, and so he died a gruesome death at the hands of Prince Johnson.

For the reader who finds the above example too contrived, it is perhaps worthwhile to look at an actual failed United States attempt to buy policy. In the run-up to the 2003 invasion of Iraq, the United States sought permission to base US troops in the predominantly Muslim nation of Turkey. Such basing rights would have improved the US Army's ability to engage the Iraqi army. Although Turkey is allied with the United States through NATO, the idea of assisting a predominately Christian nation to invade a fellow Muslim nation was domestically unpopular in Turkey. During negotiations in February 2003, the United States offered Turkey $6 billion in grants and up to $20 billion in loan guarantees. Given Turkey's population of approximately seventy million, these aid totals amounted to about $370 per capita.[14]

Turkey was pretty democratic at the time. For a quick, back-of-the-envelope calculation, let's suppose its leader needed the support of a quarter of the people. So the value of the United States' offer worked out to nearly $1,500 per essential backer. This was a substantial amount (almost 33 percent of Turkish per capita income in 2003), but then the policy concession sought was very politically risky. Indeed, it might be useful for American readers to think about how much compensation they would need before agreeing to allow foreign troops a base in the United States in order to invade Canada.

It appears that $1,500 per person was not enough. After much back-and-forth, the Turkish government rejected the offer. They were holding out for significantly more money, so we know there was a price at which the policy concession could have been granted, but it was a high price. The United States was not willing to pay more, and so the deal could not be struck. In the end, Turkey granted a much less controversial concession for a lot less money. The United States was allowed to rescue downed pilots using bases in Turkey.

Buying a policy from a democracy is expensive because many people need to be compensated for their dislike of the policy. Buying a policy from an autocracy is quite a bit easier. Suppose Turkey were an autocracy back in 2003 and its leaders were beholden to only 1 percent of the population. Under such a scenario, the value of the US offer rejected by Turkey would have approached $40,000 per essential backer. Thinking back to the challenge offered to American readers, while few might sell out their northern neighbor for $1,500, $40,000 might start looking very attractive to many. It is probably not an accident that the US invasion of Iraq was launched from the decidedly very-small-coalition monarchies of Kuwait and Saudi Arabia.

The logic of how coalitions operate gives us a good handle on who gives how much aid to whom. Getting the people what they want helps democratic leaders stay in office. It is therefore no surprise that most foreign aid originates in democracies. The price of a policy concession depends on the salience of the issue (as we'll address in a moment) and the size of the recipient leader's coalition. As coalition size grows, the recipient leader needs to compensate more and more people for the adoption of the policy advocated by the donor. That means that the price of a policy concession rises with the size of the prospective recipient's group of essential backers. This creates an interesting dynamic.

As a nation becomes more democratic, the amount of aid required to buy its policy goes up. But because the price is higher, donors are less likely to buy the policy concession from it; it just gets to be too expensive. Poor autocracies are most likely to get aid, but they don't get much. Although they may have great needs, they can be bought cheaply. We have confirmed this relationship between coalition size, the chance to get aid, and the amount of aid received (if any) in detailed statistical studies of aid giving by the United States and other wealthy democratic nations, namely all the members of the Organization for Economic Cooperation and Development (the OECD).[15]

Coalition size is not the only factor determining who gets aid or how much is spent to buy concessions from them. The salience of the issues at stake—what the policy concessions are worth—is an important determinant of how much aid gets transferred. Notice that in the formula we just described, need is not a significant factor. In fact, because an extra dollar is worth more to a poor country than to a rich one, among those receiving aid, needier countries are likely to get less aid, not more, than the less needy.

One extremely salient, and hence expensive, aid-for-policy deal was the 1979 Egyptian-Israeli peace treaty. As part of this agreement, Egypt became the first Arab nation to officially recognize Israel. Israel and Egypt ended hostilities that had been nominally ongoing since the 1948 war (and that had erupted into actual warfare in 1956, 1967, and 1973). As part of the 1979 deal, Israel withdrew from the Sinai Peninsula, which it had captured in the 1967 Six-Day War, and both sides agreed to the free passage of shipping through the Suez Canal.

Peace between Israel and Egypt was of great importance to the United States. Beyond the strong domestic support for Israel, the United States was suffering the ill effects of oil shocks in the 1970s. The sharp rise in oil prices raised inflation and harmed the US and other Western economies dependent on oil imports. The United States, desperate to avoid another oil crisis, underwrote the 1979 deal, thinking, perhaps, that doing so would help stabilize the oil situation in the region. As can be seen in Figure 7.1, the United States provided enormous economic incentives for Egyptian president Anwar Sadat to visit Israel, attend the Camp David peace summit, and sign the treaty.

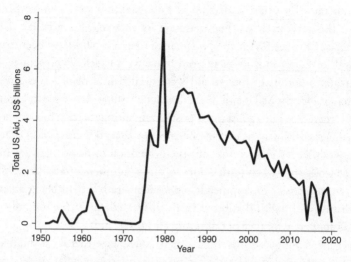

Figure 7.1: Total US Assistance to Egypt in Constant 2019 Billions US$ from USAID

The recognition of Israel was an extremely unpopular policy shift in Egypt. This is why Sadat was able to extract so much from the United States. Unfortunately for Sadat, it also contributed to his assassination in 1981. Fundamentalists threw grenades and attacked with automatic rifle fire during an annual parade. Although it officially recognizes Israel, the Egyptian government has done almost nothing to encourage the Egyptian people to moderate their hatred for Israel. In a BBC survey conducted nearly thirty years after the Camp David agreement was struck, 78 percent of Egyptians indicated that they perceived Israel as having a negative impact in the world, far above the average in other countries in the survey.[16] Of course, changing the negative attitude toward Israel in Egypt would just reduce the amount of aid the Egyptian government can extract from the United States.

The brief movement toward a more democratic government in Egypt during the Arab Spring highlights the dilemma faced by democratic donors. Those who celebrated the prospects of democracy in Egypt and favored peace with Israel had a problem. As we have noted, the aid-for-peace-with-Israel deal was possible exactly because the autocratic Egyptian leadership and its coalition were compensated for the anti-Israeli sentiment among its citizenry, a sentiment they helped preserve. With the *people* in charge, it would have been natural for Egypt to shift away from peace with Israel. To prevent that, greater amounts of foreign aid were needed in a democratic Egypt than under the Sadat and Mubarak dictatorships. As we see in Figure 7.1, there was not a substantial post–Arab Spring increase in aid when Mohamed Morsi—leader of the Muslim Brotherhood—was elected Egypt's leader. Americans tout the promotion of democracy around the world, but when push comes to shove, aid more often follows the trail of security or commercial concessions rather than being an instrument of political reform. Sadly, this statement is true not only of US foreign assistance but of nearly all OECD aid.

Depressing as all of this is, there is evidence that for a small set of countries that cannot offer meaningful commercial or security concessions, sometimes democratic donors are nevertheless willing to give aid in return for political liberalization. All democratic countries cheer others on to be democratic, and so it is sensible and reasonable that sometimes they are prepared to use aid to buy the concession of political liberalization. But political reform is hard to attain with aid even when donors are willing to use it that way (and such willingness is uncommon). The difficulty is that prospective aid recipients are much more open to selling out their people for money than they are to helping their people in ways that increase the risk that the leaders will be toppled. That, of course, is the great danger of taking aid for political reform: reform usually implies and requires expanding the winning coalition. Still, the evidence shows us that sometimes—perhaps "rarely" is a better description—the stars align and aid for political liberalization is given to recipients who offer little by way of security or commercial benefits to donors.[17]

Alas, democracy promotion is a marginal activity when it comes to foreign aid. Consider aid to Pakistan. As with aid to Egypt, US assistance to Pakistan is much easier to explain by looking at it as a payment for favors rather than a tool for alleviating poverty or promoting political reform. In 2001, the United States gave Pakistan $5.3 million and Nepal $30.4 million in aid. Pakistan's aid had been greatly reduced by congressional mandate following their test of a nuclear weapon in 1998. Yet on September 22, 2001, US president George W. Bush lifted restrictions on aid to Pakistan. It received more than $800 million in 2002. Meanwhile, Nepal, not on the front line of the fight against al-Qaeda and the Taliban, received about $37 million, just modestly more than its 2001 receipts. India, also not front and center in the battle against terrorism in 2002, received $166 million from the United States, barely up from 2001, when they received about $163 million. Poverty had not changed in any meaningful way in any of these countries between 2001 and 2002, but their importance to American voters most assuredly had.

Democrats are often perceived as being in the driver's seat and dictating terms to autocrats. However, as in other matters, they are often the ones who are constrained. They need to deliver the policies their backers want. If they try to cut back on the aid they give or impose strict conditions on it, then autocrats simply end the policy concessions.

Subsequent US relations with Pakistan offer clear evidence of this pattern of waning and waxing aid. As we saw, aid went up following the terrorist attacks of September 11, 2001, but then it began to taper as the war against the Taliban in Afghanistan seemed to have been won by 2003. Once Pakistan increasingly became a safe haven for the Taliban and al-Qaeda, everything changed. Pakistan now found itself in a tough spot. If the government opposed the Taliban, which was infiltrating the Pakistani frontier bordering Afghanistan, they were likely to face a domestic insurgency. If they supported the Taliban, they would face severe pressure from the United States. This dilemma offered an opportunity for Pakistan to make greater demands for US aid in exchange for resisting the Taliban. The demands were made, but the US Congress balked at giving Pakistan more, noting that much American aid to Pakistan was diverted to uses not intended by Congress. Some money disappeared entirely, and Pakistan channeled much of the rest to stave off India, which the Pakistanis perceived to be a greater threat than Muslim fundamentalist militants.

The United States, disgruntled with Pakistan, did not initially agree to pay the higher price needed to get the Pakistani government to pursue the Taliban and al-Qaeda militants within Pakistan. What was the upshot? As we have learned to expect, the Pakistani leadership ignored US pressure and began looking for ways to work with the Taliban. Aid is basically a pay-to-play program. The United States wouldn't pay, so Pakistan wouldn't play.

By 2008, the government of Pakistan's leader, Asif Ali Zardari, was paying only lip service to going after the militants. The Bush administration, lacking more aid to offer, proved unable to change Zardari's mind. In fact, the second half of 2008 saw only a perfunctory effort by the Zardari government to fight the militants. There was a brief military offensive against the Taliban, starting on June 28 and ending in early July, with precisely one militant killed. After that, although the Taliban aggressively pursued their own territorial expansion in Pakistan, the Zardari government mostly looked the other way. Rather than fight the militants, Zardari's regime made a deal with the Taliban in February 2009, paying them about $6 million and agreeing to the imposition of Sharia law in the Swat Valley in exchange for the Taliban's agreeing to an indefinite cease-fire. The cease-fire had unraveled by May. By this time, the Zardari government seemed in trouble, and the US government was fearful that the Taliban might take control of Pakistan altogether. In the face of such danger, the price for aid had risen, but so too had the desire in the United States to motivate the Pakistanis to try harder to beat back the Taliban.

Congress passed the Kerry-Lugar bill at the end of September 2009. It nearly tripled aid to Pakistan, increasing it to $1.5 billion. Even then the Pakistani government balked at taking the greatly increased aid because the bill included requirements that the Pakistanis be accountable for how the money was used. Facing resistance from Pakistan, Senator John Kerry clarified that the bill was not designed to interfere at all with sovereign Pakistani decisions; that is, he essentially assured the Pakistani leadership that the United States would not closely monitor use of the funds. Shortly after, the Pakistani government accepted the aid money and greatly stepped up its pursuit of militants operating within its borders. By February 2010 they had captured the number two Taliban leader, but, as we should expect, they were also careful not to wipe out the Taliban threat. Doing so would have just led to a termination of US funds.

The US government, for its part, was frustrated that even with $1.5 billion in aid, Pakistan was not sufficiently motivated to beat back the Taliban. As a result, the United States stepped up drone attacks and the use of the American military to pursue the Taliban within Pakistani territory, much to the public—but we doubt private—dismay of the Zardari government. This was all just the dance of the donors and the takers, the recipients looking for as much money as possible and the donors looking for a highly salient, costly political concession: the destruction of the Taliban.

Perhaps this is distasteful to those who would like to maintain the fiction that aid is about alleviating poverty or promoting democracy. Naturally some aid is given with purely humanitarian motives, such as that given after a natural disaster. Yet it is hard to reconcile the large scale of aid that flows to Egypt and Pakistan with idealistic goals. If aid actually helped the poor or the oppressed, then we might expect the people in recipient nations to be grateful and hold donor nations in esteem. Nothing could be further from the truth. In return for its "benevolence" to Egypt and Pakistan, the United States is widely reviled by the people in those two countries, and with good reason.

In 2010, Pew Research Center undertook a study of values and opinion in a great many other nations. One question asked about people's view of the United States. So how did Pakistanis and Egyptians feel about the United States? "Pakistan, along with Turkey and Egypt, gives America its lowest rating."[18] This was nothing new. Back in 2002 Pew's comparable study reported that in Pakistan 69 percent of people had an extremely unfavorable view of the United States. In Egypt a mere 6 percent had a favorable view of the United States.[19] In the other forty nations in that study, an average of only 11 percent of the people shared this extremely negative view of the United States. But then, Pakistan and Egypt received an average of $1.6 billion in economic and military aid from the United States in 2002, while the other forty nations averaged only $97 million in aid. The pattern is borne out in detailed statistical analyses and in survey after survey.

People in nations receiving lots of US aid seem to hate the United States.

Our account of aid may seem to paint the United States as international bad guy number one. But the United States is far from the only aid donor. While the United States is the largest overall donor, as a proportion of its economic size it gives relatively little, about 0.2 percent of GDP. Scandinavian nations give over 1 percent of their economic output in foreign aid. Provided the policy rewards that a foreign power can provide to a democrat's supporters are worth more to the supporters than the rewards that could be directly purchased with the money, democrats support aid. Other nations and agencies buy favors, too, if not perhaps on the same grand scale that the United States can afford. In fact, careful analysis shows that even the seemingly generous Scandinavians give aid in exchange for policy concessions rather than for altruistic reasons. They particularly like to use aid to gain trade concessions and prosocialist ideologies in recipient regimes.[20]

Aid agreements are notorious for being tied to conditions that help the donor. This means that the agreement often specifies how and, more importantly, where the money is spent. For instance, Germany might give a recipient nation money, but only if it uses it to buy German tractors. This might seem an inefficient way to reward tractor manufacturers. However, international trade laws often forbid direct subsidies. Further, tied aid can bring future business, such as spare parts and service. Canada is notorious for high levels of tied aid, 60–75 percent of all its aid. Scandinavia and the UK claim to have the lowest levels of tied aid, but even there, informal tying is common. For instance, Denmark had allocated $45 million to repair ferries in Bangladesh. Rather than repair the ferries locally, Denmark proposed taking the ships to Denmark and repairing them there, at four times the local cost. Amid protest from the Bangladeshi government, Denmark decided to simply cancel the whole scheme, so neither the Bangladeshis nor the Danes benefited. Ferries fixed in Bangladesh just did not deliver as many benefits for Danes as Bangladeshi ferries repaired in Denmark by Danish workers.

Just as the United States buys security and policy concessions with aid, and the Europeans trade aid for business concessions, so too does

Japan. Whales need to fear Japanese benevolence. American voters like pork. In contrast, Japanese voters like blubber, and Japanese leaders work hard to deliver. In 1986, the International Whaling Commission (IWC) instituted a moratorium on the commercial hunting of whales. While this ban was popular with the people of most nations, the citizens of Iceland, Norway, and Japan want to resume hunting. Currently the Japanese hunt whales through a loophole that allows hunting for scientific research. These whales, of course, end up being eaten. Even as demand for whale meat has fallen, Japanese fishermen promote whale hunting, arguing, as they did in 2019, that "the culture and way of life will be passed on to the next generation."[21] The Japanese government buys votes on the IWC with foreign aid. Recently, through Japan's efforts, the IWC's membership has swelled to include nations with no history of whaling. Some of these recent members, such as Laos, Mali, and Mongolia, are landlocked. Japan's efforts have been rewarded with growing support for the resumption of whale hunting.

THE IMPACT OF AID

Example after example highlight the simple fact that aid is given in exchange for policy concessions far more readily and in far larger quantities than it is given to reduce poverty and suffering. Following World War II, the rich nations seem genuinely to have thought they could free the world of poverty through their generosity. But no sooner did aid begin to flow than the demands of political survival intruded on the noble goal of reducing misery. It should not be surprising that politics prevailed over benevolence. The record is unambiguous: foreign assistance has proven ineffective at alleviating poverty and promoting economic growth.

In the aftermath of World War II, Europe faced many challenges. Even the victors had suffered enormous human and economic losses. The United States launched a widespread relief program known as the Marshall Plan. Adjusted for inflation, the United States pumped over $189 billion in economic assistance into Europe between 1946 and

1952. Britain was the largest recipient, followed by West Germany, France, and Italy.[22] The United States' goal was to build stalwart states allied against communism. To achieve these ends, the United States needed an economically strong Europe. States that were willing to combat communism and follow US-dictated economic plans got aid; those not willing to do so didn't.

Over the entire postwar period, total US economic assistance was nearly $1.3 trillion. Military aid over the same period was about $650 billion. To give some perspective, together these economic and military aid packages were roughly the size of the 2021 US stimulus package to address the COVID-19 pandemic and its dire unemployment and other disastrous economic consequences.

The success of the Marshall Plan proved hard to replicate. Trillions of dollars have been pumped into developing economies, yet there is precious little to show for it if we measure performance by assessing improvements in the quality of life. As we've seen, aid has done virtually nothing to relieve poverty.

Among policy makers, this record has prompted a fierce debate about the efficacy of aid. For critics, it is all too easy to point to many aid-dependent states in Africa that are poorer now than they were at independence. The development community likes to counter that such a direct comparison is unfair and that, while aid-dependent nations have performed poorly, they would have done even worse without aid. This defense, while wrong, is a sensible argument that needs to be taken seriously.

We cannot simply condemn the aid enterprise just because nations that received aid performed so poorly. To understand why, consider the following provocative statement: *Hospitals kill!* There is plenty of evidence to support this claim. The likelihood of dying is much higher for a person in a hospital than for a person who is not. Of course, most of us instantly see the error in the evidence. The people in hospitals are sick. Healthy people are not found in hospital beds. But this kind of error that occurs from looking at statistics without thinking about where they come from is all too common.

A colleague of ours, Peter Rosendorff, organized a petition and appealed to the Santa Monica (California) City Council to put a crosswalk at a dangerous junction near his former house. The city engineer said that the city was in fact planning to take out all the crosswalks because their study showed that pedestrians were more likely to get killed in crosswalks than anywhere else. The people of Santa Monica should be grateful to Peter. He took the time to explain that the result was not because crosswalks are inherently more dangerous but rather because that's where people cross the road.

Assessing the true impact of hospitals or of a particular treatment or drug is difficult unless we understand who is being treated. The medical community uses randomized drug trials to test the efficacy of medicines. Patients are randomly split into two groups: half get the medicine being tested and half get a placebo. The effectiveness of the drugs is determined by comparing the performance of the two groups. This is exactly the procedure followed in developing and testing the COVID-19 vaccines. If, alternatively, the medicine is given only to the sickest patients, then even if it is an effective treatment the group getting the medicine might do worse than the group that did not. Likewise, if aid agencies target aid at those nations facing the most serious problems, then aid could appear ineffective even if it was actually working.

Ideally, to assess the effectiveness of aid, the international community should undertake controlled experiments, giving aid to some randomly chosen nations and withholding it from others. But since it is unlikely aid will ever be allocated in this way, economists need to use complex (and controversial) statistical procedures to adjust the results according to which nations get treated. Rather than delve into these convoluted procedures, we offer some simple evidence based on the United Nations Security Council (UNSC).

The UNSC is composed of five permanent members (the United States, Russia, China, Britain, and France) and ten temporary members. The temporary members are elected for two-year terms on the Security Council, and they are ineligible to be reelected in the two years after their term expires. Election to the UNSC is highly prestigious—and, as it turns out, valuable too. Unfortunately, its value comes at a cost: hardship for the people in many of the countries that get elected. On average, nations elected to the UNSC grow more slowly, become less democratic, and have more restrictions on press freedoms than eligible nations that are not elected.[23] For instance, during a two-year term on the UNSC, the economy grows an average of 1.2 percent less for nations elected to the council than for nations not elected. Over a four-year period (the two years on the UNSC and the following two years of ineligibility), the difference in growth averages 3.5 percent less for elected UNSC members—that is, nearly 1 percent per year. The effects are much stronger in autocracies than democracies.

The effects of council membership on growth are fascinating and should cause us to question why the UN is held in such high regard. They also provide an important piece of evidence about the impact of aid. Nations elected to the UNSC get more aid. A UNSC seat gives leaders valuable favors to sell in the form of their vote on the Security Council, and the aid they receive results in worse performance for their economy. Recently there have been a profusion of studies that show that nations elected to the UNSC get financial rewards from the international community. They get more US and UN aid and better terms and more programs at the IMF, World Bank, and a host of other institutions.[24] Membership on the UNSC gives national leaders a say in formulating global policy. Many leaders, particularly those from autocratic nations, appear to prefer to sell this influence rather than exercise it on behalf of their people's interests.

UNSC membership comes as close to a randomized test as we are likely to get. Although who gets elected is not random, it is unrelated to the need for aid. Indeed, population size appears to be the only systematic determinant of UNSC elections. African nations, in particular, appear to have adopted a norm of rotation. Nations are elected simply because it is their turn. The key point is that prior to their election, UNSC members behave no differently from other nations. But once elected, they actually underperform. To return to the medical analogy, nations elected to the UNSC are not sicker than nations not elected. They get an extra shot of medicine (aid) and it makes them sicker (poorer, less democratic, and with more restrictions on the press).

UNSC membership gives leaders the opportunity to sell salient policy support. As we have seen over and over again, autocrats need to pay off their coalition. Aid provides the money to do so and that helps leaders survive. Further, aid encourages autocrats to reduce freedoms for two reasons. First, aid revenue means leaders are less dependent upon the willingness of people to work, so the leader does not need to take as many of the risks that arise from freedom, risks they must take when their revenue and worker productivity depend on allowing people to communicate with each other. Second, the policy concessions are generally unpopular, so leaders need to suppress dissent. UNSC membership brings prominence and prestige to a nation. For an autocratic leader, it also means more easy money. For the people of autocratic nations, UNSC membership means fewer freedoms, less democracy, less wealth, and more misery.

The historical record shows that aid has largely failed to lift nations out of poverty. It is perhaps ironic that while aid affords the resources to alleviate poverty and promote economic growth, it creates the political incentives to do just the opposite. As Edward Walker, US ambassador to Egypt (1994–1998), succinctly put it, "Aid offers an easy way out for Egypt to avoid reform."[25]

AN ASSESSMENT OF FOREIGN AID

So what are we to think of foreign aid? Is it good for policy, or just good politics?

It has certainly had its successes. Foreign aid, in the form of the Marshall Plan, lifted the predominantly democratic nations of Western Europe out of economic disaster after World War II. But the deck was stacked in the plan's favor. The United States wanted to promote an economically powerful bloc as a means of combating Soviet expansion. The plan therefore promoted economic growth. Democrats need policy success and so were happy to comply with US policy goals in exchange for substantial aid. Yet as we now know, subsequent aid donations have failed to replicate the success of the Marshall Plan.

What aid does well is help dictators cling to power and withhold freedoms. And yet, the quest to make aid work for the poor is phoenixlike in its ability to rise and rise again. Or, come to think of it, maybe, like Sisyphus, we just keep climbing the same hill only to fall down again.

Every decade or so, donor nations launch new initiatives to "get aid working." The most recent manifestation of this is the Millennium Development Goals. Set up by the United Nations Development Program and adopted by world leaders in 2000, this program set poverty, health, gender equality, education, and environmental targets to be reached by 2015. For instance, the poverty eradication goals called for reducing by half the number of people living on less than a dollar per day. Commendable as such declarations are, saying you want to make poor people richer, or at least less poor, and actually doing so are completely different things. Happily, the world saw a big reduction in the number of people living on less than a dollar a day. However, economists overwhelmingly attribute the reduction in the size of this group to the adoption of freer trade and more market orientations, not to foreign economic assistance.

Millennium Development Goals was not the first to declare a goal of ending poverty or the last. In 2021 the World Bank reported that "for almost 25 years, extreme poverty—the first of the world's Sustainable Development Goals—was steadily declining. Now, for the first time in a generation, the quest to end poverty has suffered a setback. Global extreme poverty rose in 2020 for the first time in over 20 years as the disruption of the COVID-19 pandemic compounded the forces of conflict and climate change, which were already slowing poverty reduction progress."[26] Earlier efforts as well were intended to attain "self-sustained growth" first, in the 1940s and 1950s through infrastructure development and then with the US P-4 program to make scientific and technological breakthroughs readily available to poor countries, followed in turn by John Kennedy's declaration that the 1960s would be the "Decade for Development." The goals, set back in the late 1940s, remain the same, and scant evidence suggests that the world is closer to achieving those goals than it was in the 1950s or 1960s. Economist William Easterly discussed the hope and optimism that accompany these roughly once-a-decade initiatives. He lamented that while each new plan says it will be different, it repeats the same errors of the past. He argued that the bureaucracy involved in giving aid ensures funds are given in ways that impede rather than promote economic activity. Poverty persists.[27]

Still, we don't need to be completely pessimistic about aid. Our knowledge of how it works has greatly improved. For instance, we know that aid works much better in the presence of good governance (just as we know that more often than not it goes to places with bad governance).[28] Proponents of development assistance point to the success of nongovernmental organizations (NGOs) undertaking directed programs within nations. Some of these programs have produced wonderful successes. For instance, in 1986 the Carter Center started a plan to combat Guinea worm disease, a parasite transmitted via dirty drinking water that affected about 3.5 million people in seventeen nations across Asia and Africa. By 2019, worldwide infections had been reduced to just 54, mostly in Africa.

NGOs have proven that they can effectively deliver basic health care and primary education. Yet, harking back to our discussion of public goods provided by small-coalition regimes, we can't help but notice that these benefits are precisely the kinds of public policy programs that even the most autocratic leaders want to initiate. NGOs are less successful at providing advanced education. Autocratic leaders in recipient states don't want people to be taught how to think independently lest they organize opposition to the government.

The successes of NGOs in promoting basic education, basic health care and sanitation, and other basic necessities—by, for example, digging wells, electrifying villages, and making very small business loans (at what we would describe in the United States as usurious interest rates)—all point to a fundamental failing of aid programs and to the harm being done unwittingly by many NGOs and their supporters. It is a simple fact that aid money is fungible. This means recipient governments have nearly complete discretion in moving funds from one project to another. With direct government-to-government transfers it is easy to see why this is so. Autocrats want to provide private rewards for their supporters. NGOs don't typically want to help the rich get richer, and so they provide funding for specific projects or do the work themselves. However, in practice, recipients are very skilled at converting aid into the kinds of rewards they want rather than the kinds of rewards donors want to provide.

The most sensible criterion for assessing aid's effectiveness asks not how much money is spent or even how many wells are dug, schools built, or villages electrified, but rather how many people are helped. NGOs count how much money they spend to evaluate their efficacy, but this is a flawed criterion. It encourages charities to help the easiest to reach and the more visible cases while ignoring the harder-to-reach people who might well be those in greatest need. Counting the number of people helped also encourages agencies to undertake work that the government would have otherwise done on its own. Remember that NGOs are most successful at providing basic public goods like primary education and basic health care—services even autocrats want. When aid funds substitute for government spending, then few people, maybe even no one, have actually been helped unless the government uses the freed-up money for other projects of benefit to the general population. Of course, they don't. They use the money to shore up their political position and the loyalty of their essential backers.

Cambodia is a case in point. Half of the Cambodian government's budget is made up of foreign aid. Rather than supplementing government programs, these donor funds are largely directed toward the bank accounts of government officials. Indeed, Cambodia ranks among the world's most corrupt nations. As USAID reported, "Donor funds have flowed into education and health, and some of these are passed on to ordinary citizens. But, there can be little doubt a significant portion of funds earmarked for schools, teachers and textbooks, and for clinics, health workers, and medications are diverted."[29]

In other words, the funds intended for the people are diverted to rewards for Cambodia's rich. Often when NGOs provide aid, the amount of assistance is substantially less than the numbers reflect. Suppose an NGO provides basic education to one hundred children in a village at a cost of $100 per child per year, for a total expenditure of $10,000. It sounds like one hundred people are helped by the NGO, pleasing its donors and bringing in more money. The reality of how many are helped, however, is less clear. The government might well have paid to educate half of those children (or even all of them) itself, even if there were no expectation of aid. Nominally the agency helps one hundred children. But in reality they help fifty children at twice the nominal cost and let the leaders abscond with $5,000. Is this good? Well, yes, for the fifty extra children. Is it bad? Well, yes, for all of the people, since the NGO is facilitating the government's opportunity to steal more money and the NGO is helping to further entrench a bad government in power to plague the people for many more years to come.

Even some of the simplest acts of charity have bad consequences that enhance government control and irresponsibility. To take a personal example, Alastair took his children on a tour of Kenya in 2009. One of the stops was at a primary school where they were encouraged to help paint classrooms. It seemed like a nice idea to help out, and many people enthusiastically grabbed paintbrushes, eager to brighten the classroom. Alastair objected on principle and went outside and taught some of the kids how to use a digital camera. Was he being a Grinch or was he encouraging better economic policy? From the economic perspective, having highly skilled tourists and their families paint classrooms is at best ineffective and at worst downright harmful.

Comparative advantage lies at the heart of economics. Everyone should specialize in what they are relatively good at and then trade their goods and services. This way everyone ends up with more than if everyone tried to do a little of everything by themselves. Consider the comparative advantage of Kenya relative to Britain, where most of the people on Alastair's trip were from. Education levels are low in Kenya and there are lots of unemployed manual laborers. Kenya's comparative advantage is therefore in industries requiring lots of relatively unskilled labor. Indeed, this is where it flourishes: Kenya is a huge exporter of flowers. It has a great climate for growing and lots of people to tend to the labor-intensive processes of growing, picking, and packaging flowers. The flowers are then flown to Western Europe for sale. In exchange, Europe exports goods that require human and physical capital to produce—pharmaceuticals, machinery, and computer software. Europe has a relative abundance of human and physical capital. It trades its capital-intensive products for Kenya's labor-intensive agricultural products, and both nations are better off.

So what has this to do with painting school classrooms? Well, having tourists paint classrooms, while fun, deprived a local worker of a much-needed job. If educated Westerners displace locals from manual labor jobs, then where can those workers possibly work given the current distribution of skills and capital? How can they earn enough money to make a living and perhaps send their children to school to acquire greater skills that will make them more competitive when they grow up? Rather than helping out, the wealthy tourists who took up paintbrushes made some worker worse off. Repeat that exercise thousands of times and in thousands of different ways and you can see how feel-good charitable acts can benefit the donor vastly more than they actually benefit the needy.

On a much larger scale, the means of aiding needy countries can be dramatically improved by taking stock of comparative advantage. For instance, agriculture is highly protected from competition in Europe and North America through price supports and subsidies. Agriculture was deliberately excluded from the postwar trade settlement established by the General Agreement on Tariffs and Trade and its controversial successor, the World Trade Organization. This is because rural areas are disproportionately represented in some countries and so farmers tend to be the essential backers of leaders in many European countries. Allowing farmers from developing nations to compete on the basis of comparative advantage would go much further toward promoting economic growth than providing poorly targeted and highly bureaucratized aid. Painting schools provides just one tiny example of how assistance, even when well meaning, undermines development. Bill Easterly's work shows that rather than this being the exception, it is the norm.

AID SHAKEDOWNS

We started this chapter with an account of Haile Selassie's shakedown of donors. By now it should be clear that this practice is all too common and reflects the logic of privately given aid. When private donors provide aid, governments must either strike deals with them so that the government gets its cut—that, after all, is the value of aid to a small-coalition regime—or, in the absence of such deals, they must shake down well-intentioned private donors. Either way, the government must get its piece of the action or it will make it impossible for donors to deliver assistance. That is what the Myanmar government did following Cyclone Nargis in 2008. They insisted on having United Nations aid delivered to the government and threatened to bar it from the country if it wasn't. Why? Because, as we noted earlier, the military dictatorship wanted to use the aid to enrich itself by selling food on the black market rather than distributing it to those most in need. You might think this was the odd behavior of a horrible regime, atypical of the response of government leaders following natural disasters. Not so! Consider the case of Oxfam relief for Sri Lanka in the wake of the 2004 Indian Ocean tsunami.

Following a massive earthquake on December 26, 2004, a tsunami sent huge waves of water rushing inland, killing more than 230,000 people across fourteen nations. Subsequent assistance totaled over $14 billion. Yet even though the goal of aid agencies was to relieve suffering, many recipient governments took it as an opportunity to enrich themselves.

To distribute aid, Oxfam shipped twenty-five four-wheel-drive trucks to the region. The Sri Lankan government impounded the trucks and insisted that Oxfam pay a 300 percent import duty. For over a month (the first critical month after the tsunami) the trucks sat idle and people went without food and shelter. Eventually Oxfam paid over $1 million to have its trucks released.

Before giving to a charity, many people like to assess how much of their donation goes to help people versus how much is spent on overhead. Oxfam America, for instance, gets three out of four stars from Charity Navigator, an organization that rates charities. Oxfam spends 6 percent of its revenue on administrative expenses and 14 percent on fundraising. The remaining 80 percent is spent on programs—that is, on helping people. Unfortunately, eighty cents on the dollar is not the effective amount of help provided. Remember those trucks and the 300 percent import duty: if such cases are the norm (and they usually are), the actual aid benefit may only equate to twenty cents on the dollar. If even as careful a charity as Oxfam is being shaken down, then we wonder what is happening to the rest.

It is virtually impossible to quantify how much aid gets diverted toward the recipient government's objectives rather than working toward the donor's intended goals. However, we suspect this figure is huge. The fundamental problem is that recipient governments are not appropriately incentivized to fix problems. Consider the case of flooding in Pakistan in 2010. No one could blame the government for the rains, but they were very much accountable for the subsequent devastation. Over twenty million people were affected, four million were made homeless, and nearly two thousand died.

Following severe floods in the 1970s, Pakistan set up the Federal Flood Commission. On paper this agency has completed about $900 million worth of dike construction. Of course the reality is very different. Irrigation and flood control are a source of graft, not public policy. And when the dikes are built, they serve the interests of the wealthy—that is, coalition members, not the people. As the floods swept downstream and threatened huge segments of the population, President Zardari, who was nicknamed "Mister 10 Percent" for his alleged penchant to take that portion as his cut, acted as a good autocrat should. He ignored the problem, headed off to Europe for a high-profile tour, and left his government to sacrifice the many to save the few. The government reinforced dikes to protect essential supporters while allowing flooding to continue in poor areas. Areas with ethnic minorities and large numbers of opposition supporters were particularly likely to flood.[30]

Richard Holbrooke, the late US Special Representative for Pakistan, described the flood as "an equal opportunity disaster," but this is far from the truth. Beholden to a few, Pakistani leaders sacrificed the many. They reinforced barrages and dikes to protect the homes and farms of their supporters and ignored the plight of towns and villages. A local official acknowledged, "Local government figures in the Sindh province conspired with prominent landowners to bolster the riverbank running through their property and others deemed important, at the expense of other regions, which were left vulnerable to flood waters. . . . It was not just incompetence on the part of the authorities to protect the poorest of the poor from potential floods; it was their deliberate intention that they should suffer if floods were to take place."[31]

Obviously, from a good governance stance, this behavior makes no sense. But in terms of ruling for one's own survival, it is an ingenious move. Supporters were reminded of the consequences of being outside the coalition of essential backers. That is good for loyalty. And aid agencies rushed to give money. The UN secretary general, Ban Ki-moon, described the flooding as the worst he had ever seen and called for massive foreign assistance. Many Pakistanis preferred to directly assist those affected; as one noted, "We don't donate to the government because we know it's mainly a way for government officials to make money."[32] The international community was less careful. They gave Pakistan $1.7 billion in the first three months. That equates to about $83 per affected person. Presumably much of the money was siphoned off. It certainly was not used for efficient disaster management.

Pakistan was not the only nation affected by severe floods in 2010. Benin faced historic floods that covered two-thirds of the country. Although the absolute numbers were smaller because Benin is a much smaller country, in proportion to its size, the scale of the disaster was very similar to that in Pakistan. Benin received much less assistance, only about one-twentieth of the aid per affected person that Pakistan received. Yet despite this, its response has been widely praised. But then, of course, Benin is much more democratic than Pakistan. As we have seen over and over again, democratic countries use money much more wisely than autocracies.

It is easy to understand why Zardari did so little to minimize the impact of the flood on the masses, and, some have suggested, he may have deliberately made things worse. He had strong financial incentives. As the magnitude of the disaster increased, so did the amount of aid. His survival depended on paying off the few rather than protecting the many. Aid incentivizes autocratic leaders to fail to fix problems. Had Pakistan implemented an effective flood-management program instead of just saying they had, then the people would have been much better off, but Zardari would have had no pretext to further fleece donors.

Similar incentives plagued Pakistani assistance with the war on terror. Following the terrorist attacks of 2001, the United States repeatedly sought Pakistan's assistance in fighting the Taliban and al-Qaeda and in capturing international terrorists—first and foremost, Osama bin Laden, the leader of al-Qaeda, who was believed to be hiding in the tribal regions of northwestern Pakistan. Through 2011, when bin Laden was located and killed by US forces, the US paid Pakistan $12.3 billion in economic and military aid. If Pakistan had captured bin Laden and prevented the Taliban from operating in northern Pakistan, then the United States would have been very grateful. But it would also no longer have needed to pay Pakistan. Just as effective disaster management reduces the amount of foreign aid, capturing bin Laden would have diminished the need to give aid to Pakistan's leaders—or so we speculated back in 2010 in this book's first edition. Now we can look at what happened to the amount of aid received by Pakistan after bin Laden's death. Figure 7.2 shows the annual US economic assistance to Pakistan from the year 2000 to 2020. It seems that after bin Laden's death, US assistance to Pakistan went into steep decline. No wonder the Pakistanis were so angry when the US military eliminated bin Laden, the reason for Pakistan's foreign-aid feast.

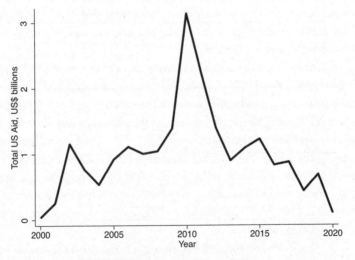

Figure 7.2: US Foreign Assistance to Pakistan

To understand how aid works, it is essential to take into account the incentives from the perspective of the leaders who enact policy. Unless aid is restructured to change these incentives, Pakistan has little reason to end insurgency and terrorism. Instead, both will be allowed to rumble on and encouraged to expand if the West tries to cut aid. Fortunately, in addition to identifying problematic incentives, our perspective offers the tools to restructure aid to create incentives to fix problems.

FIXING AID POLICY

The modus operandi of the international community is to give recipient nations money to fix problems. A common argument is that the locals know much better how to address their problems than do faraway donors. That's probably true, but knowing how to fix local problems and having the will or desire to do so is quite another matter. This policy of giving money to recipients in anticipation of their fixing problems should stop. Instead the United States should escrow money, paying it out only when objectives are achieved.

Consider the problem of capturing bin Laden. In 2009, the United States' top commander, Stanley McChrystal, testified before a Senate committee, "I don't think that we can finally defeat al-Qaeda until [bin Laden is] captured or killed."[33] Suppose the United States thought $6 billion was a reasonable reward for his capture. Remember: through 2011, the year he was located and killed by US forces, the US government had spent over $12 billion without success. Remember also that in 2011 bin Laden was living in a mansion less than a mile from the Pakistan Military Academy. We suspect that the Pakistani government had not really made an effort commensurate with $12 billion!

Rather than dole out billions of dollars each year, suppose the US escrowed $6 billion, say at a Swiss bank. Upon bin Laden's capture or death, Pakistan's government could have received these funds. The deal could perhaps have been done more cheaply by dispensing with the fiction that the money was for the Pakistani people and instead paying it directly to Pakistan's leaders.

If aid took the form of a reward-in-escrow scheme, then Zardari would have needed to hand over bin Laden to receive money. However, unlike the incentives that existed, he could have delivered without fearing that the money would dry up once his assistance was no longer needed.

Zardari might have proved unwilling or unable to capture bin Laden for $6 billion. However, had this been the case, then the United States would have lost little. The US paid $12 billion and Zardari did not help find bin Laden's compound (or at least there is no public evidence that he helped). Had he stood to gain $6 billion, he might have handed him over rather than pretend to be looking for him while the money kept flowing.

Undoubtedly there are many operational and procedural problems with implementing an aid-in-escrow scheme. And these problems would be even more difficult when it comes to designing escrowed aid relief for disaster management. Yet it is better to tackle these tricky technical issues within a framework that incentivizes leaders to solve the problem the donor wants to address than to carry on with failed policies.

NATION BUILDING

What, then, are the fundamental incentives for one institution to interfere with the institutions of another? Democracies often claim that they want to democratize other nations. They frequently justify both aid and military intervention on this basis, but the evidence that they actually promote democracy is scant (except in a very few marginal cases, as we noted earlier). Those who defend such policies tend to cite Germany and Japan after World War II, but that was more than seventy years ago, and on close examination it took many years before these nations developed (or were permitted to develop) independent foreign policies. The reality is that in most cases democracies, or any other form of government for that matter, don't want to create democracies. Remember back in Chapter 2, we discussed why Rome chose to back the autocratic Damasus for pope rather than the more democratic Ursinus. Like contemporary US presidents, Rome's emperor recognized that democrats are hard to influence and control. Promoting democracy overseas makes for great rhetoric, but it seldom enhances a leader's interests. Democrats don't want to create democracies.

In 1939, US president Franklin Delano Roosevelt famously remarked about Anastasio Somoza, a brutal Nicaraguan dictator, "He's a son of a bitch, but at least he's our son of a bitch." And herein lies the rub. Dictators are cheap to buy. They deliver policies that democratic leaders and their constituents want, and, being beholden to relatively few essential backers, autocrats can be bought cheaply. They can be induced to trade policies the democrat wants for money the autocrat needs. Buying democrats is much more expensive. Almost every US president has argued that he wants to foster democracy in the world. However, the same US presidents have had no problem undermining democratic, or democratizing, regimes when the people of those nations elect leaders to implement policies US voters don't like.

Undermining democracy was the story behind US opposition to the Congo's first democratically elected prime minister, Patrice Lumumba. He was elected in June 1960 and murdered on January 17, 1961, just half a year later. Lumumba ran into difficulty with Western democracies because of the policies he adopted, not because he usurped power. He spoke out vehemently against the years of Belgian rule over the Congo. In a speech during Congo's independence celebration less than a week after his election as prime minister, Lumumba announced, "Nous ne sommes plus vos singes" (We are no longer your monkeys).[34] In an effort to remove Belgian troops and diplomats from the Congo and to defeat the secessionist movement in Katanga Province led by Moise Tshombe, Lumumba sought Soviet military assistance. That was a big political error. The massive bulk of evidence today points to US and Belgian complicity in Lumumba's murder. Later the United States would become closely associated with the Congo's (that is, Zaire's) Mobutu Sese Seko, who, unlike Lumumba, was neither democratic nor pro-Soviet. For a price (totaling billions by the time he fell out of power thirty-two years after his ascent), Mobutu was willing to back US policy. Democratically elected Lumumba was not, and that meant he had to go.

Lumumba was not exceptional in his downfall at the hands of democratic leaders. Hawaii's Queen Liliuokalani was overthrown in 1893. Her sin? She wanted Hawaii and Hawaiians (no doubt including herself) to profit from the exploitation of farming and export opportunities pursued by large American and European firms operating in Hawaii. As these business interests organized to depose her, the United States sent in marines, ostensibly to maintain peace from a neutral stance but in fact making it impossible for the Hawaiian monarch to defend herself. And then we ought not to forget the overthrow of democratically elected Juan Bosch in the Dominican Republic at the hands of the American military in 1965. His offense: he liked Fidel Castro. Or Salvador Allende in Chile, Mohammad Mosaddegh in Iran, or US opposition to the democratically elected Hamas government in the Palestinian Authority, and the list goes on. As we write these words, we see this policy of reluctance to promote democracy at work for the US in the Persian Gulf. The United States has a long history of supporting useful autocrats. Indeed, US policy in that part of the world stands as a perfect example of the perils of democratization. Any incipient democracies in the Gulf would be unlikely to be positively inclined toward US interests, in part because of deep policy differences and in part because we've been funding for decades the oppression under which they have been governed. So the United States continued to back Saudi Arabia's monarchy even after a Saudi *Washington Post* writer, Jamal Khashoggi, was murdered in the Saudi embassy in Istanbul, Turkey.

In case after case, the story is the same. Democrats prefer compliant foreign regimes to democratic ones. Democratic interventionists, while proclaiming to be using military force to pursue democratization, have a profound tendency to reduce the degree of democracy in their targets while increasing policy compliance by easily purchased autocrats.[35]

Before reading this chapter you might have been under the impression that democrats are angels compared to their autocratic counterparts. This chapter has tarnished that image, and there will be more tarnishing to come. But rather than deplore European and Japanese prime ministers and US presidents on principle, we need to pause for a moment and consider what they are doing and why.

Democrats deliver what the people want. Because they have to stand for election and reelection, democrats are impatient. They have a short time horizon. For them, the long run is the next election, not the next twenty years. However, as long as *we the people* want cheap gasoline and an abundance of markets in which to dump agricultural products, and we want that more than we want to see genuine development in poor countries, then our leaders are going to carry out our wishes. If they don't, why, they'll be replaced with someone who will. That's what democracy is all about—government of, by, and for the people *at home*.

As a classroom experience, Bruce likes to ask his students how many of them want to help remove poverty in Nigeria or Mali. This idea produces universal support. And virtually everyone wants the government to provide aid to make it happen. Yet when push comes to shove, enthusiasm fades. For instance, he asks how many students are willing to give up their mobile phone service and have the funds sent to help Nigeria. Hardly a hand goes up. And when he asks about reducing their low-interest student loans if the money goes to the world's poor, even fewer hands go up, even though he reminds them that they are the world's incredibly rich "poor" and that they profess to want to help the world's truly poor. Not at their own expense!

Aid is a tool for buying influence and policy. Unless we the people really value development and are willing to make meaningful sacrifices toward it, then aid will continue to fail in its stated goals. Democrats are not thuggish brutes. They just want to keep their jobs, and to do so they need to deliver the policies their people want. Despite the idealistic expressions of some, all too many of us prefer cheap oil to real change in West Africa or the Middle East. So we really should not complain too much when our leaders try to deliver what we want. That, after all, is what democracy is about.

CHAPTER EIGHT

THE PEOPLE IN REVOLT

A successful leader always puts the wants of his essential supporters before the needs of the people.[1] Without the support of his coalition a leader is nothing and is quickly swept away by a rival. But keeping the coalition content comes at a price when the leader's control depends on only a few. More often than not, the coalition's members get paid at the cost of the rest of society. Sure, a few autocrats become Hall of Famers who make their citizens better off. Most don't. And those who don't will spend their time in office running down their nation's economy for the benefit of themselves and their coalition. Eventually things get bad enough that some of the people tire of their burden. Then they, too, can threaten the survival of their leader.

Although the threat of revolution is not as omnipresent as the threat posed by the risk of coalition defection, if the people take to the streets en masse, they may succeed in overwhelming the power of the state. Working out how to prevent and deal with such revolutionary threats is therefore a crucial lesson for dictators. It is also crucial for would-be revolutionaries, who must work out what the right timing is for an uprising and whether members of the regime's winning coalition will support them or the incumbent. We examine these concerns now.

TO PROTEST OR NOT TO PROTEST

In autocracies the people get a raw deal. We now know that their labor provides tax revenues that leaders lavish on essential core supporters. Leaders provide them with little beyond the essential, minimal health care, primary education, and food that they need in order to work. And if a small-coalition leader is fortunate enough to have another source of revenue, such as natural resources or a benevolent foreign donor, then he may even be able to do away with these minimal provisions. Autocrats certainly don't provide political freedoms. Life for people in most small-coalition regimes is solitary, poor, nasty, brutish, and short. The people, seeing the hopeless path they are on, invariably want change. They want a government that provides for them and under which they can live secure, happy, and productive lives.

Why, having suffered long and hard, might they suddenly and often in multitudes rise up against their government? The answer resides in a crucial moment, a tipping point, at which life in the future under the existing government is expected to be sufficiently bad that it is worth their while to risk the undoubted costs of rebellion. They must believe that some few who have come forward first in rebellion have a decent chance of success and a decent chance of making the lives of ordinary people better.

There is a delicate balance here. If a regime excels at convincing people that stepping out of line means incredible misery and even death, it is unlikely to experience rebellion. Yes, life under such a government is horrendous, but the risk of failure in a revolt and the costs of that failure are way too high for people to rise up. They might be killed or imprisoned, and they might lose their job or home, even their children. That is why the Hitlers, Stalins, and Kim Jong-Uns of the world manage to avoid revolt. If rule is really harsh, people are effectively deterred from rising up.

At first, a few especially bold individuals may rise up in revolt. They proclaim their intention to make their country a democracy. Every revolution and every mass movement begins with a promise of democratic reform, of a new government that will lift up the downtrodden and alleviate their suffering. That is an essential ingredient in getting the masses to take to the streets. Of course, it doesn't always work.

The Chinese Communists, for instance, declared the formation of a Chinese Soviet Republic on November 7, 1931. They said of their newly declared state, "It is the state of the suppressed workers, farmers, soldiers, and working mass. Its flag calls for the downfall of imperialism, the liquidation of landlords, the overthrow of the warlord government of the Nationalists. We shall establish a soviet government over the whole of China; we shall struggle for the interests of thousands of deprived workers, farmers, and soldiers and other suppressed masses; and to endeavor for peaceful unification of the whole of China."[2]

Jomo Kenyatta, the leader of Kenya's independence movement and its first head of state, likewise declared during a meeting of the Kenya African Union on July 26, 1952:

> If we unite now, each and every one of us, and each tribe to another, we will cause the implementation in this country of that which the European calls democracy. True democracy has no colour distinction. It does not choose between black and white. We are here in this tremendous gathering under the K.A.U. flag to find which road leads us from darkness into democracy. In order to find it we Africans must first achieve the right to elect our own representatives. That is surely the first principle of democracy. We are the only race in Kenya which does not elect its own representatives in the Legislature and we are going to set about to rectify this situation.... It has never been known in history that a country prospers without equality. We despise bribery and corruption, those two words that the European repeatedly refers to. Bribery and corruption is prevalent in this country, but I am not surprised. As long as a people are held down, corruption is sure to rise and the only answer to this is a policy of equality.[3]

Noble words from both Mao Zedong and Jomo Kenyatta. Neither fulfilled his promises of equality, democracy, and liberty for the average Chinese or the average Kenyan. Nor did either leader eliminate corruption and special opportunities for their party faithful. Once most revolutionaries come to power, their inclination—if they can get away with it—is to be petty dictators. After all, the democratic institutions that engender the policies the people want also make it hard for leaders to survive in office. Leaders won't acquiesce to the people's wants unless the people can compel them. And when can the people compel an old dictator, seemingly set in his ways, or a recently victorious revolutionary, newly ensconced in power, to look out for them instead of for himself? The answer to that question is the answer to when regimes choose the road to democracy rather than to sustained autocracy.

Before deciding to gamble on the promises of revolutionaries, each prospective demonstrator must judge the costs and the risks of rebellion to be tolerable relative to the conditions expected without rebellion and relative to the gains expected with a successful uprising. Thus it is that middle-of-the-road dictators, like Cuba's Fulgencio Batista, Tunisia's Ben Ali, Egypt's Hosni Mubarak, and the Soviet Union's Gorbachev (but not Stalin), are more likely to experience a mass uprising than their worst fellow autocrats. That is not to say that when the people rise up they are right in thinking life will be better. They are taking a calculated risk. They surely understand that revolutionary success holds the prospect of betterment, but not all revolutionary movements end in democracy, and not all result in an outpouring of public goods for the people.

Many revolutions end up simply replacing one autocracy with another. On some occasions the successor regime can actually be worse than its predecessor. This might well have been the case with Sergeant Doe's deposition of Liberia's True Whig government or Mao's success against Chiang Kai-shek's Kuomintang government in China. But the hope of the people when they participate is that they will improve their lot, either by enlarging the winning coalition through democratization or at least by becoming part of the new coalition.

NIPPING MASS MOVEMENTS IN THE BUD

There are two diametrically opposed ways in which a leader can respond to the threat of a revolution. He can increase democracy, making the people so much better off that they no longer want to revolt. He can also increase dictatorship, making the people even more miserable than they were before while also depriving them of a credible chance of success in rising up against their government.

The extent of expected loyalty from the military is one critical factor that shapes the direction an incumbent takes in responding to a nascent threat. Leaders know that as isolated individuals the people are no threat to their government. That is precisely why government leaders are reluctant to let people freely assemble and organize against them. If the people find a way to take to the streets en masse, the incumbent will certainly need very loyal supporters willing to undertake the decidedly dirty work of suppressing the masses if he is to survive.

We have met many leaders whose backers deserted them at just such key times. When insurgents challenged Sergeant Doe in 1990, his soldiers terrorized and stole from the people of Liberia rather than combat the threat. In 1979, the shah of Iran was deposed when his soldiers joined the supporters of Ayatollah Khomeini. Similarly, President Ferdinand Marcos in the Philippines lost power in 1986 because his security forces defected. Russia's Czar Nicholas was deposed when the people stormed his Winter Palace in St. Petersburg in 1917. The army, poorly paid and facing deployment to the front in World War I, declined to stop them. Many other crucial events in modern political history, from the French Revolution to the collapse of the Soviet Union and its satellite states, also owe their occurrence to the failure of core supporters to suppress the people at critical moments. The post–Cold War so-called colored revolutions (Georgia's Rose Revolution in 2003, Ukraine's Orange Revolution in 2004–2005, and the Tulip Revolution in Kyrgyzstan in 2005), the Jasmine revolution in Tunisia, as well as the uprisings in Egypt are also manifestations of the same phenomenon.

In each case, coalition support evaporated at the key moment because the leader could no longer promise his or her supporters an adequate flow of rewards to justify their undertaking the dirty work required to keep the regime in place. The Russian czar, France's Louis XVI, and the Soviet Union were all short of money with which to reward supporters. The Philippines' Marcos and Iran's shah were both known to be terminally ill. Ben Ali and Mubarak were both elderly and thought to be seriously ill. New leaders typically reshuffle their coalition, so key backers of the regime were uncertain whether they would be retained by the successor. Lacking assurance that they would continue to be rewarded, they stood aside and allowed the people to rebel.

Revolutionary movements may seem spontaneous, but we really need to understand that they arise when enough citizens believe they have a realistic chance of success. That is why successful autocrats make rebellion truly unattractive. They step in quickly to punish harshly those who first take to the streets. This is what we saw in Iran following the June 2009 presidential election. The regime quickly stepped in, beating, arresting, and killing protesters, until the people feared continuing to take to the streets.

A prudent dictator nips rebellion in the bud. That is why we have reiterated the claim that only people willing to engage in really nasty behavior should contemplate becoming dictators. The softhearted will find themselves ousted in the blink of an eye.

PROTEST IN DEMOCRACY AND AUTOCRACY

Dissatisfaction with what a government is doing is an entirely different matter in democracies than it is in autocracies. In a democracy, protest is relatively cheap and easy. People have the freedom and, indeed, the right to assemble. They also have easy means through which to coordinate and organize. We know from earlier chapters that governments ruled by a large coalition produce lots of public goods, including a special set of such goods that fall under the general heading of freedoms. These include a free press, free speech, and freedom of assembly. These freedom goods make it much easier for large numbers of people to exchange information about how they feel about their government and to express objections to any policies they don't like.

These freedoms also make protest easy. But since people like these freedoms, granting them can also dissipate their desire to bring down the government. Protests are common in democracies, but revolts intending to overthrow the institutions of government are not. Democrats provide the policies people want because otherwise the people will protest, and when people can freely assemble there is little a leader can do to stop them except give them what they want. Sometimes, of course, democratic leaders fail to give the people what they want. Then people are likely to take to the streets to indicate their dislike of a particular policy. That's what generally happens when a democracy goes to war, for example. Some people favor the decision and others oppose it. Those who oppose it frequently make their displeasure known by taking to the streets, and if there are enough of them and if they protest for a sufficiently sustained time, they can provoke a policy change. For instance, Lyndon Johnson chose not to seek reelection in the face of deep dissatisfaction with his Vietnam War policies.

In a democracy, protest is about alerting leaders to the fact that the people are unhappy and that, if changes in policy are not made, they'll throw the rascals out. Yet in an autocracy, protest has a deeper purpose: to bring down the very institutions of government and change the way the people are governed.

Autocrats dislike freedoms because they make it easy for people to learn of their shared misery and to collaborate with each other to rise up against the government. Given their druthers, autocrats eliminate freedom of assembly, a free press, and free speech whenever they can, thereby insulating themselves from the threat of the people. Unfortunately for autocrats, without the public goods benefits from these freedoms, people can find it hard to work effectively because they cannot easily exchange ideas even about how to improve the workplace. And if the people don't work effectively, then the leader cannot collect tax revenues.

Autocrats must find the right balance. Without enough freedom the people are less productive and do little work, but give them too many freedoms and they pose a threat to the leader. The degree to which autocrats rely on taxation to fund the government limits the extent to which they can oppress the people.

Nations awash with natural resource wealth or lavished with foreign aid rarely democratize. They are the world's most oppressive places. Their leaders have resources to reward their essential supporters without having to empower the people. In such societies, though the people really desire change, they cannot act upon these wants. Without the ability to assemble, coordinating against the government is difficult. What is more, the people know the leader can afford to pay the coalition to oppress them. With little chance of success, the people keep their heads down. Protest is rare, and when it occurs it is answered with even greater repression.

But what happens if the money dries up?

Take a look back at Figure 7.1 in the previous chapter, where we graphed Egypt's foreign aid receipts through 2020. US aid to Egypt has been dropping as Egypt's peace with Israel has aged and matured. The drop in aid has been substantial, and that means Egypt's former president, Hosni Mubarak, found himself in a weaker and weaker position when it came to buying the loyal support of the military. The global economic slowdown in 2007–2009 compounded the importance of aid for the Egyptian regime. With money drying up, a chance was created for a rebellion against Mubarak's government. And indeed, in early 2011, Mubarak, facing a poor economy and decreased aid receipts, also faced a mass rebellion.

When autocrats lack abundant resources, they have a more difficult time managing the people. First and foremost, leaders must pay their essential backers or they will be gone. Leaders without adequate revenues from aid, natural resources, or borrowing must obtain them by encouraging the people to work and by taxing them. Unfortunately for leaders, many of the public goods that increase productivity also improve the people's ability to coordinate and, therefore, protest. Further, because the leader needs the tax revenues the workers provide, such protests are more likely to be met with concessions than in a resource-rich nation or one with huge cash reserves.

The factors that lead to rebellion are relatively uncomplicated. How much a leader does to enhance the welfare of the people by providing public goods determines the desire of the people to rebel. The level of freedom determines the ease with which they can act upon these desires by taking to the streets.

Yet, though high levels of both factors are in evidence in a host of countries around the world, protests remain rare. They require a spark.

SHOCKS RAISE REVOLTS

Shocks that trigger protest come in many forms. On rare occasions protests happen spontaneously. But more often an event is needed to shake up the system and trigger protest. In the collapse of the Soviet Union and other Communist states in Eastern Europe in 1989, contagion played a major role. Once one state fell, the people in the surrounding states realized that their state was perhaps no longer invulnerable. Free elections in Communist Poland triggered protests in East Germany. When it became clear that security forces would not obey East German leader Erich Honecker's order to break up demonstrations, the protests grew. Successful protest in Germany spawned demonstrations in Czechoslovakia, and so on. As each state fell, it provided a yet stronger signal to the peoples of the remaining Communist states. The states fell like dominos. And each was suffering from a poorly performing economy, so the Eastern European dictators could no longer assure private advantages for their supporters. Quite the contrary, they had been reduced to a state in which many of their henchmen understood it was better to abandon the dictator than go down in a blaze of glory with their failed regimes. Much the same story repeated itself in the Middle East in 2011. As Tunisia fell, the people of Egypt realized that their leader might also be vulnerable. So contagious was the belief that rebellion could succeed that the once rock-steady Middle East quickly became fertile ground for mass movements. People in Bahrain, Jordan, Yemen, Syria, Libya, and elsewhere tried their luck.

A massive natural disaster, an unanticipated succession crisis, or a global economic downturn that drives the autocrat's local economy to the brink or beyond the brink of bankruptcy can also provide a rallying cry for protesters. Most crucially, as the experiences of the shah, Marcos, and Mobutu remind us, sudden serious illness is a shock that drives the coalition away from their leader, opening the door to both rebellion and coups. Still other shocks can be "planned"—that is, events or occasions chosen by an autocrat who misjudges the risks involved. One common example is a rigged election.

Dictators seem to like to hold elections. Whether they do so to satisfy international pressure (and gain more foreign aid), to dispel domestic unrest, or to gain a misleading sense of legitimacy, their preference is to rig the vote count. Elections are nice, but winning is nicer. Still, sometimes the people seize the moment of an election to shock the incumbent, voting so overwhelmingly for someone else that it is hard to cover up the true outcome.

Liberia's Sergeant Doe was foolish enough to hold an election. In doing so, he provided the impetus for protest that he was lucky to survive. In 1985, Thomas Quiwonkpa challenged Samuel Doe after it took weeks for Liberia's electoral commission to "count" the votes. Perhaps Quiwonkpa took the commission's dalliance as a sign of popular support and equally a sign of the commission's lack of support for him. As his insurgency approached the capital, Monrovia, the masses took to the streets against Doe's government. Unfortunately for them, Doe's essential supporters remained loyal. The costs of protest became very real. Doe's soldiers killed hundreds in retribution.

In post-Soviet Eastern Europe, "legitimizing" elections helped to promote citizen uprisings. Rather than sustaining the regimes in power, elections created the opportunity to replace them. In 2004, the incumbent Ukrainian leader, Leonid Kuchma, having served two terms, decided—perhaps to the surprise of his essential backers— to respect the two-term limit and retire. His chosen successor was Viktor Yanukovych. The run-up to the election looked like it came straight out of a John le Carré spy novel, with the leading opposition candidate, Viktor Yushchenko, allegedly poisoned with dioxin, which left him horribly disfigured.

In the first round of the elections in October, each of the leading candidates received about 39 percent of the vote. This necessitated a runoff election on November 21, in which the official results differed greatly from exit polls. Even before the second-round presidential runoff was complete, Yushchenko called for the people to take to the streets. The electoral commission declared Yanukovych the winner. However, protests mounted, and the security forces withdrew. Eventually the Supreme Court ruled that given the high level of fraud, another ballot was needed. Yushchenko then won the election handily.

Coalition dynamics play a key role in explaining why the security forces allowed the people to take to the streets. The president was changing. Although the retiring incumbent, Kuchma, backed Yanukovych, he could not assure core supporters within the security forces that they would be retained after the transition. As we saw with Louis XIV and many others, newly empowered leaders, even when they have been chosen by their predecessor, are wise to shake up their coalition, bring in their own loyalists, and dump many of their predecessor's erstwhile backers. The security forces, being uncertain whether they would keep their long-run privileges, declined to attack the masses, hedging their bets about who would be more likely to reward them. Without force to control the masses on the street, Yanukovych's supporters deserted. The people brought Yushchenko to power, but an essential factor in their willingness to take to the streets was the apparent lack of support for Yanukovych by the security forces.

Sometimes the shocks that spark revolt come as a total surprise. Natural disasters, while bringing misery to the people, can also empower them. One frequent consequence of earthquakes, hurricanes, and droughts is that vast numbers of people are forced from their homes. If they are permitted to gather in refugee camps, then they have the opportunity to organize against the government. You see, refugee camps have the unintended consequence of facilitating free assembly. Earthquakes, storms, and volcanoes can concentrate large numbers of desperate people with little to lose. They also can substantially weaken the state's capacity to control the people.

On the morning of September 19, 1985, an 8.1 magnitude earthquake occurred in the Pacific Ocean about 350 kilometers from Mexico City. Mexico City is geologically vulnerable because it was built on the soft foundation of the remains of Lake Texcoco. The clay silts and sands that make up the lake bed plus the soil's high water content led to liquefaction (wherein the ground behaves like a liquid) during the earthquake. The city was also built in the absence of democratic rule, so few building codes had been enforced. As a result, the distant quake caused enormous devastation throughout the city. The death toll is highly disputed but is thought to be between 10,000 and 30,000 people. An additional 250,000 were made homeless. The government did virtually nothing. Left to rescue themselves, the people formed crews to dig for survivors and organized refugee camps.

Born of necessity, these camps became the foundation for an important political force in Mexico City. Where there had been separate individuals unhappy with their government, the earthquake formed a concentrated mass of desperate people. Forced together into crowded camps, they shared their disillusionment about the government. Organizing a protest rally was suddenly relatively easy. Ready and willing participants were on hand and had little to lose. With the government largely absent, these social groups became important political forces that rapidly deployed large antigovernment demonstrations. Unable to oppose these groups, the government sought to accommodate them. It is widely believed they played a key role in Mexico's democratization.[4]

The story of Anastasio Somoza's deposition in the Nicaraguan revolution in 1979 is broadly similar. In 1972, a 6.2 magnitude earthquake struck the capital of Managua, killing around 5,000 people and rendering about 250,000 people homeless. Somoza and his cronies profited from disaster relief but did nothing to resettle the enormous number of homeless people who had gathered in refugee camps in the capital. These camps became organizing grounds for the activists who eventually ended Somoza's reign.

Not all autocrats make the mistake of ignoring disasters or ignoring the creation of refugee camps. Consider the case of Myanmar in 2008. Than Shwe was the military leader of Myanmar (formerly known as Burma). Although he has been described as an unremarkable man, he understood the essentials of staying in power.[5] On May 2, 2008, a massive cyclone named Nargis swept across the Irrawaddy Delta in southern Burma, causing havoc. The delta's residents, mainly poor fishermen and farmers, had received no advance warning of the storm, which destroyed entire towns and villages. The official death toll is 138,000, though other estimates suggest it might be as high as 500,000.

No one can blame Than Shwe for the storm or for the low-lying villages' vulnerability to storm surge. However, Myanmar's military regime provided no warning before and did nothing to help the survivors after, and for that they can be blamed. Indeed they did worse than nothing: they actively prevented help from being delivered. Many people in Rangoon, a major city in southern Myanmar that was itself heavily damaged by the storm, attempted to help those in the delta. They were not allowed. Small businessmen and traders were reduced to smuggling small amounts of food into what remained of towns and villages.

The international community rallied to offer assistance. As tens or possibly hundreds of thousands of people died of hunger and thirst in the aftermath of the storm, ships full of disaster relief supplies sat off the coast. The military junta refused to allow relief workers in. Visas were almost impossible to obtain. Information was extremely scarce. The government requested aid but asked that it be in the form of bilateral government-to-government assistance. Effectively, Than Shwe was saying, "Send cash, but you can't come in."

About a week after the disaster, the army started entering the larger towns and villages of the delta. They were not there to help. They were there to disperse survivors who had congregated in schools and temples. Even though their numbers rarely exceeded a few hundred, survivors were expelled from their shelters and told to return home. It mattered little that, in most cases, their entire village had been destroyed and they had no food, water, clothing, or shelter to return to. Indeed, one report observed, "Survivors were loaded onto boats and ferried back to the destroyed villages they had recently escaped from. In some areas the clearances happened quickly; as the emergency phase was now officially over, the authorities wanted people back in their villages by June 2, when the next school term was scheduled to begin. But survivors had no idea what they were returning to; was there even anything left at places they had once called home? And how would they get food and water there?"[6]

The government did not even attempt to answer these questions.

In the episode "Eyes of the Storm: Turning Points in Burmese History" of the PBS documentary series *Wide Angle*, a senior Burmese general is seen addressing a group of survivors.[7] Starving and destitute, they ask for a handful of rice. The general tells them that he is here now (but makes no offer of assistance) and that they must go back to their village and "work hard." While the army seized (and sold on the black market) the few relief supplies allowed in, the people were told they could eat frogs. Effectively, the government told these survivors to go away and die quietly: inhumane in the extreme, but good small-coalition politics. Dead people cannot protest.

ARE DISASTERS ALWAYS DISASTERS FOR GOVERNMENT SURVIVAL?

Earthquakes and other disasters shake up political systems. However, the nature of the shake-up is very different under different institutions. Democratic leaders are very sensitive to disaster-related casualties. Allowing people to die reveals serious policy failure. Democrats need to deliver good public policy to reward their large number of backers. When they fail to do so, they are liable to be removed. Disaster-related deaths result in protest and in the removal of leaders in democracies.

To illustrate the difference in political responses to poor disaster relief in nondemocratic and democratic settings, we contrast Cyclone Nargis with Hurricane Katrina. Katrina struck the US Gulf Coast in August 2005. This was the most costly natural disaster in US history up to that time, with damages estimated at $81 billion. The death toll was 1,836.

The government, from President George W. Bush down to New Orleans mayor Ray Nagin, were accused of mismanagement and lack of leadership. Nagin delayed the evacuation order for the city until nineteen hours before the storm struck. As a result, many people became trapped. Then, once the Superdome football stadium was set up as an emergency center, it became overwhelmed when thirty thousand rather than the anticipated eight hundred people showed up. Federal disaster relief was slow in arriving. Many of the casualties were the sick and elderly who were overcome by heat and dehydration.

The tenure of US leaders was seriously jeopardized by the disaster. Many observers think Katrina contributed significantly to the Republican Party's midterm electoral losses in 2006 and their significant losses, including the presidency, in 2008. Yet, while it is clear that the situation could have been handled much better, it bears no resemblance to Cyclone Nargis. In contrast, despite having allowed at least 138,000 people to die, Than Shwe felt sufficiently well entrenched to allow a farcical election in 2010, which the government-backed parties won easily (at least according to official sources).

As seen in the cases of Mexico and Nicaragua, disasters can serve as rallying points in autocracies. Disasters can concentrate opponents of the regime, making it easier for them to coordinate. Yet the death toll from disasters has relatively little effect on a dictator's chance of staying in power. Indeed, if anything, large numbers of people dying in disasters actually enhances the political survival of autocratic leaders.

As we know, autocrats don't buy political support with efficient public policy. Resources spent saving lives cannot be spent on cronies. In addition, as we have seen, autocrats are skilled at exploiting the international community. By letting more people die, they may be able to extract more relief assistance. The implications of these results are frightening. Small wonder, then, that far more people die in natural disasters in autocracies than in democracies.

Letting people die is good governance for autocrats, but it is disastrous for the tenure of democrats. Although a detailed statistical analysis of the relationship between disasters, deaths, and leader tenure is complex,[8] we compared what happens in a country when two hundred or more people die in a magnitude 5+ earthquake to what happens in the same size earthquake if fewer people die. In particular, we looked at the effect of such circumstances on the odds of a country's leader being removed from office within two years following the earthquake.

An earthquake alone does not threaten the survival of democrats. However, if more than two hundred people are killed by the quake, then a democratic leader is almost certain to be removed from office. Under normal circumstances, any democrat has a 40 percent chance of being ousted from office in any two-year period. But for a democrat whose country suffered two hundred or more deaths in an earthquake, those odds rise to 91 percent. We believe this is the case because democratic leaders are supposed to deliver effective public policies, and those effective policies include ensuring that good building codes are enforced and excellent rescue and recovery is implemented following a natural disaster. Many deaths in such a disaster are a signal to everyone else that the leadership has not done an adequate job of protecting the people, and so out go the leaders.

Autocrats are less vulnerable to removal than democrats, and earthquake-related deaths have little effect on their hold on power. Over a typical two-year period, 22 percent of autocrats lose power. If their country suffers a magnitude 5 or greater earthquake in the first year of this two-year window, the dictator's risk of being removed goes up to 30 percent. However, the autocrat's risk of removal rises only to 24 percent if the earthquake killed more than two hundred people. Earthquakes pose a threat to autocratic leaders when people are forced into refugee camps and can organize against the regime. People killed in an earthquake can't organize and so do not endanger a dictator's survival in office. As might be expected, given these facts and the incentives they suggest, instances of two hundred or more people dying in earthquakes is much more common in autocracies than democracies.[9]

Not all disasters are equal in the eyes of autocrats. Dictators are particularly wary of natural disasters when they occur in politically and economically important centers. Disaster management in China emphasizes this point. When an earthquake struck the remote province of Qinghai in 2010, the Chinese government's response was, at best, half-hearted. In contrast, its handling of disaster relief in the wake of a 2008 earthquake in Sichuan won the approval of much of the international community. The differences are stark and driven by politics. The Sichuan quake occurred in an economically and politically important center where a massed protest could potentially threaten the government. Qinghai is remote and of little political importance. Protest there would do little to threaten the government. The government did much less to assist people who could not threaten them.

RESPONDING TO REVOLUTION OR ITS THREAT

Whether because of an unforeseen earthquake, a succession crisis, or a financial meltdown, the threat of rebellion can rise and strike a leader like a lightning bolt. What, then, is the right response to such a threat? History teaches us that some autocrats crack down hard on rebels; some succumb to them; and some reform on their own. The rules governing politics help us understand how different circumstances lead to different choices among these options.

Successful rebellions, mass movements, and revolutions are not commonplace, but neither are they extremely rare. Successful rebellions that turn into sustained democracies are pretty rare. They do happen, but more commonly revolution replaces one small-coalition system with another. While many revolutions fail to deliver what their participants hoped for, the threat of revolution can be an important driver of political change. Leaders far prefer to rule through a small coalition; that is the essence of rule one. Yet sometimes the people create a credible threat because the leader lacks either the funds or sufficient coalition loyalty to crack enough heads to keep the people off the street. Under such conditions, leaders decide it is better to reform than be swept away. Of course, the canny leader will "democratize" according to the rules to rule by: that is to say, by minimizing the expansion of the coalition and maximizing the expansion of the selectorate.

As we write in April 2021, Myanmar is engulfed in protests following a military coup on February 1. Earlier, we saw the lengths General Than Shwe went to in order to prevent protests in the wake of Cyclone Nargis in 2008. However, he was obviously aware of the threat that the people posed. In 2008, he started talks with opposition leaders including Aung San Suu Kyi, daughter of Burmese independence leader Aung San, Nobel Peace Prize winner and leader of the National League for Democracy (NLD) party. The NLD claimed to have won the 1990 election with 58.7 percent of the popular vote and 392 out of 492 seats. At that time the military junta chose to ignore the election results and continue ruling. However, as we will see, circumstances changed, and by 2008 the junta was prepared to compromise. Talks led to constitutional reforms and elections in 2010. The NLD boycotted these elections, and so the Union Solidarity and Development Party—effectively the military in civilian clothing—won. However, in the 2015 election the NLD won an overwhelming victory, taking 235 of 330 available seats in the Lower House; the remaining 110 seats in this house were military appointments. Aung

San Suu Kyi became Myanmar's de facto leader. Her official role was state counselor (a position similar to prime minister). The military included a constitutional provision that prevented her from becoming president because her late husband and her children were foreign born. In the November 2020 election, her party gained an additional three seats. However, the day before the new parliament was to be sworn in, a military coup ended (at least for now) Myanmar's nascent democracy. Protests and rebellions shape the trajectory of nations, and, importantly, they do so both as latent threats and actualized events.

Myanmar's experience leaves us with a perplexing question. Given Than Shwe's demonstrated ability to suppress the people during his time in power, we need to question why Shwe started the reform process that led to elections that he and his backers lost. None of us would regard the 2010 elections as free and fair, and the 2008 constitution guaranteed the army 25 percent of the parliamentary seats. However, institutions clearly became more inclusive after 2008. On our 0 to 1 scale, by 2020 (the date of the most recent election) Myanmar's winning coalition had increased to 0.62: far from accountable governance, but a huge increase from the coalition size of 0.32 in 2008.

Why would Than Shwe agree to such changes? The answer, we believe, lies in a growing budget difficulty. As events in September 2007 showed, the army was perfectly capable of putting down protests, but it needed to be well compensated. Junta leaders have relatively little budgetary discretion. Sure, juntas are small-coalition systems, but they are also small-selectorate systems. Shwe needed to choose his supporters from the upper ranks of the military, which limited the availability of potential replacements. With only a small risk of replacement, Shwe's supporters expected to be well compensated for their loyalty.

In the late 2000s Myanmar's natural resource rents declined precipitously. According to World Bank data, in 2006 natural resource rents accounted for 13.5 percent of GDP. By 2010 this figure had declined to 5.9 percent.[10] We should treat these numbers with caution because lots of revenue bypassed official accounts, but the trend was clear. Shwe had a budgetary, which is to say a political, problem. With a coalition whose fickle loyalty needed to be bought and much less money coming in, Shwe needed to find a way to increase revenues and increase loyalty. Getting the people to work meant giving them more, although still limited, freedoms. Increasing loyalty meant enlarging the selectorate. Partial democratization provided Shwe and the military a way to survive their political problem. Survival came at the cost of an enlarged winning coalition, and Shwe was forced to step aside in favor of Thein Sein in 2010. But by securing 25 percent of parliamentary seats for the military as part of the deal, the junta insiders could hope to continue to receive at least some of the perks they were accustomed to.

Than Shwe allowed for limited democracy not because he wanted to empower and enrich the Burmese people but because he couldn't afford not to. Why, then, did the military seize power in 2021? One answer is: because they could. But as we write, the outcome still remains up in the air. Despite harsh clampdowns, protests continue. Burmese democracy is flawed, but the people clearly prefer it to junta rule. The military's actions are clearly a gamble, so we need to consider the timing of their choice. The COVID pandemic plays in the military's favor. Social distancing is incompatible with mass protests, especially in military regimes, and Aung San Suu Kyi and numerous other government officials were arrested for violating COVID restrictions. Yet coalition dynamics are probably the most important consideration in the military's timing.

The NLD's increased parliamentary majority meant that they might be able to push the military out of power completely, perhaps by reforming the constitution to eliminate the military's 110 automatic seats. If the upper brass sat back and allowed themselves to be replaced, then they would be powerless. If they allowed the new parliament to be sworn in, they would have been in a considerably weaker position. In 2016 Turkey's military attempted a coup against President Recep Tayyip Erdoğan. They did so when they learned that they were about to be shuffled out of the coalition. But they had waited too long; Erdoğan had already replaced enough of their numbers. Myanmar's military rolled the dice because for them it was probably now or never. Once replaced, they would be powerless, a few among many in the vastly enlarged selectorate of a relatively corrupt mass franchise electoral system.

POWER TO THE PEOPLE

A few of history's revolutionaries stand out for their success not only in overthrowing a nasty regime but also in creating a people-friendly government in its place. America's George Washington, South Africa's Nelson Mandela, India's Jawaharlal Nehru, and the Philippines' Corazon Aquino (at least for a while) are a few cases in point. Perhaps even more interestingly, a few leaders threatened with revolution have also democratized as a way to keep themselves in power. Ghana's Jerry John "J.J." Rawlings is a perfect example. Common threads run through each of these democratizers—common threads that are absent from revolutions that replaced one dictator with another, such as occurred under Mao Zedong in China, Fidel Castro in Cuba, Porfirio Díaz in Mexico, and Jomo Kenyatta in Kenya.

Democratic revolutions are most often fought by people who cannot count on great natural resource wealth to sustain them once they overthrow the predecessor regime. These "good" revolutionaries just are not as lucky as Venezuela's Nicolás Maduro or Kazakhstan's Nursultan Nazarbayev. Although economic collapse prompted an extreme threat to Maduro's political survival in 2019, his oil wealth, along with assistance from Russia, allowed him to prevail against a popular rebellion. He had the money to buy soldiers and keep them loyal, something his resource-poor Tunisian and Egyptian colleagues did not have in 2011. They, like good revolutionaries, had to rely on the productivity of the people to generate the revenues they needed to reward supporters. To encourage the people to work productively, good revolutionary leaders needed to increase the people's freedoms. If the people can meet and talk, then they can earn more. As a very simple example, if farmers have access to telephones, newspapers, and radios, then they can find out about market prices. This allows them to take the crops to the right markets at the right time. Roads and transport networks reduce transaction costs. Given the ability to earn more, farmers work harder and the economy improves. Unfortunately, for a leader, those same freedoms allow people to organize. The same media, telecommunications, and roads that increase productivity also make it much easier for the same farmers to hear about antigovernment demonstrations and join them. In much the same way that Mexico City's 1985 earthquake lowered the barriers for coordination and organization, increasing the public good of freedom makes protest more likely.

In the latter half of the 1980s, Mikhail Gorbachev faced a dilemma. The economy of the Soviet Union was failing. Without additional resources he could not continue to pay his essential backers. He might have turned to oil—of which Russia has plenty—to save the day, but oil prices were depressed in those years. His best shot at keeping rebellion at bay was to liberalize the Soviet economy, even though that also meant giving the people more power over their lives. Gorbachev showed himself willing to take that risk.

Some might suggest that Gorbachev is a better person than Myanmar's General Shwe. Probably he is, although we cannot help but notice that he cracked down on constitutionally protected secessionist movements in Azerbaijan, Latvia, Lithuania, and Estonia. The Soviet military response to the efforts of the people in those republics to gain their freedom is hardly the response of an enlightened leader. The Soviet "black beret" militia killed 14 and injured 150 people in Lithuania.[11] A week later, 4 more people were killed and 20 injured when Soviet forces cracked down on Latvia's efforts to attain independence.[12]

Why did the enlightened Gorbachev take these harsh actions? He was responding to political pressure from within his coalition. Top-ranking Soviet military officers together with others urged Gorbachev to impose direct Kremlin rule in breakaway provinces. They wrote in an open letter that was circulated at the Congress of People's Deputies, "If constitutional methods prove ineffective against separatists, criminal speculators and the paramilitary forces that are continuing to spill the blood of the people, we suggest instituting a state of emergency and presidential rule in zones of major conflicts."[13] Gorbachev understood the political risks of ignoring key military and political figures in his coalition of essentials.

Gorbachev's failure to quash the secessionist movements was a significant contributor to the decision by hard-liners in his government to launch the coup that overthrew him. He was restored to power—briefly—when the people, backed by Boris Yeltsin, occupied

Red Square and forced the coup makers to retreat. But for Gorbachev the damage was done. He returned to power and recognized the independence of Lithuania, Latvia, and Estonia, only to find himself unable to sustain his government or even the existence of the Soviet Union. The Soviet Union was formally dissolved three months later.

Gorbachev's policy of perestroika, aimed at restructuring the Soviet political and economic system, can be understood as his effort to increase the government's revenue to forestall just such problems as the secessionist movements and their political aftermath. It didn't work out for him or the Soviet form of government, but that is what it means to take risks. Sometimes they turn out your way and sometimes they don't.

Today Russia is backsliding away from democratization. While under Boris Yeltsin's post-Gorbachev government Russia maintained free and competitive elections, that is no longer true today. Vladimir Putin, former member of the Soviet secret police (the KGB) and Yeltsin's immediate successor, moved the political system sharply back from its emerging dependence on a large coalition and good governance. He made it much more difficult for opposition parties to compete by severely restricting freedom of assembly. He made it much more difficult for opposition candidates to get their message across by nationalizing television and much of the print media. He made it much more difficult for people to articulate their dissatisfaction by making it a crime to make public arguments that disparaged the government. It seems he had many of his most effective opponents murdered, even reaching beyond Russia's borders to do so. In short, he systematically reduced the availability of freedoms that compel a democratic government to attend to the wishes of the people. Why could he do this? As we have noted, Russia is awash in oil wealth. During Putin's time, unlike poor Gorbachev's, oil prices were at record highs, so he could pay key backers to help him quash opposition and possibly even have enough extra money to keep the people happy enough not to rebel against their loss of freedom. The upshot: he has been in power for more than twenty years and counting.

The expansion of freedoms is a sure sign of impending democratization. Economic necessity is one factor that produces such a concession. Another is coming to power on the back of a large coalition. This was George Washington's, Nelson Mandela's, and Jawaharlal Nehru's circumstance. For different reasons, each started out with a big coalition and was pretty much locked into trying to sustain it, at least for a while, if their government was to survive.

When Washington became president of the United States, the term "United States" was treated as a plural noun. Back then people identified more strongly with their state than with the nation. Washington headed an army that depended on recruits from thirteen distinct colonies, each with its own government and each paying for its military contingent out of its own pocketbook. Washington needed the support of a broad base of colonists, and so he was stuck with a large coalition from the get-go. In that circumstance he had to do what large coalition leaders do—disproportionately deliver public goods rather than private benefits. First among these public goods was the Bill of Rights, which guaranteed the very freedoms that are central to democratic, large-coalition governance. Without these, the colonies would not have agreed to ratify the Constitution and unite under a single government.

Nelson Mandela's story is not much different. His political movement, the African National Congress (ANC), spent decades fighting the white-dominated apartheid regimes of South Africa. Despite their efforts and the protracted use of violence, they were unable to grow strong enough to overthrow their oppressors through force. Nelson Mandela, who served twenty-seven years in prison for his antigovernment stance and who refused early release from prison on the condition of eschewing violence, eventually saw another way.

Possibly due to the effects of sanctions, the South African economy went into a sharp decline during the 1980s. In 1980, per capita income in 2010 constant US dollars was $6,722. But by 1993, the year in which F. W. de Klerk's apartheid regime passed a new constitution paving the way for elections for all races, it had fallen to $5,518.[14] De Klerk and his long-term predecessor, Pik Botha, were in trouble because with the economy in decline they did not have sufficient resources to buy the continued loyalty required to keep the people suppressed. Under those conditions, more money was needed to sustain the government. That money could only be gotten from the people, and many of them were already rebelling against the apartheid government. Faced with very tough circumstances, the apartheid regime had a choice: fight to the bitter end or cut a deal with Mandela. They chose the latter course.

The large-coalition compromise deal with Mandela and his ANC meant allowing all South Africans equal rights. In practice, this meant that the voting majority was turned over to the very people who were most discriminated against during the years of apartheid. As a result, the country became more democratic and its people freer. But, as is so often true with new democracies, as the incumbent ANC's interests have come more and more to dominate the government, democracy has been eroded. We estimate that South Africa's coalition size at the time of its first free election in 1994 was 0.87. Today, more than a quarter century later, it is down to 0.78. Competitive, democratic governance has faced, and seems to continue to face, a slow erosion. The reduction in the size of South Africa's group of essentials signals the real danger down the road that, unless the opposition wins office and leadership is swapped back and forth between different political parties, South Africa could go the way of Zimbabwe. Like South Africa, Zimbabwe started out on a positive path to democracy based on a large-coalition deal between Joshua Nkomo's ZAPU, Robert Mugabe's ZANU party, and Ian Smith's white-only UDI government. But once Mugabe became sufficiently entrenched, he, like Putin in Russia, was able to overturn the progress toward democratization. He plunged Zimbabwe back into the role of a corrupt, rent-seeking, small-coalition regime that serves the interest of the few at the expense of the many, Black and white.

The successes of Washington, Mandela, and others were duplicated from a very different starting place in the case of Ghana. There, revolution did not lead to democracy so much as the anticipation of revolution did.

Ghana's J.J. Rawlings understood well that liberalizing Ghana's economy and empowering the people could endanger his hold on power. But he also recognized that liberalization did not mean that the people would inevitably end up revolting or that the coalition would turn on its leader. Rawlings became the poster boy for the IMF and World Bank. He implemented the economic reforms they prescribed, invigorated the economy, and instituted democratic reforms, and after serving two terms as president of Ghana, he stepped down. But that is not how he started out. And the people were not as happy with him as this rosy picture would suggest; at least not if you believe what Adu Boahen, a professor and leading political opponent, had to say.

Boahen recounted Rawlings's explanation for the seeming passivity of the Ghanaian people. Here's his summation of Rawlings's stance:

> The people have faced and continue to face hardship. Naturally, people will grumble. But the fact that Ghanaians have been able to put up with shortages, transport difficulties and low salaries, and other problems without any major protest, is an indication of their confidence in our integrity, the integrity and good intentions of the PNDC [Provisional Nations Defense Council] government. Visitors from other countries have commented that in their countries there would be riots if conditions were similar to those here. But the people know that they are not suffering to make a corrupt government rich at all, we are suffering in order to concentrate all our resources in the building of a just and prosperous society.

To this, Boahen responded, "I am afraid that I do not agree with Rawlings's explanation of the passivity of Ghanaians. We have not protested or staged riots not because we trust the PNDC but because we fear the PNDC! We are afraid of being detained, liquidated or dragged before the CVC or NIC or being subjected to all sorts of molestation.... They have been [protesting] but in a very subtle and quiet way—hence the culture of silence."[15] Boahen portrays Ghana in 1989 as permeated by oppression. Yet by 1989 things were much better than they had been, as evidenced by the fact that Boahen could make such speeches in the first place.

Rawlings's seizure of power on January 11, 1982, is often described in almost biblical terms. In reference to his initials, "J.J.," he was sometimes called "Junior Jesus," and this was his second coming. He had been the figurehead for a military revolt in 1979. Rawlings had movie-star looks and exuded charisma. But charm was not what kept him in power. Oppression and rich rewards for supporters are the staples of leadership in small-coalition systems, and Rawlings was no exception. In the first six months of his rule, 180 people were killed and 1,000 more were arrested and tortured. His loyal soldiers were renowned for their thuggish brutality, and Rawlings bought their loyalty through a massive increase in military spending. J.J. knew whose support he needed, and despite the economy's collapse and a complete meltdown of government finances, he paid them first.

Rawlings had a talent for preventing protest. He stifled any critical press by restricting the supply of paper. His supporters infiltrated the trade unions and effectively made strikes impossible for many years. He avoided free assembly at every turn. Events a year into his rule demonstrate his considerable organizational talents. In January 1983, Nigeria announced the expulsion of 1.4 million Ghanaians working in Nigeria. In a few weeks 10 percent of the population, most of them young adults, flooded back into a poverty-stricken Ghana. The prospects of hundreds of thousands of disgruntled and unemployed people milling around the capital terrified many in the government, some of whom advocated closing the border to prevent them from arriving. Instead, Rawlings welcomed them with open arms, but he almost immediately ensured the returnees were transported back to their home villages. His massive transport undertaking prevented the formation of the kind of camps that overwhelmed Mexico and Nicaragua. And it was a much more humane approach than Shwe's.

Rawlings's fundamental problem was that Ghana was broke and the economy had nearly completely collapsed. Ghana's food production was the second lowest in Africa, ahead of only Chad. Rigged exchange rates lay at the heart of Ghana's economic problems and its system of political rewards. The official exchange rate for Ghana's currency, the cedi, was much higher than the black market rate. Essential backers were allowed to exchange money at the official exchange rate and then convert it on the street. Unfortunately this eroded incentives for farmers. By the early 1980s, it often cost farmers more to buy fuel to take goods to markets than they earned by selling them. Seventy percent of the crops that did make it to market were carried on people's heads. Smuggling crops across the border to the Ivory Coast became the norm. The government responded by making smuggling a capital crime. With little being produced for export, Ghana had exhausted its capacity to borrow and was going bankrupt.

Rawlings had a big problem. He had seized power and wanted to pursue a revolutionary socialist agenda, but he needed money. As Naomi Chazan phrased it, "The question was no longer where resources were located but if they existed at all."[16] To start with, Rawlings closed all the universities and had students help bring in the harvests. But such measures were not enough. The people were hungry. Ghana had insufficient funds to pay for food imports and to pay the army. As a good rule-abiding autocrat, Rawlings knew his priorities: pay the army! Soon the term *Rawlings necklace* became a popular euphemism for the protruding collarbones common among the emaciated people. He approached the Soviet Union, but they had their own financial problems, and despite his move to the political left, they declined to support him.

J.J. was between a rock and a hard place. He needed money, and the only way left to get it was to encourage the people to get back to work. At the beginning of 1983 he enacted a radical reversal of policy. The cedi was allowed to devalue. Producer prices paid to farmers were increased, and subsidies for gas, electricity, and health care were cut. International financial institutions such as the IMF and World Bank were delighted to have an adherent to their policies, but many of his closest allies were not as happy. This policy switch was accompanied by a change in personnel. Rawlings orchestrated a coup and made it a fait accompli before his targets could organize and retaliate. Overnight his closest supporters found themselves without influence. Some, such as J. Amartey Kwei, were executed (allegedly for his part in a notorious murder of judges). Others, such as the radical student activist Chris Atim, fled into exile.

It is telling that by 1985, Rawlings was the only remaining member of the original ruling PNDC council. As a further sign of the direction Rawlings's administration was taking, that council swelled from six members to ten. No leader voluntarily increases the number of people to whom he is beholden unless he thinks that doing so will help him stay in power.

As is to be expected, Rawlings was a reluctant democrat. He simply had few options left. He needed money. To get it, he implemented policies that empowered the people. Gradually, they could demand more. "Rawlings was a victim of his own success." He had given the people a voice by liberalizing the economy and opening the airwaves. There was the perception of increased confidence. With the economic crisis resolved, the people began to feel that they could "do this without someone telling [them] what to do."[17]

As we have seen, by 1989 Boahen felt comfortable openly criticizing Rawlings. Even he had to admit reforms had improved the economy. The "Rawlings necklace" had been replaced by the "Rawlings waistcoat" (a fat belly). Having had to implement policies to keep the masses happy, Rawlings allowed a gradual expansion of the coalition to accompany the expansion in public goods. In 1988 and 1989 local elections were allowed. Rather than provoke mass protest, Rawlings stayed one step ahead of the people. As a loose affiliation of political interests coalesced into the People's Movement for Freedom and Justice and called for multiparty elections, Rawlings defused their anger by organizing elections while the opposition was still disorganized. In the 1991 presidential election he decisively defeated Adu Boahen, who ran as the leader of the New Patriotic Party (NPP). Although there were some discrepancies, international observers declared the results basically fair.

Elections have been basically fair ever since. Rawlings and his National Democratic Congress party won again in 1996, beating John Kufuor. In 2000, Rawlings stepped down and John Kufuor went on to serve the constitutional limit of two terms as president. In 2008 the NDC candidate, Atta Mills, became president. Ghana held highly competitive elections. The NDC held on to power in 2012, and the NPP won in 2016 and 2020.

Rawlings needed money, and the only way he could get it was to empower the people. By allowing the people to assemble and communicate he increased their productivity. But he also made it easier for them to coordinate and organize against him. He successfully avoided protest and revolution only by remaining one step ahead of the people in terms of granting concessions. Yet he could not avoid protest indefinitely. In 1995 between fifty thousand and a hundred thousand people joined Kume Preko (which literally means "You may as well kill me," indicating "We have had enough") marches through downtown Accra, the capital. Although the government sought to prevent these marches, the courts overruled them. An independent judiciary encourages entrepreneurial zeal, but it also protects the civil liberties of the people.

Today Ghana is an economically vibrant democracy. Its transition from autocracy to democracy took place under the leadership of the larger-than-life J.J. Rawlings. Yet it should be remembered that he was a reluctant democrat. Had he had the necessary resources, he would have perpetuated his socialist revolution. Ghana recently developed an offshore oil field. Had these funds been available to J.J., or had the Soviets had the resources to back him, then it is likely he would still be in power and Ghana would be a much poorer and more oppressed land.

Revolutionary moments often arise, as in the cases of Ghana, South Africa, and the Soviet Union, when an economy is near collapse—so near, in fact, that the leadership can no longer buy the military's loyalty. Such circumstances are practically inevitable in the life of the vast majority of autocracies. Their rent-seeking, corrupt, inefficient economic ways assure it.

At such moments the threatened government is more than likely to blame the international community for its woes. After all, in exchange for policy concessions, oppressive leaders have been able to borrow on relatively easy terms from rich foreign governments and the international banks they control. Now these governments face crushing debt obligations and no money to pay them. Getting more money becomes difficult exactly because they are in such danger of defaulting on their debts. And what do many well-intentioned people cry out for them? Debt forgiveness.

We must repeat what we said earlier. Financial crises, from an autocratic leader's perspective, are political crises. The leader hasn't cared a whit about destroying his country's economy by stealing from the public. Now that money is in such short supply that he can't maintain his coalition's loyalty, there is a moment of opportunity for political change. Forgive the debts and the leader will just start borrowing again to pay his cronies and keep himself in power. Political scientist Nicolas van de Walle compared the fates of regimes in Benin and Zambia with those of regimes in Cameroon and the Ivory Coast during crises.[18] In the former cases, international financial institutions withdrew support and the nations democratized. In the latter cases, France stepped in with financial support and no reform occurred.

So the first policy recommendation for outside observers when a dictator faces national bankruptcy, and the protests likely to follow, is this: Don't save the dictator. Don't forgive indebtedness unless the dictator first puts his hold on power at real risk by permitting freedom of assembly, a free press, freedom to create opposition parties, and free, competitive elections in which the incumbent's party is given no advantages in campaign funds, rallies, or anything else. Only after such freedoms and real political competition are in place might any debt forgiveness be considered. Even the least hint of a fraudulent election or cutbacks in freedom should be met by turning off the flow of funds.

Foreign aid, as we have seen, is a boon to petty dictators and to democratic donor citizens and leaders. That makes persuading people to cut off aid to help promote democratization very difficult indeed. But if the opportunity arises, it should be seized. Just like debt forgiveness or new loans, foreign aid should be tied to the actuality of political reform and not to its promise. When leaders put themselves at risk of being thrown out by the people, then they show themselves worthy of aid. When leaders allow their books to be audited and any corruption to be publicized, then they are good candidates for aid designed to improve the well-being of their people. Those who refuse to make politics competitive or to expose and correct corruption will just steal aid and should not get it if there is not an overwhelming national security justification for continuing aid.

When a succession in leaders takes place, whether through revolution or through the unexpected death or retirement of the person in power, then there is a window of opportunity for real democratic change. We have seen that the early part of an incumbent's time in office carries the highest risk of deposition. This is especially true for autocrats. Indeed, they have a strong incentive to pretend to be democratic in their first couple of years exactly because democrats have a better chance of surviving that first period in office than autocrats. We saw just such reforms coming out of Cuba, for instance, when Raúl Castro took over from his brother Fidel. Raúl needed to consolidate his hold on power and reassure his backers that he could provide for them, and to do that he had to get Cuba's economy to grow. Solution: introduce some economic competition and a few acts of political liberalization. We will probably see a repeat of such reform now that Raúl has "retired."

Today Cubans can take greater advantage of private businesses than was true at any time since the revolution. They can have cell phones and some access to the internet, expanding their reach for information and their ability to coordinate with fellow Cubans even when they are not face to face. But will these reforms outlast Raúl? Will they be expanded upon? Or will Raúl's successor, like any newly ensconced autocrat, consolidate his control over the flow of money and the loyalty of his key backers and then pull back on reform? Sustained reform is unlikely unless the international community exploits its brief window of opportunity. It can do so by tying economic assistance to locking in political liberalization.

All the methods mentioned above are exactly the tools that liberal governments can adopt to promote lock-in of democratic reforms. But do they have the will to do it? That, sadly, is unlikely—and for that problem we have not yet found a cure.

CHAPTER NINE

WAR, PEACE, AND WORLD ORDER

The first war in the Bible arises when the kings of Shinar, Ellasar, Elam, and Goiim fight the kings of Sodom, Gomorrah, Admah, Zeboiim, and Bela, two thousand years after the world's creation. The world has not seen that long a stretch without war again. Indeed, it is fair to say that our world has had too much war, too little peace, and hardly any order. We think that a big part of why war has been such a scourge is that too many leaders get the wrong advice about how to solve international problems. Maybe, just maybe, by looking at war in our political survival terms we will see ways to construct a more peaceful and orderly world.

War is often said to transcend everyday politics, to be above the fray of partisan rancor. But the fact is that war is inherently political. Carl von Clausewitz, the nineteenth-century Prussian soldier and preeminent military thinker, expressed it best: "War is a mere continuation of politics by other means." And as we have seen, political survival is at the heart of all politics.

Georges Clemenceau, leader of France during the later stages of World War I, famously declared, "War is too important to be left to the generals." He was right. Relative to parliamentarians, generals do a lousy job of fighting wars. Although it's completely counterintuitive, the military men who lead juntas and other forms of autocratic leaders are much worse at fighting wars than their civilian counterparts who lead democratic governments. That's why it's so important for us to unpack the contrasting advice different leaders receive about how and when to fight. It turns out that autocrats and democrats should receive and follow radically different counsel. War, being about domestic politics, can be best understood, we believe, by putting it in the context of interchangeables and essentials and taking it out of the context of grand ideas about national interest and balances of power.

WAR FIGHTING

Two thousand five hundred years ago, Sun Tzu literally wrote the book on how to wage war.[1] Although his advice influenced leaders down through the centuries, leading American foreign policy advisers have contradicted his war-fighting doctrines.

Ronald Reagan's secretary of defense, Caspar Weinberger; George W. Bush's first secretary of state, Colin Powell; and, with slight modifications, Bill Clinton's second secretary of state, Madeleine Albright, all prescribed a doctrine of when and how the United States should fight. And it differed radically from the time-tested advice of Sun Tzu.

The reason Sun Tzu has served so many leaders so well over twenty-five centuries is that his is the right advice for kings, chieftains, and autocrats of every shape to follow. Until recently, with very few exceptions, small-coalition systems were the dominant form of government. But these are the wrong policies for a leader beholden to many. Democratic warfare emphasizes public welfare, exactly as should be the case for a leader who relies on a large coalition. Sun Tzu's advice is exactly right for a small-coalition leader. To see this, let's have a look at the ideas expressed by Sun Tzu and Caspar Weinberger.

Sun Tzu contended to his king, Ho Lu of Wu, that

> the skillful general does not raise a second levy, neither are his supply wagons loaded more than twice. Once war is declared, he will not waste precious time in waiting for reinforcements, nor will he turn his army back for fresh supplies, but crosses the enemy's frontier without delay. The value of time—that is, being a little ahead

of your opponent—has counted for more than either numerical superiority or the nicest calculations with regard to commissariat.... Now, in order to kill the enemy, our men must be roused to anger. For them to perceive the advantage of defeating the enemy, they must also have their rewards. Thus, when you capture spoils from the enemy, they must be used as rewards, so that all your men may have a keen desire to fight, each on his own account.[2]

In contrast to Sun Tzu's perspective, Caspar Weinberger maintained,

First, the United States should not commit forces to combat overseas unless the particular engagement or occasion is deemed vital to our national interest or that of our allies....

Second, if we decide it is necessary to put combat troops into a given situation, we should do so wholeheartedly, and with the clear intention of winning. If we are unwilling to commit the forces or resources necessary to achieve our objectives, we should not commit them at all....

Third, if we do decide to commit forces to combat overseas, we should have clearly defined political and military objectives. And we should know precisely how our forces can accomplish those clearly defined objectives. And we should have and send the forces needed to do just that....

Fourth, the relationship between our objectives and the forces we have committed—their size, composition, and disposition—must be continually reassessed and adjusted if necessary. Conditions and objectives invariably change during the course of a conflict. When they do change, then so must our combat requirements....

Fifth, before the United States commits combat forces abroad, there must be some reasonable assurance we will have the support of the American people and their elected representatives in Congress....

Finally, the commitment of US forces to combat should be a last resort.[3]

Sun Tzu's ideas can coarsely be summarized as follows: (1) an advantage in capabilities is not as important as quick action in war; (2) the resources mobilized to fight should be sufficient for a short campaign that does not require reinforcement or significant additional provisions from home; and (3) the provision of private goods is essential to motivate soldiers to fight. Sun Tzu says that if the supplies the army initially raised prove insufficient or if new supplies are required more than once, then the commanders lack sufficient skill to carry the day. In that case, he advises that it is best to give up the fight rather than risk exhausting the state's treasure.

Weinberger's doctrine does not emphasize swift victory but rather a willingness to spend however much is needed to achieve victory, a point made even more emphatically in the Powell Doctrine. Weinberger and Powell argue that the United States should not get involved in any war in which it is not prepared to commit enough resources to win. They, and Madeleine Albright too, argue for being very cautious about risking war. Once a decision is made to take that risk, then, as Weinberger and Powell recognize, the United States must be prepared to raise a larger army and to spend more treasure if necessitated by developments on the ground. War should only be fought with the confidence that victory will follow and that victory serves the interests of the American people.

Sun Tzu emphasizes the benefits of spoils to motivate combatants ("When you capture spoils from the enemy, they must be used as rewards, so that all your men may have a keen desire to fight, each on his own account"). Weinberger emphasizes the public good of protecting vital national interests. For Sun Tzu, the interest soldiers have in the political objectives behind a fight or their concern for the common good is of no consequence in determining their motivation to wage war. That is why he emphasizes that soldiers fight, "each on his own account."

Sun Tzu's attentiveness to private rewards and Weinberger's concentration on the public good of protecting the national interest (however that may be understood) represent the great divide between small-coalition and large-coalition regimes. Our view of politics instructs us to anticipate that leaders who depend on lots of essential backers only fight when they believe victory is nearly certain. Otherwise, they look for ways to resolve their international differences peacefully. Leaders who rely on only a few essential supporters, in contrast, are prepared to fight even when the odds of winning are not particularly good. Democratic leaders try hard to win if the going gets tough. Autocrats make a good initial effort, and if that proves wanting, they quit. These strategies are clearly in evidence when we consider the Six-Day War in 1967.

TO TRY HARD OR NOT

As its name tells us, the Six-Day War was a short fight, begun on June 5, 1967, and ending on June 10. On one side were Syria, Egypt (then the United Arab Republic), and Jordan; on the other was Israel. By the end of the war, Israel had captured the Sinai from Egypt; Jerusalem, Hebron, and the West Bank from Jordan; and the Golan Heights from Syria. The air forces of the Arab combatants were devastated, and Egypt accepted an unconditional cease-fire. The Israelis had easily defeated their opponents. From a conventional balance-of-power perspective, the outcome must be seen as extraordinarily surprising. From the political-survival point of view, as we shall see, it should have been perfectly predictable.

To understand the war and how our way of thinking explains it, we must first comprehend some basic facts about the adversaries. The combined armed forces of the Arab combatants on the eve of war came to 360,000, compared to Israel's 75,000; that is, the Israeli side represented only 17 percent of the available soldiers.[4] The Arab combatants accounted for 61 percent of the national military expenditures of the two sides. For starters, comparing these two sets of values already tells us something very important that reflects a fundamental difference between large-coalition and small-coalition governments. Although the Arab side had 83 percent of the soldiers, they spent considerably less per soldier than did the Israelis.

Remember that large-coalition leaders must keep a broad swath of the people happy. That means democrats must care about the people, and, of course, soldiers are people. Although conflict involves putting soldiers at risk, democrats do what they can to mitigate such risk. In autocracies, foot soldiers are not politically important. Autocrats do not waste resources protecting them.

The difference in expenditures per soldier is greater even than the numbers alone indicate. The Israeli military, like the militaries of democracies in general, spends a lot of its money on buying equipment that is heavily armored to protect soldiers. Better training and equipment enable democracies to leverage the impact of each soldier so they can achieve the same military output while putting fewer soldiers at risk.[5] The Egyptian military's tanks, troop transports, and other equipment were lightly and cheaply armored. They preferred to spend money on private rewards with which to ensure the loyalty of the generals and colonels.

Gamal Abdel Nasser, Egypt's president at the time, was not elected by the people; he was sustained in office by a small coterie of generals whose own welfare depended on the survival of his regime. For that reason, he was not beholden to the bereaved family members who scream about the avoidable deaths of their loved ones. Israeli prime ministers are elected by those family members, and this is reflected in the superior equipment, armor, and training given to Israeli soldiers. "Give our troops the best" is a democratic refrain. This is why there was such a stink about US soldiers having insufficient body armor in Iraq and Afghanistan, and why the United States rushed to fix this deficiency, even if in some cases the extra armor made some vehicles so heavy that they became close to inoperable.

A bit of close reasoning shows us that making an extra effort to win the war made tons of sense for the Israelis and no sense at all for their opponents. Let's have a look at why it is that democrats, like Israel's then prime minister, Levi Eshkol, try hard to win wars and autocrats, like Egypt's Nasser, don't. Indeed, we will see that for a small-coalition autocrat like Nasser, it could make more sense to lose the war and keep paying off his cronies than to win the war if doing so required asking the cronies to sacrifice their private rewards.

In a small-coalition regime, the military serves two crucial functions: it keeps the incumbent safe from domestic rivals, and it protects the incumbent's government from foreign threats. In a large-coalition government, the military only has to worry about the latter function. Sure, it might be called on to put down some massive domestic unrest from time to time, but its job is to protect the system of government, not the particular group running the government. Its job description does not include taking out legitimate domestic political rivals. Autocrats, of course, don't recognize any rivals as legitimate. And to do their job in an autocracy, as Sun Tzu eloquently argued, the soldiers must have their rewards. If they don't, they might turn their guns on the leadership that employed them to keep rivals at bay. With that in mind, we can begin to unravel the seeming surprise of a larger military, backed by a larger gross domestic product—$5.3 billion derived from thirty million people in 1967 Egypt, compared to $4 billion generated by only 2.6 million Israelis—losing to a puny state.

Imagine that the Israeli government spent as much as 10 percent of its revenue on private rewards, probably a high estimate. Imagine that the Egyptian government spent 30 percent of its revenue on private rewards—that is, more than the Israelis, as befits the comparison of large- and small-coalition regimes that we have seen in the earlier chapters. Then how valuable did winning have to be for Israel's coalition and for Egypt's coalition to justify trying so hard that it meant spending extra money on the war effort?

Anticipating the high risk of war, the usually fractious Israelis formed a unity government in May 1967, reflecting the national commitment to win the coming war. We know the government allocated $381 million to the military in 1967. That means, given our assumptions, that $38 million of that pot of money might have been available for private rewards to the government's winning coalition. Of course, even more would have been available across the whole economy (both in Egypt and in Israel), but we focus just on money committed to the military in 1967, thereby *understating* our case. Since Israel had a unity government, it is likely that the Israeli winning coalition was very large, but we will err on the side of conservatism and assume that the government needed just 25 percent of the population to sustain it. That puts the winning coalition's size at roughly 650,000 people. With these numbers in mind, we see that the potential value of private rewards taken from the military budget for government supporters in Israel would have been less than $60 a head ($381 million in military expenditures × 10 percent for private rewards / 650,000 coalition members = $58.62 per coalition member).

Each member of Israel's coalition could have had a choice: take the private reward or agree to put that money toward the war effort. Putting it toward the war effort would certainly have increased the odds of victory, an attractive public good to offset the small private gain that would be sacrificed by each individual in the coalition. Surely each of the relevant 650,000 Israelis would have put a greater value on military victory than a paltry $58.62!

Compare this calculation to that for Egyptians in Nasser's winning coalition. We did a pilot study a few years ago in which we surveyed country experts about the size of several governments' winning coalitions from 1955 to 2008. The experts we interviewed about Egypt placed its winning coalition in 1967 as being as small as eight members and as large as sixty-five. Wherever one comes down in that range, it is obvious that the coalition was very small. We suspect the experts may have underestimated its size, so we will err, again, on the side of conservatism and assume it consisted of as many as one thousand key military officers and essential senior civil servants. Even with our conservative estimate, each coalition member stood to get $150,000 in private rewards ($500 million in military expenditures × 30 percent for private rewards / 1,000 coalition members = $150,000 per coalition member) if the funds out of the military budget that were available for that use were turned over to them instead of being applied to making a concerted increased effort to win the war. Whereas Israeli coalition members were only asked to sacrifice about $60 to help their country win the war, Egypt's coalition members would have had to personally give up $150,000 in income to help their country win. It should be obvious that Nasser would likely have lost the loyal support of lots of his key backers if he took their $150,000 a head and spent it on the war instead of on them. He actually would have increased his chance of being overthrown in a military coup by making an all-out effort to win the war at the expense of his cronies. His backers would have had to place a value on winning the war that was worth their personally giving up $150,000. Victory is nice, but it probably isn't that nice for many people. Levi Eshkol faced no such problem. His supporters were much more likely to place a value on victory that was greater than $58.62.

Of course, Israel did not just fight Egypt. It took on Syria and Jordan at the same time. Here again the logic for its victory is the same. As journalist Ryszard Kapuscinski described, Israel simply tried harder.

> Why did the Arabs lose the 1967 war? A lot has been said on that subject. You could hear that Israel won because Jews are brave and Arabs are cowards. Jews are intelligent, and Arabs are primitive. The Jews have better weapons, and the Arabs worse. All of it untrue! The Arabs are also intelligent and brave and they have good weapons. The difference lay elsewhere—in the approach to war, in varying theories of war. In Israel, everybody takes part in war, but in the Arab countries—only the army. When war breaks out, everyone in Israel goes to the front and civilian life dies out. While in Syria, many people did not find out about the 1967 war until it was over. And yet Syria lost its most important strategic area, the Golan Heights, in that war. Syria was losing the Golan Heights and at the same time, that same day, that same hour, in Damascus—twenty kilometres from the Golan Heights—the cafes were full of people, and others were walking around, worrying about whether they would find a free table. Syria lost fewer than 100 soldiers in the 1967 war. A year earlier, 200 people had died in Damascus during a palace *coup*. Twice as many people die because of a political quarrel as because of a war in which the country loses its most important territory and the enemy approaches within shooting distance of the capital.[6]

Kapuscinski's numbers are wrong, since about 2,500 Syrians were killed in the war, but his point is not. Autocrats don't squander precious resources on the battlefield. And elite, well-equipped units are more for crushing domestic opposition than for fighting a determined foreign foe. Syrian president Hafez al-Assad did not squander precious resources on the battlefield because they were better used to protect him against his domestic foes. In February 1982, he deployed around twelve thousand soldiers to besiege the city of Hama in response to an uprising of a conservative religious group, the Muslim Brotherhood. After three weeks of shelling, the city was destroyed and tens of thousands of civilians were massacred.

When they need to, democracies try hard. However, often they don't need to. Indeed, they are notorious for being bullies and picking on weaker states, and negotiating whenever they are confronted by a worthy adversary. Thus the United States readily fights small adversaries like Grenada, Panama, and the Dominican Republic, and many democracies expanded their influence in the world by colonizing the weak. But when it came to the Soviet Union, the United States and its democratic NATO allies negotiated regardless of whether the dispute was over Cuba, issues in Europe, or elsewhere in the world. Indeed, the Cold War stayed cold precisely because the United States, a large-coalition regime, could not be confident of victory even with enormous effort. When extra effort does make victory likely, as in the Iraqi surge, democrats try hard.

Unfortunately, sometimes negotiations fail, as was the case when Britain and France sought to appease Adolf Hitler before World War II. They agreed to Germany's occupying Austria and the German-speaking part of Czechoslovakia. Even when he invaded Poland, some in Britain hesitated to declare war. No concession, however, was sufficient to satisfy Hitler's appetite for Lebensraum. This left Britain and France with a very serious fight on their hands, one in which Britain tried enormously hard. In contrast, Germany did not switch its economy onto a full war footing until the later stages of the war, when it was clear to Hitler and his cronies that their government's survival—and their personal survival—was at risk.

In other cases the fight turns out to be significantly more difficult than initially thought. US involvement in Vietnam, Iraq, and Afghanistan would be just such cases. When confronted by these kinds of difficult fights, democracies increase their effort. In Vietnam, the United States continually reassessed the resources needed to win before negotiating a settlement with North Vietnam, only to see that agreement collapse a year after American withdrawal. In both Iraq and Afghanistan, the United States needed troop surges to advance its objectives, and when, in Afghanistan, that failed to defeat the Taliban, then as in Vietnam, the United States negotiated a withdrawal settlement—that is, the United States follows Weinberger's counsel and not Sun Tzu's. Autocratic leaders are wary of expending resources on the war effort, even if victory demands it. They know their fate depends more on the loyalty of their coalition than success on the battlefield. They don't generally make that extra effort.

World War I provides a great case study in these principles. Its origins are complex and contentious, so we limit ourselves to describing the chain of events. The war started as a dispute between Austria and Serbia after Serbian nationalists murdered the heir to the Austrian throne, Archduke Franz Ferdinand, in June 1914. When Austria threatened war, Serbia's ally, Russia, became involved. This activated Germany's alliance with Austria. Given that war with Russia also meant war with its ally, France, the Germans launched a rapid invasion of France in the hope of quickly defeating it, as they had in 1871. The German invasion of France went through Belgium, and since the British had pledged to protect Belgium's neutrality, this brought Britain in on the side of the allies.

A tangled web! Although many nations were involved, the war was basically a struggle between the Central powers of Austria and Germany and the Allied powers of France, Russia, and Britain. After a dynamic beginning—the war was famously supposed to be over by Christmas—the conflict stagnated and devolved into trench warfare, particularly on the western front. Russia dropped out of the war in late 1917, after the Bolshevik Revolution. Doing so cost it enormous amounts of its western territory, but Lenin, in his political genius, knew it was better to preserve resources to pay supporters than it was to carry on fighting. In late 1917, the United States entered the war on the Allied side.[7] Allied victory was sealed with an armistice signed on the eleventh hour of the eleventh day of the eleventh month of 1918.

Figure 9.1 plots the military expenditures of the primary combatants.[8] On a per capita basis, Russia spent less than the others. It was both massive and poor. Of these nations only Britain and France were

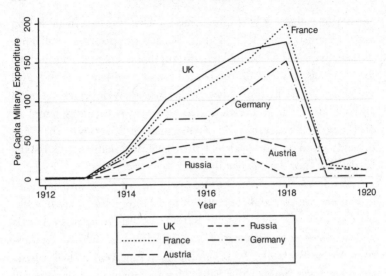

Figure 9.1: Military Expenditures in World War I

democratic. After the war started in 1914, all combatants ramped up their military spending. However, after 1915, the autocratic nations didn't increase their efforts much, and their expenditures plateaued as the war dragged on. German spending did increase again in 1917 as it became clear that defeat would mean the replacement of the German government. In contrast to the meager efforts by autocracies like Austria and Russia, the democracies continued to increase expenditures until victory was achieved.

Sun Tzu's advice to his king predicted the behavior of autocrats in World War I: they didn't make an extraordinary effort to win. The effort by the democratic powers in that same war equally foreshadowed what Caspar Weinberger and so many other American advisers have said to their president: if at first you don't succeed, try, try again.

When it comes to fighting wars, institutions matter at least as much as the balance of power. The willingness of democracies to try harder goes a long way to explaining why seemingly weaker democracies often overcome seemingly stronger autocracies. The United States was once a weak nation. And yet in the Mexican-American War (1846–1848) it defeated the much larger, better-trained, and highly favored

Mexican army. The minuscule Republic of Venice survived for over a thousand years until it was finally defeated by Napoleon in 1797. Despite its small size and limited resources, it fought above its weight class throughout the Middle Ages. It played a crucial role in the Fourth Crusade, which led to the sacking of Constantinople, in which Venice captured the lion's share of the Byzantine Empire's wealth. The smaller but more democratic government of Bismarck's Prussia defeated the larger—and widely favored—Austrian monarchy in the Seven Weeks' War in 1866. Prussia then went on to defeat Louis Napoleon's monarchical France in the 1870–1871 Franco-Prussian War. And as we have seen, tiny Israel has repeatedly beaten its larger neighbors. History is full of democratic Davids beating autocratic Goliaths.

FIGHTING FOR SURVIVAL

At one level, autocrats and democrats fight over the exact same thing: staying in power. At another level, they are motivated to fight over different things. Democrats more often than autocrats fight when all other means of gaining policy concessions from foreign foes fail. In contrast, autocrats are more likely to fight casually, in the pursuit of land, slaves, and treasure.

These differences have important implications. As Sun Tzu suggested, autocrats are likely to grab what they can and return home. On the other hand, democrats fight where they have policy concerns, be these close to home or, as can be the case, in far-flung lands. Further, once they have won, democrats are likely to hang around to enforce the policy settlement. Frequently this can mean deposing vanquished rivals and imposing puppet regimes that will do their policy bidding.[9]

Thinking back to our discussion of foreign aid, we can see that war for democrats is just another way of achieving the goals for which foreign aid would otherwise be used. Foreign aid buys policy concessions; war imposes them. Either way, this means that democrats, eager as they are to deliver desired policies to the folks back home, would much prefer to impose a compliant dictator (surely with some bogus trappings of democracy, such as elections that ensure the outcome desired by the democrat) than take their chances on the policies adopted by a democrat who must answer to her own domestic constituents.

The idea that democrats and autocrats fight for their own political survival may seem awfully cynical at best and downright offensive at worst. Nevertheless, we believe the evidence shows this is the way the world of politics, large and small, actually works. A look at the First Gulf War will validate all of our suspicions.

Before 1990, relations between Iraq and Kuwait had long been fractious. Iraq claimed that Kuwait, with its efficient modern oil export industry, had been pumping oil from under Iraq's territory. On numerous occasions it demanded compensation and threatened to invade. After misreading confused signals from US president George H. W. Bush (on previous occasions the United States had deployed a naval fleet to the region in response to Iraqi threats but had also told Iraq's government that what it did in Kuwait was of no concern to the United States), Saddam Hussein's forces invaded and occupied Kuwait in August 1990. His goal was to exploit its oil wealth for the benefit of himself and his cronies—fairly typical for an autocrat at war. However, despite initially confused signals, the United States did not look the other way: President Bush organized an international coalition and in January 1991 launched Operation Desert Storm to displace Iraqi forces.

The goals and conduct of each side in the First Gulf War differed greatly. In contrast to Hussein, President Bush did not attempt to grab oil wealth to enrich cronies. Rather, the goal was to promote stability in the Middle East and restore the reliable, undisrupted flow of oil. Protesters against the war would chant "No blood for oil." It would be naive to argue that energy policy was not a major (even *the* major) determinant of US policy in the Middle East, but for the United States, the war was not an exchange of soldiers' lives for oil wealth. The objective was to protect the flow of oil, which was and still is the energy running the machines of the world's economy. Economic stability, not private gain, was the goal of the coalition. To be sure, soldiers from the United States and other coalition members died, although in very small numbers. Of the 956,600 coalition troops in Iraq, the total number of fatalities was 358, of which nearly half were killed in noncombat accidents. In contrast, Iraq experienced tens of thousands of casualties. The coalition deaths brought concessions from Saddam Hussein, not booty.

The conduct of the First Gulf War also fits the patterns predicted by a political survival outlook. The United States first tried negotiations to get Iraqi forces to leave Kuwait. When these failed, the United States assembled an overwhelmingly powerful coalition of highly trained and superbly equipped troops. Saddam Hussein had elite troops, such as the Republican Guard, that perhaps came close to matching the training and capability of coalition forces. But his elite Republican Guard did not confront the coalition forces; Saddam had them pulled back to safety so they could protect him rather than protect Iraq. Instead, the brunt of the coalition attack was borne by raw recruits and poorly equipped units. As the casualty figures show, many of these units suffered horribly.

Facing the possibility that coalition forces would invade Baghdad to depose him, on February 28 Saddam Hussein agreed to terms of surrender. The United States retained forces in the Gulf to ensure Saddam complied with the terms to which he had agreed. Yet no-fly exclusion zones, diplomatic isolation, and economic sanctions did not stop Saddam from repeatedly violating the agreement. He also survived domestically. After his military defeat, several groups, including Shiites in the South and Kurds in the North, rebelled. Unfortunately for them, Saddam had preserved his best troops and retained enough resources to buy their continued loyalty. The suppression of these uprisings killed tens of thousands and led to the displacement of hundreds of thousands of others. Saddam remained in power until the United States deposed him in the Second Gulf War in 2003.

Saddam was not alone in placing survival and enrichment over fighting well. Dictators like to win wars if they can secure control over extra riches that way, but keeping their job takes priority over pursuing those riches. Mengistu Haile Mariam, who came to power in 1974 when he overthrew Ethiopian emperor Haile Selassie, embraced communism and was handsomely rewarded by the Soviet Union. Over a fourteen-year period the USSR gave his regime about $9 billion, much of it as military aid with which to fight Eritrean rebel forces seeking independence. Despite all this money, his war against the Eritreans did not go well. It seems Mengistu was more interested in the Soviet money as a means to enrich himself and ensure his political survival than in the successful conduct of the war. He certainly had little concern for his soldiers' welfare, as we shall see later. Michela Wrong reported that the Soviets eventually worked out that Mengistu's devotion to the fight was not all it was cracked up to be: " 'He kept telling us that if we helped him he could achieve this military victory,' remembers Adamishin, with bitterness. 'I remember how he told me with tears in his eyes: "We may have to sell our last shirt, but we will pay you back. We Ethiopians are a proud people, we settle our debts." Looking back, I almost feel I hate him. Because I believed that what mattered to him was what was best for the country. While really all that mattered to him was his own survival.' "[10]

Unfortunately for Mengistu Haile Mariam, the collapse of the Soviet Union meant the end of his gravy train. In 1989 the Soviets departed. Mengistu needed a new source of money. In an effort to salvage his situation, he decided to try to get blood money from the United States and Israel by offering to trade Falashas—Ethiopian Jews—for money and military aid. The Falashas had lived in North Africa for thousands of years and are counted among those who fled from the Babylonian captivity in 586 BCE. To resettle these people, the United States allegedly paid $20 million and Israel agreed to pay $58 million (but eventually paid only $35 million). With the money transferred, the rescued Falashas were then settled in Israel.[11] This blood money was not enough to buy the loyalty of his supporters. It was a far cry from the annual amounts doled out by the Soviets. As his military collapsed to the much weaker Eritrean forces, Mengistu fled to Zimbabwe, where he continues to live in luxury with around fifty former colleagues and family members.

WHO SURVIVES WAR

Democrats are much more sensitive to war outcomes than autocrats.[12] Indeed, even victory in war does not guarantee a democrat's political survival. For instance, within eighteen months of defeating Saddam Hussein, and the over 80 percent approval ratings that went with it, President George Herbert Walker Bush was defeated at the polls by Bill Clinton in 1992. Similarly, British voters threw Winston Churchill out of office despite his inspired leadership during World War II. Still, while it is no guarantee of political survival, military victory clearly helps. British prime minister Margaret Thatcher turned her career around with the defeat of Argentina in the Falklands War in 1982. Her economic reforms and confrontations with trade unions had led to a recession and high unemployment. Prior to the war she was deeply unpopular. At the end of 1981 her approval rating stood at 25 percent. After the war it jumped to over 50 percent, and a year later she won a decisive electoral victory that would have looked virtually impossible eighteen months earlier.

Military success helps democrats retain power while defeat makes removal a near certainty for democrats. A failure to achieve victory in Vietnam ended US president Johnson's career. French premier Joseph Laniel suffered a similar fate. His government collapsed following the French defeat by Vietnamese forces in 1954 at the Battle of Dien Bien Phu. British prime minister Anthony Eden was forced to resign after his disastrous invasion of Egypt's Suez Canal Zone in 1956.

Autocrats are much less sensitive to defeat. Despite defeat in the First Gulf War and a costly and inconclusive result in the Iran-Iraq War (1980–1988), Saddam Hussein outlasted four US presidents (Carter, Reagan, Bush, and Clinton). Only defeat in the Second Gulf War cost him his job, and that war was fought primarily to remove him. Unless they are defeated by a democracy seeking policy concessions, autocrats can generally survive military defeat provided that they preserve their resources. Autocrats even survive if their loss involves huge casualties. In contrast, even in victory democrats are liable to be deposed if they get lots of soldiers killed in the process. That presumably is why democrats do much more to protect soldiers than autocrats do.

Hermann Göring, Hitler's number two in the Nazi regime, knew that, while it is the people who do the fighting, it is leaders who start wars. "Naturally the common people don't want war. . . . But, after all, it is the leaders of the country who determine the policy, and it is always a simple matter to drag the people along, whether it is a democracy, or a fascist dictatorship, or a parliament or a communist dictatorship....All you have to do is tell them they are being attacked, and denounce the pacifists for lack of patriotism and exposing the country to danger. It works the same way in any country."[13]

Göring is right. Leaders of every flavor can deploy troops and the people in democracies are liable to rally around the flag. But democrats don't recklessly put soldiers in harm's way. And when they do put them in harm's way, they do much more to protect them. The value of a soldier's life differs drastically between small- and large-coalition systems. To illustrate this sad truth, we compare two conflicts fought a few years apart in the Horn of Africa.

The US military operates on the principle of no soldier left behind. For an accurate and gory drama of this principle, we recommend Ridley Scott's 2001 film *Black Hawk Down*, which portrays an account of the battle of Mogadishu, October 3–4, 1993. US troops entered Somalia as part of a United Nations–sponsored humanitarian mission. In 1993 Somalia was a collapsed state. Between 1969 and 1991 it had been ruled by Siad Barre, someone who understood that policy should always be subordinate to survival. As Barre bluntly stated, "I believe neither in Islam, nor socialism nor tribalism, nor Somali nationalism, nor pan-Africanism. The ideology to which I am committed is the ideology of political survival."[14] And this focus allowed him to successfully survive in office for twenty-two years before being caught up and deposed in the myriad of civil wars that plague the Horn of Africa. Following his deposition, the Somali state collapsed, with control divided between tribal warlords whose militias terrorized the people. Mohamed Farrah Aidid, who led the Habar Gidir clan, controlled one of the strongest factions. Aidid was strongly opposed to the United States' presence in Somalia because he believed the United States was backing his adversaries. After several failed attempts to capture or kill Aidid, the United States received intelligence that several of his senior colleagues were meeting at a house. The US plan was to helicopter elite troops into the building, capture the senior Habar Gidir members, and get out via a military convoy.

Unfortunately the mission went sour. Two Black Hawk helicopters went down and two others were damaged. Thousands of Somalis took to the streets and erected barricades so that the convoy became trapped. Both the helicopter crews and many in the convoy became trapped overnight and were subjected to small-arms fire, and it was not until the next day that they could be rescued. Although the operation was a debacle, the US commitment to its soldiers was unwavering. As is to be expected when soldiers' lives are highly valued, the United States sent forces in to retrieve the downed helicopter crews. We might take this for granted, but it is not the behavior of autocrats—the Ethiopian-Eritrean conflict in the Horn of Africa provides a case in point.

The Battle of Afabet (March 17–20, 1988) was an important turning point in the decades-long battle for Eritrean independence from Ethiopia. As we have seen, Ethiopia had an enormous military of about five hundred thousand men that was lavishly equipped by Soviet military aid. In contrast, virtually all the Eritreans' equipment had been captured from the Ethiopians.

In a switch from its usual guerrilla tactics, the Eritrean rebel force (the Eritrean People's Liberation Front, or EPLF) decided to challenge the Ethiopian army in a head-on battle. The Ethiopians resisted solidly for sixteen hours. On multiple occasions the EPLF commander, Mesfin, was told to withdraw but carried on pressing his attack. The Ethiopian commanders decided to withdraw to the garrison town of Afabet and assembled a convoy of seventy vehicles. Unfortunately for them, the withdrawal went through the Adi Shirum Pass, which forms a natural bottleneck. When an advancing EPLF tank hit a truck in the front of the column, the Ethiopian forces were stuck.

The Ethiopian command was concerned that their heavy weapons might fall into enemy hands. Fortunately for them they had a sizable air force. Yet rather than attempt to relieve their trapped countrymen and fellow soldiers, they embarked on a two-hour aerial bombardment that destroyed everything. The Ethiopian motto was: Leave no working tank behind. As an Ethiopian general put it, "When you lose an area you better destroy your equipment—it's a principle of war. If you cannot separate your men from their equipment then you bomb them both together."[15]

It's likely that few readers have ever heard of this battle, in which Ethiopian casualties were perhaps as high as eighteen thousand men. In contrast, many Americans are familiar with the disastrous policy failure in which, for the loss of thirteen lives, the US Army killed as many as one thousand Somali militants.

THE PEACE BETWEEN DEMOCRACIES

Democracies hardly ever (some might even say never) fight wars with each other. This is not to say they are peace loving. They are not shy about fighting other states. But the reasoning behind the tacit peace between democracies provides some clues to how the world could become more peaceful and why achieving that end is so difficult.

Democratic leaders need to deliver policy success or they will be turned out of office. For this reason they only fight wars when they expect to win. Of course they may turn out to be wrong, in which case, as we have argued, they then double down to turn the fight in their direction. That is just what happened in Vietnam, where the United States committed massive numbers of troops and huge amounts of money to no avail. Only after many long, costly years of trying did the United States settle for a negotiated peace that ultimately turned all of Vietnam over to the North Vietnamese regime. The story in Afghanistan was much the same.

If we are correct, we should hardly ever witness two large-coalition regimes fighting against each other. According to our reasoning, democrats will fight only when they are almost certain that they will win. But how can two adversaries each sustain such certainty? Autocrats, as we saw, don't need to think they have a great chance of winning. They are prepared to take bigger risks because they have good reason to think that the personal consequences of defeat are not as bad for them as the personal consequences of not paying off their few essential supporters. Now, following the logic of political survival closely, we must recognize that just because two democrats are not likely to fight with each other, we cannot say that one will not use force against another. Large-coalition nations certainly may be prepared to engage in disputes with each other, and one might even use force against the other. How does this work?

As long as a large-coalition leader believes that his dispute is unlikely to escalate fully to war, he can move partially up the escalation ladder, pressing his foe into backing down or else backing down himself, and negotiating if he concludes that the other side is prepared to fight and that his own prospects of victory are too small to justify fighting. Hence the departure from Afghanistan after twenty years of fighting but not fully defeating the Taliban. Now imagine the two disputants are both democracies dependent on a large coalition. The logic of large-coalition politics tells us that a large-coalition state will attack another large-coalition state only if the target is weak enough that it is expected to prefer to negotiate rather than fight back. Since the democratic target will also try hard if it chooses to fight back, the initiating democracy must either have (or be capable of having) a great military advantage or be confident that its rival's resources are insufficient for the target to believe it can be nearly certain of victory. Thus, the attacking democracy must be sure that its target democracy is *unsure* of victory; this is of paramount importance in a head-to-head military dispute between two democracies.[16] Here we have an explanation for the history of US attacks against very weak democratic rivals, such as Lyndon Johnson's 1965 attack and overthrow of Juan Bosch's democratically elected regime in the Dominican Republic, France's invasion of Weimar Germany in 1923, and the list goes on.

Democracies don't fight with each other, true. But big democracies pick on little opponents whether they are democratic or not, with the expectation that they won't fight back or won't put up much of a fight. Indeed, that could very well be viewed as a straightforward explanation of the history of democracies engaged in imperial and colonial expansion against weak adversaries with little hope of defending themselves.

This democratic propensity to pick on weak foes is nothing new. Looking at all wars for nearly the past two centuries, we know that about 93 percent of wars started by democratic states are won by them. In contrast, only about 60 percent of wars started by nondemocracies are won by them.[17]

DEFENDING THE PEACE AND NATION BUILDING

In his 1994 State of the Union address, US president Bill Clinton declared that "democracies don't attack each other" and therefore "the best strategy to insure our security and to build a durable peace is to support the advance of democracy elsewhere."[18] This is a common theme for US presidents. Unfortunately, actions have not matched the rhetoric. More unfortunately still, the problem lies not in a failure on the presidential level but with "we the people."

In democracies, leaders who fail to deliver the policies their constituents want get deposed. Democrats might say they care about the rights of people overseas to determine their own future, and they might actually care, too, but if they want to keep their jobs they will deliver the policies that *their people* want. Earlier we examined how democrats use foreign aid to buy policy. If that fails or gets too expensive, then force is always an option. Military victory allows the victors to impose policy.

We should dismiss any pretense that such policies are benevolent and imposed with the foreigners' long-term best interests in mind. They are not. They are done for the benefit of the democrat's supporters, and sometimes these policies can be very unpleasant. For instance, the Opium Wars (1839–1842 and 1856–1860) got their name because the British wanted to finance their purchases of Chinese exports by selling the Chinese opium grown in India. China was reluctant to become a nation of addicts. The British used force to open up China to the drug market. Hong Kong started out as a base from which the British could enforce this trade openness. It is telling that, while the settlements that ended the wars are officially known as the Treaties of Nanking and Tianjin, the Chinese often refer to them as the Unequal Treaties.

One of the problems with seeking a policy solution is that after the democrat's army leaves, the vanquished nation can renege. Enforcing the settlement can be very expensive, as was the case after the Gulf War. A common solution, and the one eventually used against Saddam Hussein, is leader replacement. Democrats remove foreign leaders who are troublesome to them and replace them with puppets.

The leaders that rise to the top after an invasion are more often than not handpicked by the victor.

A difficult leader whom democrats don't trust to honor an agreement will often find himself replaced. The Congo's Patrice Lumumba, democratically elected, didn't have policies that pleased the Belgian or American governments, and before you knew it, Lumumba was dead, replaced by horrible successors who also happened to be prepared to toe the line favored by the United States and Belgium. France was no different, stepping into its ex-colony of Chad to make sure that a French-friendly government was in charge rather than a Libyan-friendly or Arab-friendly regime.

Democratic leaders profess a desire for democratization. Yet the reality is that it is rarely in their interest. As the coalition size grows in a foreign nation, its leader becomes more and more compelled to enact policies that his people want and not the policies desired by the puppeteer's people. If a democratic leader wants a foreign leader to follow his prescribed policies, then he needs to insulate his puppet from domestic pressures. This means reducing coalition size in vanquished states. This makes it cheaper and easier to sustain puppets and buy policy. US foreign policy is awash with examples where the United States overtly or covertly undermined the development of democracy because it promoted policies counter to US interests. Queen Liliuokalani of Hawaii in 1893, Salvador Allende of Chile in 1973, Mohammad Mosaddegh of Iran in 1953, and Jacobo Arbenz of Guatemala in 1954 all suffered such fates.

Democracy overseas is a nice thing to believe in, in the abstract. In practice, it's probably not what we the people want. Let's return to reconsider Egypt and Israel and the case for democratization. Western democracies used to complain, albeit not too emphatically, about electoral malpractice in Egypt under Mubarak. With Mubarak gone, they worried that true democracy in Egypt might be contrary to the interests of friends of Israel. Buying peace with Israel under Mubarak was costly, but moves toward democracy in Egypt would make continued peace costlier, at least until (and if) Egypt becomes a full-fledged, mature democracy whose leaders will then only fight if they are virtually sure of victory. So when the Egyptian military toppled their nascent democracy led by the Muslim Brotherhood's

Mohamed Morsi, the Obama administration was careful not to call the military's action a coup. Doing so would have triggered a US law that would have cut off aid to Egypt just when a potentially more US-friendly government was taking over.

While it is true that democracies generally don't fight each other, we have also noted that they do have lopsided conflicts, and those conflicts often end with the weaker side capitulating. If Egypt were democratic and if a democratic Egypt mobilized and armed itself, tiny Israel would have little hope of resisting unless the United States or NATO was prepared to make a large effort to defend it. Anyone who thinks a democratic Egypt attacking Israel is too fanciful a scenario might ask democratic Native American tribes from the American plains about their dealings with the expanding United States in the 1800s. Democratization sounds good in principle only.

Of course, many may think that we are just too cynical. Advocates of democratization are fond of pointing out the success stories. Yet all of these cases—Germany, Japan, South Korea, and Taiwan—also happen to involve countries whose populations' values largely coincided with American values in resisting large communist neighbors for decades.

The big problem with democratizing overseas continues to lie with "we the people." In most cases we seem to prefer that foreign nations do what we want, not what they want. However, if our interests align, then successful democratization is more likely. This is particularly so if there is a rival power that wishes to influence policy. The postwar success stories fit this category well. Generally, the people of West Germany and Japan preferred what the United States wanted to the vision expounded by the Soviet Union. Creating powerful states that wanted to resist communism and would try hard was in the US interest. As occupying powers, the United States, Britain, and France might have set Germany on a course to democracy, but they did so only because it was advantageous for them. This confluence of interests is rare, and so is externally imposed democratization.

Sun Tzu exerted a lasting influence on the study of war precisely because his recommendations are the right recommendations for leaders, like monarchs and autocrats, who rule based on a small coalition. The Weinberger Doctrine—like its more recent replacements—exerts influence over American security policy precisely because it recommends the most appropriate actions for leaders who are beholden to a large coalition.

We have seen that larger-coalition nations are extremely selective in their decisions about waging war and smaller-coalition nations are not. Democracies only fight when negotiation proves unfruitful and the democrat's military advantage is overwhelming, or when, without fighting, the democrat's chances of political survival are slim to none. Furthermore, when war becomes necessary, large-coalition regimes make an extra effort to win if the fight proves difficult. Small-coalition leaders do not if doing so would use up treasure that would be better spent on the private rewards that keep their cronies loyal. And finally, when a war is over, larger-coalition leaders make more effort to enforce the peace and the policy gains they sought through occupation or the imposition of a puppet regime. Small-coalition leaders mostly take the valuable private goods for which they fought and go home, or take over the territory they conquered so as to enjoy the economic fruits of their victory for a long time.

Clausewitz had war right. War, it seems, truly is just "a continuation of" domestic "politics by other means." For all the philosophical talk of a "just war" and all the strategizing about balances of power and national interests, in the end, war, like all politics, is about leaders trying to stay in power and control as many resources as possible. It is precisely this predictability and normality of war that makes it, like all the pathologies of politics we have discussed, susceptible to being understood and fixed.

CHAPTER TEN

IS DEMOCRACY FRAGILE?

January 6, 2021, may be a day that equaled—or overtook—December 7, 1941, as a "day that will live in infamy." Democracy in the United States was threatened by a small, intense, violent group seeking to overturn the results of the presidential election two months earlier. It was the most serious assault on the American Capitol since the British burned it in 1814. The British action was an act of war. The 2021 assault on the Capitol was an act of insurrection—an action by domestic actors intended to alter the institutions of US governance. Democracy survived.

The Capitol insurrection came at the end of what many have perceived as a decade of democratic retrenchment. Concerned citizens point to Rodrigo Duterte in the Philippines, Jair Bolsonaro in Brazil, and Andrzej Duda in Poland as undermining democratic principles. Throughout the preceding chapters we outlined how leaders are only in it for themselves and why bettering themselves means contracting their coalition of supporters. You might therefore expect us to be predicting the end of democracy. Yet to the contrary, we are optimistic about the survival of large-winning-coalition (a.k.a. democratic) governments, and we believe the evidence is on our side.

Despite our admonitions to think of governance in terms of the number of essential supporters that a leader needs to stay in power, we have continually erred in equating large-coalition systems with democracy. We will certainly repeat this linguistic convenience, but we are mindful that it can lead to sloppy thinking. We have dodged the perennial question of what is democracy, and with good reason. Does democracy simply require elections, or do the elections need to be free and fair? Or does democracy require civil liberties and the right to free speech? We could fill many chapters with fruitless debate on the meaning and definition of democracy. Further, we all too often politicize the epithet: we call our friends democrats and our enemies despots. While we concede the peril that democracy faces, we shall defend the argument that when leaders rely on a sufficiently large coalition of supporters to retain power, governance institutions are robust and endure.

Our optimism does not mean that those of us fortunate enough to live in large-coalition systems can sit back because everything will be all right. Rather, we have the means to protest and organize to preserve our freedoms. And it is in our interest to do so.

January 6 reminded everyone paying any attention (and was there anyone not paying attention?) that democracy always exists atop an undercurrent of threat. Elections pick winners and create losers, and no one likes to lose. Hence, democracy presents leaders with a formidable conundrum.

Every head of state, whether a dictator or a democrat, is best off when her rule depends on pleasing just a few people. The difficulty is that democratic leaders always have to satisfy a large coalition; that is what it means to be a democracy. Such government, as we have emphasized throughout, requires the sustained support of many essentials. The problem is that the loyalty of those essentials always is unreliable. They are easily tempted away by a rival, putting the incumbent at a high risk of replacement. With such fickle support, democrats must work hard to deliver policy solutions to the problems of the day. Despite their best efforts, they are often kicked out. In the words of US president Herbert Hoover following his 1932 defeat by Franklin Delano Roosevelt, "Democracy is a harsh employer." The simple fact is that democratic states do well; democratic heads of state do not!

We have just made a distinction that too often is ignored: democratic governing institutions are robust while democratic administrations are fragile. The plain fact is that the institutions of very-large-coalition democracies are rarely overturned, but the leaders of those institutions—presidents and prime ministers—hang on to power only for a short time.

Leaders come and go, but large-coalition governance endures. Back in Chapter 3, we compared the tenure of leaders under different governance institutions. The average time in office for a leader in the smallest-coalition systems is about twelve years, while leaders in the largest-coalition systems average less than five years in office. The sad fact for democrats is that while they deliver policies that enable their citizens to enjoy long, productive, and happy lives, their reward is a short term in office and little opportunity to enrich themselves. Remember Mexican politician Hank Gonzalez's declaration that "a politician who stays poor is poor at politics."[1] That's simply not true in democratic politics. Presidents make money on book deals after they leave office. Sure, corruption happens. Bill Clinton was rightly put through the wringer for trying to take furniture from the White House, and there are allegations that Donald Trump enriched his eponymous company by accommodating government officials in his hotel chain at taxpayer expense. Certainly such actions are inappropriate and wrong, but they are so small-scale compared to what leaders do in small-coalition regimes. The Marcoses, the Mobutus, and the Gonzalezes must consider US presidents rank amateurs. They work hard, earn (or steal) little, and still get kicked out of office after all their hard work and honesty.

While the person who rules in a democracy is constantly changing, the democracies themselves hardly change. In the 232 years that have followed the introduction of the Bill of Rights (the first ten amendments), the US Constitution has been amended only seventeen times. Some of these amendments represent consequential changes to institutional rules: for instance, the Twelfth Amendment (1804) altered the rules for electing the vice president, the Fourteenth Amendment (1868) defined citizenship rules, the Twenty-Second Amendment (1951) introduced presidential term limits, the Twentieth (1933) and Twenty-Fifth (1967) Amendments clarified succession procedures, and the Fifteenth (1870), Nineteenth (1920), Twenty-Fourth (1964), and Twenty-Sixth (1971) Amendments established who could vote (allowed all races to vote, extended the franchise to women, removed poll taxes, and changed the voting age to eighteen). Other amendments, although not changes to the rules by which leaders are chosen, were of monumental importance: the Thirteenth Amendment (1865) abolished slavery, and the Sixteenth Amendment (1913) authorized income tax. The Eighteenth (1919) and Twenty-First (1933) Amendments dealt with Prohibition and its repeal, perhaps a less salient topic unless you are really partial to wine.

While we don't want to diminish the importance of these changes, and amendments fifteen, nineteen, twenty-four, and twenty-six clearly altered the size of the winning coalition and selectorate by increasing the number of voters, the electoral rules by which the US chooses leaders remain largely unchanged after more than two hundred years. In a letter to James Madison dated September 6, 1789, Thomas Jefferson argued that the Constitution needed to be revised with every generation: "No society can make a perpetual constitution, or even a perpetual law. The earth belongs always to the living generation."[2] That the system that these men and the other Founding Fathers created has endured largely unchanged is all the more surprising given the transformation of the US. Since 1790, its population has grown eighty-five-fold and its land mass has increased by a factor of 4.4 (and that includes counting territories rather than just states in 1790). The economic change is nearly incomprehensible. In 1790 the US was an economic backwater of smallholder farmers with a GDP of about $4 billion (in current dollars). Today the US economy is the largest in the world with a GDP of close to $21 trillion—that's a staggering five-thousand-fold increase (yes, we had to do the math several times to believe it). What better advertisement could there be for crafting rules for large-coalition governance? It also makes clear why the people of the United States would want to preserve democratic institutions.

The US rules of political competition have been remarkably stable, though major constitutional amendments have increased the size of the winning coalition (amendments fifteen, nineteen, twenty-four, and twenty-six, for instance). Other democracies experience significant rule changes, although, as we shall see, only modest changes in coalition size. For instance, as the result of a referendum in 1993,

New Zealand switched from a first-past-the-post (the British West-minster style) electoral system to a multimembered proportional representation system (parties get seats in proportion to their vote shares). Superficially, New Zealand politics appears much changed. Prior to 1993, there were only two major parties, but after reform the number of competitive parties increased, often necessitating coalition governments. To a political scientist who studies electoral systems, these differences are huge. In terms of selectorate theory, the referendum resulted in a small increase in the size of the winning coalition; by our measure on the 0 to 1 scale, the set of essentials increased from 0.90 in 1993 to 0.93 after the reform. Hardly an enormous change, but it was in the direction of expansion.

The rules by which leaders are chosen may remain relatively unchanged, as in the US experience, or they may change markedly, as was the case in New Zealand. In either case, once leaders are beholden to very large numbers of supporters, they remain so. Who the leaders are may change rapidly, but their dependence on a large coalition endures.

Indeed, over the past 230 years, there are not even a handful of examples of governments that depended on a winning coalition equal to at least 0.9 on our 0 to 1 coalition-measurement scale whose coalition subsequently shrank below 0.7. The few cases that do exist involve the external impact of the conquest of these nations by, for instance, Nazi Germany or the Soviet Union. In contrast, there are more than two hundred cases of at least a 0.2-point loss in coalition size for governments that did not have really big essential groups to begin with. Once a nation gets large governance institutions, these institutions survive.[3]

Figure 10.1 shows the persistence of large-coalition systems of governance. We classified regimes as being "large coalition" if they had a coalition of at least 0.9 on our 0 to 1 scale. All other regimes are classified as "smaller coalition." For the years 1970, 1980, 1990, and 2000, we compared by how much coalition size changed for initially large-coalition or initially smaller-coalition regimes over the following twenty years. We could have chosen different decades or looked at longer or shorter changes; the pattern is the same.

The white bars indicate the number of initially smaller-coalition governments whose essentials group changed by the amount shown on the horizontal axis during the twenty years periods. The black bars show the same information but for large-coalition regimes.

While many smaller-coalition nations experienced only modest change in institutions, a significant number experienced large contractions or expansions covering more than half the 0-to-1 scale. The changes in the institutions of nations that started with a large coalition (the black bars) look quite different. They are clustered around zero. That means there is very little change in the institutions of nations that start with large coalitions. The tallest black bar indicates that most systems that start with a large coalition expand slightly over the next twenty years. This is especially remarkable because when they start near the top of the scale there is very little room for improvement but a lot of potential to slip. Yet very few nations with a lot of essentials slip in their coalition size, and even fewer slip by a significant amount. The largest decline shown in the graph is Poland's.

Figure 10.1 is pretty encouraging. The historical record supports the persistence of democracy. But don't get us wrong. Even mature democracies are a little malleable, with the emphasis on the word *little*.

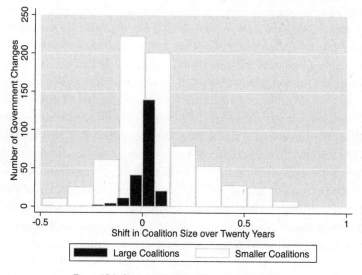

Figure 10.1: Change in Coalition Size over Twenty Years

Overturning really close elections, for example, is feasible even in the most mature of democracies. Who, after all, can truly say with confidence that Al Gore or George W. Bush clearly won Florida in 2000 and so won the Electoral College and the presidency in that remarkably close election? The margin was razor thin. In other cases, rules overturn substantial leads. In the 1824 US election Andrew Jackson beat his nearest rival, John Quincy Adams, by 12 percent in the popular vote. However, with four candidates in the race, his 43 percent vote share was not enough to win outright, and so the House of Representatives got to decide. In what is often described as the "corrupt bargain," Henry Clay, Speaker of the House, orchestrated a deal by which Adams would be elected president and in return Clay would become secretary of state. This seeming injustice angered many, and they responded by kicking out Adams and electing Jackson four years later.

Of course, who won mattered a great deal to Bush and to Gore and to Adams and to Jackson, but either way, the outcome did not materially alter the institutionally required size of a winning coalition in the United States. But when the electoral outcome is clear instead of insanely close, it is almost impossible—in fact, maybe it *is* impossible—to shrink a really-large-coalition system into a meaningfully smaller one from within so as to overturn the will of the voters. Democracies have a malleable coalition but not one that is so elastic that it can be stretched to the point that it is not recognizable.

Take a look back at Figure 1.1 in Chapter 1. That figure shows a wide range of coalition sizes in places that are regularly identified as democracies. One of the democracies in the figure, India, suffered a serious governmental setback during the 1970s when then prime minister Indira Gandhi maneuvered to shrink the governing coalition to the point that it became barely recognizable. She even amended the constitution in an effort that many interpreted as her attempt to turn herself into an autocratic ruler, much as it seems that Donald Trump was trying to do for himself in 2020. Prime Minister Gandhi was momentarily successful, but then the electorate perceived that she had gone too far. The upshot was that she, along with her Congress Party, were thrown out of office by the voters. In pretty short order, her successor restored India's large-coalition institutional requirements just as Figure 1.1 shows us.[4]

Today, India's coalition is again backsliding, as are coalition sizes in many other democracies. We think that India's voters will once again restore reliance on a larger coalition once Prime Minister Narendra Modi is out of office. We think that will happen in the United States, too, as Joe Biden restores coalitional requirements that were diminished somewhat during Donald Trump's presidency. We are optimistic about the restoration of a larger national winning coalition in the United States even though those coalition requirements are under attack in numerous states. And we think today's democratic backsliding will reverse in just about every place that has long-established, robust democratic institutions. We think that because the logic of political survival tells us for once to be optimists: big coalitions and the vast number of everyday people who benefit from them do not easily submit to the will of a coalition-shrinking leader. In fact, as Figure 10.1 showed us, the largest-coalition governments, places like modern-day Sweden, Costa Rica, the United States, Australia, South Korea, Germany, and so forth, experience a much smaller range in the swings in coalition size compared with smaller-coalition countries. This is not just a happy fact of history. The reasons that this is true explain why it is so much easier to topple large-coalition *rulers* than it is to topple large-coalition *polities*.

Democracy is facing a tough time, but the logic behind our survival way of thinking tells us that when a government's group of essentials is sufficiently large (we'll explain what that "sufficient" size is in a moment) then its governmental institutions are resilient. Sure, we anticipate that many autocratic, small-coalition regimes will persist long into the future. However, once nations have successfully transitioned to large-coalition democracies, these institutions become locked in. The future belongs disproportionately to public goods–producing large-coalition governments.

BIG AND SMALL COALITIONS ARE INSTITUTIONALLY STABLE; MIDSIZE COALITIONS ARE NOT!

Naturally, given how much easier it is to please a few people than it is to please millions, any democratic leader would like to maneuver her

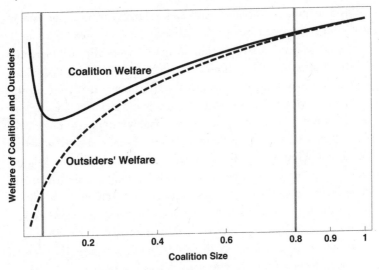

Figure 10.2: The Welfare of Citizens and Coalition Members

government into becoming more autocratic, but the changes required to achieve that goal are dangerous to execute. To see why materially shrinking the coalition is an especially tough order for democrats, let's have a look at Figure 10.2. Every detail in this figure, whether simple, obvious, subtle, complex, or counterintuitive, is rigorously derived from the game theory logic behind everything we have said and will say. And it is the story told by the details in this figure that is the essence behind our optimism that once a coalition has passed beyond a critical juncture, democratic institutions are here to stay.

Okay, we know, your eyes are glazing over—this is one complicated figure. We will, however, break it down into its critical parts, and it will be clear that it conveys a powerfully optimistic message for democracy. Let's begin by briefly explaining the horizontal and vertical axes.

The horizontal axis, coalition size, is straightforward. We want to look at the full range of possible coalitions (holding constant the size of the pool of people—the selectorate—from which it can be drawn). We are interested in knowing how the value on the vertical axis—welfare—changes as the coalition gets bigger. What do we mean by "welfare"? We mean the sum of the value of public goods and private goods that individuals receive from their government. Remember that leaders generate revenue (for example, by taxing income, borrowing, earning fees, etc.) and spend some of it on public goods in the form of policies for everyone in society, some on private goods that are enjoyed only by members of the winning coalition, and any leftover, discretionary money on whatever they want (such as themselves or pet projects).

The leader's welfare (a downward sloping curve, not shown) is greater when there is lots of discretionary money. That happens when the coalition is as small as possible and the selectorate is as large as possible.[5] Therefore, leaders want as small a coalition as possible with as big a selectorate as possible. That way, besides whatever public benefits they provide—and enjoy—they also get the maximum amount of discretionary money that they can possibly obtain.

The welfare of those outside the winning coalition, the influentials and interchangeables (the selectorate), is depicted on the rising, dashed curve in the figure. They want the coalition to be as large as possible because they benefit from a leader's hard work to produce public goods. Their welfare consists only of these public goods since, not being in the coalition, they do not get any of the private rewards provided by the government. Their welfare—the value they attach to the public goods—increases as the coalition gets bigger and bigger. Outsiders and the leader have diametrically opposed goals. But neither leaders nor outsiders can get their way without the support of insiders—those essentials who determine whether the leader can retain power or will be swept away.

The welfare of the essentials in the winning coalition is shown by the swoosh-shaped curve. That curve is a little complicated, but we have discussed all of the components in preceding chapters, and we can gain great insight into when governments are stable or unstable by understanding why the curve in Figure 10.2 looks the way it does. The benefits gained by coalition members consist of two parts: the value they attach to the public goods the government provides, and the value they attach to the private benefits (like corruption opportunities, better housing, superior schooling for their children, etc.) that they receive as an exclusive privilege of coalition membership.

To understand the logic behind the swoosh curve, let's start at the far left of the figure—that is, in a very-small-winning-coalition society. In such a society the leader provides few public benefits, so society is unproductive and poor. But while society is poor, the leader taxes the people heavily and gives lavishly to his supporters. Each supporter's loyalty is bought with private goods. So when the coalition is tiny, its very few members are rewarded—that is, bribed—with enormous amounts of private benefits.

What happens as the coalition expands? The graph shows that coalition welfare drops rapidly as the coalition starts to expand from a small base. More people need to get a share of the pie, but society has not gotten much more productive (public goods and freedoms remain rare), so each essential's share of benefits diminishes. Each supporter becomes worse off as the coalition starts to expand. However, beyond a certain point, further expansion of coalition size increases the coalition's welfare. On the right side of the figure, the solid line shows coalition welfare increasing. The expansion of the coalition still diminishes each supporter's share of private goods, but when the coalition is relatively large, private goods are simply not as important as they were in tiny-coalition systems. The dilution of private goods is less important because the coalition's overall well-being is improving.

As coalition size becomes very large, leaders must compete in the battle of good policy ideas. At the right side of the figure, expansion of the coalition means leaders must convince more people that they have good ideas about improving policy if they are to remain in power. If those good ideas do not pan out, they will lose some of their essential supporters and be out of office. To avoid such a horrific outcome, leaders who rely on a large coalition must work hard to satisfy their many supporters and cannot divert resources to their pet projects or secret bank accounts. That is great news for coalition members and society in general but terrible news for the leader.

The swoosh curve explains much about political change. Leaders always prefer to rely on a small coalition. The people prefer a leader to need many supporters. Which institutional changes the essentials within the coalition will endorse depends on how big the existing coalition is. At the extreme left of the figure (that is, in the smallest-coalition systems) the essentials only want to contract the coalition. At the far right of the figure (that is, in large-coalition systems), coalition expansion—in other words, further democratization—is the only institutional change in the coalition's interest. At intermediate coalition sizes—at the low point in the center of Figure 10.2—supporters can improve their lot through purges or coups that diminish the coalition *or* by supporting democratic expansion of the coalition. It is in this middle that institutions churn. At the extremes, supporters are happy with their lot. In the middle, they are happy to change their lot.

The welfare of the essentials who keep a leader in power is highest in very small and very large coalitions, but for very different reasons. Consider taking a stroll across the thirty-eighth parallel (although not literally, since it's covered in land mines), between North and South Korea. North Korea is a poor nation. Its total GDP is about $28.5 billion, although of course it is hard to measure it accurately. What is very clear is that its wealth is not evenly distributed over its twenty-six million people. Most of the population live isolated lives in remote towns and villages with little electrification or communications. The elites have a more rarified lifestyle in the capital, Pyongyang. They get to live in luxury high-rise buildings and buy luxury goods, such as German cars, cell phones, flat-screen TVs, designer fashion goods, and Japanese whiskey. They also get to visit water parks, fairgrounds, a science museum, and even a dolphinarium. In exchange for staying loyal, the families of Kim Jong-Un's essential supporters get to enjoy subsidized modern housing, fine dining, and luxury goods. At a material level their lives might even be better than those of the essential insiders who keep President Moon Jae-In in power below the thirty-eighth parallel, in South Korea.

Today South Korea is a rich industrial democracy with a per capita income of about $35,000. Yet until the mid-1970s there was little to distinguish it economically from the North. Of course, not coincidentally, the 1970s is when the Republic of Korea, to use its formal name, began to democratize. Today it ranks twentieth in its coalition size, with a score of 0.91 on our 0 to 1 scale. The current president, Moon Jae-In, is from the more left-leaning of the two main political parties. In the 2017 presidential election he received about 13.5 million votes, but 8 million votes would have been sufficient for him to defeat the second-place candidate—that is, he was supported by roughly 15 percent of the population, or 22 percent of the voters. That is hardly a majority of South Koreans, but it is thousands of times more supporters than Kim Jong-Un needs.

Moon promotes economic reforms and wants to break up chaebols (conglomerates that dominate much of the economy). He has increased the minimum wage by 16 percent and cut the maximum workweek from sixty-eight hours to fifty-two. The public health measures he implemented largely contained COVID even though South Korea had a substantial outbreak early in the pandemic. As you might expect, his supporters tend to be relatively poor (by South Korean standards) and his policies are designed to improve their lives. As a rough guide, let's suppose that his average supporter earns about twelve million won per year (that is, about $10,500) and represents the bottom 38 percent of wage earners. That's not a lot of money, and such a supporter surely would be priced out of downtown Seoul. However, such supporters get good basic public health care and their children get an excellent public education. They probably have to take public transport to get around; however, in stark contrast to the other side of the thirty-eighth parallel, there is an excellent transport network, people can travel wherever they want, and they say whatever they want and meet with whomever they want while they are there. Life is pretty good for essential supporters on both sides of the border, although for very different reasons.

Seoul and Pyongyang are geographically close. Yet a transition between their political systems is virtually impossible (except via military conquest). Some elites in North Korea might envy Moon's numerous healthy, educated, free but poor supporters. Equally, some members of the working class in the South might be willing to trade their freedoms for lavish living if they could be essentials in the North, a very big *if*. Yet for neither group does attempting the transition make sense. To see why, we need only look back at Figure 10.2.

Let's start in North Korea, on the left side of the figure. On the left side, the welfare of coalition members increases only if the coalition gets smaller. Kim's supporters are willing to support purges of their fellow coalition members provided, of course, that they are not among the purged. Purges result in fewer people having a share of the private goods to be distributed—the dolphinarium won't be so crowded at their next visit, and there might be vacancies on the penthouse floor. Expanding the coalition makes little sense for them because doing so would dilute their share of the goodies. The polity might start down the road to democratization, but before they get far the leader and coalition members will realize that expansion harms their welfare. On the left of the figure, the interests of the leader and his small band of cronies coincide. Provided the leader is healthy, such systems are virtually immune to change. Supporters are loyal and the people are powerless to rise up. Of course, things can get more volatile when the leader's health declines, but so long as that does not happen, the leader's and his coalition's interests are aligned, and the masses are too poor, isolated, and oppressed to do anything about it.

Now consider working-class supporters of Moon in the South who hypothetically prefer riches to freedoms. They might go to the North (virtually no one does) to try to become part of that country's winning coalition. Embarking on such a transition is a perilous journey for them. Speaking extremely generously, they have less than a one in many, many thousands chance of making it into and then remaining in the coalition. And their effort to get into the coalition comes with their own reduced welfare during their journey from South to North. Moon needs millions of supporters; Kim needs, generously, a few thousand—probably far, far fewer. They are unlikely to be among those few whose support is essential in the North.

Alternatively, some coalition members and some people in the South might try to emulate the small coalition structure that prevails in the North. But most coalition members and most of the people will resist any attempt by South Koreans to emulate North Korea's government structure. The mathematics of coalition welfare is such that essential supporters in large coalitions can make themselves better off only by continuing to expand the coalition, shifting further to the figure's right, not its left.

In large democratic systems there is some wiggle room: often coalition members don't fully realize the consequences of the policies they support. But if a leader tries to significantly and overtly contract the winning coalition, then the people will protest, supporters will start to defect, and the democratic leader will become a former leader. Donald Trump attempted to restrict the franchise by limiting immigration, making it harder for his opponents to vote, and undermining the press with claims of "fake news," not to mention leaning on voting officials and inciting his supporters to storm Congress. These were all actions intended to reduce the number of supporters he would need to rule—a contraction in the coalition's size. Yet as he tried to enact these changes, he was still constrained by the large-coalition, democratic institutions in which he operated. While we might point to differences in how law enforcement treated those who demonstrated in support of Trump and how it treated those who protested against him, the people had freedoms that allowed them to protest, and they did so.

People turned out to vote in record numbers in the 2020 presidential election; turnout was 7.5 percent higher than in 2016. In part the election was about the policies that Trump and Joe Biden each advocated. Trump's policies were extremely popular with his supporters, and by voting for him they hoped to get their preferred policies (that is, they wanted to be in the winning coalition, or at least be supporters of it), but those policies would have come at the cost of inferior democratic institutions—a smaller winning coalition moving forward. Such a contraction would have meant worse governance in the future. For many Trump supporters the package of "our guy today" and less public-spirited governance by someone else in the future was better than Biden today. But for some it was not. It is telling that Republicans in, for instance, Georgia and Wisconsin did much better in down-ballot races in 2020 than Trump did.[6] And, for those outside Trump's coalition, there was only downside in his election. Biden ran on a platform that included keeping the coalition large. Over eighty-two million voters turned out to support Biden, in part to protect the institutions that they valued.

The voters rejected Trump's overt attempt to contract the coalition. But Trump was not the first president to suffer a rebuff from the voters. That honor—probably better described as a dishonor—goes to the second president, John Adams, for his imposition of the Alien and

Sedition Acts. These acts (there were actually four of them) are pretty well described by their names. The Alien Acts discriminated against recent immigrants, making it harder for them to become citizens and, therefore, to gain the right to vote. It won't shock you to learn that recent immigrants back in 1804 disproportionately voted for Jefferson's Democratic-Republican Party and not for Adams's Federalist Party. The Sedition Acts made it a crime to defame the government and were intended to curtail criticism of the Adams administration. The backlash against these policies was enormous. In the 1800 election Adams received only 38.6 percent of the popular vote, and Jefferson became president. The voters' rebuke of Trump seems mild by comparison.

Voters in large coalitions enjoy their democracy, or rather the good policies it provides, and they reject those who openly try to undermine it. Once the coalition becomes sufficiently large, only the leader stands to gain from its contraction. As the logic presented in Figure 10.2 shows, once coalitions are very large they stay that way.

Let's have a look back at Figure 10.2 to be more precise about where the risk of coups and mass rebellions is greatest and where it is virtually nonexistent. Notice the vertical gray line near the upper bound of coalition size. That line denotes the coalition size at which the expected welfare of any coalition member is as good as their best achievable welfare when the coalition is at its smallest. If we ran a horizontal line from the high point of coalition welfare that is expected by the smallest coalition to the largest, it would intersect the swoosh curve before the possible maximum coalition size, indicating that more welfare is available for coalition members if the essential group is larger than the intersection point for the proposed horizontal line. Of course, very few people enjoy a high level of well-being when the coalition is tiny and a great many enjoy it when the coalition is as large as where the vertical gray line is located (at about 0.8 on the coalition scale).

Look a little to the left of that vertical line. Coalition welfare is declining along with coalition size. It keeps declining until we reach the lowest coalition-welfare point on the graph. Although essentials might not notice a small wiggle downward, they are in the coalition for the benefits it offers them. They are, therefore, paying attention to whether the incumbent is taking good care of them with an eye to whether they should throw their backing behind someone else. If the coalition shrinks, then some of its former members must have been purged, a fact that is not likely to be missed by those who remain. They are probably okay with a purge that left their benefits in place. But their benefits are shrinking. That, of course, is exactly what is happening as we move left of the right-hand vertical line. Look to the right of that vertical line. People in the coalition expect to be better off the bigger the coalition gets beyond that point. As a consequence, there is a huge difference in the trajectory of well-being just to the left and just to the right of the gray line.

To the left, coalition welfare can be improved in two different ways. The incumbent ruler can purge members from the coalition, shrinking the essential group, so that those who survive the purge are better off than they were before the purge. That's probably what happened after Saddam Hussein finished his videotaped purge of Ba'ath Party leaders in 1979. Or the leader can expand the coalition enough to improve the welfare of everyone in it, making the government more accountable. That was the path eventually followed by J.J. Rawlings in Ghana. Either way, those in the coalition can be well off.

Leaders naturally prefer to purge people, thereby improving their own welfare, but such purges can be risky, as we discussed in Chapter 2. If coalition members anticipate a purge and fear that they will be ousted from the coalition, then they may initiate a coup d'état to overthrow the incumbent and set up a new regime that is better for them. Likewise, if some of those excluded from the coalition anticipate that it is going to be further diminished, reducing public goods along the way, there may be a mass uprising or revolt intended to overthrow the government.

If we move to the right of the right-hand vertical line, then the incentives to stage a coup or a revolution all but disappear. Once we are even a tiny bit to the right of the vertical line, the coalition's welfare can only get worse if the coalition is diminished in size and it can only get better if it is enlarged. Hence, once a government is sufficiently democratic to be to the right of this gray line, just about no one in the winning coalition should be expected to support purges.

Sure, a leader might find some outsiders to try to overturn the existing order. Those outsiders would have to think that a revolt would probably get them into the next winning coalition, giving them access to private benefits that they otherwise could not get. But they would have an awfully hard time raising broad support for their effort, and they would need that broad support to topple the existing institutions. That, remember, is why we don't expect poor South Koreans to migrate to the North in the hope of making it into Kim Jong-Un's coalition. After all, most people in democracies like South Korea are on the dashed line. They are getting tons of public goods when their government's coalition is to the right of that right-hand vertical line. They are much more likely to end up worse off rather than better off by supporting an effort to *shrink* the coalition. As we already know, the same is true for those in the coalition. That is exactly the implication of the swoosh-shaped line in Figure 10.2, a shape determined by the logic of selectorate reasoning.[7]

When the January 6, 2021, invasion of the Capitol is looked at with an understanding of Figure 10.2, it is easy to see why the insurrectionists failed. There was no way for them to succeed: there just were not enough people who could be made better off by supporting the effort to stop certification of the 2020 presidential election. Sure, those trying to stop the certification of Biden's election were making an effort to get into or stay in the winning coalition, or at least the support coalition. Presumably, they perceived that they were being purged by those forming Biden's coalition. Their problem was that there were enough defections away from Trump that Trump no longer commanded a winning coalition. Since the winning coalition was almost certainly on the right side of the gray line, those trying to save Trump were on a hopeless fool's errand.[8] They simply could have had no reasonable expectation of mustering enough support to halt Biden's larger coalition.

Knowing the risks and the costs of purges, large-coalition leaders or aspiring leaders in large-coalition settings almost never take actions that are likely to result in attempted coups d'état or revolutions. Being survival oriented, they have the foresight to avoid actions that will lead their coalition or the general citizenry to rise up against them.

As we saw, if the group of essentials is large enough, the government is practically immune from coups and mass uprisings as a matter of logic. But how about the circumstances confronted by really-small-coalition incumbents? By looking at the left-hand gray vertical line in Figure 10.2, we learn that a region exists for sufficiently small coalitions in which the regime is also virtually immune from mass uprisings and coups. The consequence is the same as in very-large-coalition settings, but the reasoning is a bit different.

In the large-coalition environment, in places like the United States, people get so many public goods that they have little incentive to revolt; they are already getting lots of what they want. When the coalition is really small—as when it is to the left of the left-hand gray vertical line—the people are miserable and the very few coalition members are very happy. So the people would love to revolt, but they get virtually no free speech to raise complaints, no free press to know that others are unhappy too, and no freedom of assembly to make it possible for them to coordinate with each other. Sounds a lot like conditions in the Democratic People's Republic of Korea (that is, North Korea), where the government is not democratic, it is not serving the people's interests, and it is not a representative republic. Lacking the ability to organize, the people do not rebel because the costs of doing so exceed the expected benefits. Put succinctly, they know that if they rebel, they will almost certainly fail. So, to the left of the left-hand gray line, revolts do not happen because their costs are too high and the people's prospects of success are too low. And, of course, coups do not happen for the same reason that they don't happen when the coalition exceeds the size at the right-hand gray line: the coalition is flush with benefits and so its members have no incentive to overthrow the leader who is magnanimous to them.

Okay, we have seen the logic. Certainly, logic is well and good, but of course you will want to know that real governments in the real world work the way Figure 10.2 indicates.[9] Fair enough. Let's have a look at evidence. Figure 10.3 shows us the odds of actual attempted coups and revolutions across national governments from 1789 to 2020.[10] The graph covers the entire spectrum of coalition sizes in the real world. We are looking at a lot of governments and a lot of time,

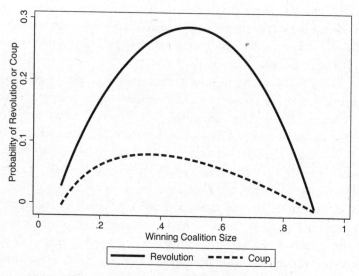

Figure 10.3: Make the Coalition Big or Small Enough and the Risk of Coups and Revolutions Disappears

so we can be pretty confident that Figure 10.3 is giving us a good, representative view of the actual odds of coups and revolutions across regimes ranging from the smallest to the largest coalitions. The picture couldn't be clearer.

The risk of violent government turnover is practically zero, nada, nil, when a government relies on a tiny or an enormous proportion of the population as essentials. The chances of a coup or revolution rise as the essential group gets bigger up to a turning point, after which, the more accountable the government becomes, the lower the chances of the regime being violently deposed whether by coup or mass revolt. At the top of the coalition scale, coups and revolutions just about never happen. This is just what the logic behind Figure 10.2 told us, and it is just what we know has actually happened across the world and across nearly a quarter of a millennium.

Knowing that it is really dangerous to gamble on wholesale reductions in coalition size, democratic rulers, who live at the right-hand end of Figure 10.2, have to operate in a narrow band of low-risk changes to the number of essentials. They have a little wiggle room, to be sure, but that is it. They may adjust the number of essentials modestly, but if they try for a big, transformative reduction, as Indira Gandhi did and as Donald Trump did, they are likely to find themselves unemployed.

Donald Trump's tacit—and sometimes even explicit—effort to shrink the size of the required US winning coalition between the run-up to Election Day, November 3, 2020, and January 6, 2021, when Congress certified the electoral outcome, illustrates the sorts of maneuvers that democratic leaders can try and how hard those maneuvers are to carry off successfully. Selectorate logic tells us why those efforts were, are, and always will be extremely unlikely to succeed. Let's go step by step through some of the efforts by leaders like Trump and others to illustrate the dangers that any democratic government may face. We start with widely used techniques to shape the postelection assessment of results and then move on to narrower and, ultimately, illegitimate efforts. As we look at these maneuvers, we should keep in mind that many of these sorts of efforts can succeed anywhere that is to the left of the right-hand gray line in Figure 10.2, but they are extremely unlikely to succeed to the right of that line, where the coalition is already very large.

The stories of Brazil, the United States, and the Philippines illustrate how small differences in the size of the essential group can dramatically alter the course of democracy. As we write, Brazil and the Philippines are governed and the United States was recently governed, until January 20, 2021, by individuals who seem strongly inclined to make themselves into autocrats. We are prepared to bet that Brazil's Jair Bolsonaro will fail in any such effort. Donald Trump has so far failed, and we believe he will continue to fail in his effort. We are not prepared, however, to say with confidence that the Philippines' president, Rodrigo Duterte, will not turn himself into a new dictator.

All three of these presidents have records of remarkable intolerance for democratic norms and have openly displayed their inclination to tolerate—or promote—governance by violence. But they face (or faced) radically different electoral rules and different coalition sizes. Those differences probably place Duterte to the left of the right-hand vertical line in Figure 10.2 while Brazil and the United States are almost certainly to the right of it. That means that Bolsonaro can tweak the rules, as Trump tried to do, but he cannot fundamentally alter them. Duterte will find it challenging, but he might be able to shift the coalition in the Philippines far to the left.

Back in 1980, Brazil had a military dictatorship and the Philippines was governed by dictator Ferdinand Marcos. Their winning coalitions were almost the same size: 0.42 under Brazil's João Figueiredo and 0.49 under Marcos. The United States back then was structured pretty much as it is today. Its winning coalition size on our scale was a hefty 0.96. By the late 1980s Brazil and the Philippines were on the move toward democracy. By 1987, with Marcos ousted from power, the Philippines' coalition shot up to 0.71, almost exactly where Brazil was two years earlier; both were well behind the United States, which was still at 0.96. But then the paths parted ways. Today, Duterte depends on a coalition of 0.71, the same size it's been in the Philippines for the past thirty-five years. Brazil's Bolsonaro, in contrast, depends on a coalition of 0.92, meaning that as much as he might wish to alter the system, he faces an extremely steep uphill struggle in trying to do so. The United States backslid slightly during the Trump years, down to 0.94. The US and Brazilian coalitions appear to be too big for a meaningful retreat from democracy.

Bolsonaro's election may have been a perfect storm: his two immediate predecessors had been caught up in corruption charges and were ousted from power. Brazil's most popular politician, Luiz Inácio Lula da Silva, had been expected to contest the election but was barred by the courts from running because of his own corruption conviction. With Lula out of the picture, Bolsonaro won a runoff election with 46 percent of the vote in the first round and 55 percent in the second. And he inherited reasonably functional legislative and judicial branches.

Trump's election was much the same as Bolsonaro's—that is, a perfect storm. He lost the popular vote by a substantial margin but won easily in the Electoral College, a peculiar coalition-reducing institution that is unique to the United States. His opponent, Hillary Clinton, was caught up in hints of scandal that turned out to be without foundation, but that allowed Trump to deflect attention from his own alleged scandals. With nearly 130 million votes cast, a shift of fewer than 80,000 would have tipped the election into Clinton's corner.

Duterte also won election to his presidency but under less demanding rules than were faced in Brazil. While Bolsonaro required a majority of the vote by the second round, Duterte only needed more votes than the second-place finisher in a one-round, first-past-the-post system. As we know, first-past-the-post elections normally translate into two-party contests, but that was not true when Duterte was elected in 2018. Five candidates ran for president, with results of 39 percent for Duterte, and 23.5 percent, 21.4 percent, 12.7 percent, and 3.4 percent for the other candidates. Obviously, Duterte needed much less support in the Philippines than Bolsonaro required in Brazil. So, with the difference in their coalition sizes in mind, what tricks can they play—what tricks can any large-coalition leader play—to improve their odds of holding office by shrinking their coalition?

WHOSE VOTES COUNT?

Democracies provide their leaders with lots of ways to shape who does or does not vote. Of course, incumbents (or their political party if there are term limits) never want to suppress votes by their backers, but they would love to reduce turnout by those who do not support them. Eliminating voters helps to diminish the size of the winning coalition—every leader's dream. However, in most democracies restricting who can vote also reduces the availability of future coalition members in proportion to the shrinking selectorate, and this diminishes loyalty. Of course, it is still better for a leader to need half of a small pool of voters than half of a large pool of voters, but nirvana for a leader is to shrink the coalition while simultaneously expanding the pool of people who can be in it.

In the good old days, before Lenin worked out the benefits of having many interchangeables along with few essentials, coalitions were kept small by preventing the riffraff—folks who might vote for "radical" politicians—from voting. The mob could easily be suppressed by requiring meaningful property ownership as an enfranchisement requirement. That definitely kept the coalition small. Rich, property-owning people have never been the bulk of any society. But then property ownership went out of fashion.

The Philippines banned property ownership as a criterion for voting in its 1987 constitution as it emerged from decades of Marcos's dictatorship. Brazil, with mandatory voting for all citizens between the ages of eighteen and seventy, has had no property requirement for voting since 1881. In the young United States, most states had eliminated property requirements for voting by the 1828 presidential election, a contest between John Quincy Adams (the first-ever National Republican Party candidate, not to be confused with Lincoln's Republicans) and Andrew Jackson (the first-ever Democratic Party candidate).

With the elimination of a property requirement for voting, turnout in the United States expanded dramatically, from 3.4 percent of the population in 1824 to a "whopping" 9.5 percent in 1828. The winning coalition had gotten bigger, but it was still darn small. Still, there must have been enormous pressure behind this change, because it almost certainly was not a big benefit for those who had previously been essentials and it surely was a deadweight loss for the incumbent, John Quincy Adams. Of course, for candidate Jackson, expanding the coalition was his ticket to winning office. That is one of the beautiful features in nascent democracies with honest elections: increasing the coalition can be the pathway to election and, as we discussed, once sufficiently increased it is hard to shrink it again.

In Brazil, fear of an expanded electorate following the elimination of a property requirement for voting led to the Savaria Law in 1881. That legislation, while nominally expanding who was eligible to vote, cleverly also restricted who could actually vote simply by requiring literacy. The literacy requirement all but eliminated the right to vote for the recently liberated former slaves in Brazil, for example. The elite had found a way to lock in a small winning coalition (of about 0.46) despite the official expansion of the selectorate to include former slaves, non-Catholics, and citizens as young as twenty-one.

Nascent democracies have plenty of tools to work with to keep voting down. Finland, the first European country to grant the right to vote to women, didn't do so until 1906. The USA's Nineteenth

Amendment, giving women the right to vote, was ratified in 1920; Brazil did not allow women to vote until 1932; the Philippines, not until 1937. Switzerland waited until 1971! The United States, like Brazil, prevented women, formerly enslaved people, and illiterate people from voting. That way, these "democracies" could keep the "wrong" prospective voters out of the ballot box. Many southern states in the United States also added a tax on voting, a poll tax, as a way to keep the poor from casting votes, just as a property and literacy requirement had done in Brazil.

Alternatively, rather than making it hard to vote, you could just not let the mob cast votes for president at all. In the same 1828 election in which property requirements had been largely dropped, Delaware and South Carolina continued to use their state legislatures to pick electors for the Electoral College. South Carolina's and Delaware's citizens had no direct say in choosing their state's electors. Remember that when we get around to the United States' 2020 election—and beyond!

Restricting who can vote in democracies keeps down the size of the essential group since, especially in a two-party race, the winning coalition's size depends significantly on the selectorate's size. So suppressing votes is entirely understandable for those, like John Quincy Adams, who could not win with an enlarged electorate. As Donald Trump, perhaps quite correctly, observed during an appearance on the TV show *Fox and Friends* in the spring of 2020, Democrats "had...levels of voting that if you'd ever agreed to it, you'd never have a Republican elected in this country again."[11]

Voter suppression is remarkably widespread to this day. Israel historically made it hard for Arab Israelis to form political parties and apparently made voting by Arab citizens unattractive. Arab Israeli turnout tends to be substantially lower than mostly Jewish, European Israeli turnout. The reduced Arab turnout is a consequence of disillusionment mixed with variation in the designation of voting days. The shifting days for voting is believed by some to be designed to suppress Arab voting, much as defeated efforts in 2021 to prevent voting on Sundays in the state of Georgia seemed intended to eliminate "souls to the polls" efforts by Black churches intent on increasing turnout by their parishioners. The selection of different, sometimes unique dates for voting, recall, is how Robert Rizzo and his crowd turned Bell, California, into a charter city through voter suppression. Efforts like Rizzo's can really work well when the required coalition is already small, but when such procedures are introduced to shrink an established large coalition, trouble is likely to follow. Rizzo and company got away with their electoral distortion for a while, but ultimately it was discovered, and he and his Bell cronies were packed off to jail.

Keeping in mind that suppressing votes *after* the coalition has been enlarged can be risky business, politicians must always be open to other ways to rig seemingly fair elections in their favor. In fact, it isn't necessary to suppress votes by opponents to win even when they are more popular than you. You can always try to arrange how votes contribute to electoral outcomes. In a series of decisions between 1962 and 1964, the United States Supreme Court determined that state electoral districts must be approximately equal to one another in population so that the principle of one person, one vote applied throughout the land. Of course, equal populations by district more or less assures that all districts have about the same number of people in their selectorate, but it does not assure that all districts have an equal number of people in their winning coalition. While courts may not distinguish between selectorate size and winning coalition size, political parties definitely do. The principle of one person, one vote is readily manipulated to shape how much any individual's vote counts toward winning, even when the votes are honestly counted. Indeed, the manipulation of district composition by political parties so as to rig election outcomes is almost as old as the United States.

Before the United States was even a quarter of a century old, Elbridge Gerry, then the governor of Massachusetts (who was later the vice president from 1813 to 1814), helped create the practice of gerrymandering. This practice is named in his "honor" and in recognition of the salamander-shaped district he created. He did so to assure victory by his Democrat-Republican Party in Massachusetts in 1810. Gerry's ability to redraw the electoral lines is all the more remarkable when you realize that Massachusetts was a Federalist stronghold. In the popular presidential vote in 1812, Democrat-Republican James Madison received only 35 percent of the vote, yet the Democrat-Republican Party took eleven of twenty congressional seats. Drawing district boundaries to give one's party an electoral advantage remains a robust practice to this very day, a practice engaged in by each American political party when it has the chance. And it is not limited to the United States. The *Manila Times* reported on April 21, 2019, that the Philippine province of Palawan had been gerrymandered.[12] And why not? It's a great way to virtually assure electoral victory.

As we saw in Chapter 3, gerrymandering helps the majority party in a state group voters so their opponents win in a very few districts by overwhelming margins and assuredly lose by closer votes in as large a share of districts as possible. Gerrymandering is great for a state's controlling party, but population relocations, shifts in party efforts to mobilize their voters or suppress the opposition's voters, and other changing conditions can weaken its beneficial effects. For instance, put a life-threatening crisis into the mix, like the COVID-19 pandemic in 2020, and other techniques may be needed to make sure the "right" party wins.

During the 2020 presidential campaign, the Trump administration made heroic efforts to delegitimize high Democratic voter turnout by condemning mail-in ballots, saying that they were rife with voter fraud. The mail-in ballots, normally mostly Republican, skewed heavily in favor of Democrats, many of whom feared voting in person because of the COVID-19 pandemic. Republicans, being less worried about COVID-19, voted more often in person. So, naturally, Republican-dominated state governments looked for ways to keep Democrats from voting. And, of course, where Democrats were in control they looked for ways to register and turn out more Democratic-leaning voters than Republican-leaning. When the Republican efforts to prevent Democratic voters from turning out failed, then president Trump focused on more inventive means by trying to alter who counted votes and how. He looked for ways to alter the size of the winning coalition so that he could win with fewer votes and so that Democrats could lose with more. As we know from Figure 10.2, his efforts were likely to fail, and they did.

HOW TO MAKE VOTES COUNT DIFFERENTLY

In its 1989 election, Kenya introduced a new voting system called queue voting. As the name suggests, voters queued up behind a sign designating the name of the candidate they supported. Then an official counted the voters behind each sign. If, by some terrible error, the "wrong" candidate looked like a winner, the problem was readily solved: the official just changed the tally.[13] Who counted the votes mattered more than how people voted.

It seems, at first blush, pretty straightforward to go from casting votes to summing up the votes and working out who the winner and the loser(s) were in each constituency, recognizing that to win in, for instance, a first-past-the-post system, all a candidate needs in any constituency is one more vote than whoever comes in second. Large-coalition governments and even rigged-election autocracies have been counting votes for centuries, albeit in quite different ways. Of course, in rigged-election regimes everyone expects the vote counter, not the actual votes, to determine who won, just as was the case in some districts in Kenya in 1989. That's how it works these days in Russia, in Turkey, in Venezuela, seemingly in Tanzania, and in lots and lots of other places, including in some situations in the United States.

Every now and then elections are super close. In such cases, votes need to be counted and recounted, not so much to manipulate the size and composition of the winning coalition but rather honestly to discover it. In 2020, however, seemingly new, surprising issues were promoted to influence vote counting in the United States for the express purpose of shrinking the coalition while altering the outcome. These efforts failed, but they scared a lot of people across the entire political spectrum. They were right to be scared. Their fear was part of the inevitable corrective pressure that prevents dishonesty from defeating the truth in large-coalition systems. And that, as we said, makes us optimistic about the future of really-large-coalition, mature democracies.

IS THE UNITED STATES' DEMOCRACY FRAGILE?

The United States Constitution sets out the essential elements for determining the size of a presidential winning coalition. The size of the Electoral College is precisely set out in the Constitution's Article II, section 1: "Each State shall appoint, in such Manner as the Legislature thereof may direct, a Number of Electors, equal to the whole Number of Senators and Representatives to which the State may be entitled in the Congress." With a few restrictions on who can be an elector, this brief statement is the essence of the Electoral College's existence.

The consequence today of this brief passage is, just as its consequence was in 1787, to produce a tremendous distortion in the notion that each citizen's vote counts equally. It absolutely defies the notion of one person, one vote when it comes to assessing the voters who were in the winning coalition. But then, in 1787 the United States had a pretty small winning coalition as a proportion of the population, and today that coalition is tremendously large.

Putting aside the phrase "Each State shall appoint, in such Manner as the Legislature thereof may direct" for the moment, back in 1787, when an enslaved person counted as three-fifths of a person for the purpose of assigning each state its apportionment of congressional seats, the enumeration of electors greatly favored states where slavery was legal: their congressional numbers were inflated because the very people who had zero say in how they were governed were counted among the population. Today, the calculation of electors hugely favors states with few people in them. For example, Wyoming gets one vote in the Electoral College for about every 194,000 of its residents. Texas, in contrast, gets one vote in the Electoral College for about every 773,000 residents. In other words, each voter in Wyoming counts as much as four voters in Texas when it comes to choosing members of the Electoral College.

The Electoral College structure is hardwired in favor of low-population states, and for whatever reason, many of those states lean Republican. The upshot is that in 2020, to win the presidency, the Democrat (Biden) needed a substantially larger voter coalition to achieve a winning coalition in the Electoral College than did the Republican (Trump). Of course, at other times in American history, the opposite would have been true. The key is that the Electoral College greatly distorts the support group needed to go from votes to election. It favors whichever political party is preferred in the less-populated states, whose voters are grossly overrepresented. It simply takes far fewer voters in less-populous states to elect the president of the United States than it takes in the more-populous states. Andrew Jackson understood this back in 1832 and so campaigned against the Electoral College. He failed, and low-population-state politicians prevent overturning the Electoral College to this day.

Because of the distortion in how many electoral votes each state has on a per capita basis—that is, on the principle of one person, one vote—the presidential winning coalition can be surprisingly small (though still very large by world standards) if the winning candidate gets her or his votes distributed just right. We already know that Abraham Lincoln was remarkably skilled on that very front. But, as Article II, section 1 of the Constitution tells us, and as the cases of South Carolina and Delaware in 1828 remind us, the Constitution does not require that voters elect the president. Indeed, the United States Supreme Court and the state supreme court in Florida could not have been clearer on this point in *Bush v. Gore* in 2000. They both echoed the judgment in the Supreme Court's ruling in *McPherson v. Blacker* (1892): "The individual citizen has no federal constitutional right to vote for Electors for the President of the United States."[14] Remember, the Constitution stipulates that "Each State shall appoint, *in such Manner as the Legislature thereof may direct*, a Number of Electors, equal to the whole Number of Senators and Representatives to which the State may be entitled in the Congress" (emphasis added). What might that mean for the size of the essential group in the United States?

Let us suppose, to keep things simple, that each legislator in each state is elected in a two-party race. Then, to win, each assemblyperson needs one-half of the vote plus one in his or her district. To control a state legislature, a party needs half the seats plus one, each seat won in half the districts by half the vote plus one. To win the Electoral College, ignoring the distortion in favor of less-populous states—a distortion that further shrinks the hypothetical coalition—half the state legislatures need to control half of their assembly plus one to vote for the winning candidate, such that the chosen electors add up to 270 Electoral College votes. To get an Electoral College majority under this set of assumptions, remembering that these assumptions enlarge the coalition relative to Constitutional requirements, we have ½ the state assemblies times ½ their members times ½ of those members' district votes, or a winning coalition equal to one-eighth of the electorate that chose state legislators!

But wait, that is still too big. This calculation assumes the whole selectorate has turned out. However, midterm elections, when many state assemblies are chosen, have low voter turnout. Turnout in 2018 was 49.4 percent, and that was the highest level for midterm elections in more than a century. Being extremely generous, we will treat turnout as 50 percent. Then we have to multiply our previous coalition-size calculation by ½ to reflect the proportion of the selectorate from which the coalition is drawn. In that case, if the state assemblies did as Trump wanted by picking the electors without regard to the popular vote for president and instead in accordance with the popular vote that chose the assembly members, then the group of essentials is reduced to 6.25 percent of the electorate—about 20 percent of the vote the loser, Donald Trump, got, and, of course, even a smaller percentage of the vote that Joe Biden received. That sure is starting to look undemocratic, and it reminds us how fragile US conditions might be for choosing the president while sticking to the strictures of the Constitution. Indeed, that is a winning coalition size akin to what was required in 1828, when well over half of the population was disenfranchised! For now at least, state laws preclude state legislators from ignoring the will of their voters in determining the allocation of electors. Changing that could be very tough since the people, already in the elector-selection winning coalition, would be loath to be removed from it. The state-granted right to vote for president makes it hard to shrink the winning coalition.

WHOSE VOTE MIGHT COUNT OUTSIDE THE US CONSTITUTION?

So far, we have seen a variety of ways to diminish the winning coalition so that it is as small as about 6 percent of the electorate. Looking back at Figure 10.2, we can see why it is really hard for these methods to succeed in the United States, or anyplace else, once the winning coalition has been enlarged enough to pass the right-hand gray line. Hardly anyone is a beneficiary from such midrange reductions in the size of the essential group. But if we can find ways to get the coalition down to or past the left-hand vertical line, then we can imagine that there is a small set of selectors who would endorse such a move because then their welfare would be substantial even as the rest of us would be cast into misery. How might the coalition, alarmingly, be reduced that much?

The Constitution of the United States, a country whose current winning coalition ranks tenth- or eleventh-largest in the world and is surely above the right-hand gray dividing line, does not require electors to vote in any particular way. Rather, state governments constrain electors by generally requiring them to vote in accordance with the voters' choice for president. Additionally, state political parties generally compel their slate of electors—that slate being what "we the people" actually vote for on Election Day—to pledge to vote for the candidate they are elected to support. In other words, there are lots of rules in place that bind electors to vote in accordance with the preference of their party's voters. The Supreme Court has ruled that such commitments are binding, so electors who vote contrary to their initial pledges will have their votes discounted or maybe even reversed.

Despite the general commitment of electors, every now and then electors deviate, voting however they please without regard to the candidate they were supposed to be bound to. As long as these few rogue votes do not alter the outcome, it is pretty common for them to be ignored. Imagine, however, that electors could routinely vote their personal preference regardless of what the voters in their state instructed them to do. That would mean that the group of essentials would be reduced to half of the 538 people who currently are chosen to be members of the Electoral College, plus one.

If electors could simply vote however they wanted to, then the winning coalition would not consist of millions of voters but rather would consist of 270 named individuals—a simple majority of the members of the Electoral College. Then we would be looking at a government approximating some petty dictatorship that is awash in corruption and private goods and suffering from a severe shortage of effective public policies. While a small group might be induced to back such a restructuring of institutions, a massively large group of selectors, whether they had been essentials or not, would balk and would be easily positioned to overwhelm the few supporting such a shift in coalition size. Tens of millions of people would face higher taxes; there would be worse health care for the young, the old, and perhaps for women; their children's educational opportunities would diminish; their lives would be less free, less prosperous, and less fulfilling. Before allowing such a collapse, these millions would demonstrate and the military probably would stand by them and the Constitution, which the military is sworn to obey. Wishful thinking? Maybe, but we believe not, given the logic of the theory and the extraordinary record of history. A coalition reversal from massive (remember coalition size in the United States was well above 0.9 in 2020) to tiny has *not happened* since at least 1789, as best as our data can tell.

Donald Trump did not focus heavily on convincing individual electors to vote his way in 2020. Probably, given how many of them were bound by state law, by party pledges, and by sincere preferences because they were doing so well in the large-coalition environment of the United States, he realized that switching individual electors was a losing proposition. He did, however, put a lot of energy into trying to get state legislatures to designate their electors without regard to how the people voted. We know his effort did not work. We think it did not work in 2020 in large part because, having already set their state rules for choosing electors, the legislatures were bound to abide by the rules they had put in place. Of course, they could change the rules for future elections much more easily than they could change them after the fact for an election that had already happened. But because the legislators have first to get elected, the winning coalition would still be too large to get down below the left-hand line in Figure 10.2, as we explained earlier.

Still, there is another mechanism that uncovers the potential fragility of the American democracy. How does any state government actually *know* who won the presidential election in their state? Each state has a procedure in place for certifying the outcome of the vote. At the end of the state voting process there is a person, usually the state's secretary of state, whose job it is to officially declare the outcome of the election by following the conclusion of an election board. Donald Trump, remember, tried to persuade several such people to certify that he won their state's election. Famously, he was recorded on the telephone with Georgia's secretary of state, asking him to reverse the electoral outcome.

There are fifty such people, whether their title is secretary of state, lieutenant governor, or something else. What if enough secretaries of state chose to ignore the certification of the state's bipartisan or nonpartisan board? Then, if enough secretaries of state agree on a candidate and agree to ignore what "we the people" said, that candidate would have a majority of electors and so would be elected to the presidency. That could be a winning coalition at or below the left vertical line in Figure 10.2, meaning that a tiny group of people—for instance, the secretaries of state making up the hypothetical new regime's winning coalition—could be so well rewarded that if they could get away with it, they would convert a very-large-coalition, democratic political system into a very-tiny-coalition, rigged-election autocracy.

Nothing beyond norms, ethics, and personal honor binds secretaries of state to certify the election outcome correctly. So, if they put aside ethics and honor, then just enough certifiers to give a candidate a majority in the electoral college (at a maximum, twenty-six of them) could theoretically be the winning coalition in the United States. If that were how the United States were governed, then it would look a lot like Kim Jong-Un's government in North Korea or Xi Jinping's regime in China. Fortunately, secretaries of state behaved honorably in 2020, but that is a thin condition to have to rely on. More reassuringly, so many currently really-well-off citizens would realize that they were about to be thrust into misery that the few secretaries of state who might contemplate such a move would be deterred by the expectation of rebellion against them, a rebellion that they could not defeat.

Wait a minute. What if the military got behind the coalition of secretaries of state? Wouldn't that assure the successful overturning of a large-coalition democracy like the United States? Was it dumb luck that the military did not side with Trump in 2020 or early 2021? No, it was not dumb luck. With the military added to the secretaries of state, the coalition would have to be appreciably larger in order to secure the loyalty of enough generals, and then we would be back toward the midrange area of Figure 10.2. That can work if one starts with a small coalition and enlarges it by adding generals to move to the upward-slope part of the figure. But it can't work when the starting place is a massively large coalition, as was the case in the United States in 2020. Then the people in the slightly enlarged coalition that includes up to twenty-six secretaries of state and a sufficient number of generals would be worse off than they are under the current large-coalition system. Such a coalition cannot garner enough support to succeed against the current political arrangements. They cannot do better than they are doing in a large-coalition system.

WHY THE US COALITION REMAINS HUGE AND MATURE DEMOCRACY IS NOT FRAGILE

Although we can imagine scenarios in which the US presidential coalition is as small as 6.25 percent of the electorate, or as small as 270 electors, or as small as twenty-six state secretaries of state, in reality the essential group in the United States remains in the many tens of millions of people. Why is that? The answer, as we have intimated, resides in the extraordinarily difficult political passage from a government with a coalition larger than the right-hand gray line in Figure 10.2 to one past the left-hand vertical line. Nothing in-between those two points is an attractive shift in governance for people who start out with a sufficiently large coalition!

What selectorate logic tells us is often couched in different terms in everyday discussion. One common explanation for the robustness of the US democracy is that most people in the United States, including most politicians, feel bound to a set of norms that assure that they abide by the will of the people. Certainly, we must say that Georgia's secretary of state in 2020, Brad Raffensperger, seems to have felt bound by norms of good conduct when he, a pro-Trump Republican, certified the state's vote in favor of Joe Biden even though that was not the outcome he wished for. And he did so despite direct requests from then president Trump to recount the votes yet again (they had already been counted three times) or recheck the ballot signatures to find for him one more vote than Biden received, meaning an extra 11,780 votes.

The belief that but for such honorable, norms-bound people, the voters' will could have been overturned is frightening for the survival of democracy and, hence, deeply unsatisfying. That explanation calls on us to probe what we mean by *norms* and how they might shape outcomes, remembering that the logic of our argument is that people do what they believe is best for them.

We have a straightforward, though atypical, understanding of what makes something a "norm." Everything we have argued depends on the tenets of game theory and especially on its understanding of what makes for stable, equilibrium, behavior. In game theory–speak—and all of selectorate thinking depends on the logic behind game theory— an equilibrium outcome, a stable result, arises when *no one* in the game believes they would be better off by choosing a different course of action on their own, without anyone else switching strategies too. Now that may seem like a very demanding standard, but if you think about it for a moment, you will realize that this description of action characterizes what just about every one of us does all the time. Sure, sometimes we may have to choose when we are not confident what the consequences of our action will be, but still we do what we believe— maybe incorrectly—will be best for us under the circumstances.

Let's take a simple norm. In the United States, everyone drives on the right side of the road. In Britain, everyone drives on the left—or, as Alastair puts it, the "correct" side of the road. Yet even Alastair drives on the right side in the United States. Why? Because he fears that he will get into a crash if he drives on the left (correct) side. The driving norm assures a stable, safe passage almost all of the time: safe in England on the left and safe in the United States on the right. A norm is stable equilibrium behavior exactly because it is what everyone believes is best under the circumstances. Then, in the same spirit, when the circumstance has produced a large coalition—when everyone is driving on the same side of the road—enforcing democratic norms is stable and secure. Trying to make a really large coalition into a small one is like driving on the left when everyone else is on the right. Just because one person switches to the other side of the road doesn't change where everybody else drives, and it probably will result in disaster for anyone foolish enough to break the norm.

If a society has a very small coalition, its leaders and its essentials are content while everybody else is miserable. Because the coalition is content, its members will do what is required to keep the leader in power and to keep the people down. The people, realizing that there is little they can do to make themselves better off, will, in fact, do little. They won't rebel; they won't work hard "on the books," and society will languish. Should something then happen to the incumbent leader—old age strikes down all of us if we live long enough to become old—then an opportunity may arise for the people to rise up, improving their welfare by increasing the coalition size.

If the coalition increases just enough to fall somewhere between really big and really small, then what happens to the society depends on whether coalition members seek to expand the coalition, thereby potentially improving their welfare, or shrink the coalition, thereby also potentially improving their welfare. The first move puts them in cahoots with the people, while the second aligns their interests with the interests of the leader. Either is a feasible adjustment, and the choice is dictated by the prospect of the leader delivering more or fewer benefits to them in the future. That's why we are unsure whether Duterte in the Philippines will become a long-serving autocrat or not. The Philippines' coalition resides in circumstances where the interests of leaders and essentials might align or essentials and the people might align. Places like the United States and Brazil are past the point where the people can be left out of the calculation.

Finally, and of most interest, if the coalition starts out sufficiently large, then even a small wiggle downward in the size of the essential group will alert the people and those who have been, or expect to be, purged from the coalition to strike back and oust the incumbent. That is what happened to Indira Gandhi; that is what happened to Donald Trump; and that is, we believe, what will happen to any ruler over a large-coalition democracy if they gamble on shrinking the coalition (driving on the wrong side of the road). Logic tells us they will fail. History tells us that those who have made such a risky attempt in the past have failed. We reiterate: there are *no examples* of truly large-coalition governments—where the coalition was at least a 0.9 on our scale—that then turned into small-coalition governments—say, below 0.6 on our scale—other than through external military conquest (for example, by Nazi Germany). There is no reason to expect democracy's future to look different. Democracy prevails and democratic would-be dictators do not. And so, when it comes to the survival of mature democracies, we are inveterate optimists!

CHAPTER ELEVEN

WHAT IS TO BE DONE?

A man always has two reasons for doing anything: a
good reason and the real reason.

—J. P. MORGAN

n late 1901, Vladimir Ilyich Lenin wrote a revolutionary essay called
"What Is to Be Done?" His question was directed at justifying the
creation of the Communist Party as the vanguard of the people.
We are more interested in his literal question than in his reason for
asking it, and, equally, we are intrigued by his unintended answer
three years later (really in a different context, but nevertheless apt) in
the title to another essay: "One Step Forward, Two Steps Back." Too
often, the real world of politics and business responds to problems
by taking one step forward and two steps back, resulting in no progress on the problem at hand. Backsliding is, and should be, the way
leaders deal with problems. It is the existing rules that have allowed
them to seize and control resources to date. A headlong plunge into
new ways of conducting politics might only heighten a leader's risk of
being overthrown.

After the past ten chapters, nine of which provide an exceedingly
cynical—but, we fear, accurate—portrayal of most politics, while
Chapter 10 gives us reason to be hopeful for democracy's future, it

is time at last to more seriously confront Lenin's first question: What is to be done? We hope that, informed by the lessons of leadership, we can offer a much better and more democratic answer than he provided.

It is an understatement to say that making the world better is a difficult task. If it were not, then it would already have been improved. The misery in which so many live would already have been overcome. The enrichment of CEOs while their stockholders lose their shirts would be a thing of the past. However, the inherent problem with change is that improving life for one group generally means making at least one other person worse off, and that other person is likely to be a leader if change really will solve the people's problems. If the individual harmed by change is the ruler or the CEO—the same person who has to initiate or implement the changes in the first place—then we can be confident that change is never going to happen.

From the beginning we said we would focus on what *is* rather than what *ought* to be. Now we need to talk a bit about what ought to be. In doing so, we want to lay down the ground rules. First among these is that we should never let the quest for perfection block the way to lesser improvement. Utopian dreams of a perfect world are just that: utopian. Pursuing the perfect world for everyone is a waste of time and an excuse for not doing the hard work of making the world better for many.

It is impossible to make the world great for everyone. Everyone doesn't want the same things. Think about what is good for interchangeables, influentials, and essentials, the three dimensions of political life: hardly ever is it true that what is good for leaders and their essential backers is good for everyone else. If everyone had the same wants, there wouldn't be misery in the world. So, even as we are trying to change the world for the better, we are tied to the dictates of political reality. A fix is not a fix unless it can actually be done! What can be done must satisfy the needs of everyone required to implement change. Wishful thinking is not a fix, and a perfect solution is not our goal and should not be any well-intentioned person's goal. Even minor improvements in governance can result in significant improvements in the welfare of potentially millions of people or shareholders.

RULES TO FIX BY

Whether we are looking at the welfare of shareholders in publicly traded corporations, the quality of life for citizens in a democracy, or the conditions under which billions live in oppressive and impoverished underdeveloped countries, there are certain common principles behind bettering the world. These commonalities need to be laid bare before we tackle the specifics of fixing particular problems in particular places.

If we have learned anything in the preceding pages, it is to be suspicious of people's motives. Appeals to ideological principles and rights are generally a cover. J. P. Morgan had it right: there is always some principled way to defend any position, especially one's own interests. In one overseas nation, our government supports protest and advocates the will of the people to determine their own future. That is a popular refrain for leaders in the United States when it comes to places like Maduro's Venezuela or Kim Jong-Un's North Korea. Elsewhere we call for stability. That's the principle invoked when people try to bring down a government that is our friend and ally, such as the governments of Bahrain and Saudi Arabia. Both freedom and stability are principled positions (the good reason) selectively asserted depending upon how we like the incumbent (the real reason). In devising fixes to the world's ills, the essential first step is to understand what the protagonists want and how different policies and changes will affect their welfare. Reformers who take what people say at face value will quickly find their reforms at a dead end.

Everyone has an interest in change, but interchangeables, influentials, essentials, and leaders don't often agree on what changes they want. Leaders, given their druthers, would always like the set of interchangeables to be very large and the groups of influentials and essentials to be very small. That's why the world of business has so many massive corporations with millions of shareholders, a few influential large owners, and a handful of essentials on the board of directors who agree to pay CEOs handsomely regardless of how the company fares. That's why so much of humanity for so much of human history has been governed by petty despots who steal from the poor to enrich the rich.

The masses—whether members of the selectorate or the wholly disenfranchised—agree that their group, the interchangeables, should be large, but they want all other groups to be big as well. Their best chance at having a better life comes from the coalition and the influential group growing in size, such that they have a realistic chance of becoming one of their members and of benefiting from the profusion of public goods such governance provides, even if they remain excluded from the coalition. As we have seen, it is this very hope of improving the people's lot that revolutionaries use as their rallying cry to get them to take to the streets. But even in a large-coalition system, these masses are unlikely to get what they want all the time. Their hope is to get what they want more of the time.

The group whose desires are most interesting from the perspective of lasting betterment is the set of essentials. We've seen a lot about how their welfare changes when the selectorate is held constant while the coalition is made bigger or smaller. But what happens when the selectorate isn't held to a fixed size? What happens when it is allowed to get bigger—enfranchising more people—or get smaller—disenfranchising more people? Leaders and their essentials share a preference for dependence upon a small coalition, but leaders want the selectorate to be as big as possible while the coalition prefers to keep their substitute group as small as possible. The welfare of essentials is enhanced if there are relatively few replacements for them. The incumbent cannot use the implicit threat of replacing them with a cheaper backer as a way to keep more benefits for himself rather than paying his essentials their due. This creates tension between a leader and his coalition. The leader would like to establish a Leninist-style, corrupt, rigged electoral system that guarantees him an eager supply of replacement supporters. The coalition prefers monarchical, theocratic, or junta-style institutional arrangements that restrict those who can be brought into the coalition to a select group of aristocrats, clerics, or military elites. Think how terrific the Iranian regime is if you happen to be an ayatollah. You have great power, lots of money, and few substitutes waiting in the wings to take your job.

The essential facts of political life are that people do what is best for them. Thus, except under extreme duress, leaders don't expand the coalition; the masses press for democratization; and essential supporters vary in what they want. This latter group can be made better off by contractions in the number of coalition members through coups and purges—provided they are the ones retained. Democratization can also make them better off. It is therefore this group that offers the greatest prospect for constructive as well as destructive change. With them lies the possibility of both one step forward and two steps back. The prospect of being dropped from the coalition encourages its members to take the single step forward rather than risk becoming a casualty of the two steps back. Times and circumstances that heighten the risk of coalition turnover engender an appreciation of democracy among political insiders.

Members of a small coalition live in luxury but also in constant fear: make the coalition smaller, as their leader wants, and they may be out; make the coalition bigger and their special privileges diminish. But decreased privileges are much better than the danger of being out altogether. So there are two times when the coalition is most receptive to the urge to improve life for the many, whether those are the people or shareholders: when a leader has just come to power, and when a leader is so old or decrepit that he won't last much longer. In these circumstances, coalition members cannot count on being retained, and so they are open to changes that can make most of society better off. It is at the beginning and the end of an incumbent's reign that the danger of being purged is greatest, and so, at these times, coalition members should be most receptive to reform. Effective reform means expanding the coalition, and that means that everyone, including the current essentials, has a good chance of being needed by tomorrow's new leader.

Not only is there a good time to look for the opportunity for reform; there also are good circumstances when reforms that can improve the people's welfare are welcomed. Coalitions whose leaders face serious economic strains understand that their days of luxury and splendor are numbered. That is one of the reasons companies sometimes commit fraud: CEOs, senior management, and board members believe they will be ousted because of the firm's failure, so they cover up how poorly the business is doing while they try to fix it and save themselves. Little white lies work well the first year, but if things do not turn around, then each year they need to lie a little bit more, until their reports are outright fiction and legally fraudulent.

As we have learned, when a country's economy is in trouble the big problem from a ruler's perspective is that she doesn't have enough money to buy continued loyalty. When the privileges enjoyed by essentials are shrinking, they are likely to be tuned in to the possibility of change. They know the leader will want to purge people so she can use what little money is around more effectively. They, not wanting to be purged, will be amenable to expanding their group, trading their privilege for their future security and well-being. Coalition members are not the only ones willing to contemplate changing the rules when circumstances warrant. If the economic crisis is severe enough (and foreign aid donors stay away), then even leaders must ponder whether they might be better off liberalizing, just as J.J. Rawlings did in Ghana. Democratization jeopardizes their long-term future, but if they don't pay their supporters today, whether they can win an election tomorrow is not a salient consideration.

Fools don't often get to rule countries or companies. Pretty much any leader worth his salt can see the dangers he faces when economic circumstances leave him bereft of funds to buy loyalty. Under such circumstances even leaders can believe that reform is their best shot at political survival. They might look for a fix even before their coalition does. Consider the experience of Chiang Kai-shek, who certainly was no fool. He was China's leader from 1928 until his defeat by Mao Zedong's forces in 1949 and then became the leader of the Republic of China on Taiwan from 1949 until his death in 1975. We might well ask why he encouraged much more successful economic policies on Taiwan than on the mainland of China. In the latter, even with extensive poverty, because there were so many people, there was plenty to enrich himself and his coalition. But when Chiang Kai-shek and his backers retreated to Taiwan, they took over an island with relatively few people and hardly any resources. Only economic success could provide the way to reward his coalition. In the process of achieving that success, he also gradually expanded the coalition, perhaps in response to pressure from his essential cronies or perhaps under pressure from the United States, until at the end of his life, Taiwan began a serious move toward becoming the democracy that it is today.

When the time or circumstances are ripe for change, coalition members must recognize that if they do not pressure for an expansion of public goods and public welfare, then others will. Provided that the chances of success are good enough and the expected gains from success outstrip the costs involved in gambling on a revolt, an intransigent coalition and leadership will find itself besieged by an uprising. In this circumstance, such as was seen in Tunisia, Egypt, Yemen, and elsewhere in the Middle East and North Africa, and as we saw in the proxy fight at Hewlett-Packard over Carly Fiorina's decision to merge with Compaq, people are willing to take big risks to improve their lot. They do so to call for exactly the same change as is widely favored by smart coalition members when and if any change becomes necessary.

A wise coalition, therefore, works together with the masses to foster an expanded coalition. The people cooperate because it will mean more public goods for them, and the coalition cooperates because it will mean less risk that they will end up out on their ear. Egypt's military leaders, essential members of the Mubarak government, understood this choice very well in the early months of 2011. They ensured their continued place as important players in Egypt's future by cooperating with the mass movement and supporting an expanded coalition rather than hunkering down and risking losing everything—or at least, they did so until the time was ripe for them to seize control.

What are the lessons here for change? First, coalition members should beware of their susceptibility to purges. Remember that it ticks up when there is a new boss, a dying boss, or a bankrupt boss. At such times, the essential group should begin to press for its own expansion to create the incentives to develop public-spirited policies, democracy, and benefits for all. Purges can still succeed if they can be mounted surreptitiously, so wise coalition members who are not absolutely close to the seat of power would do well to insist on a free press, free speech, and freedom of assembly to protect themselves from unanticipated upheaval. And should they be unlucky enough to be replaced, at least they will have cushioned themselves for a soft landing. Outsiders would be wise to take cues from the same lessons: the time for outside intervention to facilitate democratic change or improved corporate responsibility is when a leader has just come to power or when a leader is near the end of his life.

Knowing what people want and the conditions under which they will oppose reform and the circumstances under which the swing coalition members will support reform, we can now turn to concrete ideas about fixing, at least partially, the worlds of business and governance.

LESSONS FROM GREEN BAY

The Green Bay Packers, a football team based in the cold climes of Wisconsin, are remarkable for the loyalty their fans show them. In fact, win or lose, Packer fans are nearly always satisfied. Virtually every one of their home games since 1960 has been sold out. Attendance averages 98.9 percent despite often-appalling weather. The Packers have one of the longest waiting lists for season tickets among professional football teams.[1] Despite being a small-market team (Green Bay is a city of only about one hundred thousand), they have been very successful. They have won twelve championships, the most in the NFL; they rank fifth in terms of Super Bowl appearances and victories, appearing five times and winning four times.[2] They attract a larger, more loyal fan base than teams from many much-larger cities. Their successes on the field and in terms of fan loyalty stem from their institutional structure.

The Packers are the only nonprofit, community-owned franchise in American major league professional sports. Their 361,311 shareholders are mainly local fans. The ownership rules preclude a small clique taking control of the team. No one is allowed to own more than two hundred thousand shares in the Packers out of more than five million shares outstanding. The board has forty-five members.[3] Thus, a tiny band of owners cannot easily overturn the many and run the team for their personal gain at the expense of the larger, small-owners fan base. The Packers were grandfathered into the NFL. NFL rules for the other thirty-one teams state that they cannot have more than thirty owners and that one of these owners must own at least 30 percent of the team. The Packers might not be maximizing revenue for their owners (the Packers pay no dividends to their shareholders), but their fans are happy.

Indeed, they have good reasons to be happy. The two most recent stock offerings, in 1997 and 2011, increased the number of shares and shareholders. And the stock offerings were each followed by a statistically significant increase in on-field success. The winning percentage improved by more than 10 percent and the team's seasonal point spread went up over sixty points.

The concern for fan welfare is not commonplace in sports, although every team says they care. Recently European football (a.k.a. soccer) witnessed the tension created by the competing interests of fans and owners. In April 2021, twelve top football clubs (well, really eleven and Arsenal) announced the formation of a European Super League. In contrast to other (more meritocratic) European competitions for which clubs qualify by performing well in their domestic competition, the Super League planned to restrict entry. The plan envisioned huge revenues, €10 billion according to press releases.[4] Good for the owners, but probably not good for football. Even the loyal fans of these clubs appeared to prefer open competition where the top clubs are defined by performance, not by restricting competition. Their vociferous protests led to the league being abandoned after a few days. At several of the clubs involved, protests against team owners continued until the idea of the Super League was abandoned. For instance, on May 2, 2021, a much-anticipated game at Manchester United was postponed because fans, many of them wearing the original colors of the club from when it was community owned, invaded the stadium. The Manchester United Supporters' Trust, a fan organization, called for dramatic changes in the club's ownership structure: "What happened was the culmination of 16 years in which your family's ownership of the club has driven us into debt and decline, and we have felt ever more sidelined and ignored."[5] The complaints of the Manchester fans point to a trend in which many top clubs have been bought by wealthy individuals such as Russian oligarchs, Emirati royalty, and other billionaires. The fans would prefer that clubs enhance the supporters' experience, just as the Green Bay Packers do. But such a public-goods focus is incompatible with the revenue focus of a small group of owners.

The lesson to be extracted from the Green Bay Packers compared to the Super League is that if firms can be made to rely on a bigger coalition, they are likely to do a better job of serving the interests of their selectorate. But how can corporate governance be turned on its head to make this happen?

Consider what the main difficulties are for shareholders. They suffer from two big problems: First, in big corporations there tend to be millions of little shareholders, a handful of big, institutional shareholders, and a bunch of insider owners. The millions of little shareholders might as well not exist. They are not organized, and the cost for any of them to organize the mass of owners just isn't worth it. Second, the flow of information about the firm's performance comes from pretty much only two sources: the firm itself and the financial media. Few owners read annual reports or SEC filings, and the financial media doesn't spend much time reporting on any one firm unless it is in huge trouble. By then it is usually too late for the shareholders to save the day.

We live in the age of networking. Much of the world, including owners of shares, tweet on Twitter and chat with friends on Facebook; they are on LinkedIn; they can easily communicate with one another, even if they don't always do so. Surely it would be relatively simple to design firm-specific Facebook pages or other networking sites.

Companies maintain lively websites to put their view across, but few entrepreneur-owners have stepped forward to do the same to help organize the mass of little owners and to provide a way for them to share views. Sure, there are bloggers writing about anything and everything, but there don't seem to be many shareholder-controlled sites where they can exchange thoughts and ideas about a company that participants own in common. If something like this existed, the size of the influential, informed voters in any corporation would go way up. Then, for the first time, boards would really be elected by their owners, and then the board, like any leadership group, would need to be responsive to their large coalition of constituents. A simple change that exploits the internet to be a conduit for increasing coalition size can turn the Apples, Amazons, Bank of Americas, Twitters, and Teslas of the world into big-coalition regimes that serve their millions of small owners instead of a handful of senior managers.

Ah, you are thinking, senior management can thwart such efforts. They will, as they already do, hold shareholder meetings in places most owners can't afford to go, or the meetings will be so brief that it will be impossible for dissidents to express their views (the preferred shareholder meeting strategy in Japan), and, after all, proxies pour in, turning millions of votes over to a handful of board members. None of that, of course, will stop shareholder control once the millions of little owners have a cheap and easy way to exchange information. Set up a shareholder social media platform and then they will set the rules—by majority vote—for who casts proxies. They can set some of their own up to represent competing parties, and they can make the annual shareholders' meeting a purely decorative event. All such skeptics should remember that social networking websites have already successfully mobilized revolutions and brought down governments. Changing corporate governance is far easier.

Corporations don't have armies that can go out and bash in the heads of dissidents. Pursue a course of connecting and informing shareholders, and we will see whether shareholders who limit CEO salaries do better or worse; whether firms that alter behavior to meet the social expectations of their shareholders do better or worse; and whether shareholders care more about employees or about themselves. Whatever the millions of little owners decide to do, they will be responsible for their own fate. Management will serve them just as democratic leaders are more constrained than autocrats to do what their citizens want.

We also ought to comment a bit on how not to improve corporate governance. In the wake of Enron's collapse and other big frauds, Congress decided to regulate corporate governance, ostensibly to make it better. By now every reader knows that the interest of government leaders is not in making shareholders or even the man or woman on the street better off. Their interest is in making themselves better off. The regulations they imposed on corporate governance may have played well with voters, many of whom had little stake in many of the companies that were harmed by the regulations, but they have not made corporate governance better. The Sarbanes-Oxley Bill, passed in 2002, was supposed to tamp down management's greed and make companies responsive to their shareholders' interest in equity growth. The trouble is, it didn't work. There have been loads of big corporate frauds after Sarbanes-Oxley just as there were before. Just think of such big frauds as Volkswagen in 2015, Wells Fargo in 2016, Theranos in 2017, Wirecard in 2020. And this is only a brief list. Don't take our word for it.

Study after study shows that Sarbanes-Oxley did not do its job. In a brilliant summary of the statistical assessments of each of the governance planks in Sarbanes-Oxley, Yale law professor Roberto Romano shows that Sarbanes-Oxley did not do what it was supposed to do and often made things worse. Even a seemingly obvious reform—requiring an independent audit committee—turns out not to have been beneficial. Costly, yes! But it did not improve corporate governance or performance. Romano goes on to document the failings of Congress and regulators to get it right.[6] The wishes of a large coalition of shareholders with a big stake in finding the right answers to any given corporation's problems is likely to make businesses work better. A coalition of government regulators bent on improving their own electoral prospects is not.

FIXING DEMOCRACIES

For the citizens of democracies, life is good. But good does not preclude better. Our approach depends on the subtle organizational differences in the size of the three political dimensions on which we focus. For convenience, these distinctions are often dropped, but even small differences matter. It is time, then, to confront those small differences head on and see how good can be made better.

At the time of its independence, the United States was composed of thirteen states. They all had broadly the same first-past-the-post electoral rules, and yet their records of performance were remarkably different. It is easy to be sloppy and think that they all had the same political system—governed by the United States Constitution—so that their differences must have come from somewhere else. In reality, however, their political systems were not the same. The Constitution is silent on many issues that are central to governance. The Constitution tells us nothing, for instance, about how to add up votes. As we saw, just by changing this simple rule, Harvey Milk could change American politics by getting elected to San Francisco's board of supervisors in 1977, even though he could not do so in 1975 with ten times more votes than in 1977. Seemingly small differences in enfranchisement rules and districting decisions led to big disparities in the economic (and social) development of the states of the United States.

On average, the northern states developed more rapidly than the southern states. It is tempting to ascribe this to the traditional historical narratives and attribute the general difference to climate or slavery. However, a careful examination of the subtle differences between the states suggests that variations in their political institutions were the main culprit behind how they developed. Jeffrey Jensen, a former student of ours and now a faculty member at NYU, Abu Dhabi, did a very careful study of the differences in the size of the interchangeables, influentials, and essential groups across the original states.[7] He understood that many thought the differences in development depended on slavery and climate, and so he corrected for these possibilities. Jeff took the size of the enslaved population carefully into account, just as he also took carefully into account how many frost-free days there were per year in each of the original thirteen states. He investigated the distinctions in electoral rules within the early American states that created different levels of dependency on a large or small coalition drawn from a large or small set of interchangeables. His discoveries help us understand how to make our own modern democracy do better.

Who could vote differed greatly from place to place in the early United States. Some states imposed substantial property or educational qualifications for voting, while others did not. Electoral districts were typically based upon county lines. Many of these inadequately reflected the population distribution, so in some legislative districts it took vastly more votes to win a seat than in others. The modern principle of one person, one vote was not yet the acknowledged law of the land.

The upshot of these differences was that state political leaders were accountable to greatly different numbers of voters—that is, interchangeables and essentials. Through painstaking research, Jeff Jensen estimated the proportion of the states' populations that constituted the minimal winning coalition across states and across the years. It turns out that the size of the group of essentials varied enormously from a low of 8.8 percent of adult white males (and 0.9 percent of the total population) in South Carolina to a high of 23.9 percent of adult white males (and 4.9 percent of the total population) in Pennsylvania.

As the rules to rule by lead us to expect, states in which leaders required support from a larger proportion of the population developed faster. Such states built more extensive canal, rail, and road networks. They also achieved higher educational attainment and were more attractive places for other Americans to migrate into. People left small-coalition states and flocked to big-coalition states where public services were better and all manner of public goods were more extensively provided. Foreign immigrants also flocked to the larger-coalition states, even after correcting for proximity to large ports. Per capita incomes were much higher and varied almost directly with coalition size even after correcting for pre-independence differences. States with bigger coalitions simply did better.

The sorts of variations in performance that Jeff demonstrated for the original US states can be seen everywhere throughout history. In a recent study of Europe's economic and political development, for example, one of us has shown that there was greater economic growth and greater political accountability—through the formation of meaningful parliaments—where winning coalitions were larger in the Middle Ages than where they were smaller. Many of today's economic and political differences in Europe can be traced back to these early roots. Even the corruption or religiosity of medieval popes can be traced back to the size of their winning coalition.[8] The lesson here is clear. Make the coalition bigger and things will get better. One way to make coalitions bigger in the United States is to provide a meaningful alternative to gerrymandering in which voters pick their representatives instead of representatives picking their voters. When politicians pick who votes for them, it comes as no surprise that politicians are easily reelected and barely held accountable. Fixing gerrymandering is something that can be done only once a decade in the United States. It can be done more frequently in many parliamentary democracies that equally suffer from this perversion of representative politics. Whether the opportunity is ongoing or infrequent, fixing gerrymandering is conceptually, if not politically, easy, but to make it feasible the voters must take up the cause and fight for it.

Many scholars of American politics have worked out lots of better ways to allocate congressional districts than the way it is done now. All the methods come down to variations on a common theme: district boundaries should not be manipulated to squeeze some voters in here and others out there. Boundaries should reflect some basic principles of geometry and the natural constraints of the terrain, like major rivers or mountains. As a simple principle, gerrymandering could be greatly diminished by turning redistricting over to some computer programmers and mathematical political scientists, who could design rules that are *not* district specific and not partisan but that instead apply common principles of fair representation across all districts.

A successful voter initiative in Michigan in 2018 has taken a step in this direction. It calls for the appointment of a nonpartisan commission to handle redistricting. We will see how well that does at being nonpartisan. A computer program drawn up in ignorance of any specific district's distribution of political preferences would be much more likely to achieve fairness and impartiality while fulfilling the spirit as well as the letter of the Supreme Court's insistence on one person, one vote. With the right, nonpartisan computer program, the principle of one person, one vote would apply equally to the size of each district's selectorate and winning coalition, thereby correcting the current deficiency in how one person, one vote is implemented.

Along with wiping out coalition-reducing gerrymanders, the time may well have come to rethink the Electoral College. Here we have an institution whose founders' original intent is pretty clear. They wanted to ensure that the states where slavery was legal would join the United States, and that meant erecting constitutional provisions that would protect slavery.[9] The Electoral College was one of those institutions. Here is a great example where original intent most assuredly should not guide modern-day politics. Slavery has been outlawed for well over 150 years and yet the Electoral College persists, and the primary reason for its survival, even if it's rarely spoken out loud, is that it allows politicians to construct a coalition of essential supporters that is substantially smaller than would be the case under direct election.

There are at least two ways to fix the problems created by the Electoral College: amend the Constitution to get rid of it or pursue further the National Popular Vote Interstate Compact (NPVIC). Amending the Constitution is extremely hard. That's why it has been amended so infrequently. There are lots of low-population states whose leaders are not keen to give up their outsize influence over the selection of the president of the United States. Amending the Constitution requires approval by three-fourths of the states. That leaves lots of room for low-population states to quash any amendment.

The NPVIC alternative to amending the Constitution has so far garnered the support from fifteen states. Each of these states voted Democratic in the 2020 presidential election. Each of these states says it is committed to casting its electoral votes—a total of 196—to whichever presidential candidate wins the national popular vote. If this compact were implemented by states with a total of at least 270 electoral votes, then it would assure that no one would be elected president, as George W. Bush was in 2000 and Donald Trump was in 2016, while losing the popular vote. Also, under this compact, each voter's vote would count enough that candidates would be interested in each and every one of them. But there's not much hope of lower-population states joining the compact if they benefit from going against the national popular vote. That's why, presumably, no Republican states have signed on.

Immigration policy is a hot topic of debate in the United States and across much of democratic Europe. The reason for the debate is pretty much the same whether it is taking place in Phoenix or Paris, Shropshire or San Francisco. Immigration policies come in three flavors. In one, immigrants have an easy time becoming citizens in their new homeland. In another, immigrants are welcomed as guest workers but cannot gain citizenship. And in the third, immigrants just aren't welcomed. It turns out that which immigration flavor is chosen has big effects on the size of the groups that dictate whether a government, in governing for itself, also governs for the people.

Immigrants without citizenship opportunities increase the size of a country's disenfranchised group. As such, they are, barring open rebellion (which is rare among poor immigrants), an impotent source of demand for public goods. They are not in the interchangeable selectorate and they cannot become influentials or essentials. Guest worker immigration policies put immigrants in exactly this boat. The monarchies of the Middle East love this sort of immigration because it doesn't interfere with the control of the few over the many, and if any immigrant misbehaves he or she can just be deported.

We see a similar pattern of constraints that keep immigrants from having a shot at being in a winning coalition in some democracies as well. Gaining citizenship rights is extremely difficult in Japan, for instance. Although over the centuries there have been many waves of immigration to Japan (from, for instance, North Korea), the limits on access to citizenship ensures that immigrants do not compel an expansion of the winning coalition.

In places like Great Britain, immigrants from commonwealth countries like India or Pakistan who successfully enter the country can vote. This means that they are quickly made part of the selectorate. Because the size of the winning coalition in democracies is tied, at least indirectly, to how many people can vote, this also means that immigration expands the coalition. Naturally many politicians will be unhappy about this because it diminishes their control over discretionary money. Current citizens may also be unhappy, especially if they back the party in power. Expanding the coalition reduces the value of their private rewards. But for farsighted members of a current winning coalition in a democracy and for the many citizens who voted for the losing party, increased immigration combined with easy access to citizenship means increased pressure on the government to produce more public goods. That's good for just about everyone and especially for those not in the coalition of essentials.

Expanding immigrant access and rights, then, can boost the required size of the winning coalition and, in the process, improve the quality of public policy. But with so many interests aligned against immigration because of its short-term costs, it is hard to change immigration rules. Or is it?

A simple fix that lifts everyone's longer-term welfare is to grandfather in immigrants. Amnesty for illegal immigrants—a dirty word in American political circles—is a mechanism for choosing selectively those who demonstrate over a fixed period their ability to help produce revenue by working, paying taxes, and raising children who contribute to the national economy, national political life, and national social fabric. Give us your poor and let's see if they can make a better life. Give us your tired and let's see if they can be energized by participating in making a more public goods–oriented government work better. Give us your huddled masses longing to be free and let's see if their children's children don't grow up to be the foundation of a stronger, more peaceful, and more prosperous society than they first came to. For generation after generation, the waves of immigrants to the United States have made our winning coalitions bigger and better. They have turned from poor, tired, huddled masses into modern America's success story. This was no happenstance of time or place. This was the straightforward consequence of easy citizenship and, with it, an expanded winning coalition that makes for better governance.

REMOVING MISERY

Beneficial change in the underdeveloped world is among the most difficult challenges to overcome. Rampant poverty, frequent exposure to the resource curse, and long-entrenched autocratic regimes all stand in the way. But change can and does happen, as the stories of South Africa, Tunisia, Taiwan, and Mexico demonstrate. When change does happen, it can come from two sources, internal political upheaval or external threat, and between these two, external threat is far less likely to succeed in making many better off at the expense of the few.

American presidents and European prime ministers have long advocated a democratic world, and they might even claim some qualified success—the world is much more democratic today than it was fifty years ago. But it is not likely that our cries for freedom in the world—rarely backed up by effective efforts—turned many dictators into freedom lovers. As countries as diverse as Ghana, Armenia, Vietnam, and Mongolia demonstrate, effective change comes mostly from local circumstances. Each of these countries has meaningfully increased their winning coalition size and their economic growth rate. We don't think that the correlation between growth and essentials is coincidental; we have made the case that growth follows political reform, sometimes more quickly, sometimes more slowly, but practically inevitably. In contrast, after nearly two decades, the US government has spent trillions of dollars on combat and nation building in Afghanistan.[10] The resulting governments remained largely isolated from the need to improve the welfare of the people. External democratization and external drivers for economic growth rarely succeed, as we highlighted in Chapter 7. We don't mean to say that external influence can never be used effectively because it certainly can, but not in the conventional ways of armed intervention or foreign aid. What outsiders can do is to help provide soft landings for dictators as a way to facilitate their accepting defeat. South Africa's Nelson Mandela taught the world an important lesson in this regard. Alas, it is a lesson only poorly learned.

Following the collapse of the apartheid government, Mandela organized truth and reconciliation commissions. These were designed to provide people who had oppressed the apartheid regime's opponents the chance to come forward, confess their crimes, and be granted amnesty. The United Nations certainly could build a body of international law that motivates dictators facing rebellion to turn power over to the people peacefully. The UN could prescribe a process for transition from dictatorship to democracy. At the same time it could stipulate that any dictator facing the pressure to grant freedom to the people would have a brief, fixed period of time, say a week, to leave the country in exchange for a blanket perpetual grant of amnesty against prosecution anywhere for crimes committed as his nation's leader. There is clear precedence for such a policy. It is common practice to give criminals reduced sentences or immunity if they agree to testify against others, potentially then deterring future misconduct. Some victims are bound to resent that the perpetrator of heinous acts goes unpunished. Unfortunately, the alternative is to leave the dictator with few options but to gamble on holding onto power through further murderous acts. Certainly there is little justice in letting former dictators off the hook. But the goal should be to preserve and improve the lives of the many who suffer at the hands of desperate leaders who might be prepared to step aside in exchange for immunity. Remember, we urged you not to let the quest for perfection push aside feasible, practical ways of improving governance.

The incentives to encourage leaders to step aside could be further strengthened if, in exchange for agreeing to step down quickly, they would be granted the right to retain some significant amount of ill-gotten gains and safe havens for exile where the soon-to-be ex-leadership and their families can live out their lives in peace. Offering such deals might prove self-fulfilling. Once essential supporters believe their leader might take such a deal, they themselves start looking for his replacement, so even if the leader had wanted to stay and fight, he might no longer have the support to do so. The urge for retribution is better put aside to give dictators a reason to give up rather than fight. Libya's Muammar al-Qaddafi and Syria's Bashar al-Assad had none of these opportunities and so faced a stark choice: cling to power whatever the human costs, live the life of the hunted, or fight to the death. Qaddafi chose the last, to the detriment of the Libyan people. Assad chose to impose limitless costs on his society to cling to power, to the detriment of the Syrian people and much of the region.

Additional choices can be provided. Britain's transition from monarchy to constitutional monarchy provides a valuable lesson. Leaders want to survive in office and maximize their control over money. But what if their choice is to trade the power of office for the right to the money? The English monarchy once had both power and money, but it faced severe pressure that could have ended, as in so many other places, with the erstwhile royal family having neither power nor money. That is what happened to the Russian and French royal families, and for that matter the Stewart branch of the English royal family, in the wake of revolution. Imagine, instead, that they had the option of keeping the crown but turning power over to a properly elected government of the people, as William and Mary and the subsequent Hanoverian dynasty did in England. As compensation for doing so, they could have been granted the right to keep the family's wealth and even the assurance of further income from the state for a long, specified period of time (say, one hundred years). The transition to being fabulously wealthy figureheads of constitutional monarchies is an option the Saudi Arabian royal family, the Jordanian royal family, and the royal families of the Emirates might well contemplate as a better option than trying to crush future rebellion. Revolutionaries might fail today or tomorrow, but leaders have only to lose once, and by then it will be too late for them to negotiate their way to a soft landing.

FREE AND FAIR ELECTIONS: FALSE HOPE

Just as there are actions that can promote beneficial change, there are also actions that hamper progress. One of the most popular unhelpful solutions is an election. Leaders at risk often decide to hold fraudulent elections to create the impression of openness and fairness. Needless to say, bogus elections don't move a country toward better policies or more freedom for the people. Rather, fake elections empower the ruler by increasing the ranks of the interchangeables without adding in any meaningful way to the size of the influential and essential groups.

True, meaningful elections might be the final goal, but elections *for their own sake* should never be the objective. When the international community pushes for elections without being careful about how meaningful they are, all it accomplishes is to further entrench a nasty regime. International inspectors, for instance, like to certify whether people could freely go to the polling place and whether their votes were properly counted, as if that means there was a free and fair election. There's no reason to impede the opportunity to vote or to cheat when counting votes if, for instance, a regime first bans parties that might be real rivals, or if a government sets up campaign constraints that make it easy for the government's party to tell its story and make it impossible for the opposition to do the same. Russian incumbents don't need to cheat in counting votes to get the outcome they want. They don't need to block people from getting into the polling place. They deprive the opposition from having access to a free press and from holding rallies, so, sure, observers will easily conclude that elections were free and fair in the narrow sense, but we can all just as easily recognize that they were neither really free nor fair.

Ultimately, elections need to *follow* expanded freedom and not be thought of as presaging it!

Sometimes the problems of the world seem beyond our capacity to solve. Yet there is no mystery about how to eradicate much of the world's poverty and oppression. People who live with freedom are rarely impoverished and oppressed. Give people the right to say what they want, to write what they want, and to gather to share ideas about what they want, and you are bound to be looking at people whose persons and property are secure and whose lives are content. You are looking at people free to become rich and free to lose their shirts in trying. You are looking at people who are not only materially well off but spiritually and physically, too. Sure, places like Singapore and parts of China prove that it is possible to have a good material life with limited freedom—yet the vast majority of the evidence suggests that these are exceptions and not the rule. Economic success can postpone the democratic moment, but it cannot replace it.

A country's relative share of freedom is ultimately decided by its leaders. Behind the world of misery and oppression lie governments run by small cliques of essentials who are loyal to leaders who can make them rich. Behind the world of freedom and prosperity lie governments that depend on the backing of a substantial coalition of ordinary people drawn from a large pool of influentials, who are in turn drawn from a large pool of interchangeables. It is not difficult to draw a line from the poverty and oppression of the world to the corrupt juntas and brutal dictators who skim from their country's revenues to stay in power. Politics and political institutions define the bounds of the people's lives.

By now it should be clear that there is a natural order governing politics, and it comes with an ironclad set of rules. They cannot be altered. But that does not mean that we cannot find better paths to work within the laws of politics.

We have suggested some ways to work within the rules to produce better outcomes. At the end of the day, the solutions we have suggested will not be applied perfectly. There are good reasons for that. Entrenched ways of thinking make altering our approach to problems difficult. Many will conclude that it is cruel and insensitive to cut way back on foreign aid. They will tell us that all the money spent on aid is worth it if just one child is helped. They will forget to ask how many children are condemned to die of neglect because, in the process of helping a few, aid props up leaders who look after the people only after they have looked after themselves and their essential backers, if at all. But before we shift blame onto our "flawed" democratic leaders for their failures to make the world a better place, we need to remember why it is that they enact the policies that they do. The sworn duty of democratic leaders is to do precisely what we the people want.

Virtually since the nation's founding, American presidents have routinely endorsed the idea, if not the reality, of spreading democracy. President Woodrow Wilson, in calling on Congress to declare war against Germany on April 2, 1917, reflected his deeply held view that "the world must be made safe for democracy. . . . We have no selfish ends to serve. We desire no conquest, no dominion." His sentiment was echoed nearly ninety years later when George W. Bush, in his second inaugural address, proclaimed, "The survival of liberty in our land increasingly depends on the success of liberty in other lands. The best hope for peace in our world is the expansion of freedom in all the world. . . . So it is the policy of the United States to seek and support the growth of democratic movements and institutions in every nation and culture, with the ultimate goal of ending tyranny in our world." Yet Wilson set his noble sentiments aside when it came to standing up for self-determination in the colonies controlled by America's allies. In the same spirit, President Bush, during the same speech in which he called for democracy "in all the world," also noted: "My most solemn duty is to protect this nation and its people against further attacks and emerging threats."

The president's "solemn duty" highlights the problem. There is an inherent tension between promoting democratic reform abroad and protecting the welfare of the people at home. Free, democratic societies typically live in peace with each other and promote prosperity at home as well as between nations, making representative government attractive to people throughout the world. Yet democratic reform, as the experiences of the United States with Khomeini's Iran and Hamas-led Palestine make clear, does not always also enhance the security or welfare of Americans (or citizens elsewhere in the world) against foreign threats and may even jeopardize that security.

Our individual concerns about protecting ourselves from unfriendly democracies elsewhere typically trump our longer-term belief in the benefits of democracy. Democratic leaders listen to their voters because that is how they and their political party get to keep their jobs. Democratic leaders were elected, after all, to advance the current interests of at least those who chose them. The long run is always on someone else's watch. Democracy overseas is a great thing for us if, and only if, the people of a democratizing nation happen to want policies that we like. When a foreign people are aligned against our best interest, our best chance of getting what we want is to keep them under the yoke of an oppressor who is willing to do what we the people want.

Yes, we want people to be free and prosperous, but we don't want them to be free and prosperous enough to threaten our way of life, our interests, and our well-being—and that is as it should be. That, too, is a rule to rule by for democratic leaders. They must do what their coalition wants; they are not beholden to the coalition in any other country, just to those who help keep them in power. If we pretend otherwise we will just be engaging in the sort of utopianism that serves as an excuse for not tackling the problems that we can.

We began with Cassius imploring Brutus to act against Julius Caesar's despotism: "The fault, dear Brutus, is not in our stars, but in ourselves." We humbly add that the reason the fault is in ourselves is that we the people care so much for ourselves and so little for the world's underlings. But we have also seen that there is hope for the future. Every government and every organization that relies on a small coalition eventually erodes its own productivity and entrepreneurial spirit so much that it faces the risk of collapsing under the weight of its own corruption and inefficiency. When those crucial moments of opportunity arise, when the weight of bad governance catches up with despots, then a few simple changes can make all the difference.

We have learned that just about all of political life revolves around the size of the selectorate, the influentials, and the winning coalition. Expand them all, and the interchangeables no more quickly than the coalition, and everything changes for the better for the vast majority of people. They are liberated to work harder on their own behalf, to become better educated, healthier, wealthier, happier, and free. Their taxes are reduced and their opportunities in life expand dramatically. We can get to these moments of change faster through some of the fixes proposed here, but sooner or later every society will cross over from small-coalition, large-selectorate misery to a large coalition that is a large proportion of the selectorate—and peace and plenty will ensue. With a little bit of hard work and good luck, this can happen everywhere sooner, and if it does we all will prosper from it.

*T*he Dictator's Handbook is the culmination of more than two decades of research into the motivation and constraints of leaders. We owe a huge debt of gratitude to friends, colleagues, coauthors, and critics who have helped sharpen our understanding of what makes the world tick and given us insight into how it can be made to tick more smoothly.

In academic circles, our work has become known as *selectorate theory*. Together with two other founders of this way of thinking, Randolph Siverson and James Morrow, we published a comprehensive exposition of the theory, *The Logic of Political Survival*, in 2003 with MIT Press. That massive five-hundred-plus-page tome was full of mathematical models and complex statistical tests. Although we readily admit it is not an easy read, it is the most comprehensive statement of the theory. However, it was not the origin; nor was it the finale.

The genesis of selectorate theory was Bruce Bueno de Mesquita and Randy Siverson's foray into examining what happens to leaders after they fight wars. Surprisingly, no one had systematically looked at how winning or losing wars affects leader survival. Given their background in international relations, Bruce and Randy continued to pursue war-related topics and brought in James Morrow and Alastair Smith—and the collaborative team of BdM^{2}S^2 was born. In 1999 the four of us published "An Institutional Explanation of the Democratic Peace" in the *American Political Science Review*. This paper offered a solution to what at the time was the dominant question in international relations: Why don't democratic nations fight each other? Many of the existing theories relied on asserting different normative motivations for democrats and autocrats. Unfortunately, all too often democrats act contrary to these alleged higher values. In contrast, selectorate theory assumes that leaders have the same objective, to stay in power, and that what differentiates democrats from autocrats is that the former's dependence on a large coalition of supporters means democrats direct state resources to winning wars. Autocrats enhance their survival by hoarding resources to pay off cronies, even if this means losing the war. What started off as a desire to know why democracies don't fight each other ended up telling us how nations fight and what they fight over. As is supposed to happen in science, the answer to one problem provides answers to other problems and ends up posing a new set of questions.

In 2002, BdM²S² published a mathematical representation of the selectorate theory, "Political Institutions, Policy Choice and the Survival of Leaders," in the *British Journal of Political Science*. We further refined this model and then tested its predictions. This material became the basis for *The Logic of Political Survival*. Since its publication we have continued to advance the theory. In articles in the *Journal of Conflict Resolution* in 2007 and *International Organization* in 2009, we examined how nations trade aid for policy concessions. Recent extensions of the mathematical model incorporate revolutionary movements and have been published in the *Journal of Politics* in 2008, *Comparative Political Studies* in 2009, the *American Journal of Political Science* in 2010, the *Journal of Conflict Resolution* in 2015, and the *Quarterly Journal of Political Science* in 2018.

Selectorate theory offers a powerful yet simple-to-use model of politics. It forms the basis for the models in *Punishing the Prince*, for instance. In that book, Fiona McGillivray and Alastair Smith examined how leaders sanction leaders in other states. By targeting punishments at leaders rather than the nations they represent, a leader leverages the effectiveness of their state's policies in three ways. First, such mechanisms provide an explicit means through which to restore relations between states. Second, they encourage the citizens in targeted nations to remove their leaders in order to restore cooperation. Third, since leaders fear removal, the threat of such targeted punishments encourages leaders to abide by international norms in the first place. By focusing on the interactions of leaders instead of thinking of international cooperation as only between nations, Fiona enriched our understanding of interstate relations. As was characteristic of her scholarship, she asked questions that no one else had thought to ask and provided elegant answers that pushed scholarship in new directions. For instance, she examined how the dynamics of trade flows between nations depend upon the turnover of their national leaders. She found that the replacement of autocrats systematically altered trade flows in predictable ways.

Punishing the Prince was published in 2008, just a few days before Fiona died. She is missed every day by everyone who knew her, but most especially by Alastair and their three children, Angus, Duncan, and Molly. She was both our greatest supporter and harshest critic. Fiona endured a long and terrible illness, but her humor and spirit never failed even in her darkest hour. She died waiting on a transplant list. Please sign your donor card. The doctors and nurses at NewYork-Presbyterian Hospital and elsewhere, and especially Erika Berman-Rosenzweig and Nazzareno Galiè, gave us extra time with her; they have our profound thanks. Although she ruled Alastair's life with a rod of iron, Fiona was the epitome of a benevolent dictator.

Developing selectorate theory and writing this book were huge undertakings that we could never have done without the assistance of others. Randolph Siverson and James Morrow have been our collaborators from the start, and many of the ideas presented here are as much theirs as ours. Financial support is also vital for any research, and early developments of selectorate theory benefited from generous grants from the National Science Foundation. We also wish to thank Roger Hertog for his support through the Alexander Hamilton Center for Political Economy at New York University.

Hans Hoogeveen, formerly chief economist for the World Bank in Tanzania, commissioned a study applying the selectorate framework to help explain why the World Bank's efforts in Tanzania had not been as successful as they had hoped. The opportunity to do that study helped sharpen our own understanding of selectorate theory and proved essential to advancing our views on the formation of blocs of interests, whether ethnic, linguistic, geographic, or occupational. The work undertaken at Hans's request was a great stimulus for us, and we are most appreciative of his support and the opportunity he gave us. Our current employer, New York University, is a superb organization that has never hesitated to support our research and teaching. We benefited from superb research assistance by Alexandra Bear and Michal Harari.

Colleagues, students, and friends always improve any endeavor, especially when they are critics as well as supporters, and this book is no exception. We are truly fortunate to be connected to such a wonderful network of scholars and friends from whom we learn every day. Conversations with Neal Beck, Ethan Bueno de Mesquita, George Downs, William Easterly, Sandy Gordon, Lisa Howie, Jeff Jensen, Yanni Kotsonis, Mik Laver, Jim Morrow, Alex Quiroz-Flores, Shinasi Rama, Peter Rosendorff, Harry Roundell, Shanker Satyanath, John Scaife, Randy Siverson, Alan Stam, Federico Varesse, James Vreeland, Leonard Wantchekon, and many others helped shape this book.

Much of our previous work was aimed at an academic audience. Writing a "readable" book is a very different enterprise. Fortunately Eric Lupfer, our agent, took us under his wing. He worked tirelessly with us on structure, style, and presentation, and he fixed us up with a phenomenal press. PublicAffairs has been superbly supportive throughout the editorial and production process. Their entire team has helped us and supported us every step of the way. We thank Brandon Proia, who made the first edition of this book more readable, clearer, and more tightly argued than it would otherwise have been, and Erin Granville for her masterful copyediting and fact-checking of the second edition, and, in alphabetical order, Lindsay Jones, Lisa Kaufman, Jamie Leifer, Clive Priddle, Melissa Raymond, Anais Scott, Susan Weinberg, and Michelle Welsh-Horst, each of whom contributed mightily to improving our book. Benjamin Adams has been invaluable in stimulating and helping us to envision the second edition. Alas, we cannot hold them responsible for its failings, for which Alastair and Bruce each acknowledge that the other is responsible.

Of all the organizations we study, the ones we care most about are family. These are the people that brighten our world: Erin and Jason and Nathan and Clara; Ethan and Rebecca and Abraham and Hannah; Gwen and Adam and Isadore and Otis; Susan, Angus, Duncan, Molly, and Penelope. And most of all, we thank Arlene and Fiona and Susan, to whom we dedicate this book and ourselves.

Our fondest hope is for the well-being and success of those who imperil their lives to keep dictators in check.

INTRODUCTION

1. For information on Bell, California, houses and residents, see "Bell, CA (California) Houses and Residents," City-Data.com, accessed on September 15, 2021http://www.city-data.com/housing/houses-Bell-California.html.

2. The coach of Army's football team makes substantially more than the president despite Army's so-so record on the football field in recent years.

3. See "Jeff Tedford—California Football," Coaches Hot Seat (website), August 30, 2011, http://www.coacheshotseat.com/JeffTedford.htm.

4. Kim Christensen, "Bell Residents Paid Huge Tax Bills in Addition to Huge Salaries, Records Show," *Los Angeles Times*, July 29, 2010, https://latimes blogs.latimes.com/lanow/2010/07/bell-paid-huge-salaries-residents-paid-huge -tax-bills-records-show.html.

5. The council members, in turn, could target benefits to their essential voters. We can only wonder whether the people receiving housing grants, for example, made up the bulk of the city council's supporting voters. With a secret ballot there is no way to know, although if Bell's votes were reported by neighborhood we probably could come close to seeing the pairing of electoral support and the prospects of receiving special rewards, like housing grants.

6. Thomas Hobbes, *Leviathan*, ed. Richard Tuck (New York: Cambridge University Press, 1996 [1651]), 131.

7. Niccolò Machiavelli, *The Prince and the Discourses*, ed. Max Learner (New York: Modern Library, 1950 [1532]), 256.

8. James Madison, "Federalist 10," in *The Federalist*, ed. Jacob Cooke (Middletown, CT: Wesleyan University Press, 1961), 62.

9. Montesquieu, Charles de Secondat, *The Spirit of Laws*, ed. Edward Wallace Carrithers (Berkeley: University of California Press, 1977 [1748]), 176.

10. Robert Woodward, *Obama's War* (New York: Simon and Schuster, 2010); Robert F. Kennedy, *Thirteen Days* (New York: W. W. Norton, 1969).

11. Bruce Bueno de Mesquita, Alastair Smith, Randolph M. Siverson, and James D. Morrow, *The Logic of Political Survival* (Cambridge, MA: MIT Press, 2003).

CHAPTER 1: THE RULES OF POLITICS

1. Those interested in seeing rigorous proofs for the logic behind the claims made here should see Bruce Bueno de Mesquita, Alastair Smith, Randolph M. Siverson, and James D. Morrow, *The Logic of Political Survival* (Cambridge, MA: MIT Press, 2003), and subsequent works cited throughout this volume.

2. John Cloud, "The Pioneer Harvey Milk," *Time*, July 14, 1999, http://www
.time.com/time/magazine/article/0,9171,991276,00.html.

3. The sources for the fate of Castro's close allies are Volker Skierka, *Fidel
Castro: A Biography* (Cambridge, UK: Polity Press, 2004), 68–91; Georgie Anne
Geyer, *Guerrilla Prince* (New York: Little, Brown, 1991), 191–315; Frank Fer-
nandez, *Cuban Anarchism: The History of a Movement*, trans. Charles Bufe (Tuc-
son, AZ: Sharp Press, 2001), 75–93; George Dominguez, "Cuba Since 1959," in
Cuba: A Short History, ed. Leslie Bethell (New York: Cambridge University Press,
1993), 95–149; and *American Experience*, "Fidel Castro," written, produced, and
directed by Adriana Bosch, aired January 31, 2005, on PBS, https://www.pbs
.org/wgbh/americanexperience/films/castro/.

4. Emma Larkin, *Everything Is Broken: A Tale of Catastrophe in Burma* (New
York: Penguin Press, 2010), 179–205.

5. Alexandros Tegos, "To Leave or Not to Leave? On the Assumption of Political Survival" (working paper, Alexander Hamilton Center for Political Economy, Department of Politics, New York University, April 15, 2008).

CHAPTER 2: COMING TO POWER

1. We draw heavily on the following accounts of Doe's rise to power and rule:
Ryszard Kapuscinski, *The Shadow of the Sun* (New York: Vintage, 2001); Martin
Meredith, *The Fate of Africa* (New York: PublicAffairs, 2005), chapter 29; and
Gregory Jaynes, "Liberia's Young Sergeant Still Learning How to Rule," *New
York Times*, January 20, 1981, https://www.nytimes.com/1981/01/20/world/li
beria-s-young-sergeant-still-learning-how-to-rule.html.

2. Bruce Bueno de Mesquita, talk given to a large investment group's portfolio committee, May 5, 2010, New York, New York.

3. Lawrence K. Altman, "The Shah's Health: A Political Gamble," *New York
Times Magazine*, May 17, 1981.

4. Meredith, *Fate of Africa*, 150.

5. Bruce Bueno de Mesquita and Alastair Smith, "Political Loyalty and
Leader Health," *Quarterly Journal of Political Science* 13, no. 4 (2018): 333–361.

6. S. E. Finer, *The History of Government* (New York: Oxford University
Press, 1997).

7. "Zimbabwe's Robert Mugabe Urged by First Lady to Name Heir," BBC
News, July 27, 2017, http://www.bbc.com/news/world-africa-40740359.

8. "Mugabe Urged by First Lady."

9. Sources for the analysis of Pope Damasus I include Michael Walsh, *Butler's
Lives of the Saints* (New York: HarperCollins, 1991), 413; Edward Gibbon, *The
Decline and Fall of the Roman Empire*, vol. 1 (New York: Modern Library, 1932),
866n84; "Pope St. Damasus I," *Catholic Encyclopedia* (New York: Robert Apple-
ton, 1913), Letter of Jerome to Pope Damasus, vol. 2, 376; Henry Chadwick, *The
Pelican History of the Church*, vol. 1, *The Early Church* (London: Penguin, 1978);
Williston Walker, *A History of the Christian Church* (New York: General Books,

2010); Diarmaid MacCulloch, *A History of Christianity: The First Three Thousand Years* (London: Viking, 2009).

10. Averil Cameron and Peter Garnsey, eds., *The Cambridge Ancient History: The Late Empire, A.D. 337–425* (New York: Cambridge University Press, 1998), 103.

11. Ryszard Kapuscinski, *The Soccer War* (New York: Vintage, 1992), 113–114.

12. The discussion of Gorbachev's fall and Yeltsin's rise is based on the analysis in Kiron Skinner, Serhiy Kudelia, Bruce Bueno de Mesquita, and Condoleezza Rice, *The Strategy of Campaigning* (Ann Arbor: University of Michigan Press, 2007).

13. Ernesto Dal Bó, Pedro Dal Bó, and Jason Snyder, "Political Dynasties," *Review of Economic Studies* 76, no. 1 (January 2009): 115–142.

14. The champion for winning the presidency with little popular support was John Quincy Adams, who received less than 31 percent of the popular vote. He won in a multiparty race through clever maneuvering in America's odd system, in which popular votes, especially in the country's early days, did not translate directly into support in the Electoral College or, when no one wins there, in the House of Representatives.

CHAPTER 3: STAYING IN POWER

1. Italo Calvino, "A King Listens," in *Under the Jaguar Sun* (New York: Harcourt, Brace, Jovanovich, 1986), 36.

2. See, for instance, Andrew Ward, Karen Bishop, and Jeffrey Sonnenfeld, "Pyrrhic Victories: The Cost to the Board of Ousting the CEO," *Journal of Organizational Behavior* 20 (1999): 767–781; see also Joann Lublin, "CEO Tenure, Stock Gains Often Go Hand-in-Hand," *Wall Street Journal*, July 6, 2010, http://online.wsj.com/article/SB10001424052748703900004575325172681419254.html.

3. The chairman and CEO in 1999 was Lewis Platt. His board included Philip M. Condit, Patricia C. Dunn, Thomas E. Everhart, John B. Fery, Jean-Paul G. Gimon, Sam Ginn, Richard A. Hackborn, Walter B. Hewlett, George A. Keyworth II, David M. Lawrence, Susan P. Orr, David W. Packard, and Robert P. Wayman.

4. Carly Fiorina, "The Case for the Merger," speech at the Goldman Sachs Technology Conference, Palm Springs, California, February 4, 2002.

5. Fuad Matar, *Saddam Hussein: The Man, the Cause and the Future* (London: Third World Centre, 1981), 60, quoted in Edward Mortimer, "The Thief of Baghdad," *New York Review of Books*, September 7, 1990, http://www.nybooks.com/articles/archives/1990/sep/27/the-thief-of-baghdad/.

6. See Patrick Cockburn, "Chemical Ali: The End of an Overlord," *The Independent*, June 25, 2007. Part of Saddam Hussein's mercifulness was manifested in his allowing al-Bakr to resign rather than executing him, which was probably seen by Chemical Ali as a show of weakness.

7. Max Fisher, "Iraq's Security and Intelligence Gutted in Political Purges, New Cables Show," *The Atlantic*, December 3, 2010, http://www.theatlantic.com/international/archive/2010/12/iraqs-security-and-intelligence-gutted-in-political-purges-new-cables-show/67431/.

8. S. E. Finer, *The History of Government* (New York: Oxford University Press, 1997), 643.

9. Martin Meredith, *The Fate of Africa* (New York: PublicAffairs, 2005), 546.

10. Martin Meredith, *Our Votes, Our Guns: Robert Mugabe and the Tragedy of Zimbabwe* (New York: PublicAffairs, 2002).

11. Sabelo J. Ndlovu-Gatsheni, *Joshua Mqabuko Nkomo of Zimbabwe: Politics, Power and Memory* (London: Palgrave Macmillan, 2017), 332.

12. Meredith, *Our Votes, Our Guns*, 69.

13. Named for Maurice Duverger, who expressed this idea in his *Les Partis Politiques* (Paris: Librairie Armand Colin, 1951).

14. Bruce Bueno de Mesquita, *Report on Tanzania's Economic and Political Performance: Helping Tanzania Do Better*, World Bank, April 20, 2009. A revised version by Bruce Bueno de Mesquita and Alastair Smith is found in "Tanzania's Economic and Political Performance: A District-Level Test of Selectorate Theory," in *Politics in South Asia*, ed. Siegfried Wolf (Heidelberg: Springer Verlag, 2015), 31–48.

15. Alastair Smith and Bruce Bueno de Mesquita, "Contingent Prize Allocation and Pivotal Voting," *British Journal of Political Science* 42, no. 2 (2012): 371–392.

16. See Richard L. Park and Bruce Bueno de Mesquita, *India's Political System*, 2nd ed. (Englewood Cliffs, NJ: Prentice Hall, 1979); and Bruce Bueno de Mesquita, *Strategy, Risk and Personality in Coalition Politics: The Case of India* (New York: Cambridge University Press, 1975).

17. See Bueno de Mesquita, *Strategy, Risk and Personality*, 75.

18. Milton K. Rakove, *Don't Make No Waves, Don't Back No Losers: An Insider's Analysis of the Daley Machine* (Bloomington: Indiana University Press, 1975), 16.

19. Waikeung Tam, "Clientelist Politics in Singapore: Selective Provision of Housing Services as an Electoral Mobilization Strategy," University of Chicago, 2003, typescript.

20. See Amy Catalinac, Bruce Bueno de Mesquita, and Alastair Smith, "A Tournament Theory of Pork Barrel Politics: The Case of Japan," *Comparative Political Studies* 53, nos. 10–11 (2020): 1619–1655.

21. The measure of winning-coalition size is described in detail in Bruce Bueno de Mesquita and Alastair Smith, "A New Indicator of Coalition Size: Tests Against Standard Regime-Type Indicators," September 17, 2021, SSRN, https://ssrn.com/abstract=3925591. The data on leader tenure is taken from Bruce Bueno de Mesquita and Alastair Smith, "Political Loyalty and Leader Health," *Quarterly Journal of Political Science* 13, no. 4 (2018): 333–361.

CHAPTER 4: STEAL FROM THE POOR, GIVE TO THE RICH

1. Several scholars have examined how institutions affect transparency and the availability of data. See, for instance, James R. Hollyer, B. Peter Rosendorff, and James Raymond Vreeland, *Information, Democracy, and Autocracy: Economic Transparency and Political (In)Stability* (New York: Cambridge University Press,

2018); see also Bruce Bueno de Mesquita, Alastair Smith, Randolph M. Siverson, and James D. Morrow, *The Logic of Political Survival* (Cambridge, MA: MIT Press, 2003).

2. Quoted in Meredith Martin, *Our Votes, Our Guns: Robert Mugabe and the Tragedy of Zimbabwe* (New York: PublicAffairs, 2002), 17.

3. See Phumzile Ngcatshe, "Zimbabwean FA Boss Philip Chiyangwa Can't Account for $2 Million Supplied by FIFA," African Football (website), November 1, 2017, https://africanfootball.com/news/733466/Zimbabwean-FA-boss -Philip-Chiyangwa-can-t-account-for-10billion-supplied-by-FIFA.

4. Robert H. Bates, *Prosperity and Violence: The Political Economy of Development* (New York: W. W. Norton, 2001), 74.

5. Gerard Padró i Miquel, "The Control of Politicians in Divided Societies: The Politics of Fear," *Review of Economic Studies* 74 (2007): 1259–1274.

6. The figure is constructed using the kg variable from the Penn World Tables, version 6.3. See "Productivity," Groningen Growth and Development Centre, University of Groningen, accessed on September 17, 2021, https://www.rug .nl/ggdc/productivity/pwt/pwt-releases/pwt-6.3?lang=en.

7. These tax estimates are based, in the case of China, on the tax brackets for that country identified at www.worldwide-tax.com, accessed in March 2021, and for the United States by filling out US tax form 1040 using H&R Block's 2020 Tax Cut program, with only the standard deduction for our hypothetical American family of three.

8. Implicit taxation is the value associated with an activity that is lost to its producer as a result of government policy. High inflation, for instance, implicitly taxes wealth by diminishing its value.

9. Anna Fifield, "Life Under Kim Jong Un," *Washington Post*, November 17, 2017, https://www.washingtonpost.com/graphics/2017/world/north-korea-defec tors/.

10. "China's Richest Man Makes First Public Appearance Since October," Voice of America (website), January 20, 2021, https://www.voanews.com/east-asia -pacific/chinas-richest-man-makes-first-public-appearance-october. See also Raymond Zhong and Alexandra Stevenson, "Jack Ma Shows Why China's Tycoons Keep Quiet," *New York Times*, April 22, 2021, https://www.nytimes.com/2021 /04/22/technology/jack-ma-alibaba-tycoons.html.

11. William Shakespeare, *The Merchant of Venice*, ed. Barbara A. Mowat and Paul Werstine, Folger Shakespeare Library (New York: Washington Square Press, 2009), act 4, scene 1, 157.

12. Anita L. Allen and Michael R. Seidl, "Cross-Cultural Commerce in Shakespeare's 'Merchant of Venice,'" *American University Journal of International Law and Politics* 10 (1995): 843.

13. Calculations based upon SOI Tax States-Internal Revenue Service Collections, Costs, Personnel, and US Population, by Fiscal Year—IRS Data Book Table 29 for 2009. This, and all years of such data, can be found at https://www .irs.gov/statistics/soi-tax-stats-all-years-irs-data-books.

14. Daron Acemoglu and James A. Robinson, "Inefficient Redistribution," *American Political Science Review* 95, no. 3 (September 2001): 649–661.

15. Elizabeth Ohene, "Words, Deeds and Cocoa," *West Africa* 31 (August 1982): 2104, quoted in Jeffrey Herbst, *The Politics of Reform in Ghana, 1982–1991* (Berkeley: University of California Press, 1993), 111.

16. Tracy Williams, "An African Success Story: Ghana's Cocoa Marketing System," *IDS Working Papers* 2009, no. 318 (January 2009):1–47.

17. S. E. Finer, *The History of Government* (New York: Oxford University Press, 1997), 663–727.

18. Jerry Useem, "The Devil's Excrement," *Fortune*, February 3, 2003.

19. Bruce Bueno de Mesquita and Alastair Smith, "Political Survival and Endogenous Institutional Change," *Comparative Political Studies* 42, no. 2 (2009): 167–197; A. H. Gelb, *Windfall Gains: Blessing or Curse?* (New York: Oxford University Press, 1988); Michael Ross, "Political Economy of Resource Curse," *World Politics* 51 (1999): 297–322; Jeffrey D. Sachs and Andrew M. Warner, "Natural Resource Abundance and Economic Growth," Working Paper 5398, National Bureau of Economic Research, December 1995, https://doi.org/10.3386/w5398.

20. Xavier Sala-i-Martin and Arvind Subramanian, "Addressing the Natural Resource Curse: An Illustration from Nigeria," Working Paper 9804, National Bureau of Economic Research, June 2003, https://doi.org/10.3386/w9804.

21. This draws on lists of most expensive cities compiled by Mercer: "Thriving Anywhere," Mercer, accessed on November 8, 2021, https://www.mercer.com/our-thinking/career/cost-of-living.html. The United Nations figures in the paragraph above and the Human Development Index data in this paragraph are from "Human Development Reports," United Nations Development Programme, accessed on November 8, 2021, http://hdr.undp.org/en/indicators/137506#.

22. Paul Krugman, "Financing vs. Forgiving a Debt Overhang: Some Analytical Notes," *Journal of Development Economics* 29 (1988): 253–268; Jeffrey Sachs, "The Debt Overhang of the Developing Countries," in *Debt, Stabilization, and Development*, ed. Guillermo A. Calvo, Ronald Findlay, Pentti J. K. Kouri, and Jorge Braga de Macedo (Cambridge, MA: Basil Blackwell, 1989).

23. Martin Knoll, "The Heavily Indebted Poor Countries and the Multilateral Debt Relief Initiative: A Test Case for the Validity of the Debt Overhang Hypothesis" (discussion paper 2013/11, Free University Berlin, School of Business and Economics, 2013, https://www.econstor.eu/bitstream/10419/78106/1/756455243.pdf).

24. Data taken from the World Bank's World Development Indicators 2010, http://data.worldbank.org/data-catalog/world-development-indicators, accessed on March 12, 2021. Amounts reported in constant 2000 US dollars.

CHAPTER 5: GETTING AND SPENDING

1. See Bruce Bueno de Mesquita and George W. Downs, "The Rise of Sustainable Autocracy," *Foreign Affairs* 84, no. 5 (September/October 2005): 77–86. For contrary views, see Robert J. Barro, *Determinants of Economic Growth: A*

Cross-Country Empirical Study (Cambridge, MA: MIT Press, 1997); and Adam Przeworski, Michael Alvares, José Antonio Cheibub, and Fernando Limongi, *Democracy and Development: Political Institutions and Material Well-Being in the World, 1950–1990* (New York: Cambridge University Press, 2000).

2. "Literacy Rate by Country 2021," World Population Review, accessed on September 17, 2021, https://worldpopulationreview.com/country-rankings/liter acy-rate-by-country.

3. See the *U.S. News and World Report* rankings at Kelsey Sheehy, "Explore the World's Top Universities," *U.S. News and World Report*, October 8, 2013, http://www.usnews.com/articles/education/worlds-best-universities/2010/09/21 /worlds-best-universities-top-400-.html.

4. See Kiron Skinner, Serhiy Kudelia, Bruce Bueno de Mesquita, and Condoleezza Rice, *The Strategy of Campaigning* (Ann Arbor: University of Michigan Press, 2007).

5. For a comparison of leadership by one person in a small-coalition setting and in a large-coalition setting, see Bruce Bueno de Mesquita, "Leopold II and the Selectorate: An Account in Contrast to a Racial Explanation," *Historical Social Research [Historische Sozialforschung]* 32, no. 4 (2007): 203–221.

6. See Jorge Dominguez, *Cuba: Order and Revolution* (Cambridge, MA: Belknap Press of Harvard University Press, 1978); Jorge Dominguez, "The Batista Regime in Cuba," in *Sultanistic Regimes*, eds. H. E. Chehabi and Juan J. Linz (Baltimore, MD: Johns Hopkins University Press, 1998), 113–131.

7. See "Abortion Rates by Country," World Population Review, accessed on September 17, 2021, https://worldpopulationreview.com/country-rankings/abor tion-rates-by-country; Azam Ahmed, "In Cuba, an Abundance of Love but a Lack of Babies," *New York Times*, October 27, 2015.

8. See *The World Factbook*, Central Intelligence Agency, cia.gov/the-world -factbook, for comparisons of per capita income based on purchasing power parity in 2019, the latest year for which the data are available.

9. Quoted in James A. Robinson, "When Is a State Predatory?," SSRN, January 1999, https://ssrn.com/abstract=273022.

10. We have measured these distances wherever we could. If you want to estimate these distances yourself, just use Google Maps and associated tools.

11. See Bruce Bueno de Mesquita and Alastair Smith, "A New Indicator of Coalition Size: Tests Against Standard Regime-Type Indicators," September 17, 2021, SSRN, https://ssrn.com/abstract=3925591.

12. A recent study that examines the protection of property rights found that larger-coalition governments are significantly more attentive to protecting property rights than are governments that rely on smaller coalitions. Mogens K. Justesen, "Making and Breaking Property Rights: Coalitions, Veto Players, and the Institutional Foundation of Markets," *Journal of Institutional and Theoretical Economics* 171, no. 2 (June 2015): 238–262, http://www.jstor.org/stable/24549024.

13. David S. Brown and Ahmed Mushfiq Mobarak, "The Transforming Power of Democracy: Regime Type and the Distribution of Electricity," *American*

Political Science Review 103 (2009): 193–213; and Brian Min, "Who Gets Public Goods? Efficiency, Equity, and the Politics of Electrification," paper presented at the 2008 Meeting of the Working Group on Wealth and Power in the Post-Industrial Age, UCLA, February 8–9, 2008.

14. US Department of Commerce, "Comparison of U.S. and Chilean Building Code Requirements and Seismic Design Practice 1985–2010," section 4-3, https://www.nehrp.gov/pdf/nistgcr12-917-18.pdf.

15. Iranian Studies Group at MIT, "Earthquake Management in Iran," Disaster Management, Vojoudi.com, January 6, 2004, http://www.vojoudi.com/earthquake/management/management_eq_mit_eng.htm.

16. Edward Luce, *In Spite of the Gods: The Rise of Modern India* (New York: Anchor, 2006), 139–140.

CHAPTER 6: IF CORRUPTION EMPOWERS, THEN ABSOLUTE CORRUPTION EMPOWERS ABSOLUTELY

1. Henry is much admired for his victory at Agincourt during the Hundred Years' War. Unlike Genghis Khan, however, Henry V died young, at only forty-five. But then, he did not fall at the hand of some political foe; he died of dysentery while fighting in France.

2. William Shakespeare, *Henry V*, ed. Barbara A. Mowat and Paul Werstine, Folger Shakespeare Library (New York: Washington Square Press, 1995), act 3, scene 3, 97.

3. Having lost his fortune, he hankered to return to Haiti, thinking he might once again assume power and extract wealth. He finally bit the bullet and went back to Haiti in January 2011, where he was immediately charged with corruption and other crimes. Baby Doc was held under, admittedly, poorly enforced house arrest while his case was being heard. He died of a heart attack on October 4, 2014, at age sixty-three. The urge for power is great—maybe even great enough to induce Baby Doc to undertake such an imprudent decision.

4. "Corruption Perceptions Index," Transparency International, transparency.org/en/cpi/2020.

5. David Leonhardt, "Yes, 47% of Households Owe No Taxes. Look Closer," *New York Times*, April 13, 2010, http://www.nytimes.com/2010/04/14/business/economy/14leonhardt.html.

6. All quotations about the Dymovsky affair are from Clifford J. Levy, "Videos Rouse Russian Anger Toward Police," *New York Times*, July 28, 2010.

7. Martin Meredith, *The Fate of Africa* (New York: PublicAffairs, 2005), 556.

8. David Usborne, "Olympics Crackdown on Sponsorship Parasites," *The Independent*, October 23, 2011, http://www.independent.co.uk/news/business/olympics-crackdown-on-sponsorship-parasites-1612771.html.

9. See *Panorama*, "Buying the Games," produced by Howard Bradburn, reported by Justin Rowlatt, aired August 4, 2004, on BBC One, transcript, http://news.bbc.co.uk/2/hi/programmes/panorama/3937425.stm.

10. Rob Harris, "Keep Bribes Quiet for 10 years, FIFA Won't Punish You," Associated Press, August 13, 2018, https://apnews.com/article/d165d80179 aa4117a260a1a5e65eafb6.

11. *FIFA Code of Ethics*, 2019 edition, article 22.2, p. 19, accessed on September 17, 2021, https://digitalhub.fifa.com/m/1c429d1b627be00c/original/la3f5y qsox5cns9oypkg-pdf.pdf.

12. Quoted in Celia W. Dugger, "Battle to Halt Graft Scourge in Africa Ebbs," *New York Times*, January 9, 2009.

13. Dugger, "Battle to Halt Graft."

14. For background on Castellano, see Selwyn Raab, *Five Families* (New York: Thomas Dunne Books, 2005); and Peter Maas, *Underboss: Sammy the Bull Gravano's Story of Life in the Mafia* (New York: Harper Torch, 1997).

15. M. Cary and H. H. Scallard, *A History of Rome: Down to the Reign of Constantine*, 3rd ed. (Boston: Bedford/St. Martins, 1976), chapters 20 and 27.

16. Quoted in Beatriz Magaloni, *Voting for Autocracy* (New York: Cambridge University Press, 2008), 47.

17. Michela Wrong, *In the Footsteps of Mr. Kurtz: Living on the Brink of Disaster in Mobutu's Congo* (London: Fourth Estate, 2000), 4.

18. S. E. Finer, *The History of Government* (New York: Oxford University Press, 1997), 724.

19. "King of the Kleptocrats," *Economist*, July 11, 2017, https://www.econo mist.com/asia/2007/07/11/king-of-the-kleptocrats.

20. Afua Hirsch, "WikiLeaks Cables: Sudanese President 'Stashed $9bn in UK Banks,'" *The Guardian*, December 17, 2010.

21. William Taubman, *Khrushchev: The Man and His Era* (New York: W. W. Norton, 2003), 519–523.

22. "Arafat Aides Resume Talks with Israel, Fight over His Fortune," Arab-News, November 1, 2004, https://www.arabnews.com/node/257417.

23. Bruce Bueno de Mesquita and Alastair Smith, "The Political Economy of Corporate Fraud: A Theory and Empirical Tests," paper presented at NYU's Stern Business School, September 2004.

CHAPTER 7: FOREIGN AID

1. "USAID from the American People [Website]," Homeland Security Digital Library, accessed on September 17, 2021, https://www.hsdl.org/?abstract&did=30181.

2. Ryszard Kapuscinski, *The Emperor* (Boston: Harcourt, 1983), 118.

3. Kapuscinski, *The Emperor*, 111.

4. See Martin Meredith, *The Fate of Africa* (New York: PublicAffairs, 2005), chapter 19.

5. David Rieff, "Cruel to Be Kind?," *The Guardian*, June 24, 2005.

6. Associated Press, "Billions in US Aid Never Reached Pakistan Army," Fox News, October 4, 2009, https://www.foxnews.com/story/billions-in-u-s-aid -never-reached-pakistan-army.

7. See also Celia W. Dugger, "Battle to Halt Graft Scourge in Africa Ebbs," *New York Times*, June 9, 2009, https://www.nytimes.com/2009/06/10/world/africa/10zambia.html.

8. "Dirt Out, Cash In: Kenya's Anti-corruption Campaign Is Wooing Back Donors," *Economist*, November 27, 2003.

9. "Feet of Clay: More Bad News for Honest Kenyans," *The Economist*, February 12, 2005.

10. "USAID from the American People."

11. Jomo Kenyatta, *Suffering Without Bitterness: The Founding of the Kenya Nation* (Nairobi: East African Publishing House, 1968), 215.

12. Meredith, *Fate of Africa*, 555.

13. Meredith, *Fate of Africa*, 555–556.

14. "Turkey Holds Out for Extra US Aid over Iraq," CNN, February 18, 2003, http://www.cnn.com/2003/WORLD/meast/02/18/sprj.irq.erdogan/index.html. It is worth nothing that Turkey has shown robust growth over the last few years, as seen by comparing these figures with the more current ones used in Chapter 6.

15. Bruce Bueno de Mesquita and Alastair Smith, "A Political Economy of Aid," *International Organization* 63 (Spring 2009): 309–340; and Bruce Bueno de Mesquita and Alastair Smith, "Foreign Aid and Policy Concessions," *Journal of Conflict Resolution* 51, no. 2 (2007): 251–284.

16. "Israel and Iran Share Most Negative Ratings in World Poll," BBC World Service, March 6, 2007, http://news.bbc.co.uk/2/shared/bsp/hi/pdfs/06_03_07_perceptions.pdf.

17. See Bann Seng Tan, *International Aid and Democracy Promotion: Liberalization at the Margins* (London: Routledge, 2021).

18. Russell Heimlich, "Pakistanis See U.S. as an Enemy," Pew Research Center, August 11, 2010, https://www.pewresearch.org/fact-tank/0210/08/12/pakistanis-see-u-s-as-an-enemy/.

19. *What the World Thinks in 2002*, Pew Global Attitudes Project, Pew Research Center, 4–5, accessed on September 17, 2021, https://www.pewresearch.org/wp-content/uploads/sites/4/legacy-pdf/165.pdf.

20. See Peter J. Schraeder, Steven W. Hook, and Bruce Taylor, "Clarifying the Foreign Aid Puzzle: A Comparison of American, Japanese, French, and Swedish Aid Flows," *World Politics* 50, no. 2 (1998): 294–323.

21. Flora Drury, "Japan Whale Hunting: 'By-Catch' Rule Highlighted After Minke Death," BBC News, January 31, 2019, https://www.bbc.com/news/world-asia-55714815.

22. See *U.S. Overseas Loans and Grants: Obligations and Loan Authorizations, July 1, 1945–September 30, 2019* (Greenbook), USAID, May 9, 2021, usaid.gov/open/greenbook/2019.

23. Bruce Bueno de Mesquita and Alastair Smith, "The Pernicious Consequences of UN Security Council Membership," *Journal of Conflict Resolution* 54, no. 5 (2010): 667–686.

24. See, for instance, Ilyana Kuziemko and Eric Werker, "How Much Is a Seat on the Security Council Worth? Foreign Aid and Bribery at the United Nations," *Journal of Political Economy* 114, no. 5 (2006): 905–930; Axel Dreher, Jan-Egbert Sturm, and James Vreeland, "Global Horse Trading: IMF Loans for Votes in the United Nations Security Council," *European Economic Review* 53, no. 7 (2009): 742–757; Axel Dreher, Jan-Egbert Sturm, and James Vreeland, "Development Aid and International Politics: Does Membership on the UN Security Council Influence World Bank Decisions?," *Journal of Development Economics* 88 (2009): 1–18.

25. Charles Levinson, "$50 Billion Later, Taking Stock of US Aid to Egypt," *Christian Science Monitor*, April 12, 2004, https://www.csmonitor.com/2004/0412/p07s01-wome.html.

26. "Poverty: Overview," World Bank, April 15, 2021, https://www.worldbank.org/en/topic/poverty/overview.

27. William Easterly, *The Elusive Quest for Growth: Economists' Adventures and Misadventures in the Tropics* (Cambridge, MA: MIT Press, 2002); and William Easterly, *The White Man's Burden: Why the West's Efforts to Aid the Rest Have Done So Much Ill and So Little Good* (London: Penguin Press, 2006).

28. Craig Burnside and David Dollar, "Aid, Policies, and Growth," *American Economic Review* 90, no. 4 (2000): 847–868.

29. Michael M. Calavan, Sergio Diaz Briquets, and Jerald O'Brien, *Cambodian Corruption Assessment*, USAID, May–June 2004, p. 13, https://www.globalsecurity.org/military/library/report/2004/cambodian-corruption-assessment.pdf.

30. Omar Waraich, "Pakistan's Rich 'Diverted Floods to Save Their Land,'" *The Independent*, October 23, 2011, http://www.independent.co.uk/news/world/asia/pakistans-rich-diverted-floods-to-save-their-land-2069244.html. See also Shahzad Jillani and Salman Siddiqui, "Critical Decisions Ahead as Barrages Continue to Resist," *Express Tribune* (Pakistan), August 10, 2010, http://tribune.com.pk/story/37842/critical-decisions-ahead-as-barrages-continue-to-resist/; Andrew Clark and Allegra Stratton, "Pakistan Floods Are a 'Slow-Motion Tsunami'—Ban Ki-Moon," *The Guardian*, August 19, 2010, http://www.guardian.co.uk/world/2010/aug/19/pakistan-flood-ban-ki-moon.

31. Alejandro Quiroz Flores and Alastair Smith, "Pakistan's Flood of Cash: How Aid Made Flood Management Worse," *Foreign Affairs*, November 28, 2010, https://www.foreignaffairs.com/articles/pakistan/2010-11-28/pakistans-flood-cash.

32. Issam Ahmed, "Pakistan Floods Strand the Poor While Rich Go to Higher Ground," *Christian Science Monitor*, August 12, 2010, http://www.csmonitor.com/World/Asia-South-Central/2010/0812/Pakistan-floods-strand-the-poor-while-rich-go-to-higher-ground.

33. "Gen McChrystal: Bin Laden Is Key to al-Qaeda Defeat," BBC News, December 9, 2009, http://news.bbc.co.uk/2/hi/americas/8402138.stm.

34. Martin Meredith, *The Fate of Africa* (New York: PublicAffairs, 2005), 102.

35. See Bruce Bueno de Mesquita and George W. Downs, "Intervention and Democracy," *International Organization* 60, no. 3 (July 2006): 627–649.

CHAPTER 8: THE PEOPLE IN REVOLT

1. Portions of this chapter are drawn from several of our academic undertakings, including Bruce Bueno de Mesquita and Alastair Smith, "Political Survival and Endogenous Institutional Change," *Comparative Political Studies* 42, no. 2 (February 2009): 167–197; Bruce Bueno de Mesquita, *Principles of International Politics*, 4th ed. (Washington, DC: CQ Press, 2009); and Bruce Bueno de Mesquita, Alastair Smith, Randolph M. Siverson, and James D. Morrow, *The Logic of Political Survival* (Cambridge, MA: MIT Press, 2003).

2. Translated by Yung Wei in personal correspondence, drawn from Hongshe Zhong-gui (Red China), December 1, 1931. We are most grateful to Yung Wei for bringing this quotation to our attention.

3. Frank D. Cornfield, *The Origins and Growth of Mau Mau: An Historical Survey*, Sessional Paper number 5 of 1959/60 of Kenya LegCo (Nairobi: Government of Colony and Protectorate of Kenya, 1960), 301–308.

4. Julia Preston and Samuel Dillon, *Opening Mexico: The Making of a Democracy* (New York: Farrar, Straus and Giroux, 2005).

5. Emma Larkin, *Everything Is Broken: A Tale of Catastrophe in Burma* (New York: Penguin Press, 2010). We draw extensively on her account of Burmese politics.

6. Larkin, *Everything Is Broken*, 78–79.

7. *Wide Angle* (TV documentary series), "Eyes of the Storm: Turning Points in Burmese History," directed and produced by Evan Williams and Jeremy Williams for Thirteen/WNET New York, aired August 19, 2009, on PBS.

8. Alejandro Quiroz Flores and Alastair Smith, "Leader Survival and Natural Disasters," *British Journal of Political Science* 43, no. 4 (2013): 821–843.

9. This is true even though earthquakes are more likely to strike democracies than autocracies.

10. See "Total Natural Resource Rents (% of GDP)—Myanmar," World Bank, accessed on September 18, 2021, https://data.worldbank.org/indicator/NY.GDP.TOTL.RT.ZS?locations=MM.

11. Francis X. Clines, "Soviet Crackdown: Latvia; Latvia's Leader Tries to Placate the Kremlin," *New York Times*, January 17, 1991, https://www.nytimes.com/1991/01/17/world/soviet-crackdown-latvia-latvia-s-leader-tries-to-placate-the-kremlin.html.

12. Andrejs Plakans, *The Latvians: A Short History* (Stanford, CA: Hoover Institution Press, 1995).

13. Bill Keller, "Gorbachev Urged to Consider Crackdown in Republics," *New York Times*, December 20, 1990, http://www.nytimes.com/1990/12/20/world/gorbachev-urged-to-consider-crackdown-in-republics.html.

14. Data from World Bank, World Development Indicators, per capita GDP reported in constant 2010 US dollars, at worldbank.org/en/home.

15. Albert Adu Boahen, *The Ghanaian Sphinx: Reflections on the Contemporary History of Ghana, 1972–1987*, J. B. Danquah Memorial Lectures, Series 21, February 1988 (Accra, Ghana: Ghana Academy of Arts and Science, 1989), 51.

16. Naomi Chazan, "The Political Transformation of Ghana under the PNDC," in *The Political Economy of Ghana*, ed. Donald Rothchild (Boulder: Lynne Rienner Publishers, 1991), 27.

17. Nat Nuno-Amarteifio (former mayor of Accra), interview by Alastair Smith, May 2008.

18. Nicolas van de Walle, *African Economies and the Politics of Permanent Crisis, 1979–1999* (New York: Cambridge University Press, 2001), 241–242.

CHAPTER 9: WAR, PEACE, AND WORLD ORDER

1. Much of this section is based on Bruce Bueno de Mesquita, Alastair Smith, Randolph M. Siverson, and James D. Morrow, *The Logic of Political Survival* (Cambridge, MA: MIT Press, 2003), chapter 6; and Bruce Bueno de Mesquita, James D. Morrow, Randolph M. Siverson, and Alastair Smith, "Testing Novel Implications from the Selectorate Theory of War," *World Politics* 56 (April 2004): 363–388. Those interested in the logical, mathematical proofs of the claims made here should refer to these and the other publications cited throughout.

2. Sun Tzu, *The Art of War*, ed. James Clavell (New York: Delacorte Press, 1983), 9–14.

3. Caspar Weinberger, "The Use of Military Power," remarks delivered to the National Press Club, Washington, DC, November 28, 1984. See the text at "Give War a Chance" (webpage), *Frontline*, PBS, https://www.pbs.org/wgbh /pages/frontline/shows/military/force/weinberger.html.

4. See the Correlates of War Project data sets on Israel, Egypt, Jordan, and Syria for 1967, at correlatesofwar.org/data-sets.

5. Anna Getmansky, "Protecting the Protectors: A Cross-National Study of Domestic Regimes and Protection of Soldiers" (working paper, Department of Politics, New York University, 2008).

6. Martin Meredith, *The Soccer War* (New York: Vintage, 1992), 201–202.

7. In Europe in the 1980s it was a popular joke that Ronald Reagan was America's way of apologizing for being late for the first two world wars by being really punctual for the next.

8. The graph was generated using military expenditure from the Correlate of War Project's National Material Capabilities Data at correlatesofwar.org/data -sets/national-material-capabilities. We do not have data for Austria in 1919 because Austria-Hungary had ceased to exist.

9. For a more detailed and rigorous account of how our perspective explains the incentive to create puppet regimes, see Bueno de Mesquita et al., *Logic of Political Survival*, especially chapter 9; and Carmela Lutmar, "Belligerent Occupations," in *ISA Compendium of International Law*, ed. Robert J. Beck and Henry F. Carey (Oxford: Blackwell, 2009).

10. Michela Wrong, *I Didn't Do It for You: How the World Betrayed a Small African Nation* (New York: HarperCollins, 2005), 328.

11. Wrong, *I Didn't Do It for You*, 351–353.

12. Bruce Bueno de Mesquita and Randolph M. Siverson, "War and the Survival of Political Leaders: A Comparative Study of Regime Types and Political Accountability," *American Political Science Review* 89, no. 4 (December 1995): 841–855; and Bruce Bueno de Mesquita, Randolph Siverson, and Gary Woller, "War and the Fate of Regimes: A Cross-National Analysis," *American Political Science Review* (September 1992): 638–646.

13. G. M. Gilbert, *Nuremberg Diary* (New York: Farrar, Straus, 1947), 278–279.

14. Quoted in David D. Laitin and Said S. Samatar, *Somalia: Nation in Search of a State* (Boulder, CO: Westview Press, 1987).

15. Wrong, *I Didn't Do It for You*, 336.

16. In fact there are numerous cases of violent conflicts between pairs of democracies in the Correlates of War Project's militarized disputes data. None became wars because while one side used force, the other side backed down rather than fight back.

17. Dan Reiter and Allan C. Stam, *Democracies at War* (Princeton, NJ: Princeton University Press, 2002).

18. William J. Clinton, "Address Before a Joint Session of the Congress on the State of the Union," January 25, 1994, https://www.presidency.ucsb.edu/doc uments/address-before-joint-session-the-congress-the-state-the-union-12.

CHAPTER 10: IS DEMOCRACY FRAGILE?

1. Quoted in "C. Hank Gonzalez," *Los Angeles Times*, August 12, 2001, https://www.latimes.com/archives/la-xpm-2001-aug-12-me-33431-story.html.

2. Thomas Jefferson to James Madison, September 6, 1789, Founders Online, National Archives, https://founders.archives.gov/documents/Madison/01 -12-02-0248.

3. Our colleague Adam Przeworski and his coauthors make an argument that is similar in structure to ours. They argue that once democracies become rich enough (around $6,000 in terms of per capita GDP), democracy becomes locked in. For us, economic development is not as important as dependence on large coalitions. Adam Przeworski, R. Michael Alvarez, Michael E. Alvarez, Jose Antonio Cheibub, Fernando Limongi, and Fernando Papaterra Limongi Neto, *Democracy and Development: Political Institutions and Well-Being in the World, 1950–1990*, vol. 3 (New York: Cambridge University Press, 2000).

4. For a discussion of how the 1977 election in which Gandhi was defeated was an election to restore democracy and overthrow a movement toward autocracy, see Richard L. Park and Bruce Bueno de Mesquita, *India's Political System*, 2nd ed. (Englewood Cliffs, NJ: Prentice-Hall, 1979), especially pp. 72–78.

5. As we are holding the selectorate size constant in Figure 10.2, its size must be large enough to exceed the size of the largest-possible winning coalition, and hence the selectorate is assumed in the figure to be as large as possible. Smaller selectorates diminish leader welfare because the incumbent must spend more revenue to keep the coalition loyal—not defecting to a challenger—as the proportion of the selectorate in the winning coalition increases.

6. Brad Raffensperger, "Georgia Secretary of State: My Job Is to Make Sure We Have Honest and Fair Elections," interview by Joe Scarborough and Willie Geist, *Morning Joe*, MSNBC, September 21, 2021, https://www.msn.com/en-us/weather/topstories/georgia-secretary-of-state-my-job-is-to-make-sure-we-have-honest-and-fair-elections/vp-AAOF7M8.

7. For the formal, mathematical derivation of the functional form in Figure 10.2, see Bruce Bueno de Mesquita, Alastair Smith, Randolph M. Siverson, and James D. Morrow, *The Logic of Political Survival* (Cambridge, MA: MIT Press, 2003), chapter 3.

8. We say "almost certainly" because it is very hard to measure the exact location of the right-hand gray line. The same is true for the exact location, country by country, of the left-hand gray line.

9. For additional evidence behind the figure, see Bruce Bueno de Mesquita and Alastair Smith, "Political Loyalty and Leader Health," *Quarterly Journal of Political Science* 13, no. 4 (2018): 333–361.

10. Figure 10.3 is based on two regression analyses with fixed effects for country and year. The regressions match whether a coup or revolt happened against the prior year's coalition size, its squared value, and its cubed value.

11. Quoted in Sam Levine, "Trump Says Republicans Would 'Never' Be Elected Again If It Was Easier to Vote," *The Guardian*, March 30, 2020, https://www.theguardian.com/us-news/2020/mar/30/trump-republican-party-voting-reform-coronavirus.

12. "Gerrymandering Palawan," editorial, *Manila Times*, April 21, 2019, https://www.manilatimes.net/2019/04/21/opinion/editorial/gerrymandering-palawan/543102/.

13. For a more detailed discussion of Kenya's queue voting, see Bueno de Mesquita et al., *Logic of Political Survival*, 55–56.

14. *McPherson v. Blacker*, 146 U.S. 1, 35 (1892).

CHAPTER 11: WHAT IS TO BE DONE?

1. G. Scott Thomas, "Who Are the Most Loyal Fans in the NFL?," *Milwaukee Business Journal*, September 10, 2006, https://www.bizjournals.com/milwaukee/stories/2006/09/11/story12.html; "Executive Committee and Board of Directors," Green Bay Packers (website), accessed on September 17, 2021, http://www.packers.com/team/executive-committee.htm.

2. The most successful teams in terms of Super Bowls are the New England Patriots (eleven appearances and six victories), Pittsburgh Steelers (eight appearances and six victories), Dallas Cowboys (eight appearances and five victories), and San Francisco 49ers (seven appearances and five victories). The New York Giants have the same Super Bowl record as Green Bay.

3. "Executive Committee and Board of Directors."

4. "Leading European Football Clubs Announce New Super League Competition" (press release), Super League, April 18, 2021, https://thesuperleague.com/press.html.

5. Joshua Robinson, "Pressure Intensifies on Manchester United Owners After Violent Protest," *Wall Street Journal*, May 3, 2021, https://www.wsj.com/articles/manchester-united-old-trafford-glazers-protest-11620053976.

6. Robert Romano, "The Sarbanes-Oxley Act and the Making of Quack Corporate Governance," *Yale Law Journal* 114 (May 2005): 1521–1611.

7. Jeffrey L. Jensen, "Initial Institutions, Institutional Persistence, and the Promotion of Economic Development by the Original 13 States" (working paper, Department of Politics, New York University, 2007).

8. Bruce Bueno de Mesquita, *The Invention of Power: Popes, Kings and the Birth of the West* (New York: PublicAffairs, 2022).

9. Akhil Reed Amar, *America's Constitution: A Biography* (New York: Random House, 2006).

10. "Estimate of U.S. War on Terror Spending, in $ Billions FY2001–FY2020," Costs of War (website), Watson Institute for International and Public Affairs, Brown University, November 13, 2019, https://watson.brown.edu/costsofwar/figures/2019/budgetary-costs-post-911-wars-through-fy2020-64-trillion.

CREDIT: ARLENE BUENO DE MESQUITA

Bruce Bueno de Mesquita is the Julius Silver Professor of Politics at New York University. Through his New York–based consulting firm, he has served as an adviser to the US government on national security matters and to numerous corporations on questions related to forecasting and engineering outcomes in negotiations. Bueno de Mesquita received his doctorate in political science from the University of Michigan in 1971. He received honorary doctorates from the University of Groningen in 1999 and from the University of Haifa in 2016. From 2001 to 2002, he was president of the International Studies Association. He is a member of the American Academy of Arts and Sciences and the Council on Foreign Relations, and he has been a Guggenheim Fellow. Bueno de Mesquita is the author of 23 books, more than 140 articles, and numerous pieces in the *New York Times*, *Los Angeles Times*, *Chicago Tribune*, and *International Herald Tribune*, among other publications.

Alastair Smith is the Bernhardt Denmark Professor of International Politics at New York University. He previously taught at Washington University in St. Louis and at Yale University. He has a PhD in political science from the University of Rochester and a BA in chemistry from Oxford University. The recipient of three grants from the National Science Foundation, Smith was chosen as the 2005 Karl Deutsch Award winner, given biennially to the best international relations scholar under the age of forty, and he was elected to the American Academy of Arts and Science in 2013. He is the author of five books and approximately sixty articles and numerous pieces in major media outlets.

PublicAffairs is a publishing house founded in 1997. It is a tribute to the standards, values, and flair of three persons who have served as mentors to countless reporters, writers, editors, and book people of all kinds, including me.

I. F. STONE, proprietor of *I. F. Stone's Weekly*, combined a commitment to the First Amendment with entrepreneurial zeal and reporting skill and became one of the great independent journalists in American history. At the age of eighty, Izzy published *The Trial of Socrates*, which was a national bestseller. He wrote the book after he taught himself ancient Greek.

BENJAMIN C. BRADLEE was for nearly thirty years the charismatic editorial leader of *The Washington Post*. It was Ben who gave the *Post* the range and courage to pursue such historic issues as Watergate. He supported his reporters with a tenacity that made them fearless and it is no accident that so many became authors of influential, best-selling books.

ROBERT L. BERNSTEIN, the chief executive of Random House for more than a quarter century, guided one of the nation's premier publishing houses. Bob was personally responsible for many books of political dissent and argument that challenged tyranny around the globe. He is also the founder and longtime chair of Human Rights Watch, one of the most respected human rights organizations in the world.

· · ·

For fifty years, the banner of Public Affairs Press was carried by its owner Morris B. Schnapper, who published Gandhi, Nasser, Toynbee, Truman, and about 1,500 other authors. In 1983, Schnapper was described by *The Washington Post* as "a redoubtable gadfly." His legacy will endure in the books to come.

Peter Osnos, *Founder*